"The relationship between saving faith a[nd] the biblical doctrine of salvation. It is a v[...] historic Calvinism and historic Arminianism. Although one can savingly believe the gospel without rightly understanding this relationship, the integrity of the biblical witness to the grace of God in that gospel cannot be consistently maintained without recognizing the priority of regeneration in the application of salvation. Dr. Barrett sees this truth clearly and argues persuasively for the monergistic—or Calvinistic—position. His arguments are exegetically careful, theologically rigorous, and historically informed. Monergists will welcome this book as a helpful guide to the issues at stake, and synergists will not be able to ignore its devastating critique of their strongest arguments."

—**Thomas Ascol,** Pastor of Grace Baptist Church, Cape Coral, Florida; Executive Director of Founders Ministries; Editor of the Founders Journal

"Either God is sovereign or he is not. Matthew Barrett takes the bull by the horns and demonstrates that only the affirmation of complete divine sovereignty in all things can do justice to what God has done for our salvation. Attempts to water this down by finding room for human cooperation may be well-meaning, but they are bound to fail. This is a timely book on a perennially important subject, specially geared to meet current challenges. Every pastor and theologically alert Christian should read it."

—**Gerald Bray,** Research Professor of Divinity, Beeson Divinity School, Samford University, Birmingham, Alabama

"A movement that Collin Hansen identifies as young, restless, and Reformed is afoot. It entails a resurgence of Calvinist doctrine among young Christian scholars, many of whom are writing excellent PhD dissertations and recasting them as accessible books. Matthew Barrett may be young, restless, and Reformed, but even more, he is an emerging scholar and theologian who possesses great energy and passion for the gospel and for Christ's church. His book *Salvation by Grace* reflects both his passion for God's glory as revealed in the gospel and his energy to make clear for all his readers that when God calls everyone whom he purposes to save, his call is effectual and the Spirit's making us alive is solely a divine act and not of our doing at all, given the fact that we were dead in our tombs of trespasses and sins, no less than the senseless and decaying body of

Lazarus in the tomb of death. *Salvation by Grace* reaffirms a time-honored teaching of the Scriptures, carefully accounts for monergism's corollary doctrines, and freshly presents it all for a new generation of young and perhaps restless minds that Matthew Barrett would like to influence to embrace the Reformed doctrine that salvation in Christ is entirely of God's effectual grace."

—**A. B. Caneday,** Professor of New Testament Studies & Biblical Theology, Northwestern College, St. Paul, Minnesota

"A number of virtues make *Salvation by Grace* a truly outstanding piece of work. The subject is timely. Even though the issues are old, they present themselves in new guises right up to the present. Barrett writes elegantly, his style belying the complexity of the subject. It is a learned book, showing masterful knowledge of the many sources discussed. Here we have polemics at their best, and yet the book is an opportune encouragement for anyone doubting the fully sovereign nature of God's love in giving us salvation."

—**William Edgar,** Professor of Apologetics, Westminster Theological Seminary, Philadelphia, Pennsylvania

"Do we come to God or does he draw us to himself? This is the key question that divides monergism from synergism. Matthew Barrett has written an extremely helpful book and makes a strong case for monergism in the regeneration and effectual calling of sinners to Christ. This work is exegetically extensive, historically informed, and theologically thorough. Anyone who wants to understand the differences between monergism and synergism will find Barrett's work an able guide."

—**J. V. Fesko,** Academic Dean and Professor of Systematic and Historical Theology, Westminster Seminary California

"Calvin shocked the world and altered the course of history with a radical idea: God works miracles in the human heart. This, not predestination, was his signature contribution. Matthew Barrett's *Salvation by Grace* marshals a magnificent body of evidence that this explosive claim is scriptural."

—**Greg Forster,** Author, *The Joy of Calvinism*

"The doctrine of effectual calling—a better term than 'irresistible grace'—is at the heart of what it means to confess that Jesus Christ is the sole and sufficient Savior of spiritually dead sinners. Matthew Barrett has done a masterful job of describing this teaching in its biblical, historical, and theological dimensions. An important book for theologians and all Christians who seek to understand the deepest meaning of God's grace."

> —**Timothy George,** Founding Dean, Beeson Divinity School, Samford University; General Editor, Reformation Commentary on Scripture

"The issue tackled in this fine work is an ancient one: it was briefly touched on by Irenaeus in his debates with Gnostic determinists, and then fully aired in the fourth and fifth centuries by Augustine in his critique of Pelagianism. Of course, this was not the end of the story; it came up again in the writings of the Saxon theologian Gottschalk, only to be refought during the Reformation by numerous Reformation theologians in their replies to the Church of Rome. And it has been revisited a number of times since that major turning point in church history. Dr. Barrett is, then, in good company in defending this perspective on salvation. And in commending this work, we do not wish for more controversy, but hope and pray that the position recommended in the book might be pondered deeply by all who read it, and biblical truth ultimately prevail."

> —**Michael A. G. Haykin,** Professor of Church History and Biblical Spirituality, The Southern Baptist Theological Seminary; Director of The Andrew Fuller Center for Baptist Studies & Research Professor of Irish Baptist College, Constituent College of Queen's University Belfast, Northern Ireland

"The Reformed idea of God's effectual call hails from the days of Augustine. Nowadays, it is often caricatured as treating men and women like puppets. In this comprehensive study, Matthew Barrett shows that the doctrine lies at the center of the application of God's sovereign grace to men and women who are unable to help themselves, restoring them to their true selves. The treatment is informative and judicious and, above all, timely."

> —**Paul Helm,** Teaching Fellow, Regent College, Vancouver

"Matthew Barrett's *Salvation by Grace* is a compelling and much-needed reminder that the doctrine of monergistic regeneration is, as B. B. Warfield once put it, 'the hinge of the Calvinistic soteriology.' It is also a bold yet winsome challenge to the all-too-common assumption that the saving efficacy of the cross is ultimately determined not by God but by 'the will of man.' Fair, judicious, and admirably sensitive to the exegetical and theological subtleties of both classical and contemporary discussions, Barrett capably demonstrates why Reformed believers insist that synergistic views of regeneration subvert the teaching of Scripture and surrender the glory of God in salvation. Enthusiastically recommended."

—**Paul Kjoss Helseth,** Professor of Christian Thought, Northwestern College, St. Paul, Minnesota

"Matthew Barrett's *Salvation by Grace* contributes significantly to the burgeoning literature on Reformed theology by young scholars. He ably leads the reader through philosophical and historical elements of the centuries-old debate between monergism and synergism. He correctly notes, however, that the primary issue is biblical and theological. Barrett identifies monergism—that God acts alone to effectually and sovereignly regenerate depraved sinners—as the sine qua non of biblical exegesis faithful to the Bible. A tour de force defense of the Calvinist doctrine of God's sovereignty, *Salvation by Grace* illustrates the biblical concept of the unity of truth. After demonstrating that Augustinian original sin, Calvinist total depravity, and Lutheran bondage of the will correctly capture the Bible's teaching on human nature, Barrett effectively shows the indispensability of interpreting faith, repentance, and conversion monergistically through careful exegesis of biblical texts. Faithful adherence to the coherence and consistency of biblical texts guides Barrett's argument. Barrett also marshals ample confessional support for monergism from the Canons of Dort and the Westminster Confession. Finally, a careful probing of Arminian scholarship rounds out this fine book. What emerges is the vast diversity of synergistic interpretations that clutter the historical landscape, from Pelagius's humanistic synergism to an array of contemporary evangelical views. Given the complexity of synergisms in the Arminian tradition, one finds it difficult, if not impossible, to discern any unity of truth that holds the field together. I came away from Barrett's examination of monergism with a new appreciation for the benefits derived from adhering to confessional evangelicalism."

—**Andrew Hoffecker,** Emeritus Professor of Church History, Reformed Theological Seminary, Jackson, Mississippi

" 'Salvation is of the LORD.' All Christians would affirm this good news. Yet only monergism carries it through to the end, without equivocation. In this winsome and well-researched defense, Matthew Barrett clears away the brush—caricatures and distortions on both sides of the debate—to expose the wonder of God's amazing grace. After drawing a precise historical map of the

range of views, Barrett engages the relevant passages with fresh insight and energy. His goal is not to win an argument but to win brothers and sisters to a fuller, richer, and more biblical account of the application of redemption."
— **Michael Horton,** J. Gresham Machen Professor of Systematic Theology and Apologetics, Westminster Seminary California

"The Arminian controversy in the Netherlands continues to rumble on in varying forms centuries later. Recently, a number of Arminian theologians—and others attempting a middle path—have highlighted these questions again. Barrett carefully considers their arguments from both biblical and theological angles. This is a thorough and persuasive piece of work, demonstrating that only the consistent monergism of classic Reformed theology does justice to the gospel as a work of God's grace."
— **Robert Letham,** Senior Lecturer in Systematic and Historical Theology, Wales Evangelical School of Theology

"Matthew Barrett's *Salvation by Grace* provides a theological feast for its readers. Barrett shows a profound grasp of historical theology on this issue, a clear and pertinent deftness in exegesis, an impressive knowledge and understanding of the doctrinal nuances and connections, a detailed understanding of the contemporary literature on it, and a convincing way of synthesizing the vital points of argument. I agree with him; but if one does not agree with him, this is still a book to read in order to know what is at stake in the discussion."
— **Tom J. Nettles,** Professor of Historical Theology, The Southern Baptist Theological Seminary, Louisville, Kentucky

"We all desire a view on the doctrines of grace that gives the lion's share to God, both the work and the credit. Here you will find a compelling articulation of a view that does precisely that. Read this book and then rejoice in the God of our salvation, who brings about the miraculous transformation of sinners into saints—all to the praise of his glorious grace."
— **Stephen J. Nichols,** Research Professor of Christianity and Culture, Lancaster Bible College, Lancaster, Pennsylvania

"Matthew Barrett's work on regeneration represents scholarship at its best. His book is exegetically convincing and theologically profound, with significant pastoral consequences. The topic has not been explored in depth in recent scholarship, and hence this book is also timely."

—**Thomas R. Schreiner,** James Buchanan Harrison Professor of New Testament Interpretation, The Southern Baptist Theological Seminary, Louisville, Kentucky

"Writing as an evangelical to evangelicals, and particularly reflecting the sometimes-heated soteriological discussions current within his Southern Baptist setting, Matthew Barrett here addresses for a new day issues highlighted by B. B. Warfield in his *The Plan of Salvation* (1918)."

—**Kenneth J. Stewart,** Professor of Theological Studies, Covenant College, Lookout Mountain, Georgia

"This is quite simply the most thorough and convincing account of divine sovereignty, both over the new birth and over effectual calling, that I've ever read. It is historically informed, lucidly written, eminently practical, and, most important of all, biblically faithful. This book, and Matthew Barrett in particular, renews my confidence that the so-called young, restless, and Reformed are in good hands and moving in the right direction. *Salvation by Grace* merits a wide reading and will undoubtedly prove to be an indispensable resource for the serious student of God's Word. I cannot recommend it too highly."

—**Sam Storms,** Lead Pastor for Preaching and Vision, Bridgeway Church, Oklahoma City, Oklahoma

"*Salvation by Grace* approaches a deep and controversial topic with the goal of understanding it according to the Scriptures. Although very well reasoned, this is not primarily a philosophical or apologetic argument, but one that shows the biblical foundation for the linchpin of Calvinism. With an eye on the past as well as the contemporary debate, Dr. Barrett does an outstanding job of helping the reader understand why Calvinists hold their view and why they believe it really matters. The glory of God as the One who saves us from ourselves is powerfully presented so that the reader may be led to deeper worship, humility, and confidence."

—**Erik Thoennes,** Professor of Biblical and Theological Studies; Chair, Biblical and Theological Studies Theology Department, Biola University and Talbot School of Theology, La Mirada, California

"The nature of grace is central to the Christian faith, and how one defines it speaks volumes about how one understands God, Christ, salvation, and even the church. In this book, Matthew Barrett lays out the historical, theological, and biblical material, and presents a compelling case for classic anti-Pelagian theology. Very helpful."

—**Carl R. Trueman,** Paul Woolley Professor of Church History, Westminster Theological Seminary, Philadelphia, Pennsylvania

"Whether you are looking at this book because you assume that you already agree or disagree with Matthew Barrett, or perhaps aren't sure where you come down on these issues, don't assume that you are holding in your hands a run-of-the-mill defense of classic Calvinist doctrine. What Barrett has given us in this book is a careful examination of the biblical-theological case for the sovereignty of God in salvation and a fair and accurate analysis of the historical and modern debates surrounding this vital doctrine. At the end of the day, this doctrine is not simply a matter for debate—it is about what the Bible reveals as the only hope of salvation that lost sinners in rebellion against their Creator have. So put aside all bias and the personal animosity that too often marks this debate, and prayerfully read the case that Barrett makes for salvation being, from beginning to end, the work of God alone."

—**Brian Vickers,** Assistant Professor of New Testament Interpretation, The Southern Baptist Theological Seminary, Louisville, Kentucky

"Matthew Barrett has provided a tremendous resource for thoughtful Christian readers, both Arminian and Calvinist, in his careful and insightful analysis of the doctrines of God's calling and regeneration of sinners to salvation. Since these doctrinal areas are at the heart of the great divide between an Arminian and a Reformed soteriology, it is critical that we understand clearly what the Scriptures say on these matters. Barrett's illuminating discussion of the history of these doctrines, and his masterful treatment of all the relevant biblical passages, makes this book one of the most important contributions for adjudicating our differences and for leading us into a more faithful understanding of God's gracious saving work in our lives as believers. For clarity in theological understanding, and for the sake of our own souls, I heartily recommend this book."

—**Bruce A. Ware,** Professor of Christian Theology, The Southern Baptist Theological Seminary, Louisville, Kentucky

"The perennial debate regarding the relationship between God's sovereign grace and initiative and human sin and choice in our salvation continues unabated in our present day. Even so, Matthew Barrett's very helpful defense of God's sovereign and effectual grace in our salvation is much needed. In *Salvation by Grace*, Barrett not only sets the debate in historical context, but also, in a biblically faithful and theologically accurate manner, provides a convincing defense of God's sovereign initiative in salvation—a defense that ultimately and rightly underscores our triune God's incredible and amazing grace toward sinners. I highly recommend this work."

> —**Stephen Wellum,** Professor of Christian Theology, The Southern Baptist Theological Seminary, Louisville, Kentucky; Editor, The Southern Baptist Journal of Theology

"The testimony of Scripture is that 'salvation belongs to the LORD!' (Jonah 2:9). In *Salvation by Grace*, Matthew Barrett calls us to revel in this truth. As an heir of the Reformation, with the pastoral zeal and careful thinking that were part of that sixteenth-century revival, he reminds us that what we think about this subject matters. God's glory and our assurance of salvation are wrapped up in whether God chooses and saves us or whether we choose him. Barrett's work combines careful historical research, meticulous biblical exegesis, and thoughtful theological formulation. As you read it, worship the God who raises dead sinners to life in Christ!"

> —**Shawn D. Wright,** Associate Professor of Church History, The Southern Baptist Theological Seminary, Louisville, Kentucky

"Barrett's examination of this critical area of theology is historically informed, providing an accurate setting and perspective for the discussion. It is also theologically precise, providing definitive expositions of all sides of the debate. It is surprisingly exhaustive, treating all the primary arguments and counter-arguments responsibly. And most importantly, it is exegetically compelling, bringing God's own Word to bear on a doctrine designed to bring him glory. A valuable resource indeed! Highly recommended."

> —**Fred G. Zaspel,** Pastor, Reformed Baptist Church, Franconia, Pennsylvania; Adjunct Professor of Theology, Calvary Baptist Seminary, Lansdale, Pennsylvania

SALVATION BY GRACE

SALVATION BY GRACE

THE CASE FOR EFFECTUAL CALLING AND REGENERATION

MATTHEW BARRETT

P&R PUBLISHING

P.O. BOX 817 • PHILLIPSBURG • NEW JERSEY 08865-0817

Unless otherwise indicated, all Scripture quotations are from The Holy Bible, English Standard Version, copyright © 2001 by Crossway, a publishing ministry of Good News Publishers. Used by permission. All rights reserved.

Italics within Scripture quotations indicate emphasis added.

ISBN: 978-1-59638-643-3 (pbk)
ISBN: 978-1-59638-644-0 (ePub)
ISBN: 978-1-59638-645-7 (Mobi)

Printed in the United States of America

Library of Congress Cataloging-in-Publication Data

Barrett, Matthew Michael, 1982-
  Salvation by grace : the case for effectual calling and regeneration / Matthew Barrett. -- 1st ed.
      pages cm
  Includes bibliographical references and index.
  ISBN 978-1-59638-643-3 (pbk.)
  1. Salvation--Christianity. 2. Grace (Theology) 3. Regeneration (Theology) I. Title.
  BT751.3B36 2013
  234--dc23
                                        2013005490

To my wife,
Elizabeth Barrett.

"An excellent wife who can find?
She is far more precious than jewels.
The heart of her husband trusts in her,
and he will have no lack of gain."
Proverbs 31:10–11

CONTENTS

FOREWORD

One thing is clear to classical Arminians and Calvinists alike: if the grace by which we are saved is efficacious—irresistible—grace and only some and not all are saved, then this saving grace is given only to some (the elect) and not to all. And what happens as this saving, efficacious, irresistible grace, otherwise known as God's effectual calling of the elect to salvation, is extended to them? By this efficacious calling and grace—and therefore of divine necessity in the lives of the elect—they are regenerated; they express saving faith in God's atoning work for them in Christ; and they are thereby saved once and forever. Sovereign grace reigns here, as God first, in eternity past, chooses among the sinful and guilty human race those whom he, in his mercy, will save; and then in time and history he bestows on them the efficacious grace by which their dead hearts are enlivened and their blind eyes are opened. As this happens in them, they truly and savingly believe! Yet the expression of their faith, although a genuinely human expression of their natures made new by the regenerative work of the Holy Spirit, owes all that it is to the sovereign grace of God, which brought about in them both their new hearts and their newfound saving faith. As Ephesians 2:8–9 makes clear, both the "grace" and "faith" by which we are saved are, together, "the gift of God . . . that no one should boast."

If, on the other hand, the grace that comes to us assisting our salvation is grace that we can accept or reject—a grace that only makes possible our salvation, while leaving the final and decisive outcome squarely in our hands—then our salvation as not purely and fully the result of sovereign grace. In this case, not only do we have a part to play in our salvation, we have the most decisive part: providing the thumbs up or thumbs down on where we will spend eternity, despite what God wants, wills, or does, since the same grace is given to all, and that grace is equally resistible by all.

The core differences, then, between classic Arminianism and Reformed theology in the doctrine of salvation focus on the nature of the grace by which we are saved. Although there are other important differences, this is "ground zero," as it were, in the battle being waged over these two mutually exclusive understandings of the salvation of sinners.

Over a decade ago, we edited a volume intended to defend various aspects of the doctrines of grace within a Reformed soteriology.[1] One of the reasons we felt the need for this book at the time was to demonstrate the difference between Arminian and Reformed understandings of the nature of saving grace. We realized that the Arminian doctrine of prevenient grace and the Reformed doctrine of efficacious grace both function as lynch pins within their own soteriological models. Included in our volume was an essay by Schreiner in which he contended that the Arminian doctrine of prevenient grace, though essential to an Arminian soteriology, could not rightly be supported or defended from Scripture. A second essay by Ware sought to demonstrate that the Reformed doctrine of efficacious calling and grace was fully supported and upheld by Scripture. If this is true—if the Arminian conception of prevenient grace lacks biblical support and the Reformed understanding of effectual calling and grace is a biblical teaching—then the long-standing debate between these two soteriological models is virtually settled. Yes, other issues also are important to deal with, but this issue—the issue of the nature of the grace by which we are saved—is central and ultimate in the whole of this debate.

In the light of the importance of this issue, we are thrilled by the major treatment Matthew Barrett has given to this crucial and central doctrinal area of our faith. It is hard to imagine a study of the passages, positions, and issues any more carefully and thoroughly done than Dr. Barrett has provided here. Our hope and prayer is that readers on

1. Thomas R. Schreiner and Bruce A. Ware, eds., *Still Sovereign: Contemporary Perspectives on Election, Foreknowledge, and Grace* (Grand Rapids: Baker Books, 2000).

both sides of the debate—as well as many "undecided voters" tilting one way or the other as they consider various arguments—will do themselves and others the favor of giving careful consideration to the biblical case made here for a full and decisive sovereign, saving grace.

Ultimately, we are pleased for the publication of this book because we believe that the truths it puts forward and the biblically saturated articulation they are given speak loudly of the glory of God in our salvation. To God alone belongs all glory. May greater numbers of his people see his sovereign grace in their salvation and ascribe to him the glory due to his name and to his name alone. *Soli Deo Gloria*.

Thomas R. Schreiner and Bruce A. Ware
The Southern Baptist Theological Seminary
Louisville, Kentucky

ACKNOWLEDGMENTS

This project could not have been completed without the help and encouragement of others. First, I would like to thank my dissertation committee. My supervisor, Bruce Ware, was the first to hear my ideas for this project and from beginning to end his expertise has been invaluable to my writing. For years, Bruce has given to me an outstanding example of Christian scholarship in his writings defending Calvinism against Open Theism and Arminianism. I only hope to emulate his excellent ability to defend and expound the Scriptures clearly and acutely. His passion for the glory of God is unwavering, and he has given me a deep love and appreciation for the doctrines of grace and the sovereignty of God.

I would also like to thank Shawn Wright, whose superb knowledge of the Reformation and Post-Reformation periods saved me from much unnecessary labor. As a graduate of The Southern Baptist Theological Seminary himself, Shawn's excellent dissertation on Theodore Beza has provided me with a tremendous example of a dissertation well done. Finally, I want to thank Tom Schreiner, whose excitement for my topic was unrelenting. Tom has for years taught in the classroom the priority of regeneration to faith, taking on all objections, and his keen sense for biblical exegesis in this project is found throughout. Furthermore, Tom's faithful preaching of the Word each Sunday has continually nourished my soul and shown me what it means to magnify God in Christ.

Besides my dissertation committee, I would also like to express my appreciation to my external reader, Michael Horton, J. Gresham Machen Professor of Systematic Theology and Apologetics at Westminster

Seminary, California. Horton's review of this project was both illuminating and encouraging. Horton continues to be for me an excellent example of a theologian committed to seeing the biblical truths of the Reformation proclaimed once again in our own day.

Finally, the most important person in my life is my wife, Elizabeth. We met at Biola University, and together we both developed a love for theology. Her zeal for knowing God never ceases to amaze me. Elizabeth has read and commented on every page (and footnote!) of this project. Many times she did this in the midst of mothering our daughters, Cassandra and Georgia, a privilege she treasures above all. I embark on few theological adventures without Elizabeth's input and remarkable scrutiny. Therefore, it is to Elizabeth that I dedicate this project.

Matthew Barrett
Louisville, Kentucky
May 2011

ABBREVIATIONS

AB	Anchor Bible
AOTC	Apollos Old Testament Commentary
ATJ	Ashland Theological Journal
BECNT	Baker Exegetical Commentary on the New Testament
CTJ	*Calvin Theological Journal*
DBSJ	*Detroit Baptist Seminary Journal*
EBC	Expositor's Bible Commentary
ESV	English Standard Version
HCSB	Holman Christian Standard Bible
ICC	International Critical Commentary
JBTM	*Journal for Baptist Theology and Ministry*
JETS	*Journal of the Evangelical Theological Society*
KJV	King James Version
LCC	Library of Christian Classics
NAC	New American Commentary
NASB	New American Standard Bible
NIBC	New International Biblical Commentary
NICNT	New International Commentary on the New Testament
NICOT	New International Commentary on the Old Testament
NIGTC	New International Greek Testament Commentary
NIV	New International Version
NIVAC	NIV Application Commentary

NKJV	New King James Version
PNTC	Pillar New Testament Commentary
REC	Reformed Expository Commentary
RR	Review of Religion
SBC	Southern Baptist Convention
SBJT	*Southern Baptist Journal of Theology*
TNTC	Tyndale New Testament Commentaries
TOTC	Tyndale Old Testament Commentaries
WBC	Word Biblical Commentary
WTJ	*Westminster Theological Journal*
ZECNT	Zondervan Exegetical Commentary on the New Testament

PUBLISHER'S NOTE

This book is an abridged version of the author's original dissertation. To read the original, please see the e-book version from P&R Publishing, *Reclaiming Monergism: The Case for Sovereign Grace in Effectual Calling and Regeneration* (hereafter referred to as *Reclaiming Monergism*, e-book), which includes chapters on the history of the monergism-synergism debate; more extensive chapters representing and critiquing synergism; appendixes on the love of God, the will of God, and the relationship between effectual calling and regeneration in the Reformed tradition; as well as an extensive bibliography.

INTRODUCTION: THE CONTEMPORARY DEBATE

How important is the doctrine of sovereign grace, as displayed in effectual calling and regeneration, to the system of Calvinism? According to B. B. Warfield, "Monergistic regeneration—or as it was phrased by the older theologians, of 'irresistible grace' or 'effectual calling'—is the hinge of the Calvinistic soteriology, and lies much more deeply embedded in the system than the doctrine of predestination itself which is popularly looked upon as its hall-mark."[1] Such a statement by Warfield is astonishing given the enormous focus on other issues such as the problem of evil or God's election in eternity by Calvinists and Arminians. However, Warfield is not alone. Today Calvinist theologians still agree, believing that monergistic regeneration is the *sine qua non* of salvation.[2] For example, when asked what *the* difference is between an Arminian and a Calvinist, both R. C. Sproul and Sinclair Ferguson responded that it is the doctrine of monergistic regeneration. As Sproul stated, while Calvinists and Arminians can argue about many other issues, the litmus test is whether regeneration precedes faith in the *ordo salutis* or, stated otherwise, whether one has or does not have the ability to cooperate with the grace of regeneration.[3] According to Sproul, the shibboleth for deciding whether or not one is a Calvinist or an Arminian is the doctrine of monergistic regeneration, the belief that God alone acts

1. Benjamin B. Warfield, *Calvin and Calvinism*, vol. 5 of *The Works of Benjamin B. Warfield* (Grand Rapids: Baker, 2003), 359.
2. R. C. Sproul, *What Is Reformed Theology?* (Grand Rapids: Baker, 2005), 188.
3. R. C. Sproul and Sinclair Ferguson, "Questions and Answers #3" (session held at the annual meeting of the Ligonier Ministries National Conference, Orlando, FL, 21 March 2009). Also see R. C. Sproul, *Chosen by God* (Wheaton, IL: Tyndale, 1986), 72–73.

to irresistibly and effectually call and regenerate the dead and passive sinner from death to new life, thereby causing the sinner to respond in faith and repentance.[4]

Whether or not regeneration precedes faith and is accomplished by God's sovereign will alone (monergism) or is conditioned upon man's faith, requiring man's free-will cooperation for its efficacy (synergism), continues to be one of the most important (or in Warfield's opinion *the* most important) divisions between the Calvinist and the Arminian today. As Scott Warren observes, "Perhaps the doctrine that most evidently distinguishes an Arminian theological framework from a Calvinist framework can be found in the *ordo salutis*—specifically in the question of whether faith precedes or follows regeneration."[5] Warren is lucid: the doctrine of regeneration is the very hinge on which the debate turns. Yet, if Warfield, Sproul, and Ferguson are right that monergistic grace is the very hinge of Calvinistic soteriology, then it is no small issue that such a doctrine is under reconsideration by contemporary evangelicals. The traditional Calvinistic view is once again being challenged not only by Arminians but by those who wish to propose a modified scheme.

THE CONTEMPORARY DEBATE

While monergism is an old doctrine, its relevance today is apparent as the late twentieth and early twenty-first centuries have been characterized by a resurgence of Calvinism, and with it a resurgence of a predestinarian theology which exalts God's sovereignty rather than the will of man.[6] As J. Ligon Duncan III explains, "A fever for the glory of God has gotten into the bloodstream of a new generation."[7] Duncan goes on to show that the resurgence of Calvinism has occurred in part because Christians are famished with the small view of God they have

---

4. Sproul, *What Is Reformed Theology?*, 185.

5. Scott C. Warren, "Ability and Desire: Reframing Debates Surrounding Freedom and Responsibility," *JETS* 52 (2009): 551.

6. J. Ligon Duncan III, "The Resurgence of Calvinism in America," in *Calvin for Today*, ed. Joel R. Beeke (Grand Rapids: Reformation Heritage, 2009), 227–40.

7. Ibid., 227.

been fed and are hungry for the "big view of God" portrayed in the Scriptures and systematically articulated in the doctrines of grace. The doctrines of effectual calling and monergistic regeneration are but a slice of this biblical view of God and yet, as seen above, they may be the very hinge of the Calvinist position. In short, the Calvinist argues that God and man do not cooperate but God alone acts to regenerate the sinner, causing man to repent and believe in Christ. The grace that the Spirit applies to the elect is not resistible but effectual and monergistic. It is not man's will, but God's will, that is the cause of new life. Therefore, for the Calvinist, effectual calling and regeneration causally and logically precede conversion in the *ordo salutis*. Moreover, the Calvinist is convinced that monergism preserves the sovereignty and glory of God in salvation while synergism robs God of his sovereignty and glory. Sovereignty is preserved because God's will in salvation is not conditioned upon man's will nor can it be successfully resisted by man's will if God should so choose to save. God's glory is preserved because God alone is the cause of the new birth. If God's grace is dependent upon the will of man for its success, then God does not receive all of the credit.

However, with the resurgence of Calvinism has come a counter response from those within the Arminian tradition.[8] While Calvinism places an emphasis on God's sovereign grace, not only as displayed in predestination but in the application of monergistic grace in effectual calling and regeneration, Arminianism rejects monergism and instead affirms synergism, the view that God and man cooperate, making God's

8. David Basinger and Randall Basinger, eds., *Predestination and Free Will* (Downers Grove, IL: InterVarsity, 1986); Clark Pinnock, ed., *The Grace of God and the Will of Man: A Case for Arminianism* (Grand Rapids: Zondervan, 1989; repr., Minneapolis: Bethany House, 1995), and *Grace Unlimited* (Eugene, OR: Wipf and Stock, 1999); Thomas C. Oden, *The Transforming Power of Grace* (Nashville: Abingdon, 1993); Robert E. Picirilli, *Grace, Faith, Free Will: Contrasting Views of Salvation: Calvinism and Arminianism* (Nashville: Randall House Books, 2002); Jerry L. Walls and Joseph R. Dongell, *Why I Am Not a Calvinist* (Downers Grove, IL: InterVarsity, 2004); Jack W. Cottrell, "The Classical Arminian View of Election," in *Perspectives on Election: Five Views*, ed. Chad O. Brand (Nashville: B&H Publishing Group, 2006), 70–134; Roger E. Olson, *Arminian Theology: Myths and Realities* (Downers Grove, IL: InterVarsity, 2006), and *Against Calvinism* (Grand Rapids: Zondervan, 2011); David L. Allen and Steve W. Lemke, eds., *Whosoever Will: A Biblical-Theological Critique of Five-Point Calvinism* (Nashville: B&H Publishing Group, 2010).

grace conditional upon man's free will (see chapter 5). However, two types of Arminian synergism exist. First, there are those Arminians who affirm a *God-initiated synergism*. Man is totally depraved but God provides a universal prevenient grace whereby man's depravity is mitigated and man's will is enabled to either cooperate with or resist God's grace. While God initiates and enables, ultimately man has the final say as to whether or not God's grace will be effective.[9] Such a view, often labeled "classical Arminianism" or "evangelical Arminianism," was advocated by Jacob Arminius and John Wesley, and contemporary advocates include Roger Olson and Wesleyan Thomas Oden (see chapter 5).[10] Historically, such a view shares many affinities with the Semi-Augustinianism of the Middle Ages. Second, there are other Arminians who reject the doctrine of total depravity and argue that there is no such thing as prevenient grace in Scripture. Instead, while sin does have a negative effect on man, man is still able to exercise his free will and initiate grace in order to either accept or reject the grace of God. This Arminian view, which we can call a *man-initiated synergism*, was affirmed by Arminian Remonstrant Philip Limborch in the seventeenth century and is today advocated by Jack Cottrell, Bruce Reichenbach, and Clark Pinnock (see chapter 5).[11] Historically, such a view of synergism is consistent with the Semi-Pelagianism that Augustine wrote against. Nevertheless, despite these differences, both groups of Arminians agree that at the moment of decision the final determinative say is in the hands of the sinner to either accept or reject grace.

Today there has been an increasing effort by classical Arminians such as Thomas Oden and Roger Olson not only to refute contemporary Calvinists, but to clear the "Arminian" name from Pelagian and Semi-

9. See James Arminius, "Certain Articles to be Diligently Examined and Weighed," in *The Writings of James Arminius*, 3 vols., trans. James Nichols and William Nichols (Reprint, Grand Rapids: Baker, 1956), 2:497. Also see Cottrell, "Classical Arminian View of Election," 120–21.

10. Olson, *Arminian Theology*, 137–78; Oden, *Transforming Power of Grace*, 31–208.

11. Cottrell, "Classical Arminian View of Election," 116–22; Pinnock, "From Augustine to Arminius: A Pilgrimage in Theology," in *The Grace of God and the Will of Man*, 21–24; Bruce R. Reichenbach, "Freedom, Justice, and Moral Responsibility," in *The Grace of God and the Will of Man*, 286.

Pelagian accusations. Consequently, Olson has put immense effort into representing "classical Arminianism," as opposed to the Semi-Pelagian Arminianism represented by Cottrell, Reichenbach, and Pinnock, in order to make Arminianism more appealing to evangelicals today.

> Synergism is any theological belief in free human participation in salvation. Its heretical forms in Christian theology are Pelagianism and semi-Pelagianism. The former denies original sin and elevates natural and moral human ability to live spiritually fulfilled lives. The latter embraces a modified version of original sin but believes that humans have the ability, even in their natural or fallen state, to initiate salvation by exercising a good will toward God. When conservative theologians declare that synergism is a heresy, they are usually referring to these two Pelagian forms of synergism. Classical Arminians agree. . . . Contrary to confused critics, classical Arminianism is neither Pelagian nor semi-Pelagian! But it *is* synergistic. Arminianism is *evangelical synergism* as opposed to heretical, humanistic synergism. . . . I am referring to evangelical synergism, which affirms the prevenience of grace to every human exercise of a good will toward God, including simply nonresistance to the saving work of Christ.[12]

It is clear from what Olson says that Calvinism's monergism has a counteropponent in Arminianism's synergism. While there have existed and do exist today those Arminians of a Semi-Pelagian stripe, Olson is making an effort to counter contemporary monergists with a synergism that is tasteful to evangelicals. Olson is not alone, but his Arminian synergism is reiterated by others including Robert Picirilli, Kenneth Keathley, Steve Lemke, Jeremy Evans, Jerry Walls, Joseph Dongell, among others (see chapter 5).

Moreover, not only have contemporary Arminians reacted strongly to the monergism of Calvinism, but those who affirm a modified position also have responded with a model of their own. The modified position which has gained perhaps the most popularity and momentum

12. Olson, *Arminian Theology*, 17–18.

among contemporary evangelicals is that of Millard Erickson, Gordon Lewis, and Bruce Demarest.[13] Such a view, while it borrows from both Arminianism and Calvinism, never fully agrees with either. The modified view's differences are easily demonstrated through the logical ordering of salvation. In the classical Arminian view prevenient grace is primary, followed by man's free will decision in conversion, and consequently God's response in regeneration. Therefore, regeneration is causally conditioned upon man's free-will choice to accept or reject God's grace. For Calvinism, the *ordo salutis* differs drastically. God does not respond to the sinner but the sinner responds to God. God's choice does not depend on the sinner's, but the sinner's choice depends on God's mercy and grace. Therefore, God's special calling is particular and effectual (as opposed to a calling that is universal, prevenient, and resistible) and regeneration monergistic. Consequently, effectual calling and regeneration causally precede conversion.

However, the modified view borrows and diverges from both of these views. While the modified view affirms a special calling that is effectual and prior to conversion, it denies that regeneration causally precedes conversion. Instead the modified view argues that regeneration is causally conditioned upon conversion.[14] While advocates of this view readily acknowledge that they are borrowing not only from Calvinism but also from Arminianism,[15] nevertheless, they insist that they remain monergists.[16] Indeed, Demarest even includes his view ("Regeneration a Work of God in Response to Faith") as part of the *"Reformed Evangelical"* position.[17] As shall be shown in chapter 7, Erickson, Lewis, and Demarest are defining monergism differently and more broadly than the Reformed tradition has defined it in the past, and the modified scheme, which places

13. Millard J. Erickson, *Christian Theology*, 2nd ed. (Grand Rapids: Baker, 2005), 901–78; Bruce Demarest, *The Cross and Salvation: The Doctrine of Salvation*, Foundations of Evangelical Theology, vol. 4 (Wheaton, IL: Crossway, 1997), 49–96, 203–312; Gordon R. Lewis and Bruce A. Demarest, *Integrative Theology*, 3 vols. (Grand Rapids: Zondervan, 1994), 3:17–172.

14. Lewis and Demarest, *Integrative Theology*, 3:57, 104.

15. Ibid., 3:57.

16. For example, see Demarest, *Cross and Salvation*, 289.

17. Ibid., 289–91. Emphasis original. Lewis and Demarest title their view "moderately Reformed" and a "modified Calvinistic hypothesis." Lewis and Demarest, *Integrative Theology*, 3:57.

conversion between effectual calling and regeneration, is nothing short of a novelty as it is without precedent among Reformed theologians.

However, Erickson, Lewis, and Demarest are not the only ones who try to lay claim to the label of "monergism." More recently, Kenneth Keathley also claims he is justified in adopting the term "monergism," a surprising move in light of the fact that Keathley's view is almost identical to the Arminian position. Keathley rejects the modified view of Erickson, Lewis, and Demarest, as it concedes too much to the Calvinist affirmation of effectual calling.[18] Instead, Keathley puts forward a very traditional Arminian view of synergism when he rejects the distinction between the gospel call and the effectual call and in its place affirms that God's call is universal, God's grace is resistible, man's freedom is libertarian, and conversion is logically prior to regeneration. Monergism for Keathley means that God alone can be called the author of salvation, and he is not thwarted in his intention to save *as long as* man "refrains from resisting," a definition radically different from how Calvinists use the term.[19]

In summary, for the Arminian, Calvinism's doctrine of monergistic grace must be rejected, and for the modified advocate the doctrine must be qualified and altered at the very least. Such recent opposition demonstrates that while the monergism-synergism debate is an old one, it has taken on new significance in contemporary theology. Nevertheless, the question remains as to who is right. Does synergism or monergism best adhere to what Scripture says about the application of God's grace to the sinner?

WHAT THIS BOOK IS ALL ABOUT

The monergism-synergism debate is not first and foremost a *philosophical* debate, nor is it primarily a *historical* debate, as important as

18. Kenneth Keathley, *Salvation and Sovereignty: A Molinist Approach* (Nashville: B&H Publishing Group, 2010), 101–35.

19. As will become evident, Keathley's arguments are no different from those of Arminian Roger Olson, who likewise says God's grace is always successful as long as man is nonresistant (see Olson, *Arminian Theology*, 154–55). Therefore, I will interact with Keathley's objections when I address classical Arminianism.

philosophy and history are to the discussion. Rather, the debate is pri-marily a *biblical-theological* debate. While Calvinists and Arminians disagree over a range of issues, both agree that the Bible must have the ultimate authority. Nevertheless, each view purports to be the biblical position. The thesis of this project will argue that the biblical view is that God's saving grace is monergistic—meaning that God acts alone to *effectually* call and *monergistically* regenerate the depraved sinner from death to new life—and therefore effectual calling and regeneration causally precede conversion in the *ordo salutis*, thereby ensuring that all of the glory in salvation belongs to God not man. Stated negatively, God's grace is not synergistic—meaning that God cooperates with man, giving man the final, determining power to either accept or resist God's grace—which would result in an *ordo salutis* where regeneration is causally conditioned upon man's free will in conversion and, in the Calvinist's opinion, would rob God of all of the glory in salvation. As J. I. Packer states, "All Arminianisms involve a measure of synergism, if not strong (God helps me to save myself) then weak (I help God to save me)."[20] And as John R. de Witt concludes, synergism essentially is "an attack upon the majesty of God, and puts in place of it the exaltation of man."[21]

This thesis evaluates both the Arminian and modified views as unbiblical in nature and consequently as failing to do justice to the scriptural portrayal of God's sovereignty and glory in salvation. Moreover, since the glory of God is at stake, such a debate is no small matter. Perhaps nobody understood this as much as John Calvin. Commenting on Calvin's monergism, I. John Hesselink remarks, "If that grace is undercut by some form of cooperation (synergism) between a semiautonomous 'free' human being and the sovereign Lord, the glory of God is compromised, as far as Calvin is concerned."[22] The thesis of this project is in agreement with Calvin

20. J. I. Packer, "Arminianisms," in *Puritan Papers*, vol. 5: *1968–1969*, ed. J. I. Packer (Phillipsburg, NJ: P&R Publishing, 2005), 39.

21. John R. de Witt, "The Arminian Conflict and the Synod of Dort," in *Puritan Papers*, vol. 5, ed. Packer, 23.

22. John I. Hesselink, *Calvin's First Catechism: A Commentary* (Louisville: Westminster John Knox, 1997), 72.

precisely because Scripture itself denies that God's decision to regenerate his elect is conditioned upon man's cooperation. Only monergistic grace can fully preserve the sovereignty, glory, and majesty of God.[23] Therefore, while the present day Arminian and modified views seek to gain contemporary adherents, this project is relevant in that it is a call to evangelicals to reject the temptation of synergism in its various forms and return to the traditional Calvinist position, which is most faithful to Scripture.

VOCABULARY IN THE DEBATE

Too often in projects of this sort, whether it is from an Arminian or a Calvinist perspective, labels are thrown around carelessly. Consequently, caricatures result which only hinder dialogue in the debate. Therefore, it is crucial to categorize the terms that will be used throughout this project in relation to their respective parties. There are historical roots to both the monergism and synergism views.[24] Specifically, as many historians and theologians have recognized, we can identify at least four distinct positions concerning the monergism-synergism debate throughout church history: (1) humanistic monergism, (2) human-initiated synergism, (3) God-initiated synergism, and (4) divine monergism.[25] Each of these positions can be identified with certain groups within church history: (1) humanistic monergism is the view of Pelagius and Pelagianism, (2) human-initiated synergism is the view of Semi-Pelagianism, (3) God-initiated synergism is the view of the Semi-Augustinians, and (4) divine monergism is the view of Augustine and the Augustinians. Calvinism and Arminianism drew from these historical positions of the early and late Middle Ages. Calvinism appeals to Augustine for its view of efficacious grace.

23. John M. Frame, *Salvation Belongs to the Lord* (Phillipsburg, NJ: P&R Publishing, 2006), 186.

24. See chapter 2 of *Reclaiming Monergism*, e-book, to see how the four categories outlined in this section can be traced throughout church history.

25. Robert A. Peterson and Michael D. Williams, *Why I Am Not an Arminian* (Downers Grove, IL: IVP, 2004), 20–41.

On the other hand, Arminianism is diverse. Some, such as Philip Limborch and, today, Jack Cottrell and Clark Pinnock, advocate a view which aligns itself with Semi-Pelagianism. However, many Arminians have rejected Semi-Pelagianism and instead have affirmed what is the equivalent of the Semi-Augustinian view as they seek to be faithful to Arminius himself.[26]

While these groupings may not encompass every theologian or movement, they are descriptive of the majority and serve to categorize each view according to the historical context. The parameters of this project are not broad enough to include an exhaustive history of all the views mentioned above. Other very capable historians have provided such histories elsewhere. Instead, this project will limit itself primarily to the theological arguments of the Calvinist position, the Arminian views, and recent modified views, drawing secondarily from history where necessary to show the origins, developments, and arguments of each view.

CONCLUSION

With these categories in mind we are now ready to enter into the monergism-synergism debate.[27] We shall begin in chapter 1 by first examining how monergism has been defined and defended in the Calvinist tradition. In chapter 2 we will turn to Scripture's affirmation of man's

26. William Gene Witt, "Creation, Redemption and Grace in the Theology of Jacob Arminius" (PhD diss., University of Notre Dame, 1993), 2:612.

27. There are four significant presuppositions to this project that should be identified. (1) This entire discussion assumes the legitimacy of the *ordo salutis* as a theological category. (2) Union with Christ serves as an umbrella category within which the entire *ordo salutis* finds its beginning, fulfillment, and *telos*, though it is in effectual calling and regeneration that the sinner is first united to Christ in time. (3) While all three persons of the Trinity are at work in each stage of salvation, it is the Holy Spirit in particular who takes on a central role in effectual calling and regeneration. (4) While there are diverse views among Reformed theologians as to the relationship between effectual calling and regeneration, I sympathize with older Reformed confessions/theologians who see them as intimately connected, if not synonymous. For a more extensive treatment of each of these, including an entire appendix devoted to number 4, see *Reclaiming Monergism*, e-book, from P&R Publishing.

total depravity and bondage of the will. Chapters 3 and 4 will make the case that in Scripture not only is there a gospel call but an effectual call. Furthermore, when Scripture speaks of regeneration it does so in monergistic terms. Chapter 5 will transition to the Arminian view(s), seeking to represent the synergistic position, while chapter 6 will provide a critique, demonstrating that such a view is unbiblical. Finally, chapter 7 will assess contemporary attempts at a *via media*, arguing that such attempts are fundamentally flawed.

MONERGISM IN THE CALVINIST TRADITION

This chapter will enter into the historical context in which the doctrine of monergism has been defended by seeking out several key representatives from the Reformed tradition, including Augustine, Calvin, the Canons of Dort, and the Westminster Confession.[1] While these are only a small sampling of the many voices in Reformed theology, they do serve to bring out the best formulations in the Calvinist tradition. They also demonstrate that this tradition has consistently affirmed the doctrine of monergism as that which is taught in Scripture and has rejected various forms of synergism as unbiblical. By examining these specific representatives we will see *exactly how* Calvinists historically have made their case for the doctrine of monergism. To skip over the history of a debate that is almost two millennia old would be irresponsible and runs the risk of applying labels (Pelagianism, Semi-Pelagianism, etc.) inaccurately. We can avoid this error by carefully examining some of the major monergism-synergism controversies.

AUGUSTINE: *DOCTOR GRATIAE*

Sovereign grace is typically associated with Calvinism, and for good reason, since it was John Calvin and his followers who articulated the

---

1. For many other Reformed confessions, see James Dennison Jr., ed., *Reformed Confessions of the Sixteenth and Seventeenth Centuries in English Translation*, 3 vols. to date (Grand Rapids: Reformation Heritage, 2008–12). For interaction with far more secondary sources on Augustine, Calvin, Dort, and Westminster, see chapter 1 of *Reclaiming Monergism*, e-book, from P&R Publishing.

doctrine of effectual grace so clearly against the synergists of the sixteenth and seventeenth centuries. However, in reading Calvin it is immediately apparent that he was not inventing the doctrine but was himself tremendously indebted to Augustine (354–430). As Albert Outler has noted, the "central theme in all Augustine's writings is the sovereign God of grace and the sovereign grace of God."[2] Therefore, it is Augustine who is the *terminus a quo* for the debate over grace and free will.[3] However, in order to understand Augustine's gracious monergism one must first understand Pelagianism and Semi-Pelagianism.

Pelagianism, Semi-Pelagianism, and Semi-Augustinianism

Pelagius (c. 350), educated in Eastern theology (i.e., Antiochian) with a thorough knowledge of the Greek fathers, had a zeal that manifested itself in the ascetic legalism of monastery life and moral reform.[4] However, it was the theology behind the moral reform that aroused the attention of Augustine.

First, Pelagius denied *tradux peccati* (transmitted sin) and *peccatum originis* (original sin), consisting of both inherited guilt and corruption.[5] To Pelagius, it is blasphemous to think that God would transmit or impute Adam's guilt and corruption to his progeny. Instead, Adam was an isolated person, not a representative of all mankind, and his act of sin injured himself alone, merely setting a bad example for all who followed to imitate.[6]

2. Albert C. Outler, "Introduction," in Augustine, *Confessions and Enchiridion*, LCC, vol. 7, ed. Albert C. Outler (Philadelphia: Westminster, 1955), 14–15. Unless otherwise noted, all quotations from Augustine are designated by book and are taken from *Answer to the Pelagians I–IV*, ed. John E. Rotelle, trans. Roland J. Teske, part 1, vols. 23–26 of *The Works of Saint Augustine: A Translation for the Twenty-first Century*, ed. Boniface Ramsey (New York: New City, 1997–99).

3. Mark E. Vanderschaaf, "Predestation and Certainty of Salvation in Augustine and Calvin," *RR* 30 (1976–77): 1.

4. See B. R. Rees, *Pelagius: Life and Letters*, 2 vols. in one (Rochester, NY: Boydell, 1998), 1:xiv; Pelagius, *Pelagius's Commentary on St. Paul's Epistle to the Romans*, trans. Theodore De Bruyn (Oxford: Oxford University Press, 1993).

5. Rees, *Pelagius*, 1:91; William J. Collinge, "Introduction," in *Saint Augustine: Four Anti-Pelagian Writings*, trans. John A. Mourant and William J. Collinge (Washington, DC: The Catholic University of America Press, 1992), 8–9.

6. Augustine, *Nature and Grace*, in *Answer to the Pelagians I*, 10; Pelagius, *Commentary on Romans*, 92; Robert F. Evans, *Four Letters of Pelagius* (New York: Seabury, 1968), 97; J. Patout Burns, "Introduction," in *Theological Anthropology*, ed. and trans. J. Patout Burns, Sources of

Second, since no guilt or corruption is inherited by Adam's posterity, the will is free, unhindered by a depraved nature.[7] The will is not enslaved to sin or in bondage to sin, but is just as able after the fall as before to choose that which is good.[8] Therefore, Pelagius took offense at Augustine's prayer, *Da quod iubes, et iube quod vis* ("Give what you command; command what you will"), because these words "undermine moral responsibility."[9]

Third, since man is not infected by the guilt or corruption of Adam's sin and consequently man's will retains its ability to choose good or evil equally, an assisting grace lacks necessity. For Pelagius the will is not free if it is in need of God's help. Therefore, he rejected irresistible grace, as evident in his interpretation of Romans 8:29–30, "Those he foreknew would believe he called. Now a call gathers together those who are willing, not those who are unwilling."[10] Grace does not consist in a sovereign or efficacious work of the Spirit upon a depraved sinner, as it would for Augustine, but in a mere external *illuminatio* (illumination) or revelation (enlightenment) of (1) the law of God, (2) creation, and (3) the example of Christ.[11] Therefore, salvation is monergistic for Pelagius but it is a *humanistic* monergism because God's aid (*adjutorium*) is not fundamentally necessary or prevenient since man is able in and of himself to exercise works of righteousness that merit eternal life, and therefore save himself.[12]

Early Christian Thought (Philadelphia: Fortress, 1981), 5–6, 10–22; Rees, *Pelagius*, 1:35–36; Collinge, "Introduction," 8–9.

7. Augustine, *The Grace of Christ and Original Sin*, in *Answer to the Pelagians I*, 1.5; Rees, *Pelagius*, 1:35–36.

8. Pelagius, *Letter to Demetrias* 16.2, in Rees, *Pelagius*, 2:53; Collinge, "Introduction," 8.

9. Augustine, *Confessions*, trans. Maria Boulding, ed. John E. Rotelle, part 1, vol. 1 of *Works*, 10.40; idem, *Enchiridion on Faith, Hope, and Love*, trans. Bruce Harbert, in *On Christian Belief*, part 1, vol. 8 of *Works*, 32 (hereafter *Enchiridion*, in *Works*); Rees, *Pelagius*, 1:1; Evans, *Pelagius*, 82.

10. Pelagius, *Commentary on Romans*, 112. Also see Evans, *Pelagius*, 121.

11. "Caelestius was accused at Carthage in 411 of teaching that the Law had the same effect as the Gospel in introducing men into the kingdom of heaven." Pelagius ran into the same problem at the Synod of Diospolis. Rees, *Pelagius*, 1:32–36; Evans, *Pelagius*, 111–14; Collinge, "Introduction," 8–9.

12. Pelagius states in his *Letter to Demetrias*, "It is by doing his will that we may merit his divine grace." Rees, *Pelagius*, 1:92 (cf. 1:15, 32; especially 1:129).

The theology of Pelagius was adopted by Caelestius, who became one of Pelagius's foremost advocates, as well Julian of Eclanum.[13] Both affirmed a "*human* monergism" which "assumes that the power of the human will is decisive in the experience of salvation."[14] As Bonner observes, "Julian of Eclanum did not hesitate to speak of man as 'emancipated from God' by the possession of free will, while Caelestius asserted that the will could not be free if it need the help of God, since each of us has it in his power either to refrain from acting."[15] However, Pelagianism would be condemned by the Councils of Carthage (418), Mileve (418), and Ephesus (431), though, as seen at Carthage, Augustine's doctrines of predestination and effectual grace were not affirmed either.[16]

Pelagianism, however, was not the only view Augustine battled. Semi-Pelagianism—represented by John Cassian, Faustus of Riez, Vincent of Lérins, Gennadius of Massilia, and Arnobius, as well as the monks at Hadrumetum (Adrumetum) in Northern Africa and Southern Gaul—would also pose a threat to Augustine's view of grace as it sought a *via media* between Augustine and Pelagius.[17] In this view, while man does need God's universal grace due to the crippling effect of sin (contra Pelagianism), man is not so corrupted by the fall that he cannot initiate salvation in the first place (contra Augustine).[18] As Cassian states, "When he [God] notices good will making an appearance in us, at once he enlightens and encourages it and spurs it on to salvation, giving

13. Augustine summarizes the views of Caelestius in *The Deeds of Pelagius*, in *Answer to the Pelagians I*, 29–34.

14. Paul K. Jewett, *Election and Predestination* (Grand Rapids: Eerdmans, 1985), 6n2.

15. Gerald Bonner, *St. Augustine of Hippo: Life and Controversies* (Norwick: Canterbury, 1986), 361.

16. "The Canons of the Council of Carthage, A.D. 418," in Burns, *Theological Anthropology*, 57–60.

17. For an in-depth study of Semi-Pelagianism, see Rebecca H. Weaver, *Divine Grace and Human Agency: A Study of the Semi-Pelagian Controversy* (Macon, GA: Mercer University Press, 1996).

18. Augustine, *On Rebuke and Grace*, in *Answer to the Pelagians IV*, 45; John Cassian, *The Conferences*, trans. Boniface Ramsey, Ancient Christian Writers, 57 (New York: Newman, 1997), 13.9. Augustine wrote to the monks at Hadrumetum in his works *Grace and Free Choice* and *On Rebuke and Grace*. Augustine wrote to the monks in Southern France (Gaul) in his works *The Predestination of the Saints* and *The Gift of Perseverance*.

increase to what he himself planted and saw arise from our own efforts."[19] Therefore, while Pelagius taught a *humanistic* monergism and Augustine a *divine* monergism, the Semi-Pelagians taught a *human-initiated synergism*. Man is able to take the first move toward God, cooperating with or resisting his grace.[20]

Though Semi-Pelagianism won victories in Gaul at the Synods of Arles (472) and Lyons (475), it was condemned by the Synod of Orange (529), and yet Orange did not return completely to Augustinianism, refusing to accept irresistible grace, but rather, under the influence of Prosper of Aquitaine, endorsed what is today labeled Semi-Augustinianism, as did the Synod of Valence (529).[21] Semi-Augustinianism advocates a *God-initiated synergism*. While man is incapable of initiating salvation due to the bondage of his will, God provides a universal, prevenient grace, mitigating total depravity, enabling man to cooperate.[22] While God is credited with the initiation of salvation, ultimately man's will has the final say and determination. As will be seen in chapter 5, the synergism of classical Arminianism would closely parallel Semi-Augustinianism.

Augustine and the *Causa Gratiae*

When Augustine first came to affirm sovereign grace, Pelagianism was not what initially motivated him. Ten years prior to the controversy (c. 400) Augustine, reflecting on what Paul says in Romans 9, wrote *Confessions*, in which he exposes the depravity and utter inability of man's free will and exalts the sovereign grace of God.[23] Augustine's affirmation of sovereign grace was truly a reflection upon the events of his own conversion in the garden at Milan.[24] But Augustine was officially provoked when Pelagius wrote *On Nature* (*De Natura*) and *On Free Will*

---

19. Cassian, *The Conferences*, 13.8.
20. Robert A. Peterson and Michael D. Williams, *Why I Am Not an Arminian* (Downers Grove, IL: InterVarsity Press, 2004), 21–40.
21. "The Synod of Orange, A.D. 529," in Burns, *Theological Anthropology*, 109–28.
22. Peterson and Williams, *Why I Am Not an Arminian*, 38–39.
23. Augustine, *Confessions*, 10.32.
24. Bonner, *St. Augustine*, 357–58.

"since in them he had too little to say about divine grace and too much about the human will."[25]

First, contrary to Pelagius, Augustine, on the basis of passages like Psalm 51; Ephesians 2:1–3; John 3:3–5; and especially Romans 5:12, affirmed the doctrine of original sin as a universal reality making all of mankind a *massa peccati* (mass of sin) deserving damnation.[26] When Adam sinned, via pride (*superbia*), he brought all of his progeny from a *status integritatis* (state of integrity) to a *status corruptionis* (state of sin). Besides inheriting *originalis reatus* (original guilt), Adam's progeny inherited a corrupt and depraved nature, leading Augustine to say with Paul, "There is none who seeks after God" (Rom 3:11).[27] Augustine, reading Paul, argues that the corruption inherited from Adam is pervasive in nature, meaning that every aspect of man (will, mind, affections, etc.) is infected by sin so that no part of him escapes sin's pollution.

Second, one of the consequences of the fall and the transmission of corruption is the captivity of the will. The will, while previously able to choose good (meaning sin was only a *possibility* not a necessity), after the fall finds itself enslaved to sin, transgressing out of *necessity*. While before the fall the will of man possessed the *posse peccare* (the ability to sin) and the *posse non peccare* (the ability not to sin), after the fall the will of man is *non posse non peccare* (not able not to sin).[28] Consequently, though before the fall man possessed an inclination for good, after the fall man's will is inclined toward evil, making sin its master.[29] Augustine, however, does not mean that as a result of the fall man no longer has moral agency, for that would mitigate culpability. On the contrary, the

---

25. Rees, *Pelagius*, 1:9. It should be noted that Caelestius was the first target in Augustine's anti-Pelagian writings though Augustine would respond to Pelagius for the first time in 415 with *On Nature and Grace*.

26. Bonner, *St. Augustine*, 371.

27. Augustine, *Marriage and Desire*, in *Answer to the Pelagians II*, 2.47; idem, *Nature and Grace*, in *Answer to the Pelagians I*, 21; idem, *The Punishment and Forgiveness of Sins*, in *Answer to the Pelagians I*, 1.10.

28. Augustine, *On Rebuke and Grace*, in *Answer to the Pelagians IV*, 31–33.

29. Augustine, *Enchiridion*, in *Works*, 104–6; idem, *The Perfection of Human Righteousness*, in *Answer to the Pelagians I*, 9.

issue is not whether or not man has moral agency but whether moral agency after the fall is good or evil.[30]

It could be objected, however, that if man is a slave to sin, there can be no freedom of the will, for he does not sin voluntarily. However, Augustine argues that this bondage is a *willful* bondage to sin (*servum arbitrium*). Yes, without the *adiutorium Dei* the sinner is unable to will righteousness and therefore he sins necessarily. However, it is not the case that the sinner wants to will righteousness and God will not let him. Rather, the sinner does not *desire* or *want* to will righteousness at all. Therefore, he is both free and a slave simultaneously. He is free in the sense that he sins willfully according to the desires of his flesh. However, his sinful desires stem from a corrupt nature and therefore he sins out of necessity.[31] Augustine argues from John 8:36 and Ephesians 2:8 that it is only by God's saving grace that man can be set free from his slavery to sin and instead become, as Paul says, a slave to righteousness. For Augustine the sinner possesses a *liberum arbitrium captivatum* (captive free will) and is in need of a grace that liberates, resulting in a *liberum arbitrium liberatum* (liberated free will).[32] Grace, therefore, does not abolish the will but establishes it (John 8:24–26; 2 Cor. 3:17; Gal. 5:1).

Third, Augustine not only taught that grace is necessary but also that it is both particular and efficacious. God does not bestow his special, saving grace upon all of mankind and wait to see if man will cooperate with it (i.e., synergism), but God works upon his elect in an irresistible manner, giving the sinner a new heart and a renewed will so that the sinner *will* respond in faith and repentance (i.e., monergism). Therefore, it is God's grace that causes and effects man's will to respond in faith, rather than man's will that causes and effects God's grace.[33]

30. Augustine, *Grace and Free Choice*, in *Answer to the Pelagians IV*, 31.

31. Augustine, *Enchiridion*, in *Basic Writings of Saint Augustine*, 2 vols., ed. Whitney J. Oates (New York: Random, 1948), 1:675.

32. Augustine, *Answer to the Two Letters of the Pelagians*, in *Answer to the Pelagians II*, 1.9; idem, *City of God*, trans. Henry Bettenson (London: Penguin, 1984), 5.10; 14.6; idem, *Enchiridion*, in *Works*, 30, 104–6.

33. See Augustine, *Answer to the Two Letters of the Pelagians*, 2.18, 21–22, 23; 4:14; idem, *On the Grace of Christ and Original Sin*, in *Answer to the Pelagians I*, 1.27, 34; idem, *On the Predestination of the Saints*, in *Answer to the Pelagians IV*, 13, 15, 39, 41; idem, *The Punishment*

Irresistible grace is the natural consequence of an omnipotent Savior. An omnipotent God cannot have his will defeated.[34] God has "omnipotent power over human hearts to turn them where he pleased."[35] However, *gratia irresistibilis* does not mean that man does not resist God, but rather that when God so chooses to act upon his elect he overcomes all of man's resistance. Augustine demonstrates from texts like 1 Corinthians 1:24; Romans 8:28–29; 9:12–13; and 11:25–29 that there are two distinct callings, one universal and the other particular.[36] The former is the gospel call that many people reject while the latter is efficacious, so that those whom the Father draws always come to Jesus. Citing John 6:45, Augustine explains, "But everyone who has learned from the Father not only has the possibility of coming, but actually comes!"[37] As a consequence of God's special call, the sinner's heart of stone is replaced with a heart of flesh by the power of the Spirit (Ezek. 11:19–20; 36:22–27).[38] Only then can the sinner begin to love God. In other words, it is the sovereign act of the Spirit, not man's free choice, that causes the sinner to experience new affections for Christ.[39] Those who have been awakened to new life by efficacious grace have a will that has been liberated, renewed, and reoriented to desire God rather than sin.[40]

---

and *Forgiveness of Sins*, in *Answer to the Pelagians I*, 2.5, 30; idem, *Enchiridion*, in *Works*, 31–32; idem, *On the Spirit and the Letter*, in *Answer to the Pelagians I*, 52; idem, *On Grace and Free Choice*, 17, 29, 32–33, 40.

34. Augustine, *On Rebuke and Grace*, in *Answer to the Pelagians IV*, 45.

35. Ibid.

36. Augustine, *On the Predestination of the Saints*, 32–33.

37. Augustine, *The Grace of Christ and Original Sin*, 1.27. Also see idem, *On the Predestination of the Saints*, 13; idem, *The Grace of Christ and Original Sin*, 1.14–15; 1.19–22.

38. Augustine, *Grace and Free Choice*, 29; idem, *On the Predestination of the Saints*, 40–43.

39. Augustine, *The Spirit and Letter*, 5.

40. Augustine, *On Rebuke and Grace*, 3; idem, *The Gift of Perseverance*, in *Answer to the Pelagians IV*, 53; idem, *Grace and Free Choice*, 31, 32, 41; idem, *On Rebuke and Grace*, 35. Augustine also appeals to 1 Cor. 4:7; Prov. 8:35; Ps. 37:23; Phil. 2:13; and especially Rom. 9:16 to demonstrate that though our wills are evil God grants us a good will, not on the basis of anything in us but because of his own good pleasure. Augustine, *The Punishment and Forgiveness of Sins*, in *Answer to the Pelagians I*, 2.27–30; idem, *Enchiridion*, in *Works*, 32; idem, *On the Spirit and the Letter*, 11; idem, *Answer to the Two Letters of the Pelagians*, 2.21; idem, *Grace and Free Choice*, 32.

Fourth, if it is God who must liberate the will from its bondage to sin, so also it is God who must grant man faith to believe.[41] According to Augustine, Scripture teaches that faith is *gratia dei gratuita* (a gift from God) rather than a product of man's autonomous will.[42] Augustine appeals to passages like Ephesians 1:13–16; 2:8; Philippians 1:28–29; and 1 Thessalonians 2:13 to show that the *initium fidei* (beginning of faith) is all of God. Moreover, Augustine is clear that faith is not merely offered as a gift but God actually works faith within. In other words, when God calls us to faith, he does not merely make faith possible but actually makes sure we will come to faith without fail. As Augustine states, "The will itself is something God works [*operatur*] in us."[43] Therefore, Carey is right to conclude that for Augustine grace is not merely a *"necessary precondition* of faith but a *sufficient cause* of it . . . not only prevenient but *efficacious* in itself."[44] Interpreting John 6:45, Augustine argues that "God's grace gives us actualities, not mere possibilities." Grace "does not simply make faith possible; it causes us to believe."[45] And yet, coercion is nowhere in view, but rather an "ineffable sweetness" (1 Cor. 3:7).[46]

The Pelagian and Semi-Pelagian controversies thus turn upon one question: is redemption the work of God or the work of man? Stated otherwise, does grace depend upon the will of man or does the will of man depend upon grace? For Augustine, if grace is not necessary, sufficient, and efficacious, God is robbed of his glory and man given the credit in salvation.

THE REFORMATION

Augustine's understanding of sin and grace would be influential, infiltrating the theology of Prosper of Aquitaine, Fulgentius of Ruspe, Avitus of Vienne, and Caesarius of Arles, even being restated in works

41. Augustine, *The Spirit and the Letter*, 54, 57–60.
42. Augustine, *Grace and Free Choice*, 30; idem, *The Predestination of the Saints*, 16.
43. Augustine, *Revisions*, trans. Boniface Ramsey, part 1, vol. 2 of *Works*, 3.3.
44. Phillip Cary, *Inner Grace: Augustine in the Traditions of Plato and Paul* (Oxford: Oxford University Press, 2008), 55, emphasis added. Also see 56, 87–88, 95.
45. Ibid., 96.
46. Augustine, *The Grace of Christ and Original Sin*, 1.14.

like the *Indiculus* (c. 435–42).[47] However, by others "Augustine was reinterpreted, so that theologians came to call themselves 'Augustinian' while rejecting his views on irresistible grace and predestination."[48] To make matters worse, Semi-Pelagianism, despite being condemned by the Council of Orange, continued to spread during the medieval period.[49]

The Late Medieval Background

At least two scholastic schools of thought emerged in the late medieval period, one being the *via moderna* and the other the *schola Augustiniana moderna*. The *via moderna*, represented by William of Ockham, Pierre d'Ailly, Robert Holcot, and Gabriel Biel, held an optimistic view of human ability, arguing that man is able to do everything needed to be right with God.[50] In contrast, the *schola Augustiniana moderna*, represented by Thomas Bradwardine, Gregory of Rimini, and Hugolino of Orvieto, held a pessimistic view of man's ability, arguing, similar to Augustine, that man can do nothing apart from effectual grace. As Ozment and McGrath explain, the debate between these schools was a replay of the controversy between Pelagius and Augustine.[51]

---

47. Jaroslav Pelikan, *The Emergence of the Catholic Tradition (100–600)*, vol. 1 of *The Christian Tradition: A History of the Development of Doctrine* (Chicago: University of Chicago Press, 1971), 318–31. Prosper, however, would soften Augustine's views considerably. See Prosper, *Grace and Free Will*, vol. 7 of *The Fathers of the Church*, ed. Joseph Deferrari, trans. J. Reginald O'Donnell (New York: Fathers of the Church, 1947), 1.5.

48. Justo L. González, *The Story of Christianity*, 2 vols. (New York: HarperSanFrancisco, 1984), 1:215.

49. I have chosen to bypass the *early* medieval era. This does not mean that the monergism-synergism debate did not continue after Augustine (see Gregory the Great, Gottschalk, Councils of Quiercy and Valence, Anselm, Aquinas, Ockham, etc.), but only that I have chosen to focus very briefly on the late medieval ages due to the immediate context it provides to Reformers like Calvin.

50. David C. Steinmetz, *Luther in Context* (Grand Rapids: Baker, 2002), 61–62; Alister McGrath, *The Intellectual Origins of the European Reformation* (New York: Basil Blackwell, 1987), 73–74, 90–92, 178; Steven Ozment, *The Age of Reform, 1250–1550: An Intellectual and Religious History of Late Medieval and Reformation Europe* (New Haven: Yale, 1980), 40 (cf. 41, 234–37); Heiko A. Oberman, *The Harvest of Medieval Theology: Gabriel Biel and Late Medieval Nominalism* (Grand Rapids: Eerdmans, 1967), 207.

51. Ozment, *The Age of Reform*, 40–42; Alister E. McGrath, *Reformation Thought: An Introduction*, 3rd ed. (Oxford: Blackwell, 1998), 72; idem, *Intellectual Origins*, 104–5.

The position of the *via moderna* can be summarized by the slogan *facere quod in se est*, meaning "doing what lies within you" or "doing your best." In other words, the demands of God's covenant were that man is to do his best and when he does God is obligated to accept his work as sufficient for eternal life. Stated otherwise, *facienti quod in se est Deus non denegat gratiam* ("God will not deny grace to anyone who does what lies within them").

In contrast, the *schola Augustiniana moderna* reacted strongly to the *via moderna*, especially as it took root at the University of Oxford, Merton College. Bradwardine ignited the backlash with his book *De causa Dei contra Pelagium* (*The Case of God against Pelagius*), in which he attacked the *via moderna* as modern-day Pelagianism and argued for a return to Augustine's anti-Pelagian writings.[52] Bradwardine's arguments would be reiterated by John Wycliffe (1328–84) in England but it would be Gregory of Rimini (c. 1300–1358) who would be responsible for an "Augustinian renaissance," whereby salvation was considered totally the work of God.[53]

In spite of the *schola Augustiniana moderna*, the *via moderna* would have an enormous influence as the church became characterized by a Pelagianism and Semi-Pelagianism that relied heavily on a sacramental theology of merit. By the late Middle Ages, as McGrath argues, it "was widely held that salvation was something that could be earned by good works, which included fulfilling the moral law and observing a vast range of ecclesiastical rules."[54] Consequently, though there were exceptions, "popular Pelagianism was rampant"

---

52. Thomas Bradwardine, *De Causa Dei*, ed. Henry Savile (Frankfurt: Gruyter, 1964), 1.42. Also see Gordon Leff, *Bradwardine and the Pelagians: A Study of His "De Causa Dei" and Its Opponents* (Cambridge: Cambridge University Press, 1957), 69; Heiko A. Oberman, *Forerunners of the Reformation: The Shape of Late Medieval Thought*, trans. Paul L. Nyhus (Philadelphia: Fortress, 1981), 151–64; McGrath, *Reformation Thought*, 57–60; Jaroslav Pelikan, *Reformation of Church and Dogma (1300–1700)*, vol. 4 of *The Christian Tradition: A History of the Development of Doctrine* (Chicago: University of Chicago Press, 1984), 32.

53. Heiko A. Oberman, *Masters of the Reformation*, trans. Dennis Martin (Cambridge, MA: Harvard University Press, 1981), 70–71; idem, *Forerunners of the Reformation*, 151–64.

54. Alister E. McGrath, *Studies in Doctrine* (Grand Rapids: Zondervan, 1997), 386.

and pure soteriological Augustinianism was lost.[55] However, with the Reformation would come a return to an Augustinian soteriology, with an emphasis on the efficacy of grace and the sovereignty of God in salvation.

The Reformers

Augustine's anti-Pelagian writings were "a rich resource for the Reformers in establishing their views of the 'servitude' of the human will and the freeness and power of divine grace."[56] As Childs Robinson observes, "On account of its rediscovery of the doctrines of grace, the Reformation has been hailed as a revival of Augustinianism. . . . Luther, Zwingli, Calvin, Knox—all echo Augustine's conviction that grace does not find us willing; it makes us willing."[57] For example, Martin Luther, who was immersed in the theology of the *via moderna* at the University of Erfurt (1501–5) and again at the Augustinian monastery (1505), not only countered the Pelagianism and Semi-Pelagianism of the *via moderna* with his biblical understanding (cf. Rom. 1:17) of the *iustitia Dei* (initially aroused by his burning question *Wie kriege ich einen gnädigen Gott?*), but also, in his 1525 *De servo arbitrio* (*Bondage of the Will*) against Erasmus's 1524 *De libero arbitrio* (*Diatribe on Free Will*; cf. *Hyperaspistes I, II*), defended an Augustinian understanding of man's depravity and God's efficacious grace over against Erasmus's Ockhamist Semi-Pelagianism.[58]

One must not miss the close connection between justification by grace alone (*sola gratia*) through faith alone (*sola fide*) on the basis of Christ's work alone (*solus Christus*) and the doctrine of efficacious grace. If justification is by faith alone, then it is by grace not works, and if by grace, then it is the gift of God. Moreover, if it is the gift of God, then even faith itself must be the gift of God. And if faith itself is a gift of

---

55. Ibid., 387.

56. Paul Helm, *Calvin at the Centre* (Oxford: Oxford University Press, 2010), 202.

57. Childs Robinson, *The Reformation: A Rediscovery of Grace* (Grand Rapids: Eerdmans, 1962), 8. Also see Carl R. Trueman, "Calvin and Reformed Orthodoxy," in *The Calvin Handbook*, ed. Herman J. Selderhuis (Grand Rapids: Eerdmans, 2009), 476.

58. Martin Luther, *Bondage of the Will*, vol. 33 of *Luther's Works*, ed. Jaroslav Pelikan, Hilton C. Oswald, and Helmut T. Lehmann (Philadelphia: Fortress, 1957).

God, then it follows that God and God alone brings new life into the dead sinner, creating repentance and faith in Christ. As Calvin says, faith as a work itself ("I am justified *because I believe*") is ruled out completely, so that in no way can it be said that it is my decision that brings about justification.[59] McGrath explains,

> A popular misunderstanding of the Reformation doctrine of justi-fication by faith is that we are justified *because we believe*, that it is our decision to believe that brings about our justification. Here faith is understood as a human work, something which we do—and so we are justified on the basis of our works! This is actually the later doctrine, especially associated with seventeenth-century Arminian-ism, of "justification *propter fidem per Christum*," justification on account of faith through Christ (rather than "justification *per fidem propter Christum*," justification by faith on account of Christ). The Reformation doctrine affirms the activity of God and the passivity of humanity in justification. Faith is not something human we do, but something divine that is wrought within us. "Faith is the principal work of the Holy Spirit" (Calvin), and it is through faith that Christ and all his benefits are received.[60]

J. I. Packer also makes a similar observation that is telling:

> "Justification by faith only" is a truth that needs interpretation. The principle of *sola fide* is not rightly understood till it is seen as anchored in the broader principle of *sola gratia*. What is the source and status of faith? Is it the God-given means whereby the God-given justification is received, or is it a condition of justification which it is left to man to fulfill? Is it a part of God's gift of salvation, or is it man's own contribu-tion to salvation? Is our salvation wholly of God, or does it ultimately depend on something we do for ourselves? Those who say the latter (as the Arminians later did) thereby deny man's utter helplessness in sin,

59. John Calvin, *Institutes of the Christian Religion*, ed. John T. McNeil, trans. Ford Lewis Battles, LCC, vols. 20–21 (Philadelphia: Westminster John Knox, 1960), 3.11.7. Also see Helm, *Calvin at the Centre*, 214, 220.
60. McGrath, *Studies in Doctrine*, 391.

and affirm that a form of semi-Pelagianism is true after all. It is no wonder, then, that later Reformed theology condemned Arminianism as being in principle a return to Rome (because in effect it turned faith into a meritorious work) and a betrayal of the Reformation (because it denied the sovereignty of God in saving sinners, which was the deepest religious and theological principle of the Reformers' thought). Arminianism was, indeed, in Reformed eyes a renunciation of New Testament Christianity in favour of New Testament Judaism; for to rely on oneself for faith is no different in principle from relying on oneself for works, and the one is as un-Christian and anti-Christian as the other. In the light of what Luther says to Erasmus, there is no doubt that he would have endorsed this judgment.[61]

Therefore, though the doctrines of forensic justification and moral regeneration must remain distinct (the former a change in status and the latter a change in nature), they are intimately connected in attributing to God alone the efficacy in creating within us saving faith, a reality Arminianism would later struggle to explain in demanding that grace be conditioned upon man's free will.

JOHN CALVIN: THEOLOGIAN OF SOVEREIGN GRACE

While not all Reformers would adhere to Augustine's monergism (note, for example, the synergism of Philip Melanchthon), most would owe a debt to Augustine as they drew from his works in order to defend the irresistibility of grace in the elect against the papist synergism of their day. This is apparent in a host of sixteenth- and seventeenth-century Reformers.[62] First among these is the second-generation Reformer John

61. J. I. Packer, "Historical and Theological Introduction," in Martin Luther, *The Bondage of the Will*, trans. J. I. Packer and O. R. Johnston (Grand Rapids: Baker, 1957), 59. Also see Richard B. Gaffin, "Justification and Union with Christ (3.11–19)," in *A Theological Guide to Calvin's Institutes*, ed. David W. Hall and Peter A. Lillback (Phillipsburg, NJ: P&R Publishing, 2008), 259.

62. Consider Theodore Beza, Conrad Vorstius, Huldrych Zwingli, Heinrich Bullinger, Amandus Polanus, Wolfgang Capito, Peter Martyr Vermigli, Girolamo Zanchi, John à Lasco, Martin Bucer, John Knox, Zacharias Ursinus, Caspar Olevianus, Lambert Daneau, Francis Junius, William Perkins, Heinrich Bullinger; Johannes Wollebius; Franciscus Gomarus; William Ames, James Ussher, Gisbertius Boetius, Franciscus Burmannus, Herman Witsius,

Calvin. No other Reformer articulated the monergism of Augustine as well as Calvin.

Calvin's understanding of grace is explicit both in his *Institutes of the Christian Religion* (1536–59) and in *The Bondage and Liberation of the Will* (1543), which is his reply to the Dutch Roman Catholic and Louvain scholar Albertus Pighius, who represented the Vatican at Worms and Regensburg (1540/41).[63] In *The Bondage and Liberation of the Will* Calvin is responding to the first six books of Pighius's 1542 work *Ten Books on Human Free Choice and Divine Grace*. Although Pighius died before Calvin finished his entire response, the controversy between Calvin and Jerome Bolsec over predestination almost ten years later (1552) would inspire Calvin to finish his response to Pighius's last four books in *De aeterna Dei praedestinatione* (*Concerning the Eternal Predestination of God*).[64] By 1559 Calvin had completed his final edition of the *Institutes* and his understanding of grace and free will is again evident, but this time imbued with all the experience of his debates with Pighius.

Pervasive Depravity and the Bondage of the Will

Calvin begins with the first sin of Adam and, like Paul in Romans 5, draws the connection from Adam to all of humanity. When Adam sinned he "entangled and immersed his offspring in the same miseries."[65] Calvin defines original sin as "a hereditary depravity and corruption of our nature, diffused into all parts of the soul, which first makes us liable to God's wrath, then also brings forth in us those works which Scripture calls 'works

and Johannes Hericus Heideggerus. Also consider: Riissen, Maresius, Mastricht, Heidegger, Polan, Wolleb, Burmann, Crocius, Voetius, Keckermann, Bucan, Pictet, Turretin, Owen, Charnock, Flavel, and Howe. See Heinrich Heppe, *Reformed Dogmatics: Set Out and Illustrated from the Sources*, ed. Ernst Bizer, trans. G. T. Thomson (Eugene, OR: Wipf & Stock, 1950), 510–42.

63. John Calvin, *The Bondage and Liberation of the Will: A Defense of the Orthodox Doctrine of Human Choice against Pighius*, ed. A. N. S. Lane, trans. G. I. Davies, Texts and Studies in Reformation and Post-Reformation Thought (Grand Rapids: Baker, 1996).

64. John Calvin, *Calvin's Calvinism: Treatises on 'The Eternal Predestination of God' and 'The Secret Providence of God'*, ed. and trans. Henry Cole (London: Sovereign Grace Union, 1927).

65. Calvin, *Institutes*, 2.1.1.

of the flesh.' "[66] The result of descending from Adam's "impure seed" and being "born infected with the contagion of sin" is the pervasive corruption of man's nature.[67] "Here I only want to suggest briefly that the whole man is overwhelmed—as by a deluge—from head to foot, so that no part is immune from sin and all that proceeds from him is to be imputed to sin. As Paul says, all turnings of the thoughts to the flesh are enmities against God [Rom. 8:7], and are therefore death [Rom. 8:6]."[68] Calvin states elsewhere, "So depraved is [man's] nature that he can be moved or impelled only to evil."[69] If man has been corrupted as by a deluge and if sin permeates every recess so that "no part is immune from sin" then it follows that man's will is in bondage to sin. Calvin, against Pighius, writes, "For the will is so overwhelmed by wickedness and so pervaded by vice and corruption that it cannot in any way escape to honourable exertion or devote itself to righteousness."[70] Consequently, Calvin, with Augustine, does not hesitate to title the will "unfree."[71] Without the Spirit the will is not free but shackled and conquered by its desires.[72]

This does not mean, however, that man is coerced. Rather, man sins willingly, out of *necessity*, but not out of *compulsion*. Such a distinction is one of Calvin's chief points in his treatise against Pighius, who argues that *necessitas* (necessity) implies *coactio* (coercion). However, for Calvin "it does not follow from the denial of free will that what a person chooses is the result of coercion."[73] Coercion negates responsibility but *necessity* is "consistent with being held responsible for the action, and being praised or blamed for it."[74] Therefore, Calvin can state that man

---

66. Ibid., 2.1.8.

67. Ibid., 2.1.6.

68. Ibid., 2.1.9. Also see 2.2.12; 2.3.

69. Ibid., 2.3.5 [1539 edition]; Anthony N. S. Lane, "Anthropology," in *The Calvin Handbook*, 278–79.

70. Calvin, *Bondage and Liberation*, 77.

71. Calvin, *Institutes*, 2.2.7.

72. Calvin, *Bondage and Liberation*, 41–42 (cf. 141–42); idem, *Institutes*, 2.2.7.

73. Paul Helm, *John Calvin's Ideas* (Oxford: Oxford University Press, 2004), 162. Also see Wilhelm Niesel, *The Theology of Calvin*, trans. Harold Knight (Philadelphia: Westminster, 1956), 87.

74. Calvin, *Bondage and Liberation*, 150.

"acts wickedly by will, not by compulsion" (*Male voluntate agit, non coactione*).[75]

Does Calvin then affirm "free will"? If by freedom one means, as Lombard, the Papists, and Pighius argue, that man's will in no way is determined but man has the self-power to will good or evil toward God (what is today titled libertarian freedom), so that by his own strength he can will either equally, then free will is rejected by Calvin.[76] But if by free will one means, as Augustine maintained, that man wills out of *voluntary necessity* (not coercion) then willful choice can be affirmed.[77] Nevertheless, even if man wills out of necessity, such necessity is, prior to the application of effectual grace, only a necessity to sin. "For we do not say that man is dragged unwillingly into sinning, but that because his will is corrupt he is held captive under the yoke of sin and therefore of necessity wills in an evil way. For where there is bondage, there is necessity."[78] Therefore, the bondage of the will to sin remains, and yet, such slavery is a voluntary and willful captivity (*voluntariae suae electioni*).[79] Calvin shows how an agent can be both free and under necessity when he uses the example of the devil. The devil can only do evil all of the time, and yet, he is fully culpable for his actions and commits them voluntarily though out of necessity.[80]

75. Calvin, *Institutes*, 2.2.7; cf. 3.5; idem, *Bondage*, 68.

76. Calvin, *Bondage and Liberation*, 311; idem, *Institutes*, 2.2.7–8.

77. Calvin, *Institutes*, 2.3.5. For a defense of Calvin as a compatibilist, see Helm, *John Calvin's Ideas*, 157–83.

78. Calvin, *Bondage and Liberation*, 69. Also see Calvin, *Institutes*, 2.3.5 [1539 edition].

79. Calvin's statement on free will in his 1538 Catechism is one of his clearest and most precise definitions: "That man is enslaved to sin the Scriptures repeatedly testify. This means that his nature is so estranged from God's righteousness that he conceives, desires, and strives after nothing that is not impious, distorted, evil, or impure. For a heart deeply steeped in sin's poison can bring forth nothing but the fruits of sin. Yet we are not to suppose for that reason that man has been driven by violent necessity to sin. He transgresses out of a will utterly prone to sin. But because on account of the corruption of his feelings he utterly loathes all God's righteousness and is inflamed to every sort of wickedness, it is denied that he is endowed with the free capacity to choose good and evil which men call 'free will.'" John I. Hesselink, *Calvin's First Catechism: A Commentary* (Louisville: Westminster John Knox, 1997), 9–10 (cf. 69). Also see Calvin, *Institutes*, 2.3.5.

80. Calvin, *Institutes*, 2.3.5; idem, *Bondage and Liberation*, 149–50.

Special Calling and Effectual Grace

It is evident in Calvin's thought so far that grace is needed for the liberation of man's will. First, such grace comes before man's will (i.e., it is prevenient) in order to liberate him effectually from bondage rather than merely coming beside man's will to assist him.[81] In other words, unlike Semi-Augustinianism and the seventeenth-century Arminianism that would come after Calvin, grace is not prevenient in the sense that it simply makes salvation a possibility if man decides to cooperate with it. Rather, the prevenient grace Calvin speaks of is effectual, so that the conversion of the elect necessarily follows. As Calvin asserts, since the human will is only evil and needs transformation and renewal to will the good, God's grace is "not merely a tool which can help someone if he is pleased to stretch out his hand to [take] it." "That is, [God] does not merely offer it, leaving [to man] the choice between receiving it and rejecting it, but he steers the mind to choose what is right, he moves the will also effectively to obedience, he arouses and advances the endeavour until the actual completion of the work is attained."[82] Quoting Augustine, he concludes, "The human will does not obtain grace through its freedom, but rather freedom through grace."[83]

Second, the efficacious nature of grace also reveals the particularity of God's choice. Free will is "not sufficient to enable man to do good works, unless he be helped by grace, indeed by special grace, which only the elect receive through regeneration."[84] Calvin explains, "For I do not tarry over those fanatics who babble that grace is equally and indiscriminately distributed."[85] Against Pighius, Calvin argues,

> In addition this grace is not given to all without distinction or gener-
> ally, but only to those whom God wills; the rest, to whom it is not
> given, remain evil and have absolutely no ability to attain to the good
> because they belong to the mass that is lost and condemned and they

81. Calvin, *Institutes*, 2.2.12; 2.2.27; 2.3.5.
82. Calvin, *Bondage and Liberation*, 114. Also see 173.
83. Calvin, *Bondage and Liberation*, 130.
84. Calvin, *Institutes*, 2.2.6.
85. Ibid.; also see 3.22.10.

are left to their condemnation. In addition, this grace is not of such a kind as to bestow on [its recipients] the power to act well on condition that they will to, so that they thereafter have the option of willing or not willing. But it effectively moves them to will it; indeed it makes their evil will good, so that they of necessity will well.[86]

Therefore, Calvin would certainly have rejected what later Arminians would have meant in affirming a universal, prevenient grace. Rather, God's special grace is discriminate, particular, and efficacious.

Third, man's cooperation is excluded entirely from the process. Biblical support for this can be found in passages like Ezekiel 36, where God removes the heart of stone and implants a heart of flesh, causing the dead sinner to walk in new life, and Ephesians 2, where God works alone to bring about the "second creation" uniting us to Christ.[87] Salvation is a free gift; "if even the least ability came from ourselves, we would also have some share of the merit."[88] Quoting Psalm 100:3 ("And we ourselves have not done it") Calvin remarks, "Moreover, we see how, not simply content to have given God due praise for our salvation, he expressly excludes us from all participation in it. It is as if he were saying that not a whit remains to man to glory in, for the whole of salvation comes from God."[89]

However, Calvin anticipates an objection: "But perhaps some will concede that the will is turned away from the good by its own nature and is converted by the Lord's power alone, yet in such a way that, having been prepared, it then has its own part in the action."[90] Such an objection comes from the Semi-Augustinian view, arguing that while God initiates grace and prepares the will for subsequent acts of grace, ultimately man must do his own part for such grace to be finally successful. But Calvin answers that the very activity of the will to exercise faith is a free gift from God, eliminating any possible participation of man's

86. Calvin, *Bondage and Liberation*, 136.
87. Calvin, *Institutes*, 2.3.6.
88. Ibid.
89. Ibid.
90. Ibid., 2.3.7.

will. Therefore, it follows that "when we, who are by nature inclined to evil with our whole heart, begin to will good, we do so out of mere grace."[91] After expositing Ezekiel 36:26 and Jeremiah 32:39–40, Calvin concludes, "For it always follows that nothing good can arise out of our will until it has been reformed; and after its reformation, in so far as it is good, it is so from God, not from ourselves."[92]

> He [God] does not move the will in such a manner as has been taught and believed for many ages—that it is afterward in our choice *either to obey or resist the motion—but by disposing it efficaciously.* Therefore one must deny that oft-repeated statement of Chrysostom: "Whom he draws he draws willing." By this he signifies that the Lord is only extending his hand to await whether we will be pleased to receive his aid.[93]

Fourth, reflecting on the divine "calling" in Matthew 22:14, as well as Isaiah 54:13 (cf. John 6:44–45), Calvin observes the distinction between a general and effectual call.[94] "The Gospel is preached indiscriminately to the elect and the reprobate; but the elect alone come to Christ, because they have been 'taught by God,' and therefore to them the Prophet undoubtedly refers."[95] Commenting on the "efficacy of the Spirit," Calvin concludes, "Besides, we are taught by this passage [Isa. 54:13] that the calling of God is efficacious in the elect."[96] Likewise, in his commentary on John 6:44 Calvin first explains that though the gospel is preached to all, all do not embrace it for a "new understanding and a new perception are requisite."[97] Calvin goes on to explain that such a drawing does not consist in a mere external voice but is the secret operation of the Holy Spirit, whereby God inwardly teaches through

91. Ibid., 2.3.8.

92. Ibid., 2.3.8–9.

93. Emphasis added. Ibid., 2.3.10; also see 3.24.1–2; Calvin, *Bondage and Liberation*, 174.

94. Calvin, *Institutes*, 3.24.8.

95. John Calvin, *Commentary on the Book of the Prophet Isaiah 33–66*, trans. and ed. William Pringle, vol. 8 of *Calvin's Commentaries* (Reprint, Grand Rapids: Baker, 2005), 146.

96. Ibid., 146–47.

97. John Calvin, *Commentary on the Gospel according to John 1–11*, trans. and ed. William Pringle, in vol. 17 of *Calvin's Commentaries* (Reprint, Grand Rapids: Baker, 2005), 257.

the illumination of the heart. Calvin reveals his monergism when he concludes that men are not fit for believing until they have been drawn, and such a drawing by the grace of Christ is "efficacious, so that they necessarily believe."[98]

Sola Gratia and *Soli Deo Gloria*

Why is such a debate so crucial for Calvin? For him the glory of God is at stake in how one understands grace. Hesselink observes, "If that grace is undercut by some form of cooperation (synergism) between a semiautonomous 'free' human being and the sovereign Lord, the glory of God is compromised, as far as Calvin is concerned."[99] Such a compromise of God's glory was, for Calvin, not only unbiblical but also an assault to God himself. No one has articulated the Reformers' affirmation of monergism as well as J. I. Packer when he writes,

> Historically, it is simply a matter of fact that Martin Luther and John Calvin, and, for that matter, Ulrich Zwingli, Martin Bucer, and all the leading Protestant theologians of the first epoch of the Reformation, stood on precisely the same ground here. On other points, they had their differences; but in asserting the helplessness of man in sin, and the sovereignty of God in grace, they were entirely at one. To all of them, these doctrines were the very life-blood of the Christian faith. . . . The doctrine of free justification by faith only, which became the storm-centre of so much controversy during the Reformation period, is often regarded as the heart of the Reformers' theology, but this is hardly accurate. The truth is that their thinking was really centered upon the contention of Paul, echoed with varying degrees of adequacy by Augustine, and Gottschalk, and Bradwardine, and Wycliffe, that the sinner's entire salvation is by free and sovereign grace only. The doctrine of justification by faith was important to them because it safeguarded the principle of

---

98. Calvin, *John*, 256 (cf. 258–59). Also see Calvin, *Bondage and Liberation*, 176, 188.

99. Hesselink, *Calvin's First Catechism*, 72. Also see Alister E. McGrath, *A Life of John Calvin* (Cambridge, MA: Basil Blackwell, 1990), 145–73; Benjamin Breckenridge Warfield, *Calvin as a Theologian and Calvinism Today* (Grand Rapids: Evangelical, 1969), 26.

sovereign grace; but it actually expressed for them only one aspect of this principle, and that not its deepest aspect. The sovereignty of grace found expression in their thinking at a profounder level still, in the doctrine of *monergistic regeneration*—the doctrine, that is, that the faith which receives Christ for justification is itself the free gift of a sovereign God, bestowed by spiritual regeneration in the act of effectual calling. To the Reformers, the crucial question was not simply, whether God justifies believers without works of law. It was the broader question, whether sinners are wholly help-less in their sin, and whether God is to be thought of as saving them by free, unconditional, invincible grace, not only justifying them for Christ's sake when they come to faith, but also raising them from the death of sin by His quickening Spirit in order to bring them to faith. Here was the crucial issue: whether God is the author, not merely of justification, but also of faith; whether, in the last analysis, Christianity is a religion of utter reliance on God for salvation and all things necessary to it, or of self-reliance and self-effort.[100]

THE SYNOD OF DORT

Calvin would not be without a following as his view of grace would be defended by a host of Calvinists, including successors like Theodore Beza (1519–1605), William Perkins (1558–1602), and eventually Francis Turretin (1623–87). However, it is in the seventeenth century, with the uprising of Jacob Arminius and the Remonstrants, that Calvinism would find its greatest challenge, eventually rousing a response from the Synod of Dort (1618–19).

100. Packer, "Historical and Theological Introduction," 58–59, emphasis added. To clarify, Calvin did not always use the word "regeneration" in the narrow sense that some of his contemporaries did and as later Calvinists would (i.e., the inception of spiritual life; the new birth), but rather used it in the broad sense synonymous with sanctification. François Wendel, *Calvin: Origins and Developments of His Religious Thought*, trans. Philip Mairet (Grand Rapids: Baker, 1987), 242. However, though theological labels may differ, Calvin, other Reformers, and later Calvinists understood the *content* and *concept* of sovereign grace the same. For a comparison of Calvin with other Reformers and later Calvinists, see Kenneth Stewart, "The Doctrine of Regeneration in Evangelical Theology: The Reformation to 1800," *JBTM* 8, 1 (2011): 42–57.

Jacob Arminius

Arminianism bears the name of Jacob Arminius (1559–1609).[101] In 1582, at age twenty-two, Arminius moved to Geneva to attend the Geneva Academy under the teaching of Beza, Calvin's epigone and successor. However, it would become clear after Arminius left Geneva to pastor in Amsterdam from 1587 to 1603 that he would advocate a synergistic view of grace. In 1603 Arminius accepted a professorate at the University of Leiden and, while he would face opposition from many Calvinists, his most aggressive opponent was Franciscus Gomarus (1563–1641), a student of Beza, Whitaker, and Ursinus. Gomarus, believing Arminius's theology to be in agreement with the Jesuits and Pelagians, was not alone when he declared that Arminius violated the Belgic Confession (1561) and the Heidelberg Catechism (1563). Moreover, as Gerrit Jan Hoenderdaal observes, Arminius, along with his friend Johannes Uitenbogaert (1557–1644), "joined in wanting the [Belgic] Confession and the [Heidelberg] Catechism to be 'revisable and reformable.' "[102] Despite the claims of some historians that Arminius was part of the Reformed tradition, Richard Muller has successfully demonstrated that the synergism of Arminius was, in the eyes of seventeenth-century Reformers, an obvious violation of the Reformed confessions for "the basic doctrinal position advanced both in the Confession and in the synods was anti-synergistic, namely, monergistic."[103]

101. For resources on the life and theology of Arminius on which I am dependent, see chapter 5 and the bibliography. But especially see Carl Bangs, *Arminius: A Study in the Dutch Reformation* (Grand Rapids: Zondervan, 1985); Richard A. Muller, *God, Creation, and Providence in the Thought of Jacob Arminius: Sources and Directions of Scholastic Protestantism in the Era of Early Orthodoxy* (Grand Rapids: Baker, 1991); Keith D. Stanglin and Thomas H. McCall, *Jacob Arminius: Theologian of Grace* (Oxford: Oxford University Press, 2012); William den Boer, *God's Twofold Love: The Theology of Jacob Arminius (1559–1609)*, trans. Albert Gootjes, vol. 14 in Reformed Historical Theology, ed. Herman J. Selderhuis (Göttingen: Vandenhoeck and Ruprecht, 2010).

102. Gerrit Jan Hoenderdaal, "The Life and Struggle of Arminius in the Dutch Republic," in *Man's Faith and Freedom: The Theological Influence of Jacobus Arminius*, ed. Gerald O. McCulloh (New York: Abingdon, 1962), 15.

103. Richard A. Muller, "Arminius and the Reformed Tradition," *WTJ* 70 (2008): 31–47. Also see idem, *God, Creation, and Providence*, 42; Louis Praamsma, "Background of Arminian

One year before Arminius's death, his departure from the Reformed confessions would become even more explicit in his *Declaration of Sentiments* (1608; presented before the Calvinistic Estates General of Holland), which included a clear affirmation of synergism as well as a refutation of Calvinism's decretal theology. For Arminius, while it is necessary for God to provide a prevenient grace that mitigates man's pervasive depravity and enables belief, God's saving act to finally convert and regenerate the sinner is conditioned upon the free choice of man to accept or reject grace.[104] Such a synergistic view shared many similarities with the synergism of medieval theologian Gabriel Biel, which only fueled the charge, even if it be an inaccurate one, that Arminius was advocating Semi-Pelagianism (see chapter 5).

The Arminian Remonstrants

Though Arminius died in 1609, his synergism filled many churches in Amsterdam so that by 1610 there were many Arminian pastors. Perhaps two of his most important successors were Conrad Vorstius (1569–1622), opposed by King James himself, and Simon Episcopius (1583–1643), both of whom succeeded Arminius at the University of Leiden.[105] As unrest continued, forty-six Arminians, led by Johannes Uitenbogaert and Episcopius, gathered in Gouda in 1610 to write a *Remonstrance* against the Calvinists, which included five canons articulating their beliefs. The confession is consistent with the writings of Arminius, teaching that God's election is conditioned upon foreseen faith, Christ's atonement is universal in scope, and grace is resistible.[106] As for Arminius, so for the

---

Controversy," in *Crisis in the Reformed Churches: Essays in Commemoration of the Great Synod of Dort, 1618–1619*, ed. Peter Y. De Jong (Grand Rapids: Reformed Fellowship, 1968), 28–29.

104. See James Arminius, "Certain Articles to be Diligently Examined and Weighed," in *The Writings of James Arminius*, 3 vols., trans. James Nichols and William Nichols (Reprint, Grand Rapids: Baker, 1956), 2:492–501; idem, "Declaration of Sentiments," in *Writings*, 1:230–31; 252–53; idem, "Apology against Thirty-One Theological Articles," in *Writings*, 1:276–380 (especially 328, 364–73).

105. My exposition of the Remonstrant doctrine and Dort's response is brief, but see Herman Bavinck, *Saved by Grace: The Holy Spirit's Work in Calling and Regeneration*, ed. J. Mark Beach, trans. Nelson D. Kloosterman (Grand Rapids: Reformation Heritage, 2008), 19–53.

106. Jan Rohls, "Calvinism, Arminianism and Socinianism in the Netherlands until the Synod of Dort," in *Socinianism and Arminianism: Antitrinitarians, Calvinists and Cultural*

Remonstrants grace is not effectual, irresistible, causal, or monergistic, but only persuasive so that man's free will is able ultimately to determine whether or not to cooperate with God's grace (see chapter 5).

Prompted by the Calvinist Prince Maurice of Orange, six representatives of each side met in the Hague (the *Collatio Hagiensis*) in 1611 to discuss their differences, but the meeting was of no success. By 1618 a Counter Remonstrance was formed by the Calvinists in Dordrecht, presided over by Johannes Bogerman (1576–1637), which sought not only to correct the Arminian caricatures of the Calvinist position and refute the Remonstrant position, but also to set forth the "biblical" view.[107] In so doing, Dort showed, as Muller notes, that the

> Arminian doctrines were clearly beyond the bounds of Reformed confessional orthodoxy. . . . The Canons of Dort ought to be viewed as a magisterial interpretation of the extant Reformed confessional synthesis: they condemn predestination grounded on prior human choice; they deny a grace that is both resistible and acceptable by

---

Exchange in Seventeenth-Century Europe, ed. Martin Mulsow and Jan Rohls, Brill's Studies in Intellectual History 134 (Leiden: Brill, 2005), 19. Bavinck makes an important clarification: "The term 'irresistible grace' is not really of Reformed origin but was used by Jesuits and Remonstrants to characterize the doctrine of the efficacy of grace as it was advocated by Augustine and those who believed as he did. The Reformed in fact had some objections to the term because it was absolutely not their intent to deny that grace is often and indeed always resisted by the unregenerate person and therefore could be resisted. They therefore preferred to speak of the efficacy or of the insuperability of grace, or interpreted the term 'irresistible' in the sense that grace is ultimately irresistible. The point of the disagreement, accordingly, was not whether humans continually resisted and could resist God's grace, but whether they could ultimately—at the specific moment in which God wanted to regenerate them and work with his efficacious grace in their heart—still reject that grace." Herman Bavinck, *Reformed Dogmatics*, ed. John Bolt, trans. John Vriend (Grand Rapids: 2008), 4:83.

107. Before the delegates of Dort pronounced their verdict they requested that the Remonstrants, led by Episcopius, set forth their views with greater detail than they had in the *Five Articles* originally presented. The Remonstrants wrote a confession of their beliefs that more fully presented their views which came to be called the *Sententiae Remonstrantium* (the *Opinions of the Remonstrants*). For the entirety of the *Sententiae Remonstrantium*, see Appendix H in De Jong, *Crisis in the Reformed Churches*, 229. When Dort pronounced its verdict, condemning the Remonstrant views as outside the bounds of the Belgic Confession and Heidelberg Catechism and, most importantly, in conflict with Scripture itself, the pronouncement was based upon the *Five Articles* and the *Sententiae Remonstrantium*. See the bibliography for resources on the history of Dort.

25

man; they affirm the depth of original sin, argue a limited efficiency of Christ's work of satisfaction and stress the perseverance of the elect by grace. None of these views modifies the earlier Reformed position—indeed, virtually all of these points can be elicited from Ursinus's exposition of the Heidelberg Catechism.[108]

The focus of Dort is on the major difference between the two parties: conditionality versus unconditionality in salvation. Dort is clear: no aspect of God's eternal choice is conditioned upon man's free will for its efficacy or success.[109]

The Canons of Dort

Dort begins by describing the pervasiveness of depravity. Man has inherited from Adam a corrupt nature so that after the fall every man is a slave to sin.[110] In the first three articles of canons 3 and 4 it is evident that Dort affirms that (1) man's depravity pervades every aspect of his being (will, mind, affections); (2) man is dead, a slave to his sinful nature; and (3) man is in no way willing to return to God or reform his distorted nature.[111] He is in total reliance upon the saving power of God.[112]

Despite man's ruin, God has graciously provided a gospel call for all people.[113] And this gospel call is a well-meant offer. Those who are called by the gospel are called "seriously." Here Dort is responding to the objection of the Remonstrants, who argued in their *Sententiae Remonstrantium* that the Calvinist God was hypocritical to call all people by his

108. Richard A. Muller, "Arminius and Arminianism," in *The Dictionary of Historical Theology*, ed. Trevor A. Hart (Grand Rapids: Eerdmans, 2000), 35.

109. Fred H. Klooster, "Doctrinal Deliverances of Dort," in De Jong, *Crisis in the Reformed Churches*, 52–57 (cf. 174); John R. De Witt, "The Arminian Conflict," in *Puritan Papers*, vol. 5, *1968–1969*, ed. J. I. Packer (Phillipsburg, NJ: P&R Publishing, 2005), 20; Peterson and Williams, *Why I Am Not an Arminian*, 122.

110. "The Canons of the Synod of Dort," in *Creeds and Confessions of the Reformation Era*, vol. 2 of *Creeds and Confessions of Faith in the Christian Tradition*, ed. Jaroslav Pelikan and Valerie R. Hotchkiss (New Haven and London: Yale University Press, 2003), 3–4.1. Also see 3–4.2; 3–4, rejections 1–2 and 3–4.3.

111. Ibid., 3–4, rejections 3–4.

112. Ibid., 3–4.4; 3–4.5; 3–4.6.

113. Ibid., 3–4.8.

gospel when he would effectually save only his elect.[114] Dort rejects such a charge. Scripture is clear: God does indeed call all externally, though according to his decretive will he only chooses to convert internally his elect. God is in no way hypocritical for he only holds out to the sinner that which he could have (eternal life) if he would believe. However, the sinner not only cannot believe but he will not believe. Therefore, as Dort argues in article 9, the fact that the sinner does not believe is nobody's fault but his own.[115]

However, when a sinner does hear the gospel and believes, God and God alone receives all of the credit for he is the one who first gave the sinner new life to believe.

> [Article 10] The fact that others who are called through the ministry of the gospel do come and are brought to conversion must not be credited to man, as though one distinguishes himself by free choice from others who are furnished with equal or sufficient grace for faith and conversion (as the proud heresy of Pelagius maintains). No, it must be credited to God: just as from eternity he chose his own in Christ, so within time he effectively calls them, grants them faith and repentance, and, having rescued them from the dominion of darkness, brings them into the kingdom of his Son [Col 1:13], in order that they may declare the wonderful deeds of him who called them out of darkness into this marvelous light [1 Peter 2:9], and may boast not in themselves, but in the Lord, as apostolic words frequently testify in Scripture [1 Cor. 1:31].[116]

For the sinner to believe God must irresistibly and effectually, by the power of the Spirit, call that elect sinner to himself and awaken him to new life.

> [Article 11] Moreover, when God carries out this good pleasure in his chosen ones, or works true conversion in them, he not only sees to it that the gospel is proclaimed to them outwardly, and enlightens

---

114. "Appendix H: The Opinions of the Remonstrants," in De Jong, *Crisis in the Reformed Churches*, 226–27.
115. "The Canons of the Synod of Dort," 3–4.9.
116. Ibid., 3–4.10.

their minds powerfully by the Holy Spirit so that they may rightly understand and discern the things of the Spirit of God, but, by the effective operation of the same regenerating Spirit, he also penetrates into the inmost being of man, opens the closed heart, softens the hard heart, and circumcises the heart that is uncircumcised. He infuses new qualities[117] into the will, making the dead will alive, the evil one good, the unwilling one willing, and the stubborn one compliant; he activates and strengthens the will so that, like a good tree, it may be enabled to produce the fruits of good deeds.[118]

No mere moral persuasion will do, but unfailing resurrection to spiritual life is necessary.

[Article 12] And this is the regeneration, the new creation, the raising from the dead, and the making alive so clearly proclaimed in the Scriptures, which God works in us without our help. But this certainly does not happen only by outward teaching, by moral persuasion, or by such a way of working that, after God has done his work, it remains in man's power whether or not to be reborn or converted. Rather, it is an entirely supernatural work, one that is at the same time most powerful and most pleasing, a marvelous, hidden, and inexpressible work, which is not lesser than or inferior in power to that of creation or of raising the dead, as Scripture (inspired by the author of this work) teaches. As a result, all those in whose hearts God works in this marvelous way are certainly, unfailingly, and effectively reborn and do actually believe. And then the will, now renewed, is not only activated and motivated by God but in being activated by God is also itself active. For this reason, man himself, by that grace which he has received, is also rightly said to believe and to repent.[119]

117. Horton argues that this infusion of new qualities is "not a medieval notion of infused habits, but simply a manner of expressing the impartation of new life from a source external to the person who is 'dead in sins.' . . . [regeneration] is not represented here as accomplished apart from or prior to the external preaching of the gospel." Michael S. Horton, *Covenant and Salvation: Union with Christ* (Louisville: Westminster John Knox, 2007), 203n83.
118. "The Canons of the Synod of Dort," 3–4.11.
119. Ibid., 3–4.12.

Perhaps no confession since Dort has spent so much space articulating the monergistic nature of grace. In article 12, Dort is unambiguous: God works regeneration before any act of faith on our part and apart from our help. Such a work of God, not upon all but only upon his elect, is irresistible, effectual, and always successful, bringing the sinner from death to new life.[120] As Ezekiel 36:26 demonstrates, God's work is not by mere moral persuasion nor is it conditioned upon "man's power whether or not to be reborn or converted."[121] Rather, it is a work equivalent to raising the dead. Indeed, God's act of rebirth is always certain, unfailing, and effective, so that those whom God chooses to specially call and regenerate "do actually believe." Appealing to Ephesians 1:19; 2 Thessalonians 1:11; and 2 Peter 1:3, Dort's rejection of synergism is also evident in Rejection 8 of the Canons.

> Having set forth the orthodox teaching, the synod rejects the errors of those . . . 8. Who teach that God in regenerating man does not bring to bear that power of his omnipotence whereby he may powerfully and unfailingly bend man's will to faith and conversion, but that even when God has accomplished all the works of grace which he uses for man's conversion, man nevertheless can, and in actual fact often does, so resist God and the Spirit in their intent and will to regenerate him, that man completely thwarts his own rebirth; and, indeed, that it remains in his own power whether or not to be reborn. For this does away with all effective functioning of God's grace in our conversion and subjects the activity of Almighty God to the will of man; it is contrary to the apostles, who teach that we believe by virtue of the effective working of God's mighty strength, and that God fulfills the undeserved good will of his kindness and the work of faith in us with power, and likewise that his divine power has given us everything we need for life and godliness.[122]

120. Dort rejects a universal grace that is contingent upon the will of man, citing Ps. 147:19–20; Acts 14:16; and Acts 16:6–7 in support. See ibid., 3–4, rejection 5.

121. Ibid., 3–4, rejection 7.

122. Also see ibid., 3–4, rejection 9.

Notice the emphasis Dort places on making sure it is God, not man, who receives all of the credit and glory (1 Cor. 1:31). To reverse the order is to rob God of his glory and give man a ground to boast upon.

Furthermore, if man's faith is the result of God's effectual call and regenerative work, then it also follows that faith itself is a gift. However, Dort is very careful to avoid an Arminian definition of faith. Having Jeremiah 31:18, 33; Isaiah 44:3; and Romans 5:5 in mind, article 14 states,

> In this way, therefore, faith is a gift of God, not in the sense that it is offered by God for man to choose, but that it is in actual fact bestowed on man, breathed and infused into him. Nor is it a gift in the sense that God bestows only the potential to believe, but then awaits assent—the act of believing—from man's choice; rather, it is a gift in the sense that he who works both willing and acting and, indeed, works all things in all people produces in man both the will to believe and the belief itself.[123]

In other words, the Arminian defines faith in such a way that it is a gift, but only in the sense that it is offered so that whether or not it becomes actual is man's choice, not God's. To the contrary, Dort argues, faith is a gift that God wills to implant within the dead, lifeless sinner so that upon the granting of that new life he believes necessarily. As Dort states, God produces "in man both the will to believe and the belief itself."[124] Peter Toon correctly concludes that, on the basis of article 14, Dort taught "that regeneration precedes faith and is the cause of faith."[125]

Dort, however, is aware of two objections. First, the Arminian objects that if it is only God who can do this effectual and irresistible work so that without it no man can believe, then God is unjust and unfair to limit his saving work to only some rather than all. But Dort responds to this objection in the tradition of the apostle Paul in Romans 9: "God does not owe this grace to anyone. For what could God owe

---

123. "The Canons of the Synod of Dort," 3–4.14. Also see ibid., 3–4, rejection 6.
124. Ibid., 3–4.14.
125. Peter Toon, *Born Again: A Biblical and Theological Study of Regeneration* (Grand Rapids: Baker, 1987), 123.

to one who has nothing to give that can be paid back? Indeed, what could God owe to one who has nothing of his own to give but sin and falsehood?"[126]

Second, the Remonstrants also objected that if grace is irresistible, not just providing the opportunity to believe but also actually providing the will to believe, then man is reduced to a block or stone, stripped of his personal agency. Dort responds,

> However, just as by the fall man did not cease to be man, endowed with intellect and will, and just as sin, which has spread through the whole human race, did not abolish the nature of the human race but distorted and spiritually killed it, so also this divine grace of regeneration does not act in people as if they were blocks and stones; nor does it abolish the will and its properties or coerce a reluctant will by force, but spiritually revives, heals, reforms, and—in a manner at once pleasing and powerful—bends it back. As a result, a ready and sincere obedience of the Spirit now begins to prevail where before the rebellion and resistance of the flesh were completely dominant. It is in this that the true spiritual restoration and freedom of our will consists. Thus, if the marvelous Maker of every good thing were not dealing with us, man would have no hope of getting up from his fall by his free choice, by which he plunged himself into ruin when still standing upright.[127]

The grace of regeneration works upon the will not to abolish it or coerce it, but rather in a way that revives, heals, and reforms it, bending it back to love God rather than sin. Notice exactly how God revives, heals, reforms, and bends the will; it is in a "manner at once pleasing and powerful." It is pleasing because man is a sinner, deserving only wrath. It is powerful in that God does not leave salvation up to man's will but brings him into union with Christ without fail, accomplishing the redemption God intended.[128]

126. "The Canons of the Synod of Dort," 3–4.15.
127. Ibid., 3–4.16.
128. Turretin also identified effectual grace as a display of divine sweetness and omnipotence. Francis Turretin, *Institutes of Elenctic Theology*, ed. James T. Dennison Jr., trans. George

Synergism would continue to characterize Arminianism as it spread in the decades after Dort.[129] Nevertheless, Dort's emphasis on sovereign grace would be reiterated at the Westminster Assembly (1643–49). As Robert Norris observes, "the decisions of the Synod of Dort were of great import to the Assembly" and Dort "was the most significant of the recent Reformed synods."[130] Therefore, as Arminianism spread throughout England, it was no surprise that the Assembly believed it to be a great threat.

Westminster on Depravity and Free Will

Like Dort, Westminster affirmed original sin and the pervasive depravity of man. In chapter 6, "Of the Fall of Man, of Sin, and of the Punishment Thereof," the Westminster Confession of Faith states that guilt and corruption from Adam has been imputed to all mankind.[131] By Adam's sin man has fallen from his original righteousness and communion with God and has therefore become dead in sin, "wholly defiled in all the faculties and parts of soul and body."[132] It is from the original corruption man has inherited that all of his actual sins proceed, which only compound man's guilt and condemnation before a holy God.[133]

The implications of man's depravity are massive for free will. Chapter 9 of the Confession, "Of Free Will," states that God created Adam with a "natural liberty" so that his choices were not forced nor was he under "any absolute necessity of nature determined to good or evil."[134] "Man, in his state of innocency, had freedom and power to will and to do that which

---

Musgrave Giger, 3 vols., (Phillipsburg, NJ: P&R Publishing, 1992–97), 2:521, 524–25.

129. E.g., shortly after Dort, Episcopius took on a lead role in drafting a confession, which was published in 1621 as the *Confession or Declaration of the Remonstrant Pastors*.

130. Robert M. Norris, "The Thirty-Nine Articles at the Westminster Assembly," in *The Westminster Confession into the Twenty-first Century: Essays in Remembrance of the 350th Anniversary of the Westminster Assembly*, ed. J. Ligon Duncan III (Fearn, Ross-shire, Great Britain: Christian Focus, 2009), 3:161.

131. "The Westminster Confession," in Pelikan and Hotchkiss, *Creeds and Confessions of the Reformation Era*, 6.3.

132. Ibid., 6.2.

133. Ibid., 6.6.

134. Ibid., 9.1.

is good and well-pleasing to God; but yet mutably, so that he might fall from it."[135] However, after the fall man's will is in bondage to sin. "Man, by his Fall into a state of sin, hath wholly lost all ability of will to any spiritual good accompanying salvation; so as a natural man, being altogether averse from that good, and dead in sin, is not able, by his own strength, to convert himself, or to prepare himself thereunto."[136] Therefore,

> When God converts a sinner, and translates him into the state of grace, he freeth him from his natural bondage under sin, and, by his grace alone, enables him freely to will and to do that which is spiritually good; yet so as that by reason of his remaining corruption, he doth not perfectly, nor only, will that which is good, but doth also will that which is evil.[137]

Man's only hope is for God to free him from this bondage to sin by a supernatural grace.

Westminster on Effectual Calling

Westminster appropriately moves from man's willful bondage to sin and need for God's grace to the doctrine of effectual calling and regeneration in chapter 10.[138]

> 1. All those whom God hath predestinated unto life, and those only, he is pleased in his appointed and accepted time effectually to call [Rom. 8:30; 11:7; Eph. 1:10, 11], by his Word and Spirit [2 Thess. 2:13–14; 2 Cor. 3:3, 6], out of that state of sin and death in which they are by nature, to grace and salvation by Jesus Christ [Rom. 8:2; Eph. 2:1–5; 2 Tim. 1:9–10]: enlightening their minds spiritually and savingly to understand the things of God [Acts 26:18; 1 Cor. 2:10; 12; Eph. 1:17–18], taking away their heart of stone, and giving unto them an heart of flesh [Ezek. 36:26]; renewing their wills, and, by

135. Ibid., 9.2.
136. Ibid., 9.3.
137. Ibid., 9.4. Also see 9.5.
138. Also see the "Westminster Shorter Catechism," in Pelikan and Hotchkiss, *Creeds and Confessions of the Reformation Era*, Q. 31.

his almighty power determining them to that which is good [Ezek. 11:19; Phil. 2:13; Deut. 20:6; Ezek. 36:27], and effectually drawing them to Jesus Christ [Eph. 1:19; John 6:44–45]; yet so as they come most freely, being made willing by his grace [Song of Songs 1:4; Ps. 110:3; John 6:37; Rom. 6:16–18].

2. This effectual call is of God's free and special grace alone, not from anything at all foreseen in man [2 Tim. 1:9; Titus 3:4–5; Eph. 2:4–5, 8–9; Rom. 9:11], who is altogether passive therein, until, being quickened and renewed by the Holy Spirit [1 Cor. 2:14; Rom. 8:7; Eph. 2:5], he is thereby enabled to answer this call, and to embrace the grace offered and conveyed in it [John 6:37; Ezek. 36:27; John 5:25].[139]

Several observations must be noted. First, chapter 10 begins by stating that only those whom God has predestined for life are effectually called and regenerated, contrary to the Arminian view which only sees God's calling as universal. Second, God effectually calls and regenerates dead sinners to new life by his Word and Spirit and by the grace of his Son Jesus Christ.[140] Here Westminster draws from the biblical metaphors by stating that the Spirit enlightens the mind to understand (Eph. 1:17–18), takes away the heart of stone and replaces it with a heart of flesh (Ezek. 36:26), renews the will, and effectually draws the sinner to Jesus Christ (John 6:44–45).[141] Yet, though the Spirit's drawing is effectual, nevertheless, man comes most freely, "being made willing by his grace." The will, therefore, is renewed and made willing to believe.

Moreover, notice the order in which Westminster places God's grace in reference to man's faith. In 10.2 Westminster states that the effectual call is purely of God's grace so that man is absolutely passive. It is only when the sinner has been "quickened and renewed by the Holy Spirit, he is thereby enabled to answer this call, and to embrace the grace offered and conveyed in it." In other words, man's answer

139. "The Westminster Confession," 10.1–2. Also see 10.4.
140. Also see "Westminster Shorter Catechism," Q. 30.
141. O. Palmer Robertson, "The Holy Spirit in the Westminster Confession of Faith," in *The Westminster Confession into the Twenty-first Century*, 1:68.

to the call only comes after the Spirit has "quickened and renewed" and not before.[142]

Westminster's understanding of grace—which was restated by John Owen and Thomas Goodwin's Savoy Declaration (1658) and the Second London Confession (1677, 1689) of the Particular Baptists—once again demonstrates, as was the case with Augustine, Calvin, and Dort, that it is God's grace which must precede any activity (faith included) on the part of the dead sinner. Until God effectually calls and regenerates the sinner, no faith will be present. To reverse this order would be to exalt man's will over God's grace. Therefore, A. H. Pask is right when he observes that one of the main reasons the Puritans in England detested Arminianism so much was because it "inclines men to pride" by allowing "man's participation in the work of his salvation."[143]

CONCLUSION

E. Brooks Holifield is unquestionably correct when he states, "The defining mark of Reformed theology was its regard for the glory of God, which entailed a pronounced insistence on divine sovereignty."[144] This chapter has shown how Calvinists have defined and defended monergism as a necessary ingredient to the sovereignty of divine grace which alone can preserve God's glory. What then is the implication for evangelicals today? Michael Horton answers that Arminian and Wesleyan synergism can no longer be an option for Protestants committed to the Reformation.

> [T]hose who are convinced that the Reformation was essentially on the mark are not given the luxury of not taking a stand on . . . the monergistic work of the Holy Spirit granting new life. Therefore, if

142. The priority of the effectual call to faith is also evident in "The Westminster Confession," 14.1.

143. A. H. S. Pask, "The Influence of Arminius Upon the Theology of John Wesley," (PhD diss., University of Edinburgh, 1940), 105. For a treatment of Calvinism in Puritanism as a whole, see Dewey D. Wallace Jr., *Puritans and Predestination: Grace in English Protestant Theology, 1525–1695* (Chapel Hill: University of North Carolina Press, 1982); John T. McNeill, *The History and Character of Calvinism* (Oxford: Oxford University Press, 1954), 290–352.

144. E. Brooks Holifield, *Theology in America: Christian Thought From the Age of the Puritans to the Civil War* (New Haven: Yale University Press, 2003), 11.

we are really convinced of the justice in the Reformation's critique of medieval Rome, we can no longer fail to regard Arminianism within Protestant circles as any more acceptable. It is not only Rome, but the Wesleyan system, . . . which must be equally rejected to the extent that each fails to sufficiently honor God's grace.[145]

Reformation monergism is much more (though not less) than simply affirming that God is the sole author of salvation. God's sole authorship also means that grace for the elect is efficient and irresistible as seen in the doctrines of effectual calling and regeneration to which we will turn in chapters 5 and 6.

---

145. Michael S. Horton, "The *Sola*'s of the Reformation," in *Here We Stand! A Call from Confessing Evangelicals for a Modern Reformation*, ed. James Montgomery Boice and Benjamin E. Sasse (Phillipsburg, NJ: P&R Publishing, 1996), 120.

2

TOTAL DEPRAVITY AND
THE BONDAGE OF THE WILL

"Because of the bondage of sin by which the will is held bound, it cannot move toward good, much less apply itself thereto; for a movement of this sort is the beginning of conversion to God, which in Scripture is ascribed entirely to God's grace."[1] These words, written by John Calvin, are a lethal blow to the common man's optimism concerning his natural ability in matters of salvation. Calvin's words, however, parallel what Scripture says. For example, Jesus himself states in John 8:34 that "everyone who commits sin is a slave to sin." Likewise, the apostle Paul tells us that man is dead in his trespasses and sins (Eph. 2:1) and all of us are "by nature children of wrath" (Eph. 2:3). The sinner is very much like Lazarus, dead in the tomb, rotting away. As John Owen states, we have no more power than "a man in his grave hath in himself to live anew and come out at the next call."[2] Therefore, what the sinner needs is to hear the equivalent of the resurrection words of Christ, "Lazarus, come out!" (John 11:43). Only then, as Calvin says, will the sinner be converted to God entirely by God's grace.

1. John Calvin, *Institutes of the Christian Religion*, ed. John T. McNeil, trans. Ford Lewis Battles, LCC, vols. 20–21 (Philadelphia: Westminster John Knox, 1960), 2.2.16. See chapter 2 of *Reclaiming Monergism*, e-book, for how Augustine, Calvin, Dort, and Westminster defend total depravity.
2. John Owen, *A Display of Arminianism*, in *The Works of John Owen* (Edinburgh: Banner of Truth, 2000), 10:130.

ORIGINAL SIN

In order to understand properly effectual calling we must first comprehend the doctrine of total depravity and identify how depravity relates to the doctrine of original sin. Original sin (*peccator originaliter*) consists of two aspects: guilt and corruption (pollution/depravity). Guilt is a judicial and legal term, concept, or category describing man's relationship to the law of God. Guilt means that man has broken and violated God's holy law and is therefore liable to be punished, as was the case with Adam in Genesis 3. In regard to original sin, Calvinists have affirmed the hereditary nature of both guilt (*reatus*) and corruption (*vitium*). Original sin means that guilt and corruption have spread to all men. Exactly how original sin is transmitted is debated, but Calvinists have traditionally argued that the guilt of Adam's sin is imputed to all of mankind,[3] since Adam was acting as our federal head or representative when he sinned (Rom. 5:12–21).[4] The doctrine of original guilt is supported by passages such as Psalm 51:1–2; Romans 5:14–18; and 1 Corinthians 15:22–45. As Paul says, "one trespass led to condemnation for all men" (Rom. 5:18) and "by the one man's disobedience the many were made sinners" (Rom. 5:19).

While original guilt is a legal concept involving one's status, original corruption or pollution is a moral concept meaning that man's moral nature has been corrupted after the fall as a result of imputed guilt.[5] As Theodore Beza states, Adam "transmitted to his posterity a nature *in the first* place guilty, and *next* corrupted."[6] Or as Johannes Wollebius states, Adam's guilt is "imputed to the entire human race, and so it is

---

3. "Imputation" means to reckon to another person's account. See Caspar Wistar Hodge, "Imputation," *International Standard Bible Encyclopedia* (Grand Rapids: Eerdmans, 1982), 2:812; R. K. Johnston, "Imputation," in *Evangelical Dictionary of Theology*, ed. Walter A. Elwell (Grand Rapids: Baker, 1984), 554–55.

4. Thomas R. Schreiner, *Paul: Apostle of God's Glory in Christ* (Downers Grove, IL: InterVarsity, 2001), 149; Anthony A. Hoekema, *Created in God's Image* (Grand Rapids: Eerdmans, 1986), 148.

5. Hoekema, *Created in God's Image*, 149–50.

6. As quoted in Archibald Alexander Hodge, "The Ordo Salutis: Or, Relation in the Order of Nature of Holy Character and Divine Favor," *The Princeton Review* 54 (1878): 315.

corrupted by that sinfulness."[7] Therefore, Horton writes, "The *condition of sin* is the source of specific *acts* of sin, rather than vice versa."[8] It is the purpose here to limit our focus to original corruption, since this is where the doctrine of total depravity is focused.

Inherited corruption (pollution) is twofold. First, original corruption is the absence of original righteousness, and second, it is the presence of positive evil. In other words, original corruption is not merely a *privatio* but it is also *depravatio*. Corruption is no mere deficiency (though it is not less than that) but results in the plunging of oneself into sin.[9] Berkhof outlines several implications that follow from affirming both *privatio* and *depravatio*: (1) Original pollution cannot be a mere disease, as insisted by many Greek Fathers and also some Arminians.[10] While sin does infect man, sin also incorporates guilt, condemning man before God. As Schreiner says, "Human beings do not enter the world in a neutral state or slightly inclined to evil, according to Paul [Rom. 5:18–19]. They are *polluted* by the sin of Adam and enter the world as sinners, condemned and destined for death."[11] (2) Pollution or corruption should not be thought of as a substance infused into man's soul as if a metaphysical change occurs. Such a view was taught by the Manicheans in Augustine's day and also by Flacius Illyricus during the Reformation. "If the substance of the soul were sinful, it would have to be replaced by a new substance in regeneration; but this does not take place."[12] (3) Original pollution is no mere privation

---

7. Johannes Wollebius, *Compendium Theologiae Christianae*, trans. Alexander Ross (London: n.p., 1650), 10.1.5; quoted in *Reformed Dogmatics*, ed. John W. Beardslee III (New York: Oxford University Press, 1965), 69.

8. Michael S. Horton, "Sola Gratia," in *After Darkness, Light*, ed. R. C. Sproul Jr. (Phillipsburg, NJ: P&R Publishing, 2003), 120.

9. Contra Rome (see Bernard Ramm, *Offense to Reason: A Theology of Sin* [Vancouver: Regent College Publishing, 1985], 87–88) and Arminianism (see F. Stuart Clarke, *The Ground of Election: Jacob Arminius' Doctrine of the Work and Person of Christ* [Waynesboro, GA: Paternoster, 2006], 74; Carl Bangs, *Arminius: A Study in the Dutch Reformation* [Grand Rapids: Zondervan, 1985]; 338ff; James Arminius, "Seventy-Nine Private Disputations," in *The Writings of James Arminius*, 3 vols., trans. James Nichols and William Nichols [Grand Rapids: Baker, 1956], 2:77–78).

10. Louis Berkhof, *Systematic Theology* (Edinburgh: Banner of Truth, 2003), 246.

11. Schreiner, *Paul*, 149. Emphasis added.

12. Berkhof, *Systematic Theology*, 246. Also see Charles Hodge, *Systematic Theology*, 3 vols. (Reprint, Grand Rapids: Eerdmans, 1952), 3:6, 32.

(*privatio boni*). As Luther explains, it is not a mere lack of a quality in the will or intellect, but is pervasive deprivation of moral rectitude and ability. It is an inclination to evil and love for darkness.[13] These three points help qualify the negative aspects of original pollution. However, original pollution also must be stated positively and can be spoken of in two ways: total depravity and spiritual inability.

TOTAL DEPRAVITY

Before examining what total depravity actually refers to, it is imperative that we address some common caricatures and misunderstandings to clarify what it is not.[14] First, total depravity does not mean that man is as depraved as he possibly can be. Total depravity does not mean that the sinner will commit or indulge himself in every form of sin or in the worst sins conceivable. Through his common grace, God restrains evil so that man does not always commit the worst possible sin.[15] Second, total depravity does not mean that man has no innate knowledge of God's will or that man no longer possesses a conscience that can discern between good and evil. Third, total depravity does not mean that man is incapable of appreciating the good deeds or character of others. Though societies are corrupt they still retain remnants of altruism and civil good (or *civil virtue* as the Reformers titled it). God's common grace ensures that men can still perform civil responsibilities that benefit others (such as a doctor helping a patient in need of surgery). Berkhof explains, "It is admitted that even the unrenewed possess some virtue, revealing itself in the relations of social life, in many acts and sentiments that deserve the sincere approval and gratitude of their fellow-men, and that even meet with the approval of God to a certain extent."[16]

What total depravity *does* mean is that the corruption inherited from Adam extends to every aspect of the sinner's nature (i.e., it is total

13. Martin Luther, *What Luther Says*, ed. Ewald M. Plass (St. Louis: Concordia, 1959), 3:1300–1301.

14. My treatment is similar to Berkhof, *Systematic Theology*, 246–47; Hoekema, *Created in God's Image*, 150–55.

15. Hoekema, *Created in God's Image*, 152.

16. Berkhof, *Systematic Theology*, 246–47. Also see Hoekema, *Created in God's Image*, 152.

in extensiveness). As Berkhof says, inherited corruption extends to "all the faculties and powers of both soul and body."[17] No part of man (intellect, will, affections, etc.) is untouched by sin.[18] Total depravity is the *interior corruption totius hominis* (the internal corruption of the whole human being). Therefore, as Hoekema prefers, it may be better to speak of "pervasive" depravity.[19] Others have used the phrase "radical" depravity instead.[20]

Additionally, total depravity means that man cannot do anything spiritually good toward God but is rather a slave to sin. As the Heidelberg Catechism states, men "are wholly incapable of doing any good, and inclined to all evil."[21] Similarly, Berkhof states, "there is no spiritual good, that is, good in relation to God, in the sinner at all, but only perversion."[22] Therefore, while a man may perform a civil good toward his neighbor, such an act is never done purely out of love and reverence for the one true God. His actions are not God-oriented, as if he performs them out of faith in Christ. Therefore, even civil or natural deeds are nothing but filthy rags and ultimately defective of salvific good. As the Westminster Confession 16.7 states, "Works done by unregenerate men, although for the matter of them they may be things which God commands, yet because they do not proceed from faith are sinful and cannot please God." In relation to God, who is perfectly holy, even these "good" deeds are somehow and in some way tainted by sin. "Their fatal defect is that they are not prompted by love to God, or by any regard for the will of God as requiring them."[23]

17. Berkhof, *Systematic Theology*, 247.
18. Philip Hughes, "Another Dogma Falls," *Christianity Today* 23 (May 1969): 13; Roger Nicole, *Standing Forth: Collected Writings of Roger Nicole* (Fearn, Ross-shire, Great Britain: Christian Focus, 2002), 430; Thomas M. Gregory, "The Presbyterian Doctrine of Total Depravity," in *Soli Deo Gloria: Essays in Reformed Theology: Festschrift for John H. Gerstner*, ed. R. C. Sproul (Nutley, NJ: Presbyterian and Reformed, 1976), 36–54.
19. Hoekema, *Created in God's Image*, 150.
20. Nicole, *Standing Forth*, 430; R. C. Sproul, *What Is Reformed Theology? Understanding the Basics* (Grand Rapids: Baker, 1997, 2005), 118.
21. Question 8 of the Heidelberg Catechism, in *The Evangelical Protestant Creeds*, vol. 3 of *The Creeds of Christendom*, ed. Philip Schaff, revised by David S. Schaff (Reprint, Grand Rapids: Baker, 1997), 310.
22. Berkhof, *Systematic Theology*, 247.
23. Ibid.

Scripture everywhere affirms the doctrine of total depravity. Beginning in the Old Testament, the pervasiveness of man's depravity is evident after the fall of Adam.[24] Adam's descendants (Gen. 5) are multiplied on the earth, and in Genesis 6:5 we read, "The Lord saw that the wickedness of man was great in the earth, and that every intention of the thoughts of his heart was only evil continually" (Gen. 6:5; cf. 8:21). What the Lord saw in man was both the *extensiveness* and the *intensiveness* of sin. Hamilton rightly comments, "The situation is further aggravated because such depravity controls not only man's actions but also his thoughts. . . . The mind, too, has been perverted, an emphasis made again in 8:21."[25] To add to Hamilton's comment, it is not merely the "thoughts" but the thoughts of "his heart" that are continually evil. As Mathews explains, in Hebrew anthropology the "heart is the center of a human's cognitive processes (e.g., Gen. 31:20; Ps. 33:11; 1 Sam. 10:26)."[26]

Moreover, the word "only" is telling for, as Calvin says, it is "as if he [God] would deny that there was a drop of good mixed with it."[27] In other words, God could have said man's heart was corrupt, but instead he says every imagination of the thoughts of the heart was only evil continually, accentuating the intensiveness of depravity. Man's depravity is so perverse that he decided to "blot out man" (Gen. 6:7a) by a massive flood, sparing none, except Noah, who "found favor in the eyes of the Lord" (Gen. 6:8).[28] However, even after the flood man's depravity continues, as is readily apparent at the Tower of Babel (Gen. 11:1–9) and the destruction of Sodom and Gomorrah (Gen. 18–19). Even within Israel, God's chosen people, depravity characterized not only the people

24. On original sin in the Old Testament, see Richard C. Gamble, *God's Mighty Acts in the Old Testament*, vol. 1 of *The Whole Counsel of God* (Phillipsburg, NJ: P&R Publishing, 2009), 187–232, 250–76.

25. Victor P. Hamilton, *The Book of Genesis, Chapters 1–17*, NICOT (Grand Rapids: Eerdmans, 1990), 273.

26. Kenneth A. Mathews, *Genesis 1–11:26*, NAC, vol. 1a (Nashville: B&H Publishing Group, 1996), 341.

27. John Calvin, *Commentaries on the First Book of Moses Called Genesis*, 2 vols., trans. John King (Grand Rapids: Baker, 1996), 1:248.

28. John H. Sailhamer, *Genesis*, EBC, vol. 1 (Grand Rapids: Zondervan, 2008), 117; Mathews, *Genesis*, 340–41.

but also the leaders, so that Judges concludes, "In those days there was no king in Israel. Everyone did what was right in his own eyes" (Judg. 21:25; cf. 17:6). Rather than doing what is right in God's eyes (Exod. 15:26; Deut. 6:18; 12:25, 28; 13:19; 21:9; Jer. 34:15), Israel's corrupt heart led the people to do what was right in their own eyes (Deut. 12:8).[29] Therefore, David is correct when he states, "The fool says in his heart, 'There is no God.' They are corrupt, they do abominable deeds, there is none who does good. The LORD looks down from heaven on the children of man, to see if there are any who understand, who seek after God. They have all turned aside; together they have become corrupt; there is none who does good, not even one" (Ps. 14:1–3; cf. Rom. 3:10). Notice, the universality of depravity is emphasized by the words "all," "together," "none," and "not even one."

Moreover, as VanGemeren observes, the phrase "become corrupt," which in Arabic means "to make sour," shows the pollution of man (cf. Ps. 53:3).[30] As Calvin states concerning Psalm 14, depraved man is filled with "disgusting corruption or putrescence" and nothing can proceed from "apostates but what smells rank of rottenness and infection."[31] And again, "David declares that all men are so carried away by their capricious lusts, that nothing is to be found either of purity or integrity in their whole life."[32] Therefore, man is "one who is abominable and corrupt" in God's sight, and who "drinks injustice like water" (Job. 15:16).[33] Job can say accurately, "Man who is born of a woman is few of days and full of trouble. . . . Who can bring a clean thing out of an unclean? There is not one" (Job 14:1, 3). Job's words are similar to David's: "Enter not

---

29. Daniel I. Block, *Judges, Ruth*, NAC, vol. 6 (Nashville: B&H Publishing Group, 1999), 483–84.

30. Willem A. VanGemeren, *Psalms*, EBC, vol. 5 (Grand Rapids: Zondervan, 2008), 176–77. On the Arabic also see John Goldingay, *Psalms*, vol. 1, *Psalms 1–41*, BCOT (Grand Rapids: Baker, 2006), 214.

31. John Calvin, *Commentary on the Book of Psalms*, 4 vols., trans. James Anderson (Grand Rapids: Baker, 1996), 4:193.

32. Calvin, *Commentary on Psalms*, 4:193–94.

33. Despite the fact that Eliphaz in Job 15 wrongly believes that Job's suffering is the result of God's punishment for sin (since Job is vindicated in the end), his statements concerning man's depravity are true of all of mankind.

into judgment with your servant, for no one living is righteous before you" (Ps. 143:2).[34] David will also confess, after admitting to Nathan his adultery with Bathsheba, "Behold, I was brought forth in iniquity, and in sin did my mother conceive me" (Ps. 51:5). Surely, David's assertion is not true of him alone but of all mankind.[35] As David says in Psalm 58:3–5, "The wicked are estranged from the womb; they go astray from birth, speaking lies. They have venom like the venom of a serpent . . ." David's son Solomon would agree: "Who can say, 'I have made my heart pure; I am clean from my sin'?" (Prov. 20:9). The implied answer, of course, is "no one!"[36] As stated in Ecclesiastes, "Surely there is not a righteous man on earth who does good and never sins" (Eccl. 7:20; cf. Ps. 143:2).[37] And again, "The hearts of the children of man are full of evil, and madness is in their hearts while they live, and after that they go to the dead" (Eccl. 9:3). The prophet Isaiah is just as clear: "All we like sheep have gone astray; we have turned—every one—to his own way" (Isa. 53:6). And again, "We have all become like one who is unclean, and all our righteous deeds are like a polluted garment" (Isa. 64:6a). The prophet Jeremiah rightly concludes, "The heart is deceitful above all things, and desperately sick; who can understand it?" (Jer. 17:9; cf. Ezek. 36:26).

The concept of man's total depravity is found in the New Testament as well. Jesus himself affirmed the pervasive depravity of man in his dispute with the Pharisees over the necessity of washing one's hands prior to eating a meal. Jesus explains that it is not what goes into a man but what comes out of him that defiles him (Mark 7:18–20). Jesus then states, "For from within, out of the heart of man, come evil

34. John E. Hartley, *The Book of Job*, NICOT (Grand Rapids: Eerdmans, 1988), 231.

35. Owen, *A Display of Arminianism*, 10:70; Calvin, *Commentary on Psalms*, 5:290; VanGemeren, *Psalms*, 436. Contra John Goldingay, *Psalms*, vol. 2, *Psalms 42–89* BCOT (Grand Rapids: Baker, 2007), 129–30.

36. All men lack moral purity: Gen. 6:5; 8:21; 1 Kings 8:46; Job 15:14–16; Pss. 14; 19:12–13; 32; 51:5–8; 143:2; Eccl. 7:20–29; Jer. 17:9; Ezek. 18:31; Rom. 3:9–19. Bruce K. Waltke, *The Book of Proverbs, Chapters 15–31*, NICOT (Grand Rapids: Eerdmans, 2005), 135.

37. Tremper Longman observes that in the context of Ecclesiastes this verse (7:20) teaches that not even the "wise" are righteous. Tremper Longman III, *The Book of Ecclesiastes*, NICOT (Grand Rapids: Eerdmans, 1998), 198–99.

thoughts, sexual immorality, theft, murder, adultery, coveting, wicked-ness, deceit, sensuality, envy, slander, pride, foolishness. All these evil things come from within, and they defile a person" (Mark 7:21–23; cf. Exod. 20:13–15). In other words, it is the heart, "the very innermost nature of one's being, that is the problem."[38] However, as R. T. France notes, while in English "heart" usually conveys emotion, in Hebrew and Greek "heart" or "inner being" strongly conveys "spiritual and intel-lectual processes, including the will."[39] Therefore, depravity penetrates man's very essence, including not only his affections and mind but his will. While R. T. France recognizes that the defilement Jesus speaks of penetrates to the very essence, even the will, he wrongly concludes that one reads Jesus out of context to interpret Jesus as setting forth a "very radical view of the 'total depravity' of humanity."[40] Such a statement by France should be rejected since Jesus is teaching not only that sin has defiled man's innermost being but also, in piling one evil characteristic on top of another (evil thoughts, sexual immorality, theft, etc.), he is emphasizing just how bad man's heart really is. Indeed, man's depravity *is* radical.

In another debate with the Jews over healing a man on the Sab-bath (John 5:42–44), Jesus takes his understanding of man's depravity (as seen in Mark 7:21–23) and applies it directly to the Jews who were questioning his authority and refusing to believe in his identity as the Son of God. He says to them, "But I know that you do not have the love of God within you. I have come in my Father's name, and you do not receive me. If another comes in his own name, you will receive him. How can you believe, when you receive glory from one another and do not seek the glory that comes from the only God?" (John 5:42–44). At the root of man's depravity is a rejection and hatred for Jesus Christ which

38. Robert H. Stein, *Mark*, BECNT (Grand Rapids: Baker Academic, 2008), 346. Also see William L. Lane, *The Gospel According to Mark*, NICNT (Grand Rapids: Eerdmans, 1974), 255.

39. R. T. France, *The Gospel of Mark*, NIGTC (Grand Rapids: Eerdmans, 2002), 291.

40. Ibid., 293. France goes on to state that Jesus does not deny that good things may come out of the heart also. While this is true, France fails to understand that while good things may come out of the heart, they only do so *because* God through Christ has given the sinner a new heart.

reveals the root issue in man's corruption, namely, a failure to give glory to God.[41] Therefore, Schreiner is correct when he defines sin as "first and foremost a rejection of the supremacy of God and his lordship over our lives."[42] Perhaps no one makes this as apparent as the apostle Paul when he says in Romans 1:

> For although they knew God, they did not honor him as God or give thanks to him, but they became futile in their thinking, and their foolish hearts were darkened. Claiming to be wise, they became fools, and exchanged the glory of the immortal God for images resembling mortal man and birds and animals and reptiles.
>
> Therefore God gave them up in the lusts of their hearts to impurity, to the dishonoring of their bodies among themselves, because they exchanged the truth about God for a lie and worshiped and served the creature rather than the Creator, who is blessed forever! Amen.
>
> For this reason God gave them up to dishonorable passions. For their women exchanged natural relations for those that are contrary to nature; and the men likewise gave up natural relations with women and were consumed with passion for one another, men committing shameless acts with men and receiving in themselves the due penalty for their error.
>
> And since they did not see fit to acknowledge God, God gave them up to a debased mind to do what ought not to be done. They were filled with all manner of unrighteousness, evil, covetousness, malice. They are full of envy, murder, strife, deceit, maliciousness. They are gossips, slanderers, haters of God, insolent, haughty, boastful, inventors of evil, disobedient to parents, foolish, faithless, heartless, ruthless. Though they know God's decree that those who practice such things deserve to die, they not only do them but give approval to those who practice them. (Rom. 1:21–32)

As Paul explains, the wrath of God is unleashed upon these sinners because though they knew God they refused to give him thanks and

41. Andreas J. Köstenberger, *John*, BECNT (Grand Rapids: Baker, 2004), 194.
42. As Rom. 1:18–3:20 shows, "sin is fundamentally a refusal to honor and praise God," Schreiner, *Paul*, 103–4.

honor.[43] Instead, their thinking became futile and their hearts dark. They exchanged the glory of God for created images (idolatry) and indulged themselves in dishonorable passions. Here, therefore, we see a very grave picture of man's depravity, as emphasized in how Paul builds one evil characteristic on top of another, until it becomes obvious that man is hopelessly lost.[44] Paul says they were "filled with all manner of unrighteousness," showing the extent of depravity. As Murray observes, such wickedness, covetousness, and maliciousness "accentuates the totality of the depravity involved and the intensity with which it had been cultivated."[45] A similar picture is painted by Paul in Romans 3.

> As it is written: "None is righteous, no, not one; no one under-stands; no one seeks for God. All have turned aside; together they have become worthless; no one does good, not even one." "Their throat is an open grave; they use their tongues to deceive." "The venom of asps is under their lips." "Their mouth is full of curses and bitterness." "Their feet are swift to shed blood; in their paths are ruin and misery, and the way of peace they have not known." "There is no fear of God before their eyes." (Rom. 3:10–18; cf. Pss. 5:9; 10:7; 14:1–3; 36:1; 53:1–3; 140:3; Prov. 1:16; Isa. 59:7–8; Jer. 5:16)

Paul demonstrates (1) that sin is *universal* ("None is righteous, no, not one"), and (2) that this universal sin is *pervasive*, so that men's throats, tongues, and lips speak evil, their feet are swift to do evil, and their eyes lack any fear of God.[46] Paul's point is obvious: corruption and depravity are universal and utterly enslaving, so that no one can be justified by obedience to the law. Schreiner helpfully comments,

43. Ibid., 105. Also see Thomas R. Schreiner, *Romans*, BECNT (Grand Rapids: Baker, 1998), 87–88, 100; E. Käsemann, *Commentary on Romans*, trans. and ed. G. W. Bromiley (Grand Rapids: Eerdmans, 1980), 47.

44. Douglas J. Moo, *The Epistle to the Romans*, NICNT (Grand Rapids: Eerdmans, 1996), 118; John Murray, *The Epistle to the Romans*, NICNT (Grand Rapids: Eerdmans, 1959), 1:41ff.

45. Murray, *Romans*, 1:50.

46. Moo, *Romans*, 202–3.

Paul had a darker view of human ability than some Jews in that the latter believed that human beings had the capability to observe the law (cf. Laato 1991; Westerholm 1988:141–73). Judaism acknowledges that all people without exception were sinners (B. Longnecker 1991: 23–27). But Paul thought that sin had wrapped its tentacles so tightly around human beings that they could not keep the law. This state of affairs obtained not only for the Gentiles but also for the Jews, who were God's covenant people.[47]

Schreiner is right when he states that some (not all) Jews believed that man was capable of observing the law. As Laato and Schreiner observe, some Jews had a very optimistic view of human ability.[48] "The law could be obeyed if one overcame the evil impulse."[49] However, "Paul had a more somber estimate of human capability. Justification by law is ruled out because no one could keep what the law said."[50] Consequently, as Schreiner states, "Paul repudiates a synergism that was present in Jewish theology" and rightly so.[51] If Paul repudiated the synergism of some Jews, who denied total depravity in order to maintain man's ability, then so also would Paul have repudiated some Arminians today who likewise deny total depravity and affirm synergism (see chapter 5).

Paul again touches on the issue of man's slavery to sin in Romans 8.

For those who live according to the flesh set their minds on the things of the flesh, but those who live according to the Spirit set their minds on the things of the Spirit. For to set the mind on the flesh is death, but to set the mind on the Spirit is life and peace. For the mind that is set on the flesh is hostile to God, for it does not submit to God's law; indeed, it cannot. Those who are in the flesh cannot please God (Rom. 8:5–8; cf. 7:18).

47. Schreiner, *Romans*, 164–65. Contra Philip R. Davies, *Faith and Obedience in Romans: A Study of Romans 1–4*, Journal for the Study of the New Testament Supplement (London: Sheffield Academic, 1990), 80–104.

48. T. Laato, *Paulus und das Judentum: Anthropologische Erwägungen* (Åbo: Åbo Akademi Press, 1991), 185–209.

49. Schreiner, *Romans*, 173.

50. Ibid., 174.

51. Ibid. Also see Schreiner, *Paul*, 110–25.

Paul argues that the sinner without the regenerating work of the Spirit has a mind set on the flesh and consequently is hostile to God and his law.[52] It is not only the case that they won't submit to God's law but, as Paul states, they "cannot" for it is impossible for them to please God. Therefore, Moo rightly states that Paul's description of the unbeliever as "hostile to God" (8:7) "may justly be summed up in the theological categories of 'total depravity' and 'total inability.' "[53] Likewise, as Schreiner observes, there is an emphasis placed on the inability of the human will rather than on a human decision to cooperate (contra Cranfield and Dunn).[54] It is common for the Arminian to object that if man is unable then he cannot be held responsible. But this is not what Paul says. Paul affirms a moral inability to keep God's law and yet Paul still holds the sinner responsible. Schreiner comments, "He [Paul] does not conclude that those of the flesh are not responsible for their sin because of their inability. Rather, he holds them responsible for their sins even though they cannot keep God's law. Paul apparently did not believe that people were only culpable for sin if they had the 'moral' ability to keep commandments."[55] Contrary to Pelagius who tries to minimize Paul's words, Calvin appropriately states, "Let the Christian heart therefore drive far from itself the non-Christian philosophy of the freedom of the will, and let every one of us acknowledge himself to be, as in reality he is, the servant of sin, that he may be free by the grace of Christ and set at liberty."[56]

In Galatians 4:3 Paul reiterates the bondage of man: "In the same way we also, when we were children, were enslaved to the elementary principles of the world." Or, as Paul tells the Ephesians,

52. For Paul's understanding of "flesh" or *sarx*, see Schreiner, *Paul*, 140–46.

53. Moo, *Romans*, 488.

54. Schreiner, *Romans*, 411–12. Contra James D. G. Dunn, *Romans 1–8*, WBC, vol. 38A (Dallas: Word, 1988), 425; C. E. B. Cranfield, *A Critical and Exegetical Commentary on the Epistle to the Romans: Introduction and Commentary on Romans I–VIII*, ICC (Edinburgh: T&T Clark, 1975), 385–87.

55. Schreiner, *Romans*, 412–13.

56. John Calvin, *The Epistles of Paul the Apostle to the Romans and to the Thessalonians*, ed. D. W. Torrance and T. F. Torrance, trans. R. MacKenzie, vol. 8 of *Calvin's New Testament Commentaries* (Grand Rapids: Eerdmans, 1960), 163. On Pelagius, see *Pelagius's Commentary on St. Paul's Epistle to the Romans*, trans. Theodore De Bruyn, Oxford Early Christian Studies (Oxford: Clarendon, 1993), 107–8, as observed in Schreiner, *Romans*, 413.

> And you were dead in the trespasses and sins in which you once walked, following the course of this world, following the prince of the power of the air, the spirit that is now at work in the sons of disobedience—among whom we all once lived in the passions of our flesh, carrying out the desires of the body and the mind, and were by nature children of wrath, like the rest of mankind. (Eph. 2:1–3)[57]

Paul says that "by nature" man is under God's wrath, bearing the inherited status and condition every person receives at birth.[58] The guilty status all are born into ("dead in . . . transgressions and sins") results in a corrupt nature, an inescapable bondage to sin. *All* of "mankind" is *by nature* corrupt and the consequence is futility, darkness, hardness of heart, and alienation from God.[59] Thielman rightly notes that unbelievers "choose this path inevitably, in agreement with the state into which they were born (cf. Rom. 5:12; 2 Esd. [4 Ezra] 7:62–69, 116–18)."[60] Unbelievers are dead in trespasses and sins, following the course of this world and Satan himself (the prince of the power of the air), living in the passions of the flesh, and are *by nature* children of wrath (cf. Rom. 5:12). Man's impotence could not be more evident, for, as Hoehner observes, "Dead people cannot communicate and have no power to bring life to themselves."[61] Likewise, Schreiner writes, "Paul does not depict unbelievers as merely disinclined to the gospel. He says that they have no capacity at all to respond to the gospel, for they are engulfed in trespasses and sins and find their delight in the realm of sin and death rather than in doing the will of God."[62] Simpson is equally emphatic, "*All* alike, Jew and Gentile, are by natal proclivity inchoate children of wrath. We swerve from the very outset. 'An evil ground exists in my

57. See *The 1599 Geneva Bible* (White Hall, WV: Tolle Lege, 2008), 1217.
58. Clinton E. Arnold, *Ephesians*, ZECNT (Grand Rapids: Zondervan, 2010), 134.
59. See Hoekema, *Created in God's Image*, 152; James Montgomery Boice and Philip Graham Ryken, *The Doctrines of Grace: Rediscovering the Evangelical Gospel* (Wheaton, IL: Crossway, 2002), 74.
60. Frank Thielman, *Ephesians*, BECNT (Grand Rapids: Baker, 2010), 127.
61. Harold W. Hoehner, *Ephesians: An Exegetical Commentary* (Grand Rapids: Baker, 2002), 308; Owen, *A Display of Arminianism*, 10:130.
62. Schreiner, *Paul*, 138. Likewise, see Hoehner, *Ephesians*, 316, 320; Arnold, *Ephesians*, 130; Bryan Chapell, *Ephesians*, REC (Phillipsburg, NJ: P&R Publishing, 2009), 80.

will previous to any given act' (S. T. Coleridge)."[63] Consequently, says Simpson, Pelagianism and Semi-Pelagianism are antithetical to Paul.[64]

Notice how the sinner is in bondage to three powers: the world, Satan, and his own flesh (cf. James 3:15; 1 John 2:15–17; 3:7–10).[65] On the devil, O'Brien states,

> The devil is further characterized as the spirit who exercises effective and compelling power over the lives of men and women. . . . Indeed, so effective is his *present* evil working that Paul can refer to his victims as "sons of disobedience," that is, men and women whose lives are characterized by disobedience. They are rebels against the authority of God who prefer to answer the promptings of the archenemy.[66]

Paul returns to the lack of moral ability in Ephesians 4:17–19.

> Now this I say and testify in the Lord, that you must no longer walk as the Gentiles do, in the futility of their minds. They are darkened in their understanding, alienated from the life of God because of the ignorance that is in them, due to their hardness of heart. They have become callous and have given themselves up to sensuality, greedy to practice every kind of impurity.

Paul could not be more lucid. Man's spiritual depravity infiltrates not only his *heart* ("hardness of heart"; cf. Rom. 1:21) but also his *mind* ("the futility of their minds . . . darkened in their understanding").[67] Hoehner summarizes Paul, saying, "The hardness of their hearts toward God caused their ignorance. Their ignorance concerning God and his will caused them to be alienated from the life of God. Their alienation

---

63. E. K. Simpson, *Commentary on the Epistle to the Ephesians*, NICNT (Grand Rapids: Baker, 1977), 46.

64. Ibid., 49.

65. Clinton E. Arnold, *Powers of Darkness: Principalities and Powers in Paul's Letters* (Leicester: InterVarsity, 1992), 125–26.

66. Peter T. O'Brien, *The Letter to the Ephesians*, PNTC (Grand Rapids: Eerdmans, 1999), 160–61. Also see Arnold, *Powers of Darkness*, 125; idem, *Ephesians*, 131–32.

67. O'Brien, *Ephesians*, 320; Hoehner, *Ephesians*, 583–87; Thielman, *Ephesians*, 297.

caused their minds to be darkened, and their darkened minds caused them to walk in the futility of mind."[68]

Paul emphasizes the depravity of the heart again when he writes to the Colossians that before they knew Christ they "were dead in your trespasses and the uncircumcision of your heart, . . ." (Col. 2:13; cf. 1:13). Likewise, Paul warns Titus, "To the pure, all things are pure, but to the defiled and unbelieving, nothing is pure; but both their minds and their consciences are defiled. They profess to know God, but they deny him by their works. They are detestable, disobedient, unfit for any good work" (Titus 1:15–16). Knight notes, "By saying that the defilement is in 'their mind and conscience,' Paul signifies that it is internal and thus intrinsically moral and religious. . . . Paul consistently regards 'the mind' of the non-Christian as controlled by sin and therefore erroneous in its outlook (e.g., Rom. 1:28; Eph. 4:17; especially 1 Tim. 6:5 and 2 Tim. 3:8) and needing to be transformed by renewal (Rom. 12:2; Eph. 4:23)."[69]

The depravity of the heart and mind that results in spiritual slavery is again emphasized in Titus 3:3, "For we ourselves were once foolish, disobedient, led astray, slaves to various passions and pleasures, passing our days in malice and envy, hated by others and hating one another." The unbeliever is in bondage to sin, a bondage he cannot escape.[70] This bondage is evident in that the sinner not only gives in to various passions but also actively hates others.

It is important to recognize here the emphasis that many of the passages examined above place on the depravity of *both* the heart and the mind. Theologians have called this the "noetic" effect of the fall. Noetic derives from the Greek νοῦς, which means "mind." Prior to sin's entrance into the world, Adam's intellectual capabilities were pure, without defilement. However, after the fall man's mind became distorted and perverse. This does not mean that he can no longer reason or use logic in order to think critically, for, as Sproul has pointed out, while

68. Hoehner, *Ephesians*, 588–89. Also see Arnold, *Ephesians*, 282.

69. George W. Knight III, *The Pastoral Epistles: A Commentary on the Greek Text*, NIGTC (Grand Rapids: Eerdmans, 1992), 303. Also see Philip H. Towner, *The Letters to Timothy and Titus*, NICNT (Grand Rapids: Baker, 2006), 709.

70. Schreiner, *Paul*, 139.

the "faculty" remains it is the "facility" that is lost. The facility of the mind is tainted by a "sinful bias and prejudice, especially with respect to our understanding of the good and of God."[71] Calvin describes the situation well when he says, "All parts of the soul were possessed by sin after Adam deserted the fountain of righteousness. For not only did a lower appetite seduce him, but unspeakable impiety occupied the very citadel of his mind and pride penetrated to the depths of his heart." The consequence is devastating: "none of the soul remains pure or untouched by that moral disease." And "the mind is given over to blindness and the heart to depravity."[72]

SPIRITUAL INABILITY AND THE BONDAGE OF THE WILL

Man's inherited corruption places significant attention not only upon the depravity of man's heart and mind, but also upon the bondage of man's will.[73] The will of man is so impacted by pollution that he is unable to turn toward God in faith and repentance (Titus 1:16). Spiritual inability can be defined in several ways. First, it means that the sinner can in no way do anything that meets the perfect demands of the holy law of God. The unregenerate man cannot please God nor can he meet the consent or approval of God. Second, the sinner is unable to change his inclinations, preferences, and desires for sin so that he may turn to love God instead. In short, the sinner is not able to do anything spiritually good due to the fact that he is born with an evil prejudice, inevitably predisposed to sin.[74] Therefore, while man's rational faculties do remain intact (his ability to acquire knowledge, to reason, to form a conscience, etc.), man did lose his "material freedom," as Berkhof calls it. Man "has by nature an irresistible bias for evil. He is not able to apprehend and love spiritual excellence, to

71. R. C. Sproul, *Willing to Believe: The Controversy over Free Will* (Grand Rapids: Baker, 1997), 57. Also see Robert L. Reymond, *A New Systematic Theology of the Christian Faith*, 2nd ed., rev. (Nashville: Thomas Nelson, 1998), 452–53; A. W. Pink, *The Doctrine of Salvation* (Grand Rapids: Baker, 1975), 23–34.
72. Calvin, *Institutes*, 2.1.9.
73. Hoekema, *Created in God's Image*, 152.
74. Ramm, *Offense to Reason*, 88.

seek and do spiritual things, the things of God that pertain to salvation."[75] In this sense then it is best to say, as Johannes Wollebius does, that the "will has been made so evil [*factum est ad malum*] that it is better described as enslaved than as free."[76] However, as we will later see, such bondage is a *willful* bondage. Man is not forced or constrained against his will to commit sin. Rather, he loves sin, willfully and perpetually choosing to make sin his master. As Wollebius explains, "original sin consists not only of inability to do good, but also of a tendency [*proclivitas*] toward evil."[77]

Scripture is abundant with texts that prove the doctrine of spiritual inability. The prophet Jeremiah, after explaining the "greatness of [Israel's] iniquity" (Jer. 13:22), asks rhetorically, "Can the Ethiopian change his skin or the leopard his spots? Then also you can do good who are accustomed to do evil" (13:23). In other words, it is impossible for the wicked to do what is right in God's sight. As Reymond states, "Because man is totally or pervasively corrupt, he is *incapable of changing his character or of acting in a way that is distinct from his corruption*. He is unable to discern, to love, or to choose the things that are pleasing to God."[78] The root issue in man's inability is his corrupt character. As Jesus explains, a diseased tree cannot bear good fruit (Matt. 7:18). In the opening of his gospel John states, "But to all who did receive him [Christ], who believed in his name, he gave the right to become children of God, who were born, not of blood *nor of the will of the flesh nor of the will of man*, but of God" (John 1:12–13). If man is going to be born again, it will not be due to his own will. As Jesus states in John 3:5, a man cannot see the kingdom of God unless he is born again. In John 6:44 Jesus again makes man's impotence abundantly clear: "No one can come to me unless the Father who sent him draws him." Man is not spiritually capable of coming to Jesus. What is it that hinders, binds, and enslaves man's will, keeping him from following Christ? Jesus explains, "Truly, truly, I say to you,

---

75. Berkhof, *Systematic Theology*, 248.
76. Wollebius, *Compendium Theologiae Christianae*, 10.1.18.
77. Ibid., 10.1.8.
78. Reymond, *Systematic Theology*, 453.

everyone who commits sin is a slave to sin" (John 8
17, 19–20; 2 Peter 2:19).[79]

Slave, or δοῦλός, in John 8:34 is from δουλεύειν,
enslaved." The KJV translates the noun "servant," the AS
vant." However, the NASB and ESV use "slave," which prop
nicates the imprisonment of man's will. Moreover, since t⸺ ⸺ple
in John 8:34 is in the present tense, communicating continuation, Jesus
is saying that this enslavement to sin is habitual.[80] Köstenberger rightly
states, "At issue here is not so much the commission of distinct acts of
sin, but *remaining in a state of sin*."[81] Jesus exposes the bondage of those
who do not believe in him once again when he says,

> Why do you not understand what I say? It is because you cannot bear
> to hear my word. You are of your father the devil, and your will is to do
> your father's desires. . . . But because I tell the truth, you do not believe
> me. Which one of you convicts me of sin? If I tell the truth, why do you
> not believe me? Whoever is of God hears the words of God. The reason
> why you do not hear them is that you are not of God. (John 8:43–47)

Jesus is very clear; the reason they do not understand him in a saving
way is because they cannot bear to hear his word. Carson comments:

> This is shocking: Jesus does not say they fail to grasp his message because
> they cannot follow his spoken word, his idiom, but that they fail to
> understand his idiom precisely because they *cannot* "hear" his message.
> The Jews remain responsible for their own "cannot," which, far from
> resulting from divine fiat, is determined by their own desire (*thelousin*)
> to perform the lusts (*tas epithymias*) of the devil (8:44). This "cannot,"
> this slavery to sin (8:34), itself stems from personal sin. Sin enslaves.[82]

79. D. A. Carson, *The Gospel according to John*, PNTC (Grand Rapids: Eerdmans, 1991),
350; Herman Ridderbos, *The Gospel of John*, trans. John Vriend (Grand Rapids: Eerdmans,
1997), 310; Köstenberger, *John*, 262–63.

80. Hoekema, *Created in God's Image*, 232–33.

81. Köstenberger, *John*, 263.

82. D. A. Carson, *Divine Sovereignty and Human Responsibility: Biblical Perspectives in
Tension* (Eugene, OR: Wipf and Stock, 1994), 166.

...on's observation is piercing. The reason the sinner does not understand the word of Christ is because he is enslaved to the devil (8:44). However, as we will see later, while the proximate reason for unbelief is slavery to sin and the devil, the ultimate or remote reason is because sinners do not belong to God. As Jesus states, "The reason why you do not hear them is that you are not of God" (John 8:47; cf. 12:37–40; 14:17). What must be done to free man's will from this bondage to sin? According to Jesus, man willfully remains in bondage to sin until the Son sets him free (John 8:36). As John 15:1–5 explains, apart from Christ the sinner can do nothing, but "if the Son sets you free, you will be free indeed" (John 8:36).

Like Jesus, the apostle Paul is very clear that man is a willful slave to sin and unable to do anything out of faith in God. Paul states, "Do you not know that if you present yourselves to anyone as obedient slaves, you are slaves of the one whom you obey, either of sin, which leads to death, or of obedience, which leads to righteousness?" (Rom. 6:16). Those who are slaves to sin are dominated by sin, unable to escape its power (Rom. 6:18; cf. 6:20–23).[83] As Schreiner states, "Unbelievers cannot liberate themselves from sin's grip." In other words, "Sin exercises control over them so that they are in bondage to it."[84] In Romans 8:7–8 Paul again reminds us of man's slavery and spiritual inability when he says, "For the mind that is set on the flesh is hostile to God, for it does not submit to God's law; indeed, it cannot. Those who are in the flesh cannot please God." As observed already, Paul does not say that man, though maimed by sin, can still submit to God's law. Nor is it the case that the sinner simply is refusing to cooperate. Rather, Paul is certain that man is absolutely unable to please God because he, as unregenerate, is of the flesh rather than the Spirit (Rom. 8:9).[85] Therefore, Mounce correctly states, "Not only are persons apart from Christ 'totally depraved' (i.e., every part of their being has been affected by the fall) but also 'totally disabled'—in their rebellious state they cannot please God."[86] Murray

---

83. Schreiner, *Paul*, 127.
84. Ibid., 128.
85. Ibid., 135.
86. Robert H. Mounce, *Romans*, NAC, vol. 27 (Nashville: B&H Publishing Group, 1995), 178.

concludes, "Here we have nothing less than the doctrine of the total inability of the natural man, that is to say, total inability to be well-pleasing to God or to do what is well-pleasing in his sight."[87]

Paul makes the same point when writing to the Corinthians: "The natural person does not accept the things of the Spirit of God, for they are folly to him, and he is not able to understand them because they are spiritually discerned" (1 Cor. 2:14). The natural person is enslaved to the foolishness of this world and the spiritual things of God he cannot even begin to understand in a saving way (cf. 2 Thess. 2:9–12).[88] As Calvin comically but insightfully states, "Faced with God's revelation, the unbeliever is like an ass at a concert."[89]

As he said to the Corinthians, so Paul also says to the Galatians, "In the same way we also, when we were children, were enslaved to the elementary principles of the world" (Gal. 4:3). Being enslaved to the elementary principles of the world is comparable to being "under the law" (Gal. 3:23; 4:5).[90] Schreiner comments that Paul draws an important parallel between Israel's slavery under the law (Gal. 3:10, 22; 4:3–5) and the slavery of the Gentiles to idols (Gal. 4:8, 10). Notice that with the Jews and the Gentiles "sin reigned as a tyrannical power."

> Paul does not represent pre-Christian existence as one characterized by libertarian freedom, that is, the power to choose the contrary. People instead are under the thrall to sin, subjugated and mastered by alien power. The earthly Jerusalem that resists the Pauline gospel is not only misguided, "she is in *slavery* with her children" (Gal. 4:25) and her inhabitants are in bondage (Gal. 4:31).[91]

87. Murray, *Romans*, 1:287.

88. David E. Garland, *1 Corinthians*, BECNT (Grand Rapids: Baker Academic, 2003), 100; Anthony C. Thiselton, *The First Epistle to the Corinthians: A Commentary on the Greek Text*, NIGTC (Grand Rapids: Eerdmans, 2000), 271; Schreiner, *Paul*, 136.

89. Quoted in Richard B. Gaffin, "Some Epistological Reflection's on 1 Cor 2:6–16," *WTJ* 57 (1995): 114.

90. Schreiner, *Paul*, 130; Herman N. Ridderbos, *The Epistle of Paul to the Churches of Galatia*, NICNT (Grand Rapids: Eerdmans, 1953), 154; Richard N. Longenecker, *Galatians*, WBC, vol. 41 (Dallas: Word, 1990), 165–66.

91. Schreiner, *Paul*, 131–32.

It is only when Christ liberates the sinner that one becomes a son of God (Gal. 4:4–5). Moreover, if, as Schreiner argues, being enslaved to the elementary principles of the world is parallel to being "under the law" (Gal. 3:23; 4:5),[92] then it is also true, as Calvin observes, that the law does not reveal our capacity but incapacity to obey. Anthony Lane explains, "The purpose of the law is not to show us our capacity but rather to reveal our inability. The law cannot make sinners good but convicts them of guilt."[93] However, our inability does not mitigate our responsibility to obey the law.[94] Berkhof explains that

> though man tore away from God in sin and is now incapable of rendering spiritual obedience to his rightful Sovereign, his willful transgression did not abrogate the claim of God on the service of His rational creatures. The right of God to demand absolute obedience remains, and He asserts this right in both the law and the gospel.[95]

Therefore, when man fails to heed the law due to his corrupt nature and enslavement to sin, he is not excused due to his inability; rather, his continual inability actually aggravates and increases his culpability.[96] Consequently, the Arminian cannot object at this point that man's inability removes his responsibility. Such an assumption is unbiblical, as seen in Israel's history. Schreiner clarifies, "The law's commands were given to people who had no inclination or capability to keep the Torah. Those in the flesh are enslaved to sin [Rom. 8:8]. Once again, the history of Israel testifies to what Paul says. Israel was thoroughly instructed by the Torah, but they had no inclination to keep it."[97]

Paul emphasizes the inability and slavery of man again in 2 Timothy 2:24–26: "And the Lord's servant must not be quarrelsome but kind to everyone, able to teach, patiently enduring evil, correcting his

---

92. Ibid., 130.

93. Anthony N. S. Lane, "Anthropology," in *The Calvin Handbook*, ed. Herman J. Selderhuis (Grand Rapids: Eerdmans, 2009), 280.

94. Berkhof, *Systematic Theology*, 463.

95. Ibid.

96. John Cheeseman, *Saving Grace* (Edinburgh: Banner of Truth, 1999), 26.

97. Schreiner, *Paul*, 136. Also see Cheeseman, *Saving Grace*, 26–30.

opponents with gentleness. God may perhaps grant them repentance leading to a knowledge of the truth, and they may come to their senses and escape from the snare of the devil, after being captured by him to do his will." In verse 26 Paul is lucid: the unregenerate man is under the snare of the devil and captured by him to do his will.[98] Paul makes a similar statement in 2 Corinthians 4:4: "In their case the god of this world has blinded the minds of the unbelievers, to keep them from seeing the light of the gospel of the glory of Christ, who is the image of God." Murray Harris observes that while in 2 Corinthians 3:14a (see Rom. 11:8 also) the minds of the Jews "are hardened by God (by implication)," in 4:4 it is Satan who "blinds" the minds of all unbelievers.[99] However, God, not Satan, is sovereign in this text. Hafemann explains,

> Paul is not teaching a dualism in which competing gods battle one another for the lives of men and women. Paul describes Satan as limited, that is, he is only "the god of this age." When taken together with the use of the "divine passive" of 3:14 and Paul's emphasis on the active work of the Spirit in removing the "veil" in 3:17, Satan's work is clearly seen to be *subordinate to the sovereignty of the "one God"* (cf. 1 Cor. 8:6; also Rom. 11:36). "Those who are perishing" (2 Cor. 4:3) do so because God leaves them in their blinded state, cut off from his glory and without the power of the Spirit needed to escape Satan's reign over their lives.[100]

Man is not only a slave to his own passions and the sins of the world, but he is also a slave to Satan himself, doing his bidding.[101] Only a sovereign act of God granting repentance can liberate the will's bondage to the devil.

98. Towner, *Timothy and Titus*, 549–50; Knight, *Pastoral Epistles*, 425–27; William D. Mounce, *Pastoral Epistles*, WBC, vol. 46 (Nashville: Thomas Nelson, 2000), 537–38.

99. Murray J. Harris, *The Second Epistle to the Corinthians*, NIGTC (Grand Rapids: Eerdmans, 2005), 328 (cf. 329).

100. Scott J. Hafemann, *2 Corinthians*, NAC (Nashville: B&H Publishing Group, 2000), 178. Likewise, Harris, *Second Epistle to the Corinthians*, 329.

101. Hafemann, *2 Corinthians*, 177.

WILLFULLY INCLINED TO SIN: JONATHAN EDWARDS ON THE FREEDOM OF INCLINATION

With regard to the doctrine of spiritual inability, the categories of Jonathan Edwards on the freedom of the will are of great assistance.[102] Edwards is debatably the most important Calvinist philosopher-theologian in American history. His 1754 volume *Freedom of the Will* showed itself to be the central work in defense of a Calvinist view of free will.[103] Four years later, Edwards also wrote *The Great Christian Doctrine of Original Sin Defended* (1758), which would be the essential companion to *Freedom of the Will*. Edwards argues that the universal imputation of Adam's sin to humanity resulted in man being necessarily inclined toward sin. In other words, man "is depraved and ruined by propensities to sin," indeed, an "unfailing propensity" to moral evil.[104] Therefore, only the work of the Spirit in regeneration can change man's propensity toward sin.[105] Such an understanding of sin will come into play as Edwards expounds the freedom of the will.

Edwards defines the will as the mind that chooses. "The faculty of the will is that faculty or power or principle of mind by which it is capable of choosing: an act of the will is the same as an act of choosing or choice."[106] In the mind's choosing, a man chooses that which he most desires. "A man never, in any instance, wills anything contrary to his desires, or desires anything contrary to his will."[107] Therefore, one will always choose whatever the strongest desire (motive) may be at the

---

102. Jonathan Edwards, *Freedom of the Will*, ed. Paul Ramsay, vol. 1 of *The Works of Jonathan Edwards* (New Haven, CT: Yale University Press, 1957). For an extensive list of works on which I am depending, see the bibliography in *Reclaiming Monergism*, e-book.

103. Samuel Storms, "Jonathan Edwards on the Freedom of the Will," *Trinity Journal* 3, 2 (1982): 132; Benjamin B. Warfield, *Studies in Theology* (New York: Oxford University Press, 1932), 530. Contra Richard A. Muller, "Jonathan Edwards and the Absence of Free Choice: A Parting of Ways in the Reformed Tradition," *Jonathan Edwards Studies* 1, 1 (2011): 3–22.

104. Jonathan Edwards, *The Great Christian Doctrine of Original Sin Defended*, in *The Works of Jonathan Edwards*, 2 vols. (Edinburgh, PA: Banner of Truth, 1979), 1:145, 152.

105. Ibid., 1:210–14. Calvin also uses the language of the "faculty of the will" in *Institutes*, 3.2.5.

106. Edwards, *Freedom of the Will*, 137.

107. Ibid., 139.

moment of choice. Such desires or motives provide reasons for why a person chooses *A* instead of *B*.

If, as Edwards says, man's choice is necessitated by his strongest desire or motive, then freedom is compatible with divine determinism. Edwards explains,

> By "determining the will," if the phrase be used with any meaning, must be intended, causing that the act of the will or choice should be thus, and not otherwise: and the will is said to be determined, when, in consequence of some action, or influence, its choice is directed to, and fixed upon a particular object.[108]

Determinism means that when a person acts he must necessarily choose one option rather than another and the chosen action is exactly what God had ordained beforehand. Such a view is contrary to Arminianism's indeterminism, which argues, as chapter 5 will show, that no one thing, external (God) or internal (depravity) to man, determines, necessitates, or causes his choice. For the indeterminist, man can always choose otherwise, or could have chosen other than he did. While there may be influences on his choice, no one influence is so influential that man *must* choose *A* instead of *B*. Edwards sees such a view as nonsense because it is a freedom of indifference, which makes the agent's choices arbitrary, lacking decisive motive for any given action. In short, such a view is irrational, says Edwards. To the contrary, the will is never "indifferent" but there is always a cause which results in a certain effect. "To talk of the determination of the will, supposes an effect, which must have a cause."[109] To disagree would be to argue that the will is not caused and therefore is an "uncaused effect." However, such a view cannot explain why there are effects that issue forth from man's will.[110]

According to Edwards, the will is both a determiner and is determined. "If the will be determined, there is a determiner. This

108. Ibid., 141.
109. Ibid.
110. Ibid. Also see Sproul, *Willing to Believe*, 159.

61

must be supposed to be intended even by them that say, the will determines itself. If it be so, the will is both determiner and determined; it is a cause that acts and produces effects upon itself, and is the object of its own influence and action."[111] For Edwards, the will is a determiner in that the will produces certain effects. However, the will is also determined in that the choices it makes are choices that are caused by certain desires or motives. The will always chooses the strongest desire and so is determined. Edwards calls this the will's "strongest motive," for "the will is always determined by the strongest motive."[112] There can never be an act of the will which is uncaused, but rather the act is always caused by the will's greatest motive. If then by free will one means a will which chooses that which it most desires, then yes the will is free. However, if by free will one means (as the Arminians do) that the will is uncaused and man can always choose otherwise (i.e., has the power of contrary choice or contra-causal choice) then such a definition of free will must be rejected for the will is never free in this manner.[113] Here Edwards is simply reiterating the Reformers before him, especially Calvin, who argued that "the will is never indifferent" as if man possessed a *libertas contrarietatis* (freedom of contrariety).[114] Such a view is also affirmed by many Reformed theologians today in the position called "compatibilism."[115]

How does this philosophical discussion on the will by Edwards relate to sin and grace? If, as Edwards says, the will is always caused by its "strongest motive," then it is proper to call free will the freedom of inclination, for the will always does that which it is most inclined to do, or that which it most desires. However, in light of the corruption of Adam inherited by all of mankind, man's nature is polluted.

---

111. Sproul, *Willing to Believe*, 158–59.

112. Edwards, *Freedom of the Will*, 142.

113. For Edwards's treatment of the Arminian view, see *Freedom of the Will*, 164–65.

114. Richard A. Muller, "Liberum Arbitrium," in *Dictionary of Latin and Greek Theological Terms*, by Richard A. Muller (Grand Rapids: Baker, 1985).

115. For extensive definition of compatibilism, see Robert Kane, *A Contemporary Introduction to Free Will* (New York: Oxford University Press, 2005), 13, 18–21.

Consequently, man's inclinations are evil. What this means for the will is that its "strongest motive" after the fall is toward sin. Man's will is necessitated by his sinful nature so that he chooses that which is evil, and yet, since this is the will's strongest motive, it is exactly what he most wants to choose.[116] Man is not forced or coerced to sin but sins willingly because his will finds its strongest desire not in God but in sinful pleasures.

It is at this point that Arminians will object that man's will is not free nor can man be held responsible. How can such an understanding of freedom be reconciled with man's duty to repent and believe? Surely if man is unable to repent and believe he cannot be held responsible for not doing so. Edwards is able to answer such an objection by distinguishing, as Francis Turretin did before him, between natural and moral ability and natural and moral necessity.

> What has been said of natural and moral necessity, may serve to explain what is intended by natural and moral *inability*. We are said to be *naturally* unable to do a thing, when we can't do it if we will, because what is most commonly called nature don't allow of it, or because of some impeding defect or obstacle that is extrinsic to the will; either in the faculty of understanding, constitution of body, or external objects. *Moral* inability consists not in any of these things; but either in the want of inclination; or the strength of a contrary inclination; or the want of sufficient motives in view, to induce and excite the will, or the strength of apparent motives to the contrary. Or both these may be resolved into one; and it may be said in one word, that moral inability consists in the opposition or want of inclination.[117]

116. Some object that necessity is inconsistent with liberty. However, Edwards denies such an inconsistency. See his defense in Edwards, *Freedom of the Will*, 152.

117. Ibid., 159. Not all Calvinists have agreed with Edwards on this distinction. For example, see Berkhof, *Systematic Theology*, 247–48. This is unfortunate for it seems as though Berkhof is reacting not so much against Edwards as against those who came after Edwards (e.g., those of the New Divinity) who used his distinctions to support synergism. It is important, therefore, to distinguish between Edwards's Calvinism and the neo-Arminianism of those who followed.

If man's will was constrained by nature, then yes, man's will would not be free. However, the bondage of the will to sin is not a *natural* or physical inability of the will, but a *moral* inability. Edwards states that moral ability consists in the "want of inclination." The problem after the fall, however, is that man does not want and is not inclined toward righteousness. The will, in other words, is morally necessitated to choose evil rather than good, but since the will always chooses according to the "strongest motive" such a choice is freely chosen, respecting man's liberty. When the sinner chooses to sin he does so out of moral necessity and yet he is free because he is choosing according to his strongest inclination, namely, sin.[118] Therefore, as Edwards would argue in *Efficacious Grace*, left to himself man will not and morally cannot choose God until his inclinations are changed by a sovereign act of effectual grace.[119] It is in the sovereign work of regeneration that man's disposition is changed and his inclinations reoriented. God alone can liberate man from his willful bondage to sin.[120]

However, before moving into a discussion of the doctrine of effectual calling it is necessary to show that the philosophical categories Edwards appropriates have biblical warrant. Consider two texts: 1 Corinthians 2:14 and 2 Thessalonians 2:9–12. Thomas Schreiner explains the dilemma: "Paul says there [in 1 Cor. 2:14] that unbelievers *cannot* accept the things of the Spirit, whereas in 2 Thessalonians 2 he says merely that they *do not* accept the truth. In 1 Corinthians 2:14 their inability (cf. also 2 Cor. 4:4 below) seems to exist *before* they hear the truth, whereas in 2 Thessalonians 2:10–12 delusion is a *consequence* of their forsaking the gospel."[121] In other words, in 1 Corinthians 2:14 the sinner is incapable of obeying whereas in 2 Thessalonians 2 the sinner, it

---

118. Edwards, *Freedom of the Will*, 164. Such a distinction is adopted by Michael Horton, *For Calvinism* (Grand Rapids: Zondervan, 2011), 106.

119. Jonathan Edwards, *Efficacious Grace*, in *Writings on the Trinity, Grace, and Faith*, ed. Sang Hyun Lee, vol. 21 of *The Works of Jonathan Edwards* (New Haven, CT: Yale University Press, 2003), 149–468.

120. See Sproul, *Willing to Believe*, 165; Wilhelmus à Brakel, *The Christian's Reasonable Service*, ed. Joel R. Beeke, trans. Bartel Elshout (Grand Rapids: Reformation Heritage, 1993), 2:209–10.

121. Schreiner, *Paul*, 137.

seems, chooses not to obey. Schreiner is right to respond that no logical contradiction exists, for "Paul consistently maintains both that people *cannot* respond to the gospel and that they *do not* respond to it."[122] If we appropriate a freedom of inclination the texts are further reconciled. Remember, freedom of inclination shows that while man's choices are determined and necessitated by his strongest motive, nevertheless, he chooses that which he most wants and therefore his choice remains free. In light of depravity, man's strongest motive is toward sin and so his choice is determined and necessitated by his corrupt nature; yet, since sinning is exactly what he most wants to do his choice remains free. So is this the case in these texts. In 1 Corinthians 2:14 we see that man cannot obey because he is not spiritual. He is enslaved to his sin, determined by his corrupt nature. Yet, 2 Thessalonians 2:10–12 tells us that he willfully chooses sin, showing that this is what he most wants to do. On the one hand he cannot obey because he is not spiritual, while on the other hand he does not obey because he refuses to love the truth and be saved (2 Thess. 2:10–12; cf. Exod. 4:21, 23). Stated otherwise, on the one hand he does not believe because he is necessitated by his corrupt nature (natural man), while on the other hand he does not believe because he refuses to, loving sin more than truth. The former highlights how man's freedom is determined by his sinful nature and the latter highlights how man sins willfully and freely, for this is his strongest inclination. Thus,

> We should not conceive of bondage to sin as if unbelievers are forced or compelled to sin against their will. People manifest their captivity to sin when they do precisely what they wish to do. The dominion of sin is so complete that unbelievers are unaware of their servitude to sin. They believe that they are "free" because they do what they wish and follow the inclination of their mind. Such desires, however, stem from people who are dead in trespasses in sins, who are actually under the tyranny and dominion of sin.[123]

122. Ibid.
123. Ibid., 139.

COMMON OBJECTIONS

We must recognize and address here several objections to the doctrines of "total depravity and spiritual inability" (TDSI). First, some object that TDSI leads sinners to despair and ruins any motivation for turning to God. In response we may say that unless man is driven to see his utter corruption he will never throw himself before Christ in despair, knowing his need of a Savior. As Reymond explains, "It is only when a man knows that he is sinful and incapable of helping himself that he will seek help outside of himself and cast himself upon the mercies of God."[124] Ironically, it is one's rejection of TDSI that discourages repentance. Again, Reymond elaborates,

> Nothing is more soul-destroying than the sinner's belief that he is righteous and/or is capable of remedying his situation himself. And precisely this attitude is fostered by the teaching that man is natively able to do whenever he desires to do so what is good in God's sight. To encourage such a conviction is truly to plunge men into self-deception, and that is indeed a counsel of despair.[125]

A second objection is that TDSI is in direct tension with God's command to repent and believe. God would not give this command, the argument goes, if man were unable to fulfill it. In short, "ought implies can." A lengthy response here is unnecessary since this objection has already been addressed above. However, we should note that Reymond is right when he observes that "God deals with man according to his *obligation*, not according to the measure of his ability."[126] While Adam had both the obligation and the ability, after the fall man lost the ability yet the obligation remains as God's perfect standard cannot be compromised or lowered. Reymond concludes for us,

> Man's inability to obey, arising from the moral corruption of his nature, does not remove from us his obligation to love God with

124. Reymond, *Systematic Theology*, 454.
125. Ibid.
126. Ibid.

66

all his heart, soul, mind, and strength, and his neighbor as himself. His obligation to obey God remains intact. If God dealt with man today according to his ability to obey, he would have to reduce his moral demands to the vanishing point. Conversely, if we determined the measure of man's ability from the sweeping obligations implicit in the divine commands, then we would need to predicate *total ability* for man, that is to say, we would all have to adopt the Pelagian position, for the commands of God cover the entire horizon of moral obligation.[127]

127. Ibid.

3

THE SCRIPTURAL AFFIRMATION
OF EFFECTUAL CALLING

n the previous chapter we saw that in Scripture man is portrayed as
pervasively depraved and that this depravity has resulted in the bondage of his will.[1] As J. Gresham Machen explains, "Man, according
to the Bible, is not merely sick in trespasses and sins; he is not merely in
a weakened condition so that he needs divine help: but he is dead
in trespasses and sins. He can do absolutely nothing to save himself,
and God saves him by the gracious, sovereign act of the new birth."[2]
Consequently, the sinner is utterly reliant upon the supernatural act of
God for liberation. Such an act is not in the form of a universal, prevenient grace (as the Arminian supposes), but is specific to the elect and
absolutely efficacious in nature. While God has a gospel call to all, he
also has a special, effectual call for his elect by which the Father draws
sinners to his Son. Perhaps no one expresses the thesis of this chapter
better than John Murray, who wrote,

> The fact that calling is an act of God, and of God alone, should impress
> upon us the divine monergism in the initiation of salvation in actual
> procession. We become partakers of redemption by an act of God
> that instates us in the realm of salvation, and all the corresponding

1. See chapter 2 of *Reclaiming Monergism*, e-book, for how Augustine, Calvin, Dort, and
Westminster defend effectual calling.
2. J. Gresham Machen, *The Christian View of Man* (Edinburgh: Banner of Truth, 1984), 244.

changes in us and in our attitudes and reactions are the result of the saving forces at work within the realm into which, by God's sovereign and efficacious act, we have been ushered. The call, as that by which the predestinating purpose begins to take effect, is in this respect of divine monergism after the pattern of predestination itself. It is of God and of God alone.[3]

EFFECTUAL CALLING IN SCRIPTURE

Nineteenth-century Arminian William Pope wrote in his *Christian Theology*, "Of a *Vocatio Interna*, as distinguished from the *Vocatio Externa*, there is no trace in Scripture: internal calling and effectual calling are phrases never used. The distinction implies such a difference as would have been clearly stated if it existed."[4] As we will see, Pope is grievously mistaken, for there is every trace in Scripture of a distinction between a gospel call to all people and an effectual call only to the elect.[5]

The general call, also referred to as the *vocatio externa*, refers to the call to all people to pay heed to the revelation of God.[6] The *vocatio externa* consists of two parts: *vocatio realis* and *vocatio verbalis*.[7] The *vocatio realis* refers to a call to all people to acknowledge and honor their Creator (Ps. 19:1–4; Acts 17:24; Rom. 1:19–21; 2:14–15). The *vocatio realis*, call from things, occurs through general revelation (cre-

3. John Murray, "The Call," in *Collected Writings of John Murray* (Edinburgh: Banner of Truth, 1976), 2:166; idem, *Redemption Accomplished and Applied* (Grand Rapids: Eerdmans, 1955), 93–94.

4. William B. Pope, *A Compendium of Christian Theology* (New York: Phillips & Hunt, n.d.), 2:345.

5. Other terms used to compare these two include: material and formal, revealed call and call of God's good pleasure, common and personal, universal and special, external and internal. See Amandus Polanus, *Syntragma theologiae christianae*, 5th ed. (Hanover: Aubry, 1624), 6, chap. 32; Herman Bavinck, *Reformed Dogmatics*, ed. John Bolt, trans. John Vriend (Grand Rapids: 2008), 4:42.

6. Bruce A. Ware, "Effectual Calling and Grace," in *Still Sovereign: Contemporary Perspectives on Election, Foreknowledge, and Grace*, ed. Thomas R. Schreiner and Bruce A. Ware (Grand Rapids: Baker, 2000), 210.

7. These distinctions can be found in greater detail in Bavinck, *Reformed Dogmatics*, 4:33–35; Louis Berkhof, *Systematic Theology* (Edinburgh: Banner of Truth, 2003), 457–58; Ware, "Effectual Calling and Grace," 210–11; Richard A. Muller, "Vocatio," in *Dictionary of Latin and Greek Theological Terms*, by Richard A. Muller (Grand Rapids: Baker, 2004).

ation and conscience). The *vocatio verbalis* (call from words) refers to the call to all people through the proclamation of the gospel of Jesus Christ. The *vocatio verbalis* calls sinners to repentance and faith in Christ so that they may receive eternal life and be forgiven of their trespasses (Matt. 28:18–20; Acts 1:6–8; 26:16–23; Rom. 10:8–15; 1 Cor. 15:1–8). As we will see, the gospel call goes to all people but it is clearly not intended to be effectual for all of them, for we know that not all do in fact believe. In contrast, Scripture also teaches that there is an effectual call or *vocatio interna*. As the label suggests, the *vocatio interna*, unlike the *vocatio externa*, is invincible and irresistible. It is "God's inward and ultimately persuasive summons to repent of sin and to turn to Christ for salvation."[8] However, unlike the *vocatio externa* which is for all, the *vocatio interna* is designed by God to be only for those whom he has unconditionally elected (Rom. 8:28–30; 1 Cor. 1:22–24). The particularity of the *vocatio interna* is evidenced by the fact that not all are chosen to be saved.

THE GOSPEL CALL

Despite man's depravity God is outrageously gracious to sinners, sending forth his gospel message to the ends of the earth. Hoekema, building off of Berkhof, helpfully defines the gospel call as the "offering of salvation in Christ to people, together with an invitation to accept Christ in repentance and faith, in order that they may receive the forgiveness of sins and eternal life."[9] Hoekema's definition reveals two aspects of the gospel call: (1) it consists of the gospel of Jesus Christ and (2) it is meant to be universal in its extent. Concerning the former, Hoekema observes three essential components: (a) A presentation of the facts of the gospel and of the way of salvation. (b) An invitation to come to Christ in repentance and faith (Matt. 11:28; Luke 14:23). (c) A promise of forgiveness and salvation for those who do come to Christ.[10] The second and

---

8. Ware, "Effectual Calling and Grace," 211.

9. Anthony Hoekema, *Saved by Grace* (Grand Rapids: Eerdmans, 1989), 68. See Berkhof, *Systematic Theology*, 459–61.

10. Hoekema, *Saved by Grace*, 70.

third aspects, for our purposes, deserve considerable attention, as does the universality of the gospel call, which we shall first address.

A Call to Sinners Everywhere to Repent and Believe

The first truth to understand about the gospel call is that it is an invitation for everyone who hears the gospel. Hence, sometimes the gospel call is labeled the *general* or *universal* call, meaning that the gospel is preached indiscriminately to people of any age, race, or nation. Several passages demonstrate the universality of the gospel call. Consider Isaiah 45:22: "Turn to me and be saved, all the ends of the earth! For I am God, and there is no other." Here the Lord invites sinners to turn to Yahweh so that they might find salvation. Notice that Yahweh is the only God who can save for "there is no other." Isaiah again teaches a call to all people in 55:1: "Come, everyone who thirsts, come to the waters; and he who has no money, come, buy and eat! Come, buy wine and milk without money and without price." Here again we see an invitation to everyone to come to Yahweh empty-handed to receive true spiritual salvation. Jesus will use this same language in the New Testament when he says to the woman at the well that he has living water which he gives as a gift from God (John 4:10). Jesus promises that the living water that he gives becomes a spring welling up to eternal life (John 4:14), so that one never thirsts again (John 4:13). Likewise, Jesus uses the imagery of Isaiah when he says, "I am the bread of life" (John 6:35, 48, 51) and invites sinners to come and eat of his flesh that they may live (John 6:54–56). Such an invitation is consistent with the words of Joel 2:32a, "And it shall come to pass that everyone who calls on the name of the Lord shall be saved."

In the New Testament, the general call to all people is specifically referenced to Jesus, the Christ, who is God with us (Matt. 1:23; Isa. 7:14). Like Yahweh in the Old Testament, Jesus is the source of salvation and redemption and it is through him and him alone that eternal life can be found (John 14:6; Acts 4:12; Rom. 10:10–12). Therefore, Jesus says in Matthew 11:28, "Come to me, all who labor and are heavy laden, and I will give you rest." Jesus calls all people to come to him, to trust in him, and to believe in him (cf. Matt. 10:32–33; Luke 12:8; 16:24–26; Mark 8:34–35; Luke 9:23–24). Likewise, John 7:37 states, "On the last day of the feast, the great day, Jesus stood up and cried out, 'If anyone thirsts, let him come to me and drink'" (cf. John 4:13). And again Jesus proclaims, "Truly, truly, I say to you, if anyone keeps my word, he will never see death" (John 8:51). Such a promise is consistent with John 3:16, "For God so loved the world, that he gave his only Son, that whoever believes in him should not perish but have eternal life" (cf. John 6:40; 11:26; 12:46). Such invitations parallel Revelation 22:17, "The Spirit and the Bride say, 'Come.' And let the one who hears say, 'Come.' And let the one who is thirsty come; let the one who desires take the water of life without price."

The parables of Jesus also describe a gospel call. For example, Matthew 22:1–14 and Luke 14:16–24, which are meant to illustrate the kingdom of heaven, both describe instances where somebody in the parable (Matthew: a king; Luke: a certain man) invites guests to his banquet and then sends out his servant(s), telling his guests to come.[11] Similarly, God sends out the message of his Son, inviting people everywhere to come and enter into the kingdom. This is also the purpose of the great commission in Matthew 28:19–20 where Jesus commands his disciples, "Go therefore and make disciples of all nations, baptizing them in the name of the Father and of the Son and of the Holy Spirit, teaching them to observe all that I have commanded you. And behold, I am with you always, to the end of the age." The words of Jesus here demonstrate that the gospel is to be preached to all, without hesitation or reservation. We do not know who will believe and who will not. We do not know who the elect are. We are to preach the gospel to all, desiring to see all come to repentance and faith.

Furthermore, many times the invitation of the gospel call takes on the form of a command. Consider the words of Jesus in Matthew 4:17: "From that time Jesus began to preach, saying, '*Repent*, for the kingdom of heaven is at hand.'" Likewise, Acts 17:30 says, "The times of ignorance God overlooked, but now he *commands* all people

11. Ibid., 70–71.

everywhere to repent, because he has fixed a day on which he will judge the world in righteousness by a man whom he has appointed; and of this he has given assurance to all by raising him from the dead." Here again we see that God commands people everywhere to repent of their sins for a day of judgment is coming. What is important to note at this point is that these commands demonstrate that it is man's duty to repent and believe. In other words, regardless of whether or not man has the spiritual ability to repent and trust in Christ (which, as we saw previously, the sinner does not), nevertheless, it is still man's duty to do so. Therefore, the indiscriminate preaching of the gospel is necessary.

Besides the Gospels, the epistles also present a gospel call to all people. Using the language of Joel 2:32, Peter proclaims in Acts 2:21, "And it shall come to pass that everyone who calls upon the name of the Lord shall be saved" (cf. Rom. 10:13). Such a promise is not only for Jews but for Gentiles also as exemplified in Peter's words to the household of Cornelius in Acts 10. The promise of life is held out to those who trust in Christ: "And he commanded us to preach to the people and to testify that he [Jesus] is the one appointed by God to be judge of the living and the dead. To him all the prophets bear witness that *everyone who believes in him receives forgiveness of sins through his name*" (Acts 10:42–43). Similarly, the apostle Paul, explaining how salvation has come to the Gentiles, also holds out the promise of the gospel in Romans 9:33, as he quotes from Isaiah 28:16, "Behold, I am laying in Zion a stone of stumbling, and a rock of offense; and *whoever believes in him will not be put to shame*" (cf. Rom. 10:11–13; 1 Peter 2:6). Therefore, John rightly asserts in 1 John 4:15, "Whoever confesses that Jesus is the Son of God, God abides in him, and he in God."

God's Desire for All to Believe. As seen in the passages above, God offers the gospel freely to both Jew and Gentile, promising salvation if they believe. Such an offer is consistent with God's desire to see sinners repent and be saved. As Peter states, the Lord is patient toward sinners, "not wishing that any should perish, but that all should reach repentance" (2 Peter 2:9). Likewise, Paul tells Timothy that God our Savior "desires all people to be saved and to come to the knowledge of the truth" (1 Tim. 2:4). Such passages as these reflect God's will of disposition (not his decretive will) in which he not only offers salvation but desires that lost sinners repent and be saved.[12] Consider the following texts:

> Have I any pleasure in the death of the wicked, declares the Lord God, and not rather that he should turn from his way and live? (Ezek. 18:23)

> Say to them, As I live, declares the Lord God, I have no pleasure in the death of the wicked, but that the wicked turn from his way and live; turn back, turn back from your evil ways, for why will you die, O house of Israel? (Ezek. 33:11)

> "O Jerusalem, Jerusalem, the city that kills the prophets and stones those who are sent to it! How often would I have gathered your children together as a hen gathers her brood under her wings, and you would not!" (Matt. 23:37; cf. Luke 13:34)

> Therefore, we are ambassadors for Christ, God making his appeal through us. We implore you on behalf of Christ, be reconciled to God. (2 Cor. 5:20)

> This is good, and it is pleasing in the sight of God our Savior, who desires all people to be saved and to come to the knowledge of the truth. (1 Tim. 2:3–4)

> The Lord is not slow to fulfill his promise as some count slowness, but is patient toward you, not wishing that any should perish, but that all should reach repentance. (2 Peter 3:9)

Here we see several examples of God's desire that all people be saved, a desire which is manifested in his indiscriminate offer of the gospel to all people.

12. See Appendix 2 of *Reclaiming Monergism*, e-book.

The Well-Meant Offer of the Gospel. The preaching of the gospel to all people comes out of a real, genuine desire to see all people repent and be saved (Num. 23:19; Ps. 81:13–16; Prov. 1:24; Isa. 1:18–20; Ezek. 18:23, 32; 33:11; Matt. 23:37; 2 Tim. 2:13). The gospel call is a *bona fide* calling that is seriously given. As Berkhof states, "When God calls the sinner to accept Christ by faith, He earnestly desires this; and when He promises those who repent and believe eternal life, His promise is dependable."[13] Or as Johannes Wollebius states, "He calls both [elect and non-elect] in earnest [*serior*] and without any deceit."[14] Arminians often object that this cannot be the case in light of the Calvinist belief that God chooses to give his effectual grace only to his elect. This would make God's gospel offer "disingenuous" and "cynical."[15] However, there is no inconsistency here for several reasons.

(1) Such an offer is not superfluous because it is the gospel call which is the *very means* by which God converts sinners.[16]

(2) God never makes a promise in the gospel offer that he does not keep. God promises that eternal life will be granted on the condition of faith. However, God never promises that he will bestow faith on everyone. As Bavinck explains, in "that offer he does not say what he himself will do—whether or not he will bestow that faith. He has kept that to himself. He only tells us what he wants us to do: that we humble ourselves and seek our salvation in Christ alone."[17] Or as Wollebius argues,

> As to the reprobate, although they are not called "according to his purpose," or to salvation, nevertheless they are called in earnest, and salvation is offered them *on condition of faith.* Nor are they mocked

13. Berkhof, *Systematic Theology,* 462.

14. Johannes Wollebius, *Compendium Theologiae Christianae,* trans. Alexander Ross (London: n.p., 1650), 20.2.7.

15. Steve W. Lemke, "A Biblical and Theological Critique of Irresistible Grace," in *Whosoever Will: A Biblical-Theological Critique of Five-Point Calvinism,* ed. David L. Allen and Steve W. Lemke (Nashville: B&H Publishing Group, 2010), 120.

16. Michael Horton, *Putting Amazing Back into Grace,* 2nd ed. (Grand Rapids: Baker, 2002), 134; John Owen, *A Display of Arminianism,* in *The Works of John Owen,* ed. William H. Goold (Edinburgh: Banner of Truth, 2000), 10:48; Berkhof, *Systematic Theology,* 462.

17. Herman Bavinck, *Reformed Dogmatics,* ed. John Bolt, trans. John Vriend (Grand Rapids: Baker, 2008), 4:37.

because they have been deprived of the grace of believing. Rather, because they destroyed the original grace of their own accord, and also, by their evil passion, despised the means of grace, God therefore has the right to demand faith from them and uses it no less justly than do other creditors, so that their mouths are closed, they are without excuse, and the justice of God is upheld. Therefore, he does not call them to mock them, but in order to declare and reveal his justice.[18]

Turretin says the same: "For a serious call does not require that there should be an intention and purpose of drawing him, but only that there should be a constant will of commanding duty and bestowing the blessing upon him who performs it (which God most seriously wills)."[19]

(3) The gospel call is seriously meant regardless of the fact that man cannot fulfill it. It is objected that since sinners do not have the ability to believe (due to depravity), a gospel call cannot be genuinely offered. Some take this objection so far as to say that God would be deceptive to make an offer that he knows man cannot fulfill. However, as Wilhelmus à Brakel states, the "fact that man is not able to repent and believe is not God's fault, but man is to be blamed."[20] God will not lower the conditions of the gospel (faith and repentance) because man, by his own depravity, cannot fulfill them. Moreover, God is not obligated to bestow his grace on anyone. Man is a sinner, deserving only judgment, and for God to fulfill the gospel condition on anyone's behalf is sheer grace.

(4) The well-meant offer is just as problematic (if not more problematic!) for the Arminian. As Bavinck notes,

> If it be objected that God nevertheless offers salvation to those to whom he has decided not to grant faith and salvation, then this is an objection equally applicable to the position of our opponents. For in that case, *God also offers salvation to those whom he infallibly knows will not believe.* . . . The outcome of world history is eternally

18. Wollebius, *Compendium Theologiae Christianae*, 20.2.7, emphasis added.

19. Francis Turretin, *Institutes of Elenctic Theology*, ed. James T. Dennison Jr., trans. George M. Giger, 3 vols. (Phillipsburg, NJ: P&R Publishing, 1992–97), 2:504–10.

20. Wilhelmus à Brakel, *The Christian's Reasonable Service*, ed. Joel R. Beeke, trans. Bartel Elshout (Grand Rapids: Reformation Heritage, 1992–95), 2:207 (cf. 2:208).

and unchangeably certain. The only difference is that the Reformed have had the courage to say that the outcome corresponds to God's will and purpose.[21]

Or as Turretin explains, "It is repugnant for God simply and absolutely to will and intend what he himself decreed should never happen."[22] As it turns out, it is the Arminian who has the real problem of a *well-meant* offer of the gospel.

Unfortunately, the Calvinist's affirmation of the well-meant offer of the gospel not only raises conflict with the Arminian but with the hyper-Calvinist as well. This is evidenced in eighteenth-century hyper-Calvinism, as represented by men such as Joseph Hussey (d. 1726) and John Brine (1703–65), though scholars now recognize that, due to their various theological nuances, it is inaccurate to "lump together indiscriminately" all hyper-Calvinists.[23] Nevertheless, hyper-Calvinism was refuted by Particular Baptist Andrew Fuller in *The Gospel Worthy of All Acceptation.*[24] In the nineteenth century, the hyper-Calvinist view once again received support from men like James Wells (1803–72), but again was refuted in the Fullerism of Charles H. Spurgeon (1834–92).[25] In the twentieth century, hyper-Calvinism has shown its head yet again in the work of Herman Hoeksema (1886–1965), creating controversy both in the Netherlands and in England.[26]

Hoeksema argued that the gospel call is not an "offer" since this would mean that everyone to whom the gospel went would be capable of accepting it, which is clearly not the case.[27] Since everyone cannot accept it, but only the elect, the gospel call is not an offer of salvation

21. Bavinck, *Reformed Dogmatics*, 4:37, emphasis added.

22. Turretin, *Institutes*, 2:510.

23. Timothy George, "John Gill," in *Theologians of the Baptist Tradition*, ed. Timothy George and David S. Dockery (Nashville: B&H Publishing Group, 2001), 29.

24. Andrew Fuller, *The Complete Works of Reverend Andrew Fuller*, ed. Joseph Belcher (Reprint, Harrisonburg, VA: Sprinkle, 1988), 1:360, 376.

25. Iain H. Murray, *Spurgeon versus Hyper-Calvinism* (Edinburgh: Banner of Truth, 1995).

26. Herman Hoeksema, *The Protestant Reformed Church in America*, 2nd ed. (Grand Rapids: Baker, 1947), 317–53; idem, *Reformed Dogmatics* (Grand Rapids: Reformed Free Publishing Association, 1966), 465–68; idem, *Whosoever Will* (Grand Rapids: Eerdmans, 1945).

27. My summary is similar to Anthony Hoekema, *Saved by Grace*, 72–74.

to sinners. Building off of his views on election and reprobation, Hoeksema argues that there can be no well-meant offer of the gospel, which would imply that God intends and desires the salvation of the nonelect, for Scripture is clear that God determines to harden the hearts of the nonelect, not to save them. In fact, says Hoeksema, God does not even desire the salvation of the nonelect, nor does he act favorably toward the reprobate, but only acts to further their sentence to eternal torment. Thus grace, even in the gospel call, is never for the reprobate but only for the elect.[28] Moreover, when the gospel is preached it is not a free offer of grace to whomever will believe, but rather is simply a promise meant only for the elect. The only thing the nonelect receive in hearing this message is condemnation.

As we have seen in the Scriptures discussed already, Hoeksema's view is deeply unbiblical. Contrary to Hoeksema, Scripture everywhere affirms the well-meant offer of the gospel or, as Caspar Olevian (1536–87) termed it, an *evangelium oblatum* (gospel offered), whereby God freely offers the gospel of his Son Jesus Christ and genuinely desires the conversion of the lost (2 Peter 3:9; 1 Tim. 2:4).[29] Moreover, notice that in many of the passages discussed already the gospel call is given by Jesus himself. Jesus *did know* who the elect and nonelect were and yet he offered the gospel freely (Matt. 22:3–8, 14; Luke 14:16–21; John 5:38–40).

It is unfortunate that some Arminians accuse Calvinists of not affirming the well-meant offer of the gospel. Perhaps this is because hyper-Calvinists like Hoeksema are wrongly used as representatives of Calvinism instead of the traditional Reformed theologians.[30] However, Calvinists throughout history have embraced and taught the well-meant offer. For example, consider the Canons of Dort:

28. Hoeksema, *Whosoever Will*, 148.

29. R. Scott Clark, "Janus, the Well-Meant Offer of the Gospel, and Westminster Theology," in *The Pattern of Sound Doctrine: Systematic Theology at the Westminster Seminaries: Essays in Honor of Robert B. Strimple*, ed. David VanDrunen (Phillipsburg, NJ: P&R Publishing, 2004), 169.

30. For example, see Lemke, "A Biblical and Theological Critique of Irresistible Grace," 143–44; Kenneth Keathley, *Salvation and Sovereignty: A Molinist Approach* (Nashville: B&H Publishing Group, 2010), 49–50.

It is the promise of the gospel that whoever believes in Christ crucified shall not perish but have eternal life. This promise, together with the command to repent and believe, ought to be announced and declared without differentiation or discrimination to all nations and people, to whom God in his good pleasure sends the gospel. (V.5)[31]

All who are called through the gospel are called seriously (*serio vocantur*). For seriously and most genuinely (*serio et verissime*) God makes known in his Word what is pleasing to him: that those who are called should come to him. Seriously (*serio*) he also promises rest for their souls and eternal life to all who come to him and believe. (III–IV.8)[32]

In these statements Dort is responding to the accusation by the Arminian Remonstrants that they could not affirm the well-meant offer of the gospel. However, Calvinists have and continue to affirm the offer right alongside of the effectual call.[33] Scripture teaches both of these truths and we must let Scripture be our authority on this matter. Sounding much like Andrew Fuller in the eighteenth century, Anthony Hoekema explains the rationalizing that occurs when one tries to compromise on one of these two essential biblical truths:

The Bible teaches . . . that God seriously desires that all who hear the gospel should believe in Christ and be saved. The same Bible also teaches that God has chosen or elected his own people in Christ from before the creation of the world. To our finite minds it seems impossible that both of these teachings could be true. A kind of rational solution of the problem could go into either of two directions: (1) To say that God wants all who hear the gospel to be saved; that therefore he gives to all who hear sufficient grace to be saved if they so desire; this grace, is, however, always resistible; many do resist and thus frustrate God's design. This is the Arminian solution, which leaves us with a God who is not sovereign, and which thus denies a truth

31. As translated by Anthony Hoekema in *Saved by Grace*, 77.
32. Ibid.
33. John Murray and Ned Stonehouse, *The Free Offer of the Gospel* (Phillipsburg, NJ: Lewis J. Grotenhuis, 1948).

clearly taught in Scripture. (2) The other type of rational solution is that of Hoeksema and the Hyper-Calvinists: Since the Bible teaches election and reprobation, it simply cannot be true that God desires the salvation of all to whom the gospel comes. Therefore we must say that God desires the salvation only of the elect among the hearers of the gospel. This kind of solution may seem to satisfy our minds, but it completely fails to do justice to Scripture passages like Ezekiel 33:11, Matthew 23:37, 2 Corinthians 5:20, and 2 Peter 3:9.[34]

Hoekema's point could not be better stated. As we shall see in chapter 6, the Arminian way of rationalizing this biblical tension between God's sovereignty and the well-meant offer of the gospel fails. But notice, both the Arminian and the hyper-Calvinist have the same objection, namely, if man is unable to repent and believe then a well-meant offer cannot be genuine.[35] The Arminian responds that man must therefore have ability (whether it be natural to him or enabled by prevenient grace), while the hyper-Calvinist responds by affirming inability but concludes that there can then be no well-meant offer of the gospel. Scripture does not permit us to go in either direction.

To summarize, Scripture simultaneously affirms four truths: (1) man's inability, (2) God's well-meant offer, (3) man's duty to repent, and (4) God's sovereign, effectual grace only for the elect (see below).[36] Arminians and hyper-Calvinists may not like the tension between these four truths but the reality is that this is a *biblical* tension; therefore, not one of these four tenets can be excused.[37] Rather, we must say with Augustine, "Command what you wish, but give what you command."[38]

The Resistibility of the Gospel Call

Finally, it must be observed that unlike the effectual call, which will be discussed below, the gospel call can be successfully resisted by

34. Hoekema, *Saved by Grace*, 79. Also see Fuller, *Works*, 2:379.
35. Clark, "Well-Meant Offer," 175.
36. Hoekema, *Saved by Grace*, 79.
37. See Fuller, *Works*, 2:381.
38. Augustine, *Confessions*, trans. R. S. Pine-Coffin (New York: Penguin, 1961), 40.

sinners. All those whom God has not elected will and do resist the gospel call and consequently further their condemnation before a holy God. Consider the following Old Testament passages where many in Israel reject Yahweh.

If you turn at my reproof,
behold, I will pour out my spirit to you;
    I will make my words known to you.
Because I have called and you refused to listen,
    have stretched out my hand and no one has heeded,
because you have ignored all my counsel
    and would have none of my reproof. (Prov. 1:23–25)

When Israel was a child, I loved him,
    and out of Egypt I called my son.
The more they were called,
    the more they went away;
they kept sacrificing to the Baals
    and burning offerings to idols. (Hos. 11:1–2)

They did not keep God's covenant,
    but refused to walk according to his law. (Ps. 78:10)

But my people did not listen to my voice;
    Israel would not submit to me.
So I gave them over to their stubborn hearts,
    to follow their own counsels.
Oh, that my people would listen to me,
    that Israel would walk in my ways! (Ps. 81:11–13)

For he is our God,
    and we are the people of his pasture,
    and the sheep of his hand.
Today, if you hear his voice,
    do not harden your hearts, as at Meribah,
    as on the day at Massah in the wilderness. (Ps. 95:7–8)

What more was there to do for my vineyard,
    that I have not done in it?
When I looked for it to yield grapes,
    why did it yield wild grapes? (Isa. 5:4; cf. 65:12; 66:4)

Yet they did not listen or incline their ear, but stiffened their neck, that they might not hear and receive instruction. (Jer. 17:23; cf. 7:13, 16; 35:17)

They have turned to me their back and not their face. And though I have taught them persistently, they have not listened to receive instruction. (Jer. 32:33)

In these passages it is clear that not all in Israel were truly Israel. Stated otherwise, not all who belonged to the exterior nation of Israel were inwardly regenerated by the Spirit. Rather, many in Israel rejected Yahweh as Lord over them and instead followed the idolatry of the nations.[39] Though Yahweh called out to them to repent and turn to him, they refused.

Such resistance to God's gospel call comes to its climax in the New Testament as many of the Jews reject Jesus Christ himself, the Son of God. One passage that makes such resistance especially evident is Acts 7 where Stephen is martyred for his faith in Christ. Stephen gives a biblical theology of God's redemptive purpose through Israel, and when he comes to the end he reminds the Jews who are putting him on trial that they have failed to understand what the Scriptures have said concerning the "coming of the Righteous One" (Acts 7:52). Stephen accuses the Jews of being just like their fathers, who persecuted the prophets. "You stiff-necked people, uncircumcised in heart and ears, you always resist the Holy Spirit. As your fathers did, so do you" (Acts 7:51; cf. Ps. 95:7–11; Heb. 3:8–13). Stephen's statement is telling because he not only states that the Jews persecuting him are stiff-necked, uncircumcised, and resisting the Spirit, but also that their fathers were the same, failing to heed the

---

39. John Frame, *The Doctrine of God*, A Theology of Lordship (Phillipsburg, NJ: P&R Publishing, 2002), 317–34.

message of the prophets who proclaimed the gospel that would come through Christ (Deut. 32:9; Jer. 6:10; 9:26; Ezek. 44:7–9; Mal. 3:7). Indeed, the martyrdom of Stephen by men who resisted God's Holy Spirit sits within the shadow of the crucifixion, in which evil men, who had resisted the ministry of Jesus for years (Matt. 22:3; Luke 7:30; Mark 6:5–6; John 6:63), rejecting his invitations to receive eternal life, finally put him to death on a cross (Luke 23:1–49). Therefore, Jesus can rightly cry out, "O Jerusalem, Jerusalem, the city that kills the prophets and stones those who are sent to it! How often would I have gathered your children together as a hen gathers her brood under her wings, and you would not!" (Matt. 23:37; cf. Luke 13:34).

It is important to reiterate the resistibility of the gospel call because opponents often assume that Calvinists deny the resistibility of grace. However, Calvinists affirm that God's grace *in the gospel call* can be resisted. It is *when God so chooses to effectually call his elect* for his purposes in saving them that such a calling cannot be finally resisted; such a call *must* come to fruition.[40] The difference here is in God's intention and design. As John Owen says, "Where any work of grace is not effectual, God never intended it should be so, nor did put forth that power of grace which was necessary to make it so."[41] Welty also states the matter precisely,

> In reply, to be sure, men *do* reject God's grace again and again. Indeed, the Calvinistic doctrine of an outer, external call describes a call that can and often is successfully resisted by those to whom it comes . . . But the question is whether a man can successfully resist *when God's individual purpose* toward that man is to draw him to Himself? . . . The Calvinistic doctrine of effectual calling was never meant to preclude the phenomenon of all men resisting God (see Rom. 1:18). Rather, it precludes the notion that, once God has set His purpose of saving grace upon a person (so that he is made willing by God's grace), that person can somehow *continue* successfully to resist. This the doctrine of effectual calling denies.[42]

40. Turretin, *Institutes*, 2:547.
41. John Owen, *Pneumatologia: or, A Discourse Concerning the Holy Spirit*, in *Works*, 3:318.
42. Greg Welty, "Election and Calling: A Biblical Theological Study," in *Calvinism: A Southern Baptist Dialogue*, ed. E. Ray Clendenen and Brad J. Waggoner (Nashville: B&H Publishing Group, 2008), 240, emphasis added. Also see Turretin, *Institutes*, 2:548.

THE EFFECTUAL CALL

Why do some believe when they hear the gospel call but others do not? For the Arminian, while God may enable and initiate grace, ultimately the decision as to whether to believe or not is man's. As we shall now see, such a view is contrary to Scripture, which teaches that the only reason anyone believes is because God chooses sovereignly to call his elect effectually. As the Canons of Dort state, "The fact that some receive from God the gift of faith within time, and that others do not, stems from his eternal decision."[43] Arminians reject such a statement because it implies that God, not man, is in control of salvation, irresistibly and effectually drawing those whom he has determined to save. For the Arminian, God cannot in any way determine who will and will not believe in the gospel. While God's (prevenient) grace is *necessary* to bring the sinner to Christ, it is not *sufficient* to bring about faith and repentance, for the will of man must act to do so.[44] However, as will become evident, this is a clear breach of God's sovereignty in calling his elect to himself. Scripture teaches that when the gospel call goes out to all people, God secretly, irresistibly, and effectually calls his elect and only his elect through this gospel to new life, faith, and repentance. Frame explains, "So, in effectual calling, God acts on us first, before we offer him any response. He acts sovereignly, calling us into fellowship with his Son. This calling is the ultimate source in time of all the blessings of salvation."[45] The grace in effectual calling is not only *necessary* but also *sufficient* to bring about repentance and faith.[46] The reason for transformation is not to be found in man's will but in God's effectual grace. Piper writes,

43. Canons of Dort 1.6, in *Creeds and Confessions of the Reformation Era*, vol. 2 of *Creeds and Confessions of Faith in the Christian Tradition*, ed. Jaroslav Pelikan and Valerie Hotchkiss (New Haven: Yale University Press, 2003), 572.

44. Welty, "Election and Calling," 235; Turretin, *Institutes*, 2:514. For the Arminian view, see Roger E. Olson, *Arminian Theology: Myths and Realities* (Downers Grove, IL: InterVarsity, 2006), 20, 35, 76.

45. John M. Frame, *Salvation Belongs to the Lord*, A Theology of Lordship (Phillipsburg, NJ: P&R Publishing, 2006), 185.

46. Welty, "Election and Calling," 234–35; John L. Dagg, *Manual of Theology* (Reprint, Harrisonburg, VA: Gano Books, 1990), 332.

The internal call is God's sovereign, creative, unstoppable voice. It creates what it commands. God speaks not just to the ear and the mind, but he speaks to the heart. His internal heart-call opens the eyes of the blind heart, and opens the ears of the deaf heart, and causes Christ to appear as the supremely valuable person that he really is. So the heart freely and eagerly embraces Christ as the Treasure that he is.[47]

In this section we will show how the Reformed doctrines of effectual calling and irresistible grace are ingrained in Scripture.

The Pauline, Petrine, and Johannine Epistles

Scripture is replete with references to the effectual call (Rom. 1:6–7; 8:30; 11:29; 1 Cor. 1:2, 9, 24, 26; 7:18; 2 Thess. 2:13–14; Heb. 3:1–2; 2 Peter 1:10).[48] Summarizing the language of calling in Pauline literature, Schreiner states, "The word should not be defined as an 'invitation' that can be accepted or refused. Calling is performative, in which the call accomplishes what is demanded."[49] In other words, when Paul refers to calling he is not referring to a gospel call which is a mere invitation that can be resisted, but rather is referring to that calling which is effective, performing and fulfilling exactly that which it was sent to do. Schreiner's point is made evident in Paul's words in Romans 8:28–30,

> And we know that for those who love God all things work together for good, for those who are called according to his purpose [τοῖς κατὰ πρόθεσιν κλητοῖς οὖσιν]. For those whom he foreknew he also predestined to be conformed to the image of his Son, in order that he might be the firstborn among many brothers. And those whom he predestined he also called [οὓς δὲ προώρισεν, τούτους καὶ ἐκάλεσεν], and those whom he called he also justified, and those whom he justified he also glorified.

47. John Piper, *Finally Alive* (Fearn, Ross-shire, Great Britain: Christian Focus, 2009), 84.
48. Contra Richard Watson, *Theological Institutes* (New York: Lane and Scott, 1851), 2:353.
49. Thomas R. Schreiner, *Paul: Apostle of God's Glory in Christ* (Downers Grove, IL: InterVarsity, 2001), 241.

Paul states in verse 30 that those who have been predestined have also been called and those whom God called he also justified. Moo, contra John Wesley, correctly states,

> The exact correspondence between those who are the objects of pre-destining and those who experience this calling is emphasized by the demonstrative pronoun "these" [*toutous*]: "it was precisely those who were predestined who also (*kai*) were called." This leaves little room for the suggestion that the links in this chain are not firmly attached to one another, as if some who were "foreknown" and "predestined" would not be "called," "justified," and "glorified."[50]

In other words, Paul has the same exact group of people in mind throughout his entire description of the chain of salvation, which also means that he does indeed affirm an unbreakable chain, one in which each link leads inevitably to the next. The link we want to pay special attention to is the verb "he called" which, as Moo says, "denotes God's effectual summoning into relationship with him."[51] Those predestined are the same ones who are called and likewise those called are the same ones as those justified, etc. Murray concludes from this, "Determinate efficacy characterizes the call because it is given in accordance with eternal purpose." The calling proceeds necessarily from God's eternal election.[52] Furthermore, Paul must be referring to a calling other than the gospel call because in the gospel call it is not true that all those called are justified.[53] Indeed, with the gospel call many disbelieve and are never justified. Paul does not say that out of all those whom God calls some are justified and then glorified. No, Paul is clear: those God calls are indeed justified and also glorified. Therefore, since many reject the gospel call and are not justified, let alone glorified, Paul must be referring to a calling which unfailingly and immutably leads to and

---

50. Douglas J. Moo, *The Epistle to the Romans*, NICNT (Grand Rapids: Eerdmans, 1996), 535.

51. Ibid.

52. John Murray, *The Epistle to the Romans*, NICNT (Grand Rapids: Eerdmans, 1959), 1:315.

53. Ware, "Effectual Calling and Grace," 226.

results in justification.[54] It is this effectual call which is grounded in predestination and results in justification and glorification (cf. 1 Cor. 1:9; Heb. 9:12, 15; Eph. 4:4; 1 Thess. 2:12).

Moreover, Paul cannot have in mind here the gospel call because those who are "called" are promised that not only will all things work according for good, but also that they will be glorified (Rom. 8:30), demonstrating that calling produces perseverance. Paul in verse 28 shows that the called he has in mind are only those who love God. These are "called according to his purpose," predestined, and promised that all things work together for good. Now it is true that the gospel call is also a call that is "according to his purpose," but it is not true that the gospel call only goes to those who love God and those for whom all things work for good.[55] Therefore, Paul is referring to a call that *works*.

Additionally, we should note here the difficulty Arminians have with Romans 8:28–30. Take Richard Watson, for example, who insists that all references to calling in the New Testament, including Romans 8:28–30, must refer to a general gospel call to all people. But notice, Watson reads Paul as saying, "They are therefore CALLED, invited by it [the gospel] to this state and benefit: the calling being obeyed, they are JUSTIFIED; and being justified, and continuing in that state of grace, they are GLORIFIED. . . . The apostle supposes those whom he speaks of in the text as 'called,' to have been obedient . . ."[56] Watson has added to Paul's words the phrase "those whom he called, *and who obeyed the call*, he justified." However, Paul never says this! Watson is reading into the text his Arminian view, which conditions the efficacy of the call on man's will. As Hoekema concludes, "Watson can maintain his interpretation only by reading into the text words which are not there."[57]

Furthermore, notice the implications that Romans 8:28–30 has for the *ordo salutis*. All those who are called are then justified. Paul states in Romans 5:1 that justification is by faith. Two points must be made.

54. Hoekema, *Saved by Grace*, 84; Dave Hunt and James White, *Debating Calvinism: Five Points, Two Views* (Sisters, OR: Multnomah, 2004), 147–48.
55. See Hoekema, *Saved by Grace*, 84.
56. Watson, *Theological Institutes*, 2:359–60.
57. Hoekema, *Saved by Grace*, 84.

First, since not all have faith, once again we see that Paul does not have in mind all people but only the elect. As Schreiner states, "We can conclude from this that calling is restricted only to some and that it does not merely involve an invitation to believe."[58] Second, since calling comes before justification, and since justification is by faith, it follows that for Paul it is calling which produces faith. As Schreiner explains, "Calling must create faith since all those who are called are also justified. Thus, God does not call *all* people but only some, and those whom he calls are given the power to believe."[59] We are safe to conclude, therefore, that calling precedes faith in the *ordo salutis*. As Murray states, this is "divine monergism" and "God alone is active in those events which are here mentioned and no activity on the part of men supplies any ingredient of their definition or contributes to their efficacy."[60]

Finally, we must also observe that Paul's reference to an effectual call rules out the Arminian reading of "foreknowledge" in verse 29, which they argue is proof for the doctrine of conditional election. While it is outside the parameters of this study to explore in depth the meaning of foreknowledge, we should recognize that not only does the word's use in verse 29 refer to the believer being "relationally foreloved" rather than "God's cognitive foreknowledge of faith,"[61] but also Paul's affirmation of effectual calling in verse 30 dismisses the Arminian reading of foreknowledge as the two doctrines are mutually exclusive. Bruce Ware explains the dilemma,

> Many Arminians see foreknowledge in this text as God seeing in advance those who will believe in Christ when presented with the gospel ("foreseen faith," as it is sometimes called). That is, from the vantage point of eternity past, God looks down the corridors of history and sees those who, in time, put faith in Christ when it was in their power to reject Christ. They could have believed or disbelieved, but

---

58. Schreiner, *Paul*, 241.
59. Ibid.
60. Murray, *Romans*, 1:321.
61. E.g., Thomas R. Schreiner, "Does Romans 9 Teach Individual Election to Salvation?" in *Still Sovereign: Contemporary Perspectives on Election, Foreknowledge, and Grace*, ed. Thomas R. Schreiner and Bruce A. Ware (Grand Rapids: Baker, 2000), 89–106.

God saw in advance who would believe. But if this is true, it makes no sense later for Paul to say that those whom God foreknew he then called—if this calling is effectual. For if God's calling of them to salvation is effectual, they *must believe*; but if the foreknowledge of God is what Arminians claim, then those whom God foresees as believing *could instead have not believed*. In short, there is no way to reconcile the Arminian notion of foreknowledge in Romans 8:29 if the calling of Romans 8:30 is effectual. Since the calling of Romans 8:30 is indeed effectual ("those He called, He also justified" HCSB), foreknowledge cannot mean what these Arminians claim.[62]

Ware's point is significant, and we shall return to it later. For now, we can say simply that the Arminian doctrine of conditional election, which is based on their reading of "foreknow" in Romans 8:29, is not a biblical option, when taken with what Paul says about the effectual call in 8:30. Thus we see that Scripture further supports the Calvinist understanding of soteriology.

Moreover, Paul's unbreakable chain between election and calling as well as perseverance is also seen in passages such as Romans 9:11–12, 24–26; 1 Corinthians 1:9; 2 Timothy 1:9; 1 Thessalonians 5:23–24; and 2 Thessalonians 2:13–14. Schreiner explains,

God's election is not based on seeing what human beings would do or what in fact they actually perform (Rom. 9:11). God's saving promise "is not based on works but on the one who calls" (Rom. 9:12). We might expect Paul to say, "It is not of works but of faith," since the contrast between faith and works is common in his writings. He certainly is not denying such an idea here. And yet he reaches back to something that precedes human faith, to God's call, which creates such faith. Similarly, in 2 Timothy 1:9 God's call is opposed to works ("who saved us and called us to a holy calling, not according to our works but according to his own purpose and grace") and is linked with

---

62. Bruce A. Ware, "Divine Election to Salvation," in *Perspectives on Election: Five Views*, ed. Chad O. Brand (Nashville: B&H Publishing Group, 2006), 18n23. Also see Thomas Goodwin, *A Discourse of Election*, in *The Works of Thomas Goodwin* (Grand Rapids: Reformation Heritage, 2006), 9:279.

God's eternal purpose and grace, which were given to believers before time began. In 2 Thessalonians 2:14 God's call, which is exercised in history through the gospel, is closely conjoined with his choosing people for salvation (2 Thess. 2:13; cf. Rom. 9:24–26; 1 Cor. 1:9). Nor should we fail to see that the call guarantees the outcome. Those who are called through the gospel will possess eschatological glory (2 Thess. 2:13). The one who called believers will see to it that they obtain the sanctification needed to stand before the Lord (1 Thess. 5:23–24). Since God is faithful, he will confirm to the end those who are called as blameless (1 Cor. 1:8–9).[63]

In other words, Paul shows that the reason salvation is not by works is not just because it is of faith, but first and foremost it is because those whom God has chosen he effectually calls and unfailingly preserves to the end.

Paul's description of the effectual call in Romans 8:30 is also referenced elsewhere in Romans. At the beginning of the epistle, he addresses his readers as those "who are called to belong to Jesus Christ" (Rom. 1:6) and to those in Rome who are loved by God and "called to be saints" (Rom. 1:7). The call here is again the effectual call as it belongs only to those who are saints and those who belong to Jesus Christ. Paul again mentions the effectual call in Romans 9 when he labels those whom God has predestined "vessels of mercy" (as opposed to the reprobate who are "vessels of wrath prepared for destruction" in verse 22), "even us whom he has called," including both Jews and Gentiles (Rom. 9:23–24). These called ones are not all those who hear the gospel, but only those whom God "has prepared beforehand for glory" (Rom. 9:23).

Reference to the effectual call occurs again in Paul's first letter to the Corinthians. Paul begins his letter by identifying himself as one who has been "called by the will of God to be an apostle of Christ Jesus" (1 Cor. 1:1). He then identifies believers as those "called to be saints together with all those who in every place call upon the name of our Lord Jesus Christ" (1 Cor. 1:2). Paul gives thanks to God for the Corinthian

---

63. Schreiner, *Paul*, 241–42.

believers "because of the grace of God that was given you in Christ Jesus" (1 Cor. 1:4), a grace which enriched them in all speech and knowledge. This same God who gave them grace, Paul says in 1 Corinthians 1:8, also "will sustain you to the end, guiltless in the day of our Lord Jesus Christ." God's preservation of his elect, Paul says, shows that God is faithful. "God is faithful, by whom you were called into the fellowship of his Son, Jesus Christ our Lord" (1 Cor. 1:9). Paul cannot be referring in 1 Corinthians 1:9 to a general gospel call which can be rejected, but must instead be referring to an effectual call by which all those whom God calls experience fellowship with Christ, something that cannot be said of those who reject the general gospel call. The call Paul addresses here is one that brings the elect into union with Christ, a fellowship reserved only for those whom the Father has chosen. Paul's use of "call" to refer to the effectual call in 1 Corinthians 1:9 is similar to his use of "call" in Romans 1:7; 9:23–24; 1 Corinthians 1:26; Galatians 1:15; and Ephesians 4:1, 4.

Paul continues to speak of an effectual call in 1 Corinthians 1:18–31.

For the word of the cross is folly to those who are perishing, but to us who are being saved it is the power of God. For it is written,

"I will destroy the wisdom of the wise,
and the discernment of the discerning I will thwart."

Where is the one who is wise? Where is the scribe? Where is the debater of this age? Has not God made foolish the wisdom of the world? For since, in the wisdom of God, the world did not know God through wisdom, it pleased God through the folly of what we preach to save those who believe. For Jews demand signs and Greeks seek wisdom, but we preach Christ crucified, a stumbling block to Jews and folly to Gentiles, *but to those who are called*, both Jews and Greeks, Christ the power of God and the wisdom of God. For the foolishness of God is wiser than men, and the weakness of God is stronger than men. *For consider your calling*, brothers: not many of you were wise according to worldly standards, not many were powerful, not many were of noble birth. But God chose what is foolish in the world to shame the wise; God chose what is weak in the world to shame the strong; God chose what is low and despised in the world, even things that are not, to bring to nothing things that are, so that no human being might boast in the presence of God. And because of him you are in Christ Jesus, who became to us wisdom from God, righteousness and sanctification and redemption, so that, as it is written, "Let the one who boasts, boast in the Lord."

The gospel Paul preached (the word of the cross) is both the power and wisdom of God to those who are saved (1 Cor. 1:18, 21, 24; cf. Rom. 1:16) and at the same time is a gospel which is foolishness to those who disbelieve and perish (1 Cor. 1:18, 23, 25). Notice, there is no change in the gospel. The gospel remains the same. However, some hear this gospel and see it as folly, while others hear this gospel and see it as the power of life. Paul's words here are similar to 2 Corinthians 2:15–16 where the gospel is a fragrance of Christ. To those being saved it is an aroma of eternal life, but to those perishing it is an aroma of eternal death (2 Cor. 2:15–16). Ware helpfully observes, "The gospel, or aroma, is the same! The difference is in those smelling the fragrance and not in the fragrance itself."[64]

So, if it is not the gospel itself that accounts for the fact that some reject the gospel and see it as folly while others, who hear the same message of Christ crucified, accept the gospel as life, then what does account for this difference? The answer is found in 1 Corinthians 1:23–24: "But we preach Christ crucified, a stumbling block to Jews and folly to Gentiles, but to those who are called, both Jews and Greeks, Christ the power of God and the wisdom of God."[65] The specific group mentioned here ("the called ones") is in contrast to the larger group of Jews and Greeks whom Paul says received the message of Christ crucified and saw it as a stumbling block (Jews) and as folly (Gentiles).[66] On the other hand, to the "called ones" Christ is the power and wisdom of God. Such a

---

64. Ware, "Effectual Calling and Grace," 220n32.
65. Ibid., 222.
66. Hoekema, *Saved by Grace*, 83.

contrast precludes any idea that Paul is referring only to a general gospel call.[67] Ware explains, "It makes no sense to contrast Jews and Greeks generally with those Jews and Greeks who are called (as 1:23–24 does) if the difference between believing Jews and Greeks and disbelieving Jews and Greeks is in their respective choices only."[68] To the contrary, the contrast "is made between those called from disbelieving Jews and Greeks and, by implication, those not called, making up the general class of Jews and Greeks who regard the gospel as weakness and folly."[69] Therefore, any Arminian attempt to read into these verses prevenient grace is in vain. If Paul has in mind merely a general call, one is unable to then explain why some believe and others do not. But if we understand that Paul is comparing those who reject Christ with those whom God calls to Christ effectually, then the contrast makes perfect sense and the reason for belief as opposed to unbelief can be identified in the call of God, not in any wisdom of man.

Moreover, Paul must have in mind a calling that is irresistible because those identified as "the called" believe as a result of being called. In contrast to those who are not "the called," and therefore can only see the cross as folly, those who are identified as "the called" (both Jews and Greeks) consequently see Christ as the power and wisdom of God. Being called inevitably results in submitting to the lordship of Christ. Morris explains, "The important thing is the divine initiative, the call of God. Here, as usually in Paul's writings, *called* implies that the call has been heeded; it is an effectual call. Those *called* know that the crucified Christ means power. Before the call they were defeated by sin; now there is a new power at work in them, *the power of God*."[70]

Furthermore, verses 26–31 rule out an Arminian interpretation which would view the success of God's call as being based on the free will of the sinner. Paul explains that those called are not chosen because of anything in them, their own wisdom or power, for example. How could

---

67. Schreiner, *Paul*, 241.
68. Ware, "Effectual Calling and Grace," 222.
69. Ibid.
70. Leon Morris, *1 Corinthians*, TNTC (Downers Grove, IL: InterVarsity, 2008), 52.

this be when God purposefully chose those who were weak, lowly, and despised, so that "no human being might boast in the presence of God" (1 Cor. 1:29)? If it were the case, as the Arminian believes, that certain Jews and Gentiles were regenerated because they themselves believed, and if it were the case that certain Jews and Gentiles were elected and chosen because of what they themselves did to believe, then Paul could not exclude all boasting. Man would then have something to boast about "in the presence of God" (1 Cor. 1:29). Rather, it is "because of him you are in Christ Jesus" and therefore if anyone is to boast he is to "boast in the Lord" (1 Cor. 1:31). Ware summarizes such a point well when he says, "The basis for boasting in the Lord is not that he made our salvation possible but that he saved us by his calling (1:24, 26) and his choosing (1:27–28, 30). Therefore any and all human basis for boasting is eliminated (1:29), and all honor and glory is owing solely to him (1:31)!"[71]

Paul's other letters also exemplify the effectual call. In Galatians 1:15 Paul says that God not only set him apart before birth but also "called me by his grace" and "was pleased to reveal his Son to me, in order that I might preach him among the Gentiles" (Gal. 1:15–16; cf. 5:13; Jer. 1:5). Here Paul shows the Galatians that God elected him before he was born by his good pleasure and then at the proper time called him by his grace. The divine but gracious determinism in this passage is unavoidable. Ridderbos appropriately comments, "The *good pleasure* gives expression to the sovereign freedom as well as the infinite riches of the divine disposition . . . The emphasis falls on the sovereignty of the divine grace manifested to Paul. What the apostle is talking about here is the counsel of God which governs all things, most especially his work of redemption."[72] Likewise, Schreiner asserts, "The word 'calling' here clearly means a call that is effective, a call that convinces the one who is summoned."[73] The calling Paul has in mind refers to the Damascus road, where God called Paul to himself by revealing his Son to him by

---

71. Ware, "Effectual Calling and Grace," 224.
72. Herman N. Ridderbos, *The Epistle of Paul to the Churches of Galatia*, NICNT (Grand Rapids: Eerdmans, 1953), 63.
73. Thomas R. Schreiner, *Galatians*, ZECNT (Grand Rapids: Zondervan, 2010), 101.

"immediate intervention." "The film was, so to speak, removed from his eyes."[74]

Similarly, Paul exhorts the Ephesians,

> I therefore, a prisoner for the Lord, urge you to walk in a manner worthy of the calling to which you have been called, with all humility and gentleness, with patience, bearing with one another in love, eager to maintain the unity of the Spirit in the bond of peace. There is one body and one Spirit—just as you were called to the one hope that belongs to your call—one Lord, one faith, one baptism, one God and Father of all, who is over all and through all and in all (Eph. 4:1–6).

Call or calling, which "arises out of the gracious, saving purpose of God," is used four times in this passage, reminding the Ephesians that because they have been called by God, their life should be one of faith, hope, unity, and peace.[75] Thielman detects that here "God has called Paul's readers to be part of his people not because of anything they have done but as a free gift."[76]

Likewise, Paul writes to the Colossians, "And let the peace of Christ rule in your hearts, to which indeed you were called in one body. And be thankful" (Col. 3:15). Again, believers have been effectually called into one body characterized by the peace of Christ. Moo highlights the sovereignty of God in such a calling: "*You were called* picks up the language of election that Paul used in v. 12—'God's chosen people.' Paul frequently uses the verb 'call' (*kaleō*) to denote God's gracious and powerful summons to human beings, by which they are transferred from the realm of sin and death into the realm of righteousness and life."[77]

---

74. Ibid.

75. Peter T. O'Brien, *The Letter to the Ephesians*, PNTC (Grand Rapids: Eerdmans, 1999), 274. Also see Harold W. Hoehner, *Ephesians: An Exegetical Commentary* (Grand Rapids: Baker, 2002), 504–5; Frank Thielman, *Ephesians*, BECNT (Grand Rapids: Baker, 2010), 252; Clinton E. Arnold, *Ephesians*, ZECNT (Grand Rapids: Zondervan, 2010), 233.

76. Thielman, *Ephesians*, 252.

77. See Rom. 8:30; 9:24; 1 Cor. 1:9; 7:15–24; Gal. 1:6; 5:8, 13; Eph. 4:1, 4; 1 Thess. 2:12; 4:7; 5:24; 2 Thess. 2:14; 1 Tim. 6:12; 2 Tim. 1:9. Douglas J. Moo, *The Letters to the Colossians and to Philemon*, PNTC (Grand Rapids: Eerdmans, 2008), 284.

Moo is correct, for Paul says elsewhere, "God has called us in peace" (1 Cor. 7:15), "you were called to freedom" (Gal. 5:13), "you were called in one hope" (Eph. 4:4), "God did not call us to uncleanness but for holiness" (1 Thess. 4:7; cf. 2:12), and "God has saved us and called us to a holy life" (2 Tim. 1:9).[78]

Additionally, to Timothy Paul writes, "Fight the good fight of the faith. Take hold of the eternal life to which you were called and about which you made the good confession in the presence of many witnesses" (1 Tim. 6:12). Calling here is a summons to salvation (in the passive voice; cf. Gal. 5:13; Eph. 4:1, 4).[79] In his second letter to Timothy, Paul charges Timothy not to be ashamed of the gospel or of the Lord Jesus Christ "who saved us and called us to a holy calling, not because of our works but because of his own purpose and grace, which he gave us in Christ Jesus before the ages began" (2 Tim. 1:9). Again, calling here is not deemed successful due to anything in us ("not because of our works), but purely because of God's "own purpose and grace," which Paul says is rooted in the eternal act ("before the ages began") of election ("he gave us in Christ Jesus").[80] Mounce states, "It [calling] expresses the belief in God's prior election based solely on his desire and grace, totally apart from human works, a call that drives believers toward a holy life."[81] Like election, calling is not based on anything in us (not even faith), but purely on God's good purpose and grace. Paul in 2 Timothy 1:9 sounds much like he does in Romans 8:28, where calling is said to be "according to his purpose," and Romans 9:11–12, where God's choice of Jacob over Esau is prior to them doing anything good or bad so that election would not be on the basis of works but "because of him who calls." Here we see in Paul both an unconditional election and an unconditional call, both of which are inseparable and accomplished apart from man's will to believe.

78. Charles A. Wanamaker, *The Epistles to the Thessalonians*, NIGTC (Grand Rapids: Eerdmans, 1990), 107.

79. Philip H. Towner, *The Letters to Timothy and Titus*, NICNT (Grand Rapids: Baker, 2006), 411.

80. Ibid., 469.

81. William D. Mounce, *Pastoral Epistles*, WBC, vol. 46 (Nashville: Thomas Nelson, 2000), 482.

Not only Paul, but Peter also writes of an effectual call for the elect. According to Peter, Christians are those whom God has caused to be born again to a living hope (1 Peter 1:3). Therefore, Christians are not to be "conformed to the passions of your former ignorance, but as he who called you is holy, you also be holy in all your conduct" (1 Peter 1:14–15). Schreiner rightly identifies this calling as effectual: " 'Calling' refers to God's effectual call in which he infallibly brings people to himself (1 Peter 2:9, 21; 3:9; 5:10). . . . Calling does not merely 'invite' but conveys the idea of God's power in bringing people from darkness to light. Just as God's call creates light when there was darkness, so he creates life when there was death."[82] Schreiner explains the importance of this call:

> The reference to "calling" is important, for again grace precedes demand. Otherwise the Petrine paraenesis could be confused with the idea that human beings attain their own righteousness or that they live morally noble lives in their own strength. All holiness stems from the God who called them into the sphere of the holy.[83]

Peter mentions the effectual call in 1 Peter 2:9–10 as well: "But you are a chosen race, a royal priesthood, a holy nation, a people for his own possession, that you may proclaim the excellencies of him who called you out of darkness into his marvelous light. Once you were not a people, but now you are God's people; once you had not received mercy, but now you have received mercy." Christ is credited with calling his elect ("chosen race," cf. Isa. 43:3, 20–21; "a people for his own possession," cf. Exod. 19:5; Hos. 2:23–25) out of darkness (depravity and bondage to sin) and into the marvelous light of salvation. This "chosen and precious" people of God (1 Peter 2:4) were once dead in their trespasses and sins but Christ, through his calling, rescued them from the domain of darkness to experience new life. There is no possibility of a general gospel call here since the called are referred to as God's "chosen people." The

---

82. Thomas R. Schreiner, *1, 2 Peter, Jude*, NAC, vol. 37 (Nashville: B&H Publishing Group, 2003), 80.
83. Ibid.

monergistic nature of this calling is apparent in how Peter's language parallels Genesis 1:3–5, in which God simply speaks and light appears in the midst of darkness. Paul does the same in 2 Corinthians 4:6, in which he says that God shines directly into the heart of his elect, giving them a saving knowledge of Christ. Schreiner rightly concludes that in 1 Peter 2:9 "the calling described here is effectual." Just as "God's word creates light, so God's call creates faith. Calling is not a mere invitation but is performative, so that the words God speaks become a reality."[84]

The effectual call is again emphasized by Peter in 1 Peter 2:21: "For to this you have been called, because Christ also suffered for you, leaving you an example, so that you might follow in his steps." Peter is affirming an effectual call that results in faith. Those called follow in the steps of Christ. In other words, just as calling is given and appointed by God so also is suffering.[85] Those called to Christ will suffer as Christ suffered and in this way they will receive eternal life. Indeed, Peter takes the example of Christ's suffering so seriously that he can say that believers have been called not to repay evil for evil but instead have been called to bless those who have insulted and injured them, that they may obtain a blessing (1 Peter 3:9).

The effectual call is so important to Peter that he closes his first letter saying, "And after you have suffered a little while, the God of all grace, who has called you to his eternal glory in Christ, will himself restore, confirm, strengthen, and establish you" (1 Peter 5:10). Earlier we saw how election and effectual calling were inseparable and now we see how effectual calling and perseverance are indivisible. As Schreiner writes, "Here it should simply be said (see esp. 2:9) that 'calling' refers to God's effective work by which he inducts believers into a saving relationship with himself. That the calling is to salvation is clear since believers are called to God's 'eternal glory.' "[86] The fact that Peter is referring to a calling that is salvific is not only manifested by its reference to "eternal glory" but also by the phrase "in Christ." Schreiner again comments,

84. Ibid., 116.
85. Ibid., 141.
86. Ibid., 244.

The words "in Christ" [should] be understood as modifying the entire clause, "eternal glory" or "called." . . . Peter thereby emphasized that God's saving calling is effectual in and through Christ. The theme of calling to glory reminds the readers that endtime salvation is sure, for God himself is the one who initiated and secured their salvation. As the rest of the verse will demonstrate, God will certainly complete what he has inaugurated. Their calling to glory is not questionable but sure.[87]

For Peter, effectual calling is a doctrine that not only stems from our unconditional election, but also unites us to Christ and guarantees our perseverance unto glory.

Peter again uses language to refer to the effectual call in his second letter. He opens by saying, "His divine power has granted to us all things that pertain to life and godliness, through the knowledge of him who called us to his own glory and excellence, by which he has granted to us his precious and very great promises, so that through them you may become partakers of the divine nature, having escaped from the corruption that is in the world because of sinful desire" (2 Peter 1:3–5). Is this calling a mere gospel call and invitation for all people? Schreiner responds to contemporary misconceptions,

English readers are apt to understand calling in terms of an invitation that can be accepted or rejected. Peter had something deeper in mind. God's call is effective, awakening and creating faith. Paul referred to calling in this way regularly (e.g., Rom. 4:17; 8:30; 9:12, 24–26; 1 Cor. 1:9; 7:15; Gal. 1:6, 15; 5:8, 13; 1 Thess. 2:12; 4:7; 5:24; 2 Thess. 2:14; 1 Tim. 6:12; 2 Tim. 1:9). More significantly, the word "called" also has this meaning in 1 Peter (1:15; 2:9, 21; 3:9; 5:10). First Peter 2:9 indicates that conversion is in view, for God called believers out of darkness into his marvelous light. The terminology reminds us that God is the one who called light out of darkness (Gen. 1:3).[88]

87. Ibid., 244–45.
88. Ibid., 292.

Schreiner is indubitably right. Calling, for Peter, refers to a particular and effectual call.

In 2 Peter 1:10 Peter also says, "Therefore, brothers, be all the more diligent to make your calling and election sure, for if you practice these qualities you will never fall." Notice, calling is identified alongside of election, so much so that we could translate them as one: "elective call."[89] Election and calling here are inseparably linked together, precluding the possibility of a general gospel call. The combination of election and calling by Peter "highlights God's grace," namely, that "he is the one who saves."[90] Moreover, grammatically, as Hoekema observes, "There is only one definite article (*tēn*) before the two nouns, *klēsin* (calling) and *eklogēn* (election). This means that these two are treated as one unit and are to be thought of as such: not your calling as somehow separate from our election, but your calling and election together."[91] Hoekema is building off of A. T. Robertson, who says, "Sometimes groups more or less distinct are treated as one for the purpose in hand, and hence use only one article. Cf . . . 2 Peter 1:10." Hoekema and Robertson are grammatically right which leads to only one conclusion: the unity of calling and election in 2 Peter 1:10 demands that an effectual call is in view.

> Obviously, therefore, "calling" (*klēsin*) here cannot refer to the gospel call alone, for two reasons: (1) It is linked with "election" (*eklogēn*) by a single definite article, and "election" can only refer to God's choosing of his own from eternity. A calling which is of one piece with election can only be effectual calling. (2) There is no particular point in telling someone to make sure or to confirm his or her gospel call; once having heard the gospel or once having read the gospel message, she has been called in that sense. "Making your calling sure" must therefore mean: make sure that you have been effectually called—that is, that you have been elected to eternal life in Christ.

89. Ibid., 304.
90. Ibid.
91. Hoekema, *Saved by Grace*, 85. See A. T. Robertson, *Grammar of the Greek New Testament in the Light of Historical Research* (Nashville: Broadman, 1934), 787; F. Blass and A. Debrunner, *A Greek Grammar of the New Testament*, trans. R. W. Funk (Chicago: University of Chicago Press, 1961), sec. 276.

You can make sure of this, Peter explains, by "making every effort to add to your faith goodness; and to goodness, knowledge; and to knowledge, self-control," and so on (vv. 5–7). By observing the fruits of effectual calling in your lives, Peter is saying, you can make sure that you have been effectually called.[92]

Since Peter links calling with election it follows that an effectual call is present.

Effectual Calling in Jude and Revelation

Paul and Peter are not the only biblical writers to emphasize the effectual call. Jude in the opening verse of his letter says, "Jude, a servant of Jesus Christ and brother of James, To those who are called, beloved in God the Father and kept for Jesus Christ: May mercy, peace, and love be multiplied to you" (Jude 1:1–2). Calling here cannot be the general gospel call to all because Jude identifies the called as those who are beloved in God the Father and kept for Jesus Christ, characteristics not true of all those who receive the gospel call. Not everyone who receives the gospel call is kept by Christ and loved by the Father in a saving way.

John also speaks of the effectual call when he writes in Revelation 17:14, "They will make war on the Lamb, and the Lamb will conquer them, for he is Lord of lords and King of kings, and those with him are called and chosen and faithful." Like Jude, John here identifies those called as those who are with the Lamb, who is Christ. Those "called and chosen and faithful" represent the "vindication of the persecuted saints" (cf. Dan. 7:21; Rev. 6:9–11; 12:11; 13:10–17).[93] Also, similar to 2 Peter 1:10, here once again we see calling and election spoken of together. Those with the Lamb "are called and chosen." Not everyone who hears the general gospel call is both called and chosen, found to be faithful to the Lamb.[94]

92. Hoekema, *Saved by Grace*, 85–86.
93. G. K. Beale, *The Book of Revelation*, NIGTC (Grand Rapids: Eerdmans, 1999), 880.
94. Another passage to consider is Heb. 9:15.

Effectual Calling Taught by Jesus

Perhaps one of the most important passages on effectual calling is John 6:35–64.[95] In the context of the passage (John 6:22–34), Jesus is interacting with the Jews who did not believe in him. After Jesus instructs them not to labor for food that perishes but for food that endures to eternal life, food which only the Son of Man can give (John 6:27), the Jews respond, "What must we do, to be doing the works of God?" (John 6:28). Jesus responds, "This is the work of God, that you believe in him whom he [the Father] has sent" (John 6:29). However, rather than believing, they demand a sign if they are to believe that Jesus is from God. "So they said to him, 'Then what sign do you do, that we may see and believe you? What work do you perform? Our fathers ate the manna in the wilderness; as it is written, "He gave them bread from heaven to eat"'" (John 6:30–31). Jesus responds, "Truly, truly, I say to you, it was not Moses who gave you the bread from heaven, but my Father gives you the true bread from heaven. For the bread of God is he who comes down from heaven and gives life to the world" (John 6:32–33). When the Jews ask for this bread, Jesus replies, "I am the bread of life; whoever comes to me shall not hunger, and whoever believes in me shall never thirst" (John 6:35; cf. Isa. 49:10; 55:1; Rev. 7:16). Ware explains the words of Jesus here, "In other words, God has indeed performed the sign that the multitudes were seeking. Jesus, the bread out of heaven, is here in their midst! All that is required of them is that they believe in him, and yet they remain in their unbelief."[96]

However, Jesus is not unaware of their unbelief, noting, "But I said to you that you have seen me and yet do not believe" (John 6:36). He continues,

> All that the Father gives me will come to me, and whoever comes to me I will never cast out. For I have come down from heaven, not to do my own will but the will of him who sent me. And this

95. James White, *Drawn by the Father: A Study of John 6:35–45* (Southbridge, MA: Crowne, 1991).
96. Ware, "Effectual Calling and Grace," 212.

is the will of him who sent me, that I should lose nothing of all that he has given me, but raise it up on the last day. For this is the will of my Father, that everyone who looks on the Son and believes in him should have eternal life, and I will raise him up on the last day. (John 6:37–40)

How can it be the case that some see the signs of Jesus and believe, while others, seeing the very same signs, disbelieve? Both have the same knowledge before them and yet some trust in Christ while others hate him. What is the cause of this difference? What is to account for belief and unbelief? Notice that Jesus does not explain why some believe and others do not by saying that some choose him while others do not. While he holds out the promise of life to all (John 6:35–37, 40, 47, 51), he never says that all are able to believe, as the Arminian assumes. He tells his hearers what will happen if they do believe: they will never go hungry or be thirsty (John 6:35), they will receive eternal life (John 6:40, 47), and they will live forever (John 6:51).

However, though Jesus explains the rewards to be received for believers, he never says that the reason why some accept and others reject is free will. Arminians will argue at this point that the promises themselves must imply that those who hear can turn and believe, otherwise why would Jesus hold out such promises to them (see chapter 5)? Why would Jesus hold out eternal life unless those who hear were able to take it by faith? Ware expresses how the Arminian argument goes: "The 'ought' of believing in Christ to be saved implies the 'can' of common human ability to believe. Therefore, the answer as to why some believe and others disbelieve is that some choose to believe while others choose to disbelieve. . . . Ought implies can."[97] Yet, as Ware goes on to explain, "Our text devastates the logic of this position. . . . What is deniable is that this ought of belief implies the can of common human ability to believe. Our text never explicitly makes this logical inference upon which so much of Arminian soteriology rests, nor is it implied by anything said by Jesus here. What our text does tell us precludes the possibility of this

97. Ibid., 213.

ought-implies-can view."[98] Jesus makes no reference to the logic of ought implies can in John 6. There is much "ought" in John 6, but there is no "can" to be found. To the contrary, Jesus only affirms a "cannot." As Ridderbos states, Jesus "demonstrates the powerlessness of the natural person ('no one') to come to the salvation disclosed in Christ unless the Father who sent him 'draws' that person."[99]

Notice what Jesus says in verse 37: "All that the Father gives me will come to me, and whoever comes to me I will never cast out." Köstenberger recognizes, contra Ben Witherington, that divine predestination is in view.[100] Likewise, Carson makes two observations worthy of consideration. First, the verb "cast out" (ἐκβάλω; cf. John 2:15; 9:34; 10:4; 12:31) "implies the 'casting out' of something or someone already 'in.' The strong litotes in 6:37f., therefore, does not mean 'I will certainly receive the one who comes,' but 'I will certainly preserve, keep in, the one who comes'; while the identity of the 'one who comes' is established by the preceding clause."[101] Carson is right, Jesus' promise that he will never "cast out" implies that there is a set number already chosen, already "in" and it is clear that these are only those whom the Father has given to Jesus. Second, Carson observes that the causal *hoti* and telic *hina* in John 6:38 "give the reason for this keeping action by Jesus, in terms of the will of the Father, viz. that Jesus should not lose one of those given to him (6:38f.)." In other words, "6:37 argues not only that the ones given to Jesus will inevitably come to him, but that Jesus will keep them individually (*ton erchomenon* as opposed to *pan ho*) once there."[102] To summarize, Jesus is teaching (1) that if one has been given to him by the Father, then coming to him is inevitable (effectual), and (2) those given to Jesus he will unfailingly keep. Carson states, "Jesus is repudiating any idea that the

98. Ibid. Also see Loraine Boettner, *The Reformed Doctrine of Predestination* (Philadelphia: Presbyterian and Reformed, 1963), 178.

99. Herman Ridderbos, *The Gospel according to John*, trans. John Vriend (Grand Rapids: Eerdmans, 1997), 232.

100. Andreas J. Köstenberger, *John*, BECNT (Grand Rapids: Baker, 2004), 211. Contra Ben Witherington III, *John's Wisdom* (Louisville: Westminster John Knox, 1995), 158.

101. D. A. Carson, *Divine Sovereignty*, 184.

102. Ibid.

Father has sent the Son forth on a mission which could fail because of the unbelief of the people."[103]

The implication for those Jews who disbelieve is startling: the Father has not given you to Christ, which is what is needed for you to come to Christ.[104] Or as Carson states, "You have not been given to the Son by the Father for life and therefore you will not have life but will continue in your unbelief."[105] Jesus makes this same point in John 10:26: "But you do not believe because you are not part of my flock." Notice, Jesus does not say, "You are not part of my flock because you do not believe," as the Arminian argues (see chapter 5). The Arminian must condition being part of the flock upon man's free will to believe. But Jesus says the exact opposite, thereby dismantling the Arminian's logic. Unbelievers do not believe because they are not of Jesus' flock. And why exactly are they not of his flock? As Jesus states in John 6:37, they are not of his flock because they have not been given to Jesus by the Father. Jesus makes this same point in John 8:47: "Whoever is of God hears the words of God. The reason why you do not hear them is that you are not of God." Again, the Arminian must have it the other way around: the reason why you are not of God is that you do not hear the words of God. But Jesus says the exact opposite: you do not hear because you are not of God. Free will is nowhere the cause of becoming part of God's flock. Rather, it is God's sovereign choice to give certain sheep to his Son that results in belief.[106] As Ware so clearly states the matter,

> Implicit is the idea that only those given by the Father can come (an idea made explicit by Jesus), while explicit is the idea that all those given by the Father do come. The multitudes' disbelief is evidence that they are not among those given to Christ by the Father. . . . The point is not that they are not his sheep because of their disbelief, but their disbelief is owing to the fact they are not his sheep. Coming to

103. Ibid.
104. Ridderbos, *John*, 233.
105. Carson, *Divine Sovereignty*, 184.
106. James Montgomery Boice and Philip Graham Ryken, *The Doctrines of Grace: Rediscovering the Evangelical Gospel* (Wheaton, IL: Crossway, 2002), 159; Carson, *Divine Sovereignty*, 166.

Christ is causally linked by Jesus to having been given by the Father; all those who come do so precisely because the Father has given them to the Son.[107]

Likewise, Leon Morris states,

Before men can come to Christ it is necessary that the Father give them to Him. This is the explanation of the disconcerting fact that those who followed Jesus to hear Him, and who at the beginning wanted to make Him a king, were nevertheless not His followers in the true sense. They did not belong to the people of God. They were not among those whom God gives Him.[108]

So also John Calvin, "That their unbelief may not detract anything from his doctrine, he says, that the cause of so great obstinacy is, that they are reprobate, and do not belong to the flock of God."[109]

We must also note, lest the Arminian object at this point that coming to Christ is not the same as believing in Christ, that Jesus in John 6:35–37 equates the two. As Carson states, "Coming to Jesus is equivalent to believing in Jesus (6:35)."[110] All those who come to him will not hunger and all those who believe in him will not thirst. The parallel is obvious: hungering is to thirsting as coming is to believing. But continuing on in the passage we see Jesus reiterate his point again as the Jews are enraged by his words.

So the Jews grumbled about him, because he said, "I am the bread that came down from heaven." They said, "Is not this Jesus, the son of Joseph, whose father and mother we know? How does he now say, 'I have come down from heaven'?" Jesus answered them, "Do not

107. Ware, "Effectual Calling and Grace," 214. Also see D. A. Carson, *The Gospel according to John* (Grand Rapids: Eerdmans, 1991), 290; Hunt and White, *Debating Calvinism*, 118–25; Thomas R. Schreiner and Ardel B. Caneday, *The Race Set Before Us: A Biblical Theology of Perseverance and Assurance* (Downers Grove, IL: InterVarsity, 2001), 128–29.

108. Leon Morris, *The Gospel according to John*, NICNT (Grand Rapids: Eerdmans, 1971), 367.

109. John Calvin, *Commentary on the Gospel according to John*, trans. William Pringle (Grand Rapids: Eerdmans, 1948), 1:251.

110. Carson, *Divine Sovereignty*, 184.

grumble among yourselves. *No one can come to me unless the Father who sent me draws him.* And I will raise him up on the last day. It is written in the Prophets, 'And they will all be taught by God.' Everyone who has heard and learned from the Father comes to me—not that anyone has seen the Father except he who is from God; he has seen the Father. Truly, truly, I say to you, whoever believes has eternal life. I am the bread of life. Your fathers ate the manna in the wilderness, and they died. This is the bread that comes down from heaven, so that one may eat of it and not die. I am the living bread that came down from heaven. If anyone eats of this bread, he will live forever. And the bread that I will give for the life of the world is my flesh." (John 6:41–51)

Here again we see Jesus explain that it is impossible for anyone to come to him unless the Father has already given them over to him (John 6:44; cf. 6:65). Stated otherwise, it is absolutely necessary for the Father to give a sinner to Christ if that sinner is to believe. If the sinner is not given to Christ by the Father then he or she will not believe. Or as Boice and Ryken state, "If they fail to believe, it is because God has withheld that special, efficacious grace that he was under no obligation to bestow."[111] The only reason some come to Christ is because they were already given to the Son by the Father. Such a teaching by Jesus in no way precludes the fact that all "ought" to come to Christ and believe (cf. John 6:51). Yet, "ought" does not imply "can" for Jesus is clear that no one "can" come to him unless they are drawn to him by the Father. As Morris states, "Men like to feel independent. They think that they come or that they *can* come to Jesus entirely of their own volition. Jesus assures us that this is an utter impossibility. No man, no man at all can come unless the Father draw him."[112]

This brings us to the precise nature of such a drawing of the Father to Christ in John 6:37, 44, and 65. These three passages read:

111. Boice and Ryken, *The Doctrines of Grace*, 159. Also see Carson, *Divine Sovereignty*, 166.
112. Morris, *John*, 372.

All that the Father gives me will come to me, and whoever comes to me I will never cast out. (John 6:37)

No one can come to me unless the Father who sent me draws him. And I will raise him up on the last day. (John 6:44)

And he said, "This is why I told you that no one can come to me unless it is granted him by the Father." (John 6:65)

Is such a drawing effectual and irresistible? Or, as the Arminian believes, can this drawing be resisted successfully? For the Arminian (see chapter 5), while God initiates the drawing, unless the drawing is resistible, man's free will is compromised. As Ware explains, "Whether they believe or not is their doing, not God's. God must draw, to be sure; his drawing, however, only makes possible but not actual (or effectual) a believing response. This is the essence of the Arminian doctrine of prevenient grace."[113] And again,

In the Arminian view, what separates belief and unbelief is not the drawing of the Father; the Father draws all. Belief and unbelief, rather, is owing to what particular individuals (all of whom are drawn by the Father and so enabled to believe) freely choose to do. They may come, or they may refuse to come. God has drawn all, so it is up to them.[114]

The major problem with the Arminian interpretation of John 6, however, is that Jesus is not talking about a universal drawing of all men to himself. Prevenient grace is nowhere to be found here. Moreover, not only is a universal grace absent, but so also is a grace that is resistible and defeatable. To the contrary, Jesus teaches that the grace he is speaking of here is one that is both particular to the elect and effectual. Several observations bear this out.

In John 6, especially 6:44, the drawing of the Father necessarily results in a coming to Christ. In other words, contrary to Arminianism,

113. Ware, "Effectual Calling and Grace," 215.
114. Ibid., 218.

this is not a drawing that merely *makes possible* a coming to Christ, but rather is a drawing that *inevitably and irresistibly leads* to Christ. Or as Hendriksen says, "The Father does not merely beckon or advise, he *draws*!"[115] All those drawn do in fact believe.[116] As Jesus explains in John 6:44, "No one can come to me unless the Father who sent me draws him [ἑλκύσῃ αὐτόν]. And I will raise him up on the last day." Arminians view 6:44 as saying that while it is true that no one can come to Christ unless the Father draws him, such a drawing can be resisted (see chapter 5). However, such an interpretation fails in two ways: (1) it ignores the fact that "no one can come to me" (i.e., inability), and (2) it fails to finish the verse—"I will raise him up on the last day."

Each of these points deserves consideration. First, in John 6 the grammatical language is in support of an irresistible, effectual drawing. The word "draw" in Greek is *elkō*, which, as Albrecht Oepke explains, means "to compel by irresistible superiority."[117] Though the Arminian rejects such a notion, the word linguistically and lexicographically means "to compel."[118] Therefore, Jesus cannot be saying that the drawing of the Father is a mere wooing or persuasion that can be resisted. Rather, this drawing is an indefectible, invincible, unconquerable, indomitable, insuperable, and unassailable summons.[119] As John Frame explains, the word "summons" captures the efficacy of this call well. "That word summons brings out God's sovereignty. You might be able to refuse an invitation, but you can't refuse a summons. A summons is an offer you cannot refuse."[120] In short, this summons does not fail to accomplish what God intended. *Elkō* is also used in James 2:6, which says, "But you have dishonored

115. William Hendriksen, *Exposition of the Gospel according to John*, NTC (Grand Rapids: Baker Academic, 2002), 1:238.

116. Ware, "Effectual Calling and Grace," 216.

117. Albrecht Oepke, "*Elkō*," in *Theological Dictionary of the New Testament*, ed. Gerhard Kittel, ed. and trans. Geoffrey W. Bromiley (Grand Rapids: Eerdmans, 1964), 2:503. J. Ramsey Michaels agrees in his *The Gospel of John*, NICNT (Grand Rapids: Eerdmans, 2010), 386.

118. R. C. Sproul makes this point in *What Is Reformed Theology?* (Grand Rapids: Baker, 1997), 153–54.

119. See à Brakel, *The Christian's Reasonable Service*, 2:225, 230–32.

120. Frame, *Salvation Belongs to the Lord*, 184.

the poor man. Are not the rich the ones who oppress you, and the ones who drag [elkō] you into court?" And again in Acts 16:19, "But when her owners saw that their hope of gain was gone, they seized Paul and Silas and dragged [elkō] them into the marketplace before the rulers." As R. C. Sproul observes, to substitute "woo" in the place of drag in these passages would sound ludicrous. "Once forcibly seized, they could not be enticed or wooed. The text clearly indicates they were *compelled* to come before the authorities."[121] Sproul is right; this is not a mere external effort by God to persuade, but is an internal compelling that cannot be thwarted.

Second, the Father's drawing will indeed result in final salvation, the resurrection on the last day, as is evident in John 6:44. Jesus comes down from heaven to do the will of the Father and what is this will but to lose none of all those whom the Father has given to him but to raise them up on the last day (John 6:39–40)? Surely, Jesus cannot be referring to a universal call that is resistible, for this would mean that Jesus is promising to raise all up on the last day, a promise he has failed to accomplish since so many die in a state of disbelief. Moreover, as Carson observes, "The combination of v. 37a and v. 44 prove that this 'drawing' activity of the Father cannot be reduced to what theologians sometimes call 'prevenient grace' dispensed to every individual, for this 'drawing' is selective, or else the negative note in v. 44 is meaningless."[122] In other words, Jesus is referring only to those whom the Father has given him and these only will Jesus give eternal life and the resurrection to glory. Here we see once again that the Father's giving of the elect to the Son invincibly leads to final salvation. Therefore, the drawing Jesus speaks of must be effectual.

Nevertheless, Arminian Grant R. Osborne objects.[123] He argues that if the drawing in John 6:44 is effectual and irresistible then universalism

---

121. Sproul, *What Is Reformed Theology?*, 154.
122. Carson, *John*, 293.
123. Grant R. Osborne, "Soteriology in the Gospel of John," in *The Grace of God and the Will of Man: A Case for Arminianism*, ed. Clark H. Pinnock (Minneapolis: Bethany House, 1989), 248–49; idem, "Exegetical Notes on Calvinist Texts," in *Grace Unlimited*, ed. Clark H. Pinnock (Eugene, OR: Wipf and Stock, 1999), 171, 184–85.

is true, for Jesus says in John 12:32 that when he is lifted up he will draw all men to himself. However, as will be further demonstrated in chapter 6, the drawing in John 12:32 does not refer to all people without *exception*, but to all people without *distinction*. The context makes this clear as Jews and Greeks both come to Jesus. As Carson and Schreiner argue, Jesus has in mind all *types* and *kinds* of people (cf. Joel 2:28ff.), not all people without exception.[124]

To summarize our findings, we can conclude the following:

(1) The Father's drawing precedes any belief on the sinner's part.

(2) The reason a sinner believes is because he has been drawn by the Father to Christ, not vice versa.

(3) The reason a sinner does *not* believe is because he has not been drawn by the Father to Christ, not vice versa.

(4) The Father's drawing is effectual because (a) *elkō* means "to compel by irresistible superiority"[125] and (b) Jesus assures us that those drawn will be raised up on the last day, something not true of all people who receive the gospel call. Therefore, the drawing does not make belief a possibility but an inevitable reality.

(5) The efficacy of the drawing precludes that it is universal. Rather the drawing is particular, limited to the elect.[126]

It is crucial to observe how the narrative ends, namely, with everyone leaving Jesus because such a teaching is so offensive and difficult to understand (John 6:60–65; note the exception of Peter in John 6:66–69). How Jesus responds is telling. "It is the Spirit who gives life; the flesh is no help at all. The words that I have spoken to you are spirit and life. But there are some of you who do not believe. . . . This is why I told you that no one can come to me unless it is granted him by the Father" (John 6:63–65). Two observations are relevant.

---

124. Carson, *John*, 293, 444; idem, *Divine Sovereignty*, 185–86; Thomas R. Schreiner, "Does Scripture Teach Prevenient Grace in the Wesleyan Sense?," in *Still Sovereign: Contemporary Perspectives on Election, Foreknowledge, and Grace*, ed. Thomas R. Schreiner and Bruce A. Ware (Grand Rapids: Baker Academic, 2000), 241–42. Also see Ware, "Effectual Calling and Grace," 216n24; Michaels, *John*, 698–70.

125. Oepke, "*Elkō*," 503.

126. John Calvin, *Institutes of the Christian Religion*, ed. John T. McNeil, trans. Ford Lewis Battles, LCC, vols. 20–21 (Philadelphia: Westminster John Knox, 1960), 3.24.1.

First, Jesus once again emphasizes the inability of the sinner when he says it is "the Spirit who gives life; the flesh is no help at all." Ridderbos writes,

> Only the Spirit, as the author of God's renewing and redeeming work, makes alive, creates and imparts life. But the Spirit does so in the way and manner of the Spirit (cf. 3:8). The flesh cannot touch it! The words Jesus has spoken "are Spirit and life"; they are from God, hence life-giving for whoever believes. But the flesh—in its reflections and powerlessness—is of no avail here; it cannot hear that word, it takes offense at it, and it lapses into unbelief (vss. 64, 65).[127]

Such inability is affirmed again in John 14:17 when Jesus says, "the world *cannot accept him* [the Holy Spirit], because it neither sees him nor knows him."

Second, if, as the Arminian believes, all are drawn, why does Jesus stress his point concerning their persistence in unbelief? Jesus shows in John 6:65 that once again their unbelief serves as evidence that they have not been drawn by the Father. But none of this makes sense if Jesus is talking about a universal call that only makes salvation possible. As Ware comments, "Clearly there would be no point to it, and it certainly would not prompt those listening to Jesus to depart permanently from him."[128] A calling common to all people is *not* offensive and surely would not lead his hearers to be angered and eventually abandon Jesus. To the contrary, the reason his teaching is so offensive is because he explains their unbelief by appealing to the Father's sovereign choice, not man's free will.[129] Those not drawn by the Father and selected remain in their unbelief.

Before concluding our discussion, it is necessary to look briefly at three other passages, namely, John 12:37–40; 17:24; and 10:14ff.

In John 12:37–40 we see perhaps the most outstanding instance in all of John's gospel where emphasis is placed on divine sovereignty.

127. Ridderbos, *John*, 246.
128. Ware, "Effectual Calling and Grace," 219.
129. Carson, *Divine Sovereignty*, 186.

Though Jesus had accomplished many miraculous signs, still the people did not believe in him (12:37; cf. Deut. 29:2–4). Why exactly did they not believe? John answers,

> Though he had done so many signs before them, they still did not believe in him, so that the word spoken by the prophet Isaiah might be fulfilled:

> > "Lord, who has believed what he heard from us,
> >   and to whom has the arm of the Lord been revealed?"

> Therefore they could not believe. For again Isaiah said,

> > "He has blinded their eyes
> >   and hardened their heart,
> > lest they see with their eyes,
> >   and understand with their heart, and turn,
> >   and I would heal them."

Why is it that those following Jesus, though seeing his signs, did not believe? John, quoting Isaiah 58:1 and then 6:10, says it is because God himself "has blinded their eyes and hardened their heart" so that they will not believe. Köstenberger comments, "This kind of reasoning places human unbelief ultimately within the sphere of God's sovereignty, and more specifically his (positive or negative) elective purposes. While not rendering people free from responsibility, their unbelief is ultimately shown to be grounded not in human choice but in divine hardening."[130] Or as Michaels states, "Not only has God not 'drawn' these people or 'given' them faith, but he has 'blinded their eyes and hardened their hearts' to make sure they would *not* repent and be healed!"[131] Stated otherwise, while man's own sinfulness may be the *proximate* cause of his

130. Andreas J. Köstenberger, *A Theology of John's Gospel and Letters: The Word, the Christ, the Son of God*, Biblical Theology of the New Testament (Grand Rapids: Zondervan, 2009), 459–60.
131. Michaels, *John*, 710.

unbelief, God is the *ultimate* cause of unbelief for it is he who hardens the heart (cf. Exod. 4:21; 7:3; 9:12; 10:1, 20, 27; 11:10; 14:4, 17; Deut. 2:30; Josh. 11:20; 2 Chron. 36:13; Isa. 63:17; Rom. 9:18; 11:7, 25).[132] As Paul says in Romans 9:18, "So then he has mercy on whomever he wills, and he hardens whomever he wills." While the Arminian may detest such a claim, John saw such a hardening of the heart by God as a fulfillment of Isaiah's prophecy, again demonstrating that divine determinism is in view. Therefore, Köstenberger rightly concludes that while humans may question how God can remain just and man remain culpable if God is the one who hardens the heart, "John clearly does not condone this kind of reasoning and has no problem affirming both divine sovereignty and human responsibility in proper proportion to one another, with divine sovereignty serving as the comprehensive framework within which human agents are called to make responsible choices."[133]

Finally, in John 17 Jesus gives his "high priestly prayer" in which he asks his Father to "give eternal life to all whom you have given him [the Son]" (John 17:2). Jesus goes on to say that he has manifested the Father's name to "the people whom you gave me out of the world" (John 17:6). The predestinarian tone of Jesus' words is emphasized even further when he says, "Yours they were, and you gave them to me, and they have kept your word" (John 17:6). Most commentators agree that Jesus is referring to his disciples, as is evident in John 17:9: "I am not praying for the world but for those whom you have given me, for they are yours." Here we see that not all are chosen but only some are chosen to be given to the Son. Notice that the "giving" of these disciples to the Son is not merely for service but for salvation. Jesus is not merely praying for their earthly ministry, but is praying for the safe keeping of their very souls. This is evident in the fact that the language used here ("you have given me") parallels the language used in John 6:36–65. The salvific nature is also obvious in Jesus asking the Father to sanctify them in the truth (John 17:17, 19). Moreover, Jesus is acting as the believers' mediator and

132. Bavinck, *Reformed Dogmatics*, 4:41–42. On God's hardening, see Carson, *John*, 448–49. Also see Köstenberger, *John*, 391; Ridderbos, *John*, 444–45.

133. Köstenberger, *A Theology of John's Gospel and Letters*, 460.

high priest, praying on their behalf, holding them up before the throne of the Father as those whom he has successfully kept (see John 17:12, "While I was with them, I kept them in your name, which you have given me"). Christ is the faithful Son who keeps all those entrusted to him by the Father. Jesus, however, does not stop with his disciples, but continues to pray for the elect who will believe after he has been glorified. "I do not ask for these only, but also for those who will believe in me through their word" (John 17:20). Carson states,

> Christ's prayer is not for the believers alone, but also for those who will become such through their witness (17:20f.). These too will believe in Jesus. There is an inescapable note of certainty: Jesus is praying for the elect who are not yet demonstrably such (cf. Acts 18:10). All believers, those presently such and those who will become such, constitute those given by the Father to Jesus (17:24), and will see Jesus' glory.[134]

Those who have not yet heard the message of the disciples, but will soon enough, are already given to Jesus by the Father. Both the particularity and the determinism in this passage are inescapable. The particularity is present in that Jesus is not praying for all the world but *only* for those who will believe. The efficacy or determinism is present in that Jesus prays for those who *will* believe. Jesus is praying for the elect who have not yet heard the gospel and believed but nonetheless *will certainly do so* since Jesus himself intercedes on their behalf. Though the faith of these future believers is not yet a reality, the Father has guaranteed it in giving them to the Son, and the Son has verified it by praying on their behalf to the Father. Here again we see that belonging to Christ or being given to Christ by the Father is what determines whether or not one will believe.

John 17 shares many similarities with John 10. In John 10:14–18 Jesus says that he is the good shepherd who knows his own sheep and lays down his life for them. Here Jesus is speaking of those Jews who believe in Jesus because they have been given to him by the Father.

---

134. Carson, *Divine Sovereignty*, 187.

However, Jesus also says that he has "other sheep that are not of this fold," and he "must bring them also" and they will listen to his voice (John 10:16). Jesus is now referring to the Gentiles who would one day believe.[135] For them also Jesus lays down his life because they are his sheep as well (John 10:17). But as we saw in John 17, Jesus is here also guaranteeing that certain Gentiles will in fact believe. How can he make such a guarantee? Jesus can make such a promise *because* the Father has given these sheep to his Son, as becomes plain in John 10:24–29.

> So the Jews gathered around him and said to him, "How long will you keep us in suspense? If you are the Christ, tell us plainly." Jesus answered them, "I told you, and you do not believe. The works that I do in my Father's name bear witness about me, but you do not believe because you are not part of my flock. My sheep hear my voice, and I know them, and they follow me. I give them eternal life, and they will never perish, and no one will snatch them out of my hand. My Father, who has given them to me, is greater than all, and no one is able to snatch them out of the Father's hand. I and the Father are one."

Once again we see that the Father has sheep that he gives to the Son. The reason some do not believe is that the Father has not given them to the Son.[136] The reason others believe and the reason others *will believe in the future* (Gentiles included; cf. John 10:16) is that the Father has given them to the Son.

EFFECTUAL CALLING AND UNCONDITIONAL ELECTION

So far we have given a defense for the doctrine of effectual calling from specific passages of Scripture. However, we must recognize that if effectual calling is a biblical doctrine (which it is, as we have seen), then the doctrine of unconditional election of individuals is entailed as well (cf. John 17:2, 6, 9, 24; Acts 13:48; Rom. 9:10–16 [Exod. 33:19];

---

135. Ibid., 190.
136. Ibid.; Carson, *John*, 393; Charles Hodge, *Systematic Theology*, 3 vols. (Reprint, Grand Rapids: Eerdmans, 1952), 2:678.

11:5–7; Eph. 1:3–6, 11; 2 Thess. 2:13; 2 Tim. 1:8–9; Eph. 1:4; Titus 1:1–2). As Ware states,

> Rightly understood, these two doctrines are mutually entailing. That is, if effectual calling is true, it entails the truthfulness of unconditional election, and if unconditional election is true, it entails the truthfulness of effectual calling. Put differently, you cannot have one without the other.[137]

Ware explains exactly why this is the case:

> If God effectually calls only some to be saved, and if this calling, by its nature, is granted only to some such that all of those called actually and certainly are saved, then it follows that God must select those to whom this calling is extended. That is, God's effectual calling cannot be based on how people respond to the general call since the general call includes no certainty of the salvation of those called. But since the effectual call does include the certainty of salvation of all those called, then it follows that God must grant the effectual call to specifically selected individuals only, such that when they are called (effectually), they are surely and certainly saved. So, what name shall we give to this "selection" by God of those specific individuals to whom he extends the effectual call? Surely we could speak of these persons as those "chosen" or "elected" by God to be the recipients of the effectual call. Therefore, if the doctrine of the effectual call is true, it follows that God has previously elected just those specific persons to whom he extends this call. Effectual calling, then, entails unconditional election.[138]

While it is not the purpose of this project to provide a robust, detailed defense of unconditional election, we should note that since effectual calling entails unconditional election— simultaneously precluding Arminian prevenient grace—this only adds support to Calvinist

137. Bruce A. Ware, "Divine Election to Salvation," 17.
138. Ibid.

soteriology as a whole.[139] We have already illustrated this point in the previous exposition of Romans 8:28–30, where we saw that the Arminian reading of "foreknowledge" as proof for a conditional election is absolutely at odds with the effectual call described in that passage.

IRRESISTIBLE GRACE

Effectual calling has also been expressed by the term "irresistible grace," most famously identified as the "I" in the acronym TULIP,[140] giving the impression that Calvinists invented the label. Herman Bavinck explains otherwise,

> The term "irresistible grace" is not really of Reformed origin but was used by Jesuits and Remonstrants to characterize the doctrine of the efficacy of grace as it was advocated by Augustine and those who believed as he did. The Reformed in fact had some objections to the term because it was absolutely not their intent to deny that grace is often and indeed always resisted by the unregenerate person and therefore could be resisted. They therefore preferred to speak of the efficacy or of the insuperability of grace, or interpreted the term "irresistible" in the sense that grace is ultimately irresistible. The point of the disagreement, accordingly, was not whether humans continually resisted and could resist God's grace, but whether they could ultimately—at the specific moment in which God wanted to regenerate them and work with his efficacious grace in their heart—still reject that grace. The answer to this question, as is clearly evident from the five articles of the Remonstrants, is most intimately tied in with the doctrine of the corruption of human nature; with election (based or not based on foreseen faith); the

139. Bruce A. Ware, "Effectual Calling and Grace," 203.

140. Edwin W. Palmer, *The Five Points of Calvinism: A Study Guide*, 2nd ed. (Grand Rapids: Baker Academic, 2010); David N. Steele and Curtis C. Thomas, *The Five Points of Calvinism: Defined, Defended, and Documented*, 2nd ed. (Phillipsburg, NJ: P&R Publishing, 2004). Also see Arthur C. Custance, *The Sovereignty of Grace*, (Brockville, ON: Doorway, 1979), 175–90. On the origins of TULIP as an acronym, see Kenneth J. Stewart, *Ten Myths about Calvinism: Recovering the Breadth of the Reformed Tradition* (Downers Grove, IL: InterVarsity, 2011), 291.

universality and particularity of Christ's atonement; the identification of, or the distinction between, the sufficient call (external) and the efficacious call (internal); and the correctness of the distinction between the will of God's good pleasure and the revealed will in the divine being. Whereas the Remonstrants appealed to Isa. 5:1–8; 65:2–3; Ezek. 12:2; Matt. 11:21–23; 23:37; Luke 7:30; John 5:34; and Acts 7:51, and to all the exhortations to faith and repentance occurring in Scripture, the Reformed theologians took their cue from the picture Scripture offers of fallen humanity as blind, powerless, natural, dead in sins and trespasses (Jer. 13:23; Matt. 6:23; 7:18; John 8:34; Rom. 6:17; 8:7; 1 Cor. 2:14; 2 Cor. 3:5; Eph. 2:1; etc.), and from the forceful words and images with which the work of grace in the human soul is described (Deut. 30:6; Jer. 31:31; Ezek. 36:26; John 3:3, 5; 6:44; Eph. 2:1, 6; Phil. 2:13; 1 Peter 1:3; etc.). So they spoke of the efficacy and invincibility of God's grace in regeneration and articulated this truth in confession at the Synod of Dort.[141]

As with the doctrine of effectual calling, so with the doctrine of irresistible grace, there must be qualification as to what exactly is meant by "irresistible." As already discussed, Calvinists do not believe that there is no sense in which grace is resistible. Calvinists readily affirm that there are places in Scripture where grace is spoken of as resistible (Acts 7:51). Nevertheless, in none of the cases where grace is successfully resisted are Calvinists claiming that God has called his elect or sought to draw them to himself irresistibly. All of these cases are examples of sinners resisting God's *general* gospel call to *all* people. As van Mastricht states, Scripture "plainly speaks of resistance made not to regeneration, but to the external call."[142] It is only when the Spirit chooses to act effectually, a divine act that he only executes on

141. Bavinck, *Reformed Dogmatics*, 4:83. Also see John Murray, "Irresistible Grace," in *Soli Deo Gloria: Essays in Reformed Theology: Festschrift for John H. Gerstner*, ed. R. C. Sproul (Nutley, NJ: Presbyterian and Reformed, 1976), 55–62; Hoekema, *Saved by Grace*, 105.

142. Peter Van Mastricht, *A Treatise on Regeneration*, ed. Brandon Withrow (Morgan, PA: Soli Deo Gloria, 2002), 45.

God's elect, that the manner of grace is then called irresistible and effectual. Ware explains,

> When Calvinists refer to irresistible grace, they mean to say that the Holy Spirit is able, when he so chooses, to overcome all human resistance and so cause his gracious work to be utterly effective and ultimately irresistible. In soteriology, the doctrine of irresistible grace refers to the Spirit's work to overcome all sin-induced resistance and rebellion, opening blind eyes and enlivening hardened hearts so that sinners understand and embrace the gospel of salvation through faith in Christ (Acts 16:14; 2 Cor. 4:4–6; 2 Tim. 2:24–25). Such is the grace by which we are saved.[143]

Understood rightly, the phrase "irresistible grace" indicates that when God so chooses to call an elect sinner to himself, God will indeed be successful in doing so.[144] As John Owen states, the Spirit's regenerating work is "infallible, victorious, irresistible, or always efficacious," and it "removeth all obstacles, overcomes all oppositions, and infallibly produces the effect intended."[145] As we saw in John 6, when the Father calls an elect sinner to Christ, that elect sinner inevitably comes. When God decides to bring or draw his elect to his Son, such a drawing cannot be successfully resisted. As Cornelius Plantinga says, "Nobody can finally hold out against God's grace. Nobody can outlast Him. Every elect person comes . . . to 'give in and admit that God is God.' "[146]

But the label "irresistible grace" can be misunderstood in a second way as well; some construe it to mean that God coerces the sinner. As Carson explains, "The expression is misleading, because it suggests what the theologians themselves usually seek to avoid, viz. the idea that the inevitability of the coming-to-Jesus by those given

---

143. Ware, "Effectual Calling and Grace," 211. Also see Hodge, *Systematic Theology,* 2:687–88; Owen, *A Display of Arminianism,* 10:134–35.

144. Sproul, *What Is Reformed Theology?* 189; Turretin, *Institutes,* 2:526.

145. Owen, *Holy Spirit,* 3:317.

146. Cornelius Plantinga Jr. *A Place to Stand: A Reformed Study of Creeds and Confessions* (Grand Rapids: CRC Publications, 1979), 151.

121

to Jesus means they do so *against* their will, squealing and kicking as it were."[147] However, J. Gresham Machen helps to correct such a misunderstanding,

> The Biblical doctrine of the grace of God does not mean, as caricatures of it sometimes represent it as meaning, that a man is saved against his will. No, it means that a man's will itself is renewed. His act of faith by which he is united to the Lord Jesus Christ is his own act. He performs that gladly, and is sure that he never was so free as when he performs it. Yet he is enabled to perform it simply by the gracious, sovereign act of the Spirit of God.[148]

Therefore, while God's grace for the elect does work effectually, since God renews the will, the sinner not only comes inevitably but willingly. Packer, quoting the Westminster Confession of Faith 10.1, states the matter astutely: "Grace is irresistible, not because it drags sinners to Christ against their will, but because it changes men's hearts so that they 'come most freely, being made willing by his grace.' "[149]

Therefore, the term irresistible grace can be used synonymously with that of effectual calling. One could just as easily say God *irresistibly* calls as one could say God utilizes his *effectual* grace. Since these two phrases are synonymous, it is unnecessary to rehash here the previous defense of effectual calling.

CONCLUSION

The doctrine of effectual calling can be found throughout the New Testament. It is not only a Pauline doctrine but also a doctrine

147. Carson, *Divine Sovereignty*, 185. Also see Michael Horton, *For Calvinism* (Grand Rapids: Zondervan, 2011), 105–10.

148. Machen, *The Christian View of Man*, 244. However, as Welty observes, there are many instances where coercion is commendable, like when someone snatches another person, without his consent, from a burning house. No one complains that he has been rescued from a burning building without his consent, so why would one think otherwise when God redeems sinners from slavery to sin? Welty, "Election and Calling," 241.

149. J. I. Packer, *A Quest for Godliness: The Puritan Vision of the Christian Life* (Wheaton, IL: Crossway, 1990), 295.

taught by Jesus himself. We must recognize that at this point in the presentation of sovereign grace, we have not yet discussed the doctrine of monergistic regeneration (see chapter 4). Nor have we looked at a refutation of the Arminian view as a whole (see chapter 6). Nevertheless, already we can see that the Calvinist view best comports with Scripture, and the Arminian system can be seen to be erroneous. In other words, if the doctrine of effectual calling is biblical, which we have seen in detail that it is, then prevenient grace and synergism (two doctrines upon which the Arminian view is dependent) cannot be true, for each of these doctrines is in direct conflict with the scriptural affirmation of efficacious grace.

4

THE SCRIPTURAL AFFIRMATION OF MONERGISTIC REGENERATION

"How can a person who is dead in trespasses and sins, whose mind is enmity against God, and who cannot do that which is well-pleasing to God answer a call to the fellowship of Christ? . . . The answer to this question is that the believing and loving response which the calling requires is a moral and spiritual impossibility on the part of one who is dead in trespasses and sins."[1] This statement by John Murray is biblically on target for, as we saw in the previous chapter, man *is* dead in his sins and spiritually unable to make any move toward God in a salvific way (John 6:44; Rom. 8:8).[2] Therefore, as Murray observes, the sinner cannot answer the call of God, but God must apply his calling effectually, regenerating the sinner so that he is born again.

> God's call, since it is effectual, carries with it the operative grace whereby the person called is enabled to answer the call and to embrace Jesus Christ as he is freely offered in the gospel. God's grace reaches down to the lowest depths of our need and meets all the exigencies of the moral and spiritual impossibility which inheres in our depravity and inability. And that grace is the grace of regeneration.[3]

1. John Murray, *Redemption Accomplished and Applied* (Grand Rapids: Eerdmans, 1955), 95.
2. See Robert L. Reymond, *A New Systematic Theology of the Christian Faith*, 2nd ed., rev. (Nashville: Thomas Nelson, 1998), 450.
3. Murray, *Redemption Accomplished and Applied*, 96.

As in the last chapter, we will focus here on the grace of regeneration, which reaches down to the dead sinner and raises him to new life in Christ. Grace in regeneration, however, is not contingent upon man's will for its efficacy, nor can man cooperate with it. To the contrary, Scripture tells us that man is absolutely and totally passive in effectual calling and regeneration. God alone is the actor; man is acted upon. Therefore, it is only appropriate to label regeneration "monergistic."

DEFINING REGENERATION

A discussion of regeneration flows naturally from effectual calling.[4] Those whom God effectually calls to himself are made alive (Rom. 8:7–8; Eph. 2:1, 5; Col. 2:13). The word "regeneration" (*palingenesia*) is only used in Matthew 19:28 and Titus 3:5, and only the latter uses the word in the narrow sense, namely, as referring to the first instance of new life. In church history, however, the term has been used differently. The Reformers used it in a very broad sense. For instance, Calvin used "regeneration" to refer to the believer's renewal, covering everything from conversion to sanctification.[5] The Belgic Confession (1561) does the same, as do many Reformed theologians of the sixteenth century.[6] However, Reformed theologians since then have also used the term in a narrower sense to refer to the initial implanting of new life rather than to the entire process of sanctification. Regeneration in this narrow sense is affirmed throughout Scripture, for even if the word itself is not used, the idea is prevalent (John 1:12–13; 3:3–8; Gal. 6:15; Eph. 2:5–6, 10; 4:22–24; Col. 2:11–14; Titus 3:5; James 1:18; 1 Peter 1:3–5; 1 John 2:29; 3:9; 4:7; 5:1, 4).

4. See chapter 2 of *Reclaiming Monergism*, e-book, for how Augustine, Calvin, Dort, and Westminster defend monergistic regeneration.

5. John Calvin, *Institutes of the Christian Religion*, ed. John T. McNeil, trans. Ford Lewis Battles, LCC, vols. 20–21 (Philadelphia: Westminster John Knox, 1960), 3.3. Also see Anthony Hoekema, *Saved by Grace* (Grand Rapids: Eerdmans, 1989), 93–94.

6. See "The Belgic Confession" in *Creeds and Confessions of the Reformation Era*, vol. 2 of *Creeds and Confessions of Faith in the Christian Tradition*, ed. Jaroslav Pelikan and Valerie Hotchkiss (New Haven: Yale University Press, 2003), article 24; "The Canons of Dort" in *Creeds and Confessions*, 3–4.11–12.

That said, it is appropriate to define regeneration in this narrow sense more precisely. But first it is necessary to recognize what regeneration is *not*. First, there is no addition to or subtraction from the "substance" of man's nature in regeneration. Such was the view of the Manicheans with whom Augustine dealt, as well as that of Flacius Illyricus, with whom the Reformers debated. But as Berkhof explains, no "new physical seed or germ is implanted in man; neither is there any addition to, or subtraction from, the faculties of the soul."[7] Second, regeneration is not limited to only one faculty in the person, but impacts the entire human nature, piercing the very core. Third, while regeneration is a transformation of the entire human nature, it is not a perfect change, as if the sinner after regeneration is now incapable of sinning.

As to what regeneration *is*, I offer the following definition:

> Regeneration is the work of the Holy Spirit to unite the elect sinner to Christ by breathing new life into that dead and depraved sinner so as to raise him from spiritual death to spiritual life, removing his heart of stone and giving him a heart of flesh, so that he is washed, born from above and now able to repent and trust in Christ as a new creation. Moreover, regeneration is the act of God alone and therefore it is monergistic in nature, accomplished by the sovereign act of the Spirit apart from and unconditioned upon man's will to believe. In short, man's faith does not cause regeneration but regeneration causes man's faith.[8]

This definition assumes several characteristics about regeneration.[9] First, regeneration is an *instantaneous* change. Regeneration is not like sanctification, progressing gradually in time, which is the view of the Roman Catholic Church. Rather, regeneration is a momentary or snapshot action (Acts 16:14; Eph. 2:5). In other words, regeneration is punctiliar.

---

7. Louis Berkhof, *Systematic Theology* (Edinburgh: Banner of Truth, 2003), 468. The points listed above can be found in Berkhof.

8. My definition is similar to Hoekema, *Saved by Grace*, 94; Murray, *Redemption Accomplished and Applied*, 96; Berkhof, *Systematic Theology*, 469.

9. In what follows I am following Charles Hodge, *Systematic Theology* (Grand Rapids: Eerdmans, 1952), 2:675ff.; Berkhof, *Systematic Theology*, 468–69; Hoekema, *Saved by Grace*, 102–4.

Second, regeneration is a change in the *very inner core* or root of man's nature.[10] Just as total depravity is pervasive, penetrating the very essence of man's heart, so also is regeneration a change within the sinner's deepest recess. Like total depravity, not only does regeneration strike at the very essence of man but it also extends to every aspect, affecting the entire person.

Third, regeneration occurs *below consciousness*. John Stott helpfully explains,

> There is no biblical warrant for the view that regeneration is a conscious process, that is to say, that the person being born again is conscious of what is happening inside of him. Jesus himself indicated the opposite when in his conversation with Nicodemus he drew an analogy between the Spirit's work in the new birth and the blowing of the wind [John 3:8] . . . Although the effects of the wind are seen, heard and felt, there is something secret and mysterious about the operation of the wind itself. The effects of the new birth are evident too (in a changed life), but there is something secret and mysterious about the regenerating work of the Holy Spirit. Of course, "conversion" (the sinner's turning to Christ in repentance and faith), which is also a work of the Spirit is normally conscious, as he grasps certain things with his mind and acts with his will. But regeneration is the implantation of new life into a soul dead in trespasses and sins. We are no more conscious of this infusion of spiritual life, called rebirth or spiritual birth, than we are of our physical birth. In both cases self-consciousness, consciousness of being alive, develops later.[11]

Likewise, Loraine Boettner states,

> The regeneration of the soul is something which is wrought in us, and not an act performed by us. It is an instantaneous change from spiritual death to spiritual life. It is not even a thing of which we

10. Loraine Boettner, *The Reformed Doctrine of Predestination* (Philadelphia: Presbyterian and Reformed, 1932), 165.

11. John Stott, *Baptism and Fullness: The Work of the Holy Spirit Today*, 3rd ed. (Downers Grove, IL: InterVarsity, 2006), 84.

are conscious at the moment it occurs, but rather something which lies lower than consciousness. At the moment of its occurrence the soul is as passive as was Lazarus when he was called back to life by Jesus.[12]

As we shall see later, Stott and Boettner are right; regeneration is not a conscious synergism between God and the sinner, but rather regeneration occurs beneath the sinner's consciousness, which results in the sinner consciously turning to Christ in faith and repentance as a result of God's awakening work.

Fourth, Regeneration is not only a supernatural change but an *immediate* change.[13] It is immediate in two ways.

(1) Regeneration is immediate in that it is not a mere moral persuasion by the Word, as many in the Semi-Pelagian and Arminian traditions have said. Against the Remonstrants, the Synod of Dort rejected those "who teach that the grace by which we are converted to God is nothing but a gentle persuasion."[14] Rather, "it is an entirely *supernatural* work, one that is at the same time *most powerful* and most pleasing, a marvelous, hidden, and inexpressible work, which is not lesser than or inferior in power to that of creation or of raising the dead. . . ."[15] Bavinck explains that Dort rejected the view that "between God's activity and its effect in the human heart (which is regeneration) is thus the free human will," and instead argued that regeneration is *immediate*, meaning that "God's Spirit itself *directly* enters the human heart and with infallible certainty brings about regeneration without in any way being dependent

12. Boettner, *Reformed Doctrine of Predestination*, 165.
13. See Francis Turretin, *Institutes of Elenctic Theology*, ed. James T. Dennison, Jr., trans. George M. Giger, 3 vols. (Phillipsburg, NJ: P&R Publishing, 1992–97), 2:530–32; Hodge, *Systematic Theology*, 2:684–85, 2:702–3; 3:31.
14. Canons of Dort, 3–4, Rejection of Errors, Par. 7, quoted in Hoekema, *Saved by Grace*, 102. Also see Peter Toon, *Born Again: A Biblical and Theological Study of Regeneration* (Grand Rapids: Baker, 1987), 118–20, 162–65, 171–73, 177–80.
15. Canons of Dort, 3–4 article 12, quoted in Hoekema, *Saved by Grace*, 103, emphasis added. The Puritans would use the word "physical" to convey this same truth. See J. I. Packer, *A Quest for Godliness: The Puritan Vision of the Christian Life* (Wheaton, IL: Crossway, 1990), 295; John Owen, *A Discourse Concerning the Holy Spirit*, in *The Works of John Owen* (Edinburgh: Banner of Truth, 2000), 3:316ff.

on the human will."[16] Bavinck elsewhere explains that the immediate nature of regeneration is not meant to "exclude the Word as a means of grace from the operation of the Holy Spirit" but simply is meant to "uphold against the Remonstrants that the Holy Spirit, though employing the Word, himself with his grace entered into the heart of humans and there effected regeneration without being dependent on their will and consent."[17] Charles Hodge makes the same point, comparing the immediate nature of regeneration to the miracle of a blind man seeing. While light is key to the faculty of seeing, it does not produce sight; that is reserved to the almighty power of Christ himself. So it is with regeneration. Truth and the Word are essential, but in themselves they do nothing. Rather, it is the inward power of the Spirit with the Word that enacts the miracle of new birth.[18]

(2) The Reformed have also titled such a change immediate in response to those such as John Cameron (1580–1625), who influenced those in the school of Saumur (Amyraut, Placaeus, Cappellus, Pajon). Cameron and his followers reduced regeneration to an illumination of the mind by the Word, believing that if the mind is changed the will naturally follows. So while there is an immediate work of God on the intellect, there is not one on the will.[19] Over against Cameron, Saumur, and Pajonism, "the Reformed generally claimed that the Holy Spirit not only impacted the human will through the intellect, but also that it penetrated the will directly and there instilled new habits immediately."[20] Again, as Bavinck points out, the Reformed do not exclude the instrumentality of the Word but simply "assert against the

16. Herman Bavinck, *Reformed Dogmatics*, ed. John Bolt, trans. John Vriend (Grand Rapids: Baker, 2008), 4:81, emphasis added (cf. 3:580).

17. Ibid., 3:580. Also see Herman Bavinck, *Saved by Grace: The Holy Spirit's Work in Calling and Regeneration*, ed. Mark Beach, trans. Nelson D. Kloosterman (Grand Rapids: Reformation Heritage, 2008), 34.

18. Hodge, *Systematic Theology*, 2:703; 3:31.

19. Bavinck, *Reformed Dogmatics*, 4:81; 3:580; idem, *Saved by Grace*, 49–51. For a more extensive study, see Stephen Strehle, "Universal Grace and Amyraldianism," *WTJ* 51 (1989): 345–57.

20. Bavinck, *Reformed Dogmatics*, 4:81. Also see Louis Berkhof, *The History of Christian Doctrine* (Grand Rapids: Eerdmans, 1949), 221; Toon, *Born Again*, 129–30.

theology of Saumur that in regeneration the Holy Spirit does not merely by the Word illumine the intellect but also directly and immediately infuses new affections in the will."[21] This is another reminder of our previous point, namely, that regeneration is a change that is *total*, like depravity, in the sense that it impacts *all* of a person's faculties, the will included.[22]

This leads us to the fifth point: as Johannes Wollebius and Sinclair Ferguson observe, while the *efficient* cause of regeneration is the Holy Spirit, the *instrumental* cause of regeneration is the "word of God" (1 Peter 1:23) or the "word of truth" (James 1:18; cf. John 15:3; 2 Thess. 2:14).[23] While Cameron and Saumur overplayed the intellect and mind to the neglect of the will, we do not want to swing this pendulum to the other extreme and deny the change that regeneration has on the mind through the Word. In Scripture it is the Word of God that is absolutely necessary for the salvation and redemption of fallen sinners, as the Belgic Confession (Article 24) and Heidelberg Catechism (Lord's Day 25) make so clear. And yet, this Word must be accompanied by the Spirit if it is to be applied effectually.

Calvin understood this well. While he acknowledged the gift of the mind even to unbelievers due to God's common grace, which enables them to excel in the liberal arts, yet when it comes to God "the greatest geniuses [e.g., Plato, Aristotle] are blinder than moles."[24] Without God's Word *and* Spirit man is left in utter darkness, lacking the effectual application of the saving content of the gospel of Jesus Christ. Calvin states, "The mind of man is blind until it is illuminated by the Spirit of God [and] the will is enslaved to evil, and wholly carried and hurried to evil, until corrected by

21. Bavinck, *Reformed Dogmatics*, 3:581. Also see idem, *Roeping en wedergeboorte* (Kampen: Zalsman, 1903), 47–72.

22. Bavinck, *Reformed Dogmatics*, 4:91–92, 124.

23. Sinclair B. Ferguson, *The Holy Spirit* (Downers Grove, IL: InterVarsity, 1996), 53, 125; Johannes Wollebius, *Compendium Theologiae Christianae*, trans. Alexander Ross (London, 1650), 28.1.2; quoted in *Reformed Dogmatics*, ed. John W. Beardslee III (New York: Oxford University Press, 1965), 158. Also see Peter Van Mastricht, *A Treatise on Regeneration*, ed. Brandon Withrow (Morgan, PA: Soli Deo Gloria, 2002), 16; Turretin, *Institutes*, 2:526, 529.

24. Calvin, *Institutes*, 2.2.18. Cf. Anthony N. S. Lane, "Anthropology," in *The Calvin Handbook*, ed. Herman J. Selderhuis (Grand Rapids: Eerdmans, 2008), 282.

the same Spirit."[25] Therefore, no mere assistance or moral suasion will do, nor a mere enlightening of the mind. The preaching of God's Word does nothing if the Spirit does not work effectually to open blind eyes, deaf ears, and hard hearts to the gospel. On John 6:44 Calvin says,

> But nothing is accomplished by preaching him if the Spirit, as our inner teacher, does not show our minds the way. Only those men, therefore, who have heard and have been taught by the Father come to him. What kind of learning and hearing is this? Surely, where the Spirit by a wonderful and singular power forms our ears to hear and our minds to understand . . . it therefore remains for us to understand that the way of the Kingdom of God is open only to him whose mind has been made new by the illumination of the Holy Spirit. . . . Because these mysteries are deeply hidden from human insight, they are disclosed solely by the revelation of the Spirit. Hence, where the Spirit of God does not illumine them, they are considered folly.[26]

Calvin again explains the vital connection between Word and Spirit, "If anyone wants a clearer answer, here it is: God works in his elect in two ways: within, through his Spirit; without, through his Word. By his Spirit, illuminating their minds and forming their hearts to the love and cultivation of righteousness, he makes them a new creation (*nova creatio*). By his Word, he arouses them to desire, to seek after, and to attain that same renewal."[27] This is simply another way of saying that the gospel call is made effectual for the elect.

As Paul states in 2 Thessalonians 2:14, "To this *he called you through our gospel*, so that you may obtain the glory of our Lord Jesus Christ." Therefore, it is appropriate to say that the effectual call works through the general gospel call.[28] What differentiates the gospel call, however,

---

25. John Calvin, *Ecclesiae Reformandae Ratio*, quoted in Lane, "Anthropology," 283.

26. Calvin, *Institutes*, 2.2.20. Also see idem, *Commentary on the Gospel according to John*, 2 vols., trans. William Pringle (Grand Rapids: Baker, 2005), 2:93.

27. Calvin, *Institutes*, 2.5.5. Cf. Joseph A. Pipa, "Calvin on the Holy Spirit," in *Calvin for Today*, ed. Joel R. Beeke (Grand Rapids: Reformation Heritage, 2009), 62.

28. James Boice and Philip Graham Ryken, *The Doctrines of Grace: Rediscovering the Evangelical Gospel* (Wheaton, IL: Crossway, 2002), 142.

from the effectual call is that in the effectual call the Spirit accompanies the Word, making it effectual for the elect, while in the gospel call there is the absence of the Spirit and his effectual work for those not chosen. But the Word of the gospel not only has an instrumental role in effectual calling, but also in regeneration as well. James 1:18 and 1 Peter 1:22–23 make this especially clear.[29] James states, "Of his own will he brought us forth by the word of truth, that we should be a kind of firstfruits of his creatures." Peter says, "Having purified your souls by your obedience to the truth for a sincere brotherly love, love one another earnestly from a pure heart, since you have been born again, not of perishable seed but of imperishable, through the living and abiding word of God." The instrumentality of the Word is also evident in the regeneration of Lydia. "The Lord opened her heart [regeneration] to pay attention to what was said by Paul" (Acts 16:14). Likewise, Saul/Paul is converted when he is met by the Word, Christ Jesus, himself with the truth and reality of his resurrection and lordship (i.e., "Saul, Saul, why are you persecuting me? . . . I am Jesus, whom you are persecuting" in Acts 9:4b–5). Here we see not only the reality of the gospel (the Word) confronting Saul but also Jesus himself, who is the Word (John 1:1–3), confronting the infamous persecutor of the church. In both Saul's and Lydia's cases, the former dramatic and the latter subtle and discrete, it is when they are confronted with the Word of truth that regeneration occurs.

Unfortunately, some have used the instrumentality of the Word to undermine the sovereignty of God. Such a move shifts the Word's role from instrumentality to efficacy. The efficient cause is no longer the Spirit but the Word itself. The Spirit is then demoted to a mere instrumental role rather than being the efficient cause. Berkhof, having Lyman Beecher (1775–1863) and Charles G. Finney (1792–1875) in

---

29. I am assuming here that the Word is the gospel itself. See Thomas R. Schreiner, *1, 2 Peter, Jude*, NAC, vol. 37 (Nashville: B&H Publishing Group, 2003), 95; Peter H. Davids, *The First Epistle of Peter*, NICNT (Grand Rapids: Eerdmans, 1990), 78; Douglas J. Moo, *The Letter of James*, PNTC (Grand Rapids: Eerdmans, 2000), 79–80; Alexander Ross, *The Epistles of James and John*, NICNT (Grand Rapids: Eerdmans, 1954), 36; Dan McCartney, *James*, BECNT (Grand Rapids: Baker Academic, 2009), 110; Daniel M. Doriani, *James*, REC (Phillipsburg, NJ: P&R Publishing, 2007), 40–41; Peter Davids, *The Epistle of James*, NIGTC (Grand Rapids: Eerdmans, 1982), 89.

mind, explains, "According to this view the truth as a system of motives, presented to the human will by the Holy Spirit, is the immediate cause of the change from unholiness to holiness. . . . It assumes that the work of the Holy Spirit differs from that of the preacher only in degree. Both work by persuasion only."[30] Berkhof responds, "But this theory is quite unsatisfactory. The truth can be a motive to holiness only if it is loved, while the natural man does not love the truth, but hates it, Rom. 1:18, 25. Consequently the truth, presented externally, cannot be the efficient cause of regeneration."[31] Calvin also states, "the Word will not find acceptance in men's hearts before it is sealed by the inward testimony of the Spirit."[32] Consequently, one should not think that the instrumentality of the Word subtracts from the sovereignty of God in regeneration.[33] Ferguson insightfully comments,

> But how can regeneration take place through the word without this diluting the notion of the Spirit's monergistic, sovereign activity? . . . For the New Testament writers, however, there is no hint of a threat to divine sovereignty in the fact that the word is the instrumental cause of regeneration, while the Spirit is the efficient cause. This is signaled in the New Testament by the use of the preposition *ek* to indicate the divine originating cause (e.g., John 3:5; 1 John 3:9; 5:1) and *dia* to express the instrumental cause (e.g., John 15:3; 1 Cor. 4:15; 1 Peter 1:23).[34]

As we will see in this next section, what the Westminster Catechism calls "savingly enlightening their minds" by "his word and Spirit" (i.e., *spiritus cum verbo*, the Spirit working with the Word)

---

30. Berkhof, *Systematic Theology*, 473. Also see Hodge, *Systematic Theology*, 3:8–11, 16–17.

31. Berkhof, *Systematic Theology*, 473. Also see Bavinck, *Reformed Dogmatics*, 4:81.

32. Calvin, *Institutes*, 1.7.4.

33. Ferguson, *The Holy Spirit*, 125. In an effort to preserve the Spirit's sovereignty many in the Reformed tradition have made the following distinction: "Regeneration, taken in the strict, narrow sense as the quickening of the spiritual dead, takes place *cum verbo*, that is along with the Word, but not *per verbum*, through the Word." Typically the former is the Reformed view while the latter the Lutheran view. Herman Kuiper, *By Grace Alone: A Study in Soteriology* (Grand Rapids: Eerdmans, 1955), 48.

34. Ferguson, *The Holy Spirit*, 125. Also see Turretin, *Institutes*, 2:431.

is something which is God's sovereign prerogative, independent of man's will.[35]

THE CIRCUMCISION AND GIFT OF A NEW HEART

Deuteronomy 30:6

In Deuteronomy 30 Israel faces and anticipates the reality of coming exile and judgment for the people's disobedience. However, inspired by God, Moses foretells of a time to come when Israel will experience restoration, redemption, genuine repentance, and new spiritual life rather than judgment and condemnation. Included in such a future restoration is liberation from the slavery of sin. However, this liberation comes only through the circumcision of the heart. In Deuteronomy 30:6 we read, "And the LORD your God will circumcise your heart and the heart of your offspring, so that you will love the LORD your God with all your heart and with all your soul, that you may live." Eugene Merrill is correct to state that circumcision of the heart here refers to the "radical work of regeneration." Merrill further explains,

> Just as circumcision of the flesh symbolized outward identification with the Lord and the covenant community (cf. Gen. 17:10, 23; Lev. 12:3; Josh. 5:2), so circumcision of the heart (a phrase found only here and in Deut. 10:16 and Jer. 4:4 in the OT) speaks of internal identification with him in what might be called regeneration in Christian theology.[36]

If the circumcision of the heart refers to regeneration (cf. Rom. 2:25–27), then to what purpose does Yahweh promise to circumcise the heart? Yahweh circumcises the heart "so that" they will love the Lord.[37] The

---

35. The role of the Word in effectual calling and regeneration is more extensively studied in *Reclaiming Monergism*, e-book. "The Westminster Larger Catechism," question 67, in *Creeds and Confessions*.

36. Eugene H. Merrill, *Deuteronomy*, NAC, vol. 4 (Nashville: B&H Publishing Group, 1994), 388. Also see Mark A. Snoeberger, "The Logical Priority of Regeneration to Saving Faith in a Theological *Ordo Salutis*," *DBSJ* 7 (2002): 70.

37. J. A. Thompson, *Deuteronomy*, TOTC, vol. 5 (Downers Grove, IL: IVP Academic, 2008), 311.

Lord does not circumcise their hearts "because" they acted in repentance and faith by loving the Lord. Rather, it is Yahweh's sovereign act of circumcising the heart that causes the sinner to love him. As Hoekema states, "Since the heart is the inner core of the person, the passage teaches that God must cleanse us within before we can truly love him."[38] Therefore, Yahweh's promise of renewal and restoration is characterized by a sovereign act upon the uncircumcised heart of his elect. Nowhere in Deuteronomy 30:6 do we see any indication that Yahweh's sovereign act of circumcising the heart is conditioned upon the will of man to believe. Rather, it is quite the opposite. Yahweh must first circumcise the heart so that the sinner can exercise a will that believes.

In Deuteronomy 29:2–4 Moses summons all of Israel and says, "You have seen all that the LORD did before your eyes in the land of Egypt, to Pharaoh and to all his servants and to all his land, the great trials that your eyes saw, the signs, and those great wonders. But to this day the LORD has not given you a heart to understand or eyes to see or ears to hear." Why is it that those in Israel, who saw the many miracles God performed in saving them from Pharaoh, do not believe? Verse 4 gives the answer, "To this day the LORD has not given you a heart to understand or eyes to see or ears to hear." It is remarkable how much Deuteronomy 29 parallels John 10:26. As Israel saw the miracles and failed to hear and see spiritually so also did the Jews in the Gospels see the miracles of Jesus and fail to hear and see spiritually. But again, notice the reason Jesus gives as to why they do not believe: "The works that I do in my Father's name bear witness about me, but you do not believe because you are not part of my flock" (John 10:25–26). As in Deuteronomy 29:2–4, the reason they do not see or hear is because God did not give them "a heart to understand or eyes to see or ears to hear." It is not man's choice or will which determines whether he will have a spiritual heart to hear and see, but it is God's sovereign choice to give the sinner a heart to hear and see that is the cause and reason for belief.[39]

38. Hoekema, *Saved by Grace*, 95; John Owen, *A Display of Arminianism*, 10:105, 136.
39. Snoeberger, "Logical Priority of Regeneration," 74.

Jeremiah 31:33 and 32:39–40

The concept of a new heart is also illustrated by the prophet Jeremiah: "But this is the covenant that I will make with the house of Israel after those days, declares the LORD: I will put my law within them, and I will write it on their hearts. And I will be their God and they shall be my people" (Jer. 31:33; cf. Heb. 8:10; 10:16). Similarly the Lord says in Jeremiah 32:39–40, "I will give them one heart and one way, that they may fear me forever, for their own good and the good of their children after them. I will make with them an everlasting covenant, that I will not turn away from doing good to them. And I will put the fear of me in their hearts, that they may not turn from me." Unlike Deuteronomy 30:6, in Jeremiah the phrase "circumcise your heart," with the heart being "the organ of understanding and will," is not used.[40] Nevertheless, the phrase is used in Jeremiah 4:4, and the concept is present in 30:6 and 32:39–40, for the text does speak of the Lord writing his law on the people's hearts (in contrast to writing his law on tablets of stone), giving his people one heart, and putting the fear of the Lord in their hearts. As in Deuteronomy, in Jeremiah regeneration is in view.[41]

Notice, it is only when God writes his law within, on the heart, and places within a fear of himself that the sinner can follow after him. As Turretin explains, Jeremiah "denotes not a resistible, but an invincible action which most certainly obtains its effect."[42] Only when Yahweh circumcises the heart can the sinner obey. Thompson states, "Yahweh himself proposes to bring about the necessary change in the people's inner nature which will *make them capable* of obedience."[43] Likewise, Hamilton states, "Circumcision of the heart does seem to result in the *ability* to love God and live (Deut. 30:6). The spiritual circumcision (circumcised

---

40. J. Andrew Dearman, *Jeremiah and Lamentations*, NIVAC (Grand Rapids: Zondervan, 2002), 85.

41. F. B. Huey Jr., *Jeremiah, Lamentations*, NAC, vol. 16 (Nashville: B&H Publishing Group, 1993), 285; Bavinck, *Reformed Dogmatics*, 4:52.

42. Turretin, *Institutes*, 2:551. Also see Owen, *A Display of Arminianism*, 10:105.

43. J. A. Thompson, *The Book of Jeremiah*, NICOT (Grand Rapids: Eerdmans, 1980), 581, emphasis added.

heart and ears) *enables* people to incline to Yahweh."[44] Hamilton points to Jeremiah 6:10 where Yahweh asks, "Who shall I speak to or warn that they might listen? Behold, their ear is uncircumcised, and they are *not able* to pay attention. Behold, the word of Yahweh has become a reproach to them; they do not delight in it." He concludes, "An 'uncircumcised ear' indicates an *inability* to interest oneself in the word of Yahweh."[45] Therefore, Paul can say in Romans 2:29 that what saves is not a mere external, physical circumcision, but an inward, spiritual circumcision that is "by the Spirit, not by the letter." Consequently, "His praise is not from man but from God." Only when God circumcises the heart does a new ability to believe result.

Ezekiel 11:19–21 and 36:26–27

The concept of a circumcised heart in Deuteronomy 30:6 and a new heart in Jeremiah 31:33 is also taught by the prophet Ezekiel. Yahweh again promises a day to come when his people will experience restoration and renewal.

> And I will give them one heart, and a new spirit I will put within them. I will remove the heart of stone from their flesh and give them a heart of flesh, that they may walk in my statutes and keep my rules and obey them. And they shall be my people, and I will be their God. But as for those whose heart goes after their detestable things and their abominations, I will bring their deeds upon their own heads, declares the Lord God. (Ezek. 11:19–21)

> And I will give you a new heart, and a new spirit I will put within you. And I will remove the heart of stone from your flesh and give you a heart of flesh. And I will put my Spirit within you, and cause you to walk in my statutes and be careful to obey my rules. (Ezek. 36:26–27)

44. James M. Hamilton Jr., *God's Indwelling Presence: The Holy Spirit in the Old and New Testaments*, NAC Studies in Bible and Theology, vol. 1 (Nashville: B&H Publishing Group, 2006), 47.
45. Ibid.

Yahweh explains that in order for a sinner to walk in his statutes, keep his rules, and obey his law, he must first remove the dead, cold, lifeless heart of stone[46] and replace it with a heart that is alive, namely, a heart of flesh.[47] Yahweh does not give the sinner a heart of flesh because the sinner obeys, but rather the sinner obeys *because* Yahweh surgically implants a heart of flesh. Such an order is indicated at the beginning of Ezekiel 11:20. Yahweh removes the heart of stone and gives the people a heart of flesh "that they may" obey (Ezek. 11:21; 36:27).[48] The same causal order is even more apparent in Ezekiel 36, where Yahweh states that he will "cause you to walk in my statutes and be careful to obey my rules" (Ezek. 36:27).[49] Once again, God does not put a new heart and spirit within in reaction to or because of the sinner's faith, but it is God's sovereign act of implanting a new heart, a new spirit, that causes the sinner to turn in faith and obedience.[50]

Ezekiel 37:1–14

In Ezekiel 11 and 36 the sovereignty of God in regeneration is conveyed through imagery of a heart of stone that is replaced by a heart of flesh. This picture of God's sovereignty and man's passivity is brought into even sharper focus when the reader approaches Ezekiel 37, which presents the vision of the valley of dry bones. The hand of the Lord brings Ezekiel out in the Spirit and sets him down in the middle of a valley that is full of dry bones.

> And he said to me, "Son of man, can these bones live?" And I answered, "O Lord God, you know." Then he said to me, "Prophesy over these bones, and say to them, O dry bones, hear the word of the Lord.

46. Gerard Van Groningen, *Messianic Revelation in the Old Testament* (Grand Rapids: Baker, 1990), 750.

47. Daniel I. Block, *The Book of Ezekiel, Chapters 25–48*, NICOT (Grand Rapids: Eerdmans, 1998), 355. Also see Hans W. Wolff, *Anthropology of the Old Testament* (Mifflintown, PA: Sigler, 1996), 29, 40–41, 54; Iain M. Duguid, *Ezekiel*, NIVAC (Grand Rapids: Zondervan, 1999), 415.

48. The language used here is so blatantly "causal" in nature that Block says it highlights "divine coercion." Block, *Ezekiel*, 356. Also see Owen, *A Display of Arminianism*, 10:105.

49. Lamar E. Cooper Sr., *Ezekiel*, NAC, vol. 17 (Nashville: B&H Publishing Group, 1994), 317.

50. Hamilton, *God's Indwelling Presence*, 53; Turretin, *Institutes*, 2:551.

Thus says the Lord God to these bones: Behold, I will cause breath to enter you, and you shall live. And I will lay sinews upon you, and will cause flesh to come upon you, and cover you with skin, and put breath in you, and you shall live, and you shall know that I am the Lord."

So I prophesied as I was commanded. And as I prophesied, there was a sound, and behold, a rattling, and the bones came together, bone to its bone. And I looked, and behold, there were sinews on them, and flesh had come upon them, and skin had covered them. But there was no breath in them. Then he said to me, "Prophesy to the breath; prophesy, son of man, and say to the breath, Thus says the Lord God: Come from the four winds, O breath, and breathe on these slain, that they may live." So I prophesied as he commanded me, and the breath came into them, and they lived and stood on their feet, an exceedingly great army.

Then he said to me, "Son of man, these bones are the whole house of Israel. Behold, they say, 'Our bones are dried up, and our hope is lost; we are indeed cut off.' Therefore prophesy, and say to them, Thus says the Lord God: Behold, I will open your graves and raise you from your graves, O my people. And I will bring you into the land of Israel. And you shall know that I am the Lord, when I open your graves, and raise you from your graves, O my people. And I will put my Spirit within you, and you shall live, and I will place you in your own land. Then you shall know that I am the Lord; I have spoken, and I will do it, declares the Lord." (Ezek. 37:1–14)[51]

As in Ezekiel 11:19–21 and 36:26–27, we again see imagery of God taking that which is dead and making it alive.[52] The Lord takes bones that are dead, dry, and sitting in a heap and breathes new life into them. As Ezekiel 37:5 says, "Thus says the Lord God to these bones: Behold, I will cause breath to enter you, and you shall live." The Lord prophecies

51. Some have interpreted Ezekiel 37 as referring to the future resurrection of the dead. While we would not want to eliminate any hint of a future resurrection, I think it is better to interpret this as primarily referring to a spiritual reality that Yahweh will work in the sinner's heart, as is apparent when he uses the same language he used in chapter 36 to say, "I will put my Spirit within you, and you shall live, and I will place you in your own land. Then you shall know that I am the Lord."

52. Duguid, *Ezekiel*, 427.

that he will "lay sinews" upon these dead, dry bones and "will cause flesh to come upon you, and cover you with skin, and put breath in you, and you shall live, and you shall know that I am the LORD" (Ezek. 37:6). When Ezekiel begins to prophecy to these dead bones as he was commanded, suddenly the bones rattle and come to life, enveloped with flesh. At the command of the Lord, breath comes from the four winds and suddenly "they lived and stood on their feet" (Ezek. 37:10).[53] The Lord interprets for Ezekiel exactly what has happened. The bones represent the whole house of Israel, without hope, spiritually dead, cut off (Ezek. 37:11). However, the breath of the Lord resurrecting these bones is the restoration to new life. When the Lord breaths new spiritual life into his people, the result is that they know that he is the Lord (Ezek. 37:13–14). God's act to breathe new life is not conditioned upon the will of the dead. Dead, dry bones are lifeless (cf. Jer. 34:17–20) until God breathes new life into them (flesh, sinews).[54]

OBJECTIONS FROM DEUTERONOMY 10:16; EZEKIEL 18:31; AND JEREMIAH 4:4

Though the passages studied so far present a picture of God's monergistic work in regeneration, Arminians will object that the exact opposite is taught in Deuteronomy 10:16, Ezekiel 18:31, and Jeremiah 4:4, in which it is the unregenerate sinner who, seemingly, is supposed to circumcise his own heart.[55] As Deuteronomy 10:16 says, "Circumcise therefore the foreskin of your heart, and be no longer stubborn."[56] Likewise, Ezekiel 18:31 says, "Cast away from you all the transgressions that you have committed, and make yourselves a new heart and a new spirit! Why will

---

53. Block, *Ezekiel*, 377.

54. Ezekiel Hopkins, "The Nature and Necessity of Regeneration; or, the New-Birth," in *The Works of Ezekiel Hopkins*, ed. Charles W. Quick, 3 vols. (Reprint, Morgan, PA: Soli Deo Gloria, 1997), 2:245.

55. For example, see Thomas O. Summers, *Systematic Theology: A Complete Body of Wesleyan Arminian Divinity*, 2 vols. (Nashville: Methodist Episcopal Church, South, 1888), 2:85.

56. For a statement of the dilemma and comparison with Deut. 30:6, see Peter C. Craigie, *The Book of Deuteronomy*, NICOT (Grand Rapids: Eerdmans, 1976), 364; Steven Tuell, *Ezekiel*, NIBC (Peabody, MA: Hendrickson, 2009), 119.

you die, O house of Israel?" And again, Jeremiah 4:4 reads, "Circumcise yourselves to the LORD; remove the foreskin of your hearts, O men of Judah and inhabitants of Jerusalem; lest my wrath go forth like fire, and burn with none to quench it, because of the evil of your deeds." On the surface, these passages could be interpreted to say that the sinner has the ability in and of himself to change his heart. However, it is essential to notice that though Yahweh commands the sinner to circumcise his heart, he never says the sinner is *able* to do so.[57] The Arminian objects that a command implies ability ("ought implies can"), but as demonstrated already this is a faulty assumption that not only reads into the text but also contradicts a multitude of other texts which explicitly say that man cannot in any way turn toward God of his own accord.

But we do not even have to turn to other books of the Bible to discover the inability of man. For example, take the apparent tension between Deuteronomy 30:6 and 10:16. In Deuteronomy 30:6 it is the Lord, Yahweh, who must circumcise the heart, a miracle performed by God so that his people would have the ability to love and obey him. Merrill makes a keen observation,

> This is an obvious reference to the demand of the Shema (Deut. 6:4–5), adherence to which was at the very core of the covenant commitment. *This impossible standard* was always understood as the ideal of covenant behavior, *one to be sought but never fully achieved* (cf. Matt. 22:40; Mark 12:33). Here, however, Moses did not command or even exhort his audience to obedience. He promised it as a natural by-product of the renewal of the heart. People can love God with all their heart *only after the heart itself has been radically changed to a Godward direction.*[58]

Notice how Merrill states that Deuteronomy 30:6 is a reference to the Shema and therefore it is an "impossible standard" not because the

---

57. Contra Augustus Hopkins Strong, *Systematic Theology: Three Volumes in One* (Philadelphia: Judson, 1907; repr. Old Tappan, NJ: Fleming H. Revell, 1976), 830.

58. Merrill, *Deuteronomy*, 389. Emphasis added. Also see Owen, *Discourse Concerning the Holy Spirit*, 3:336.

law is flawed but because man is depraved. Therefore, the command in Deuteronomy 10:16 is also impossible to achieve. Yet, when Moses gives the command in Deuteronomy 10:16 and in 30:6 he reveals that it is not man who fulfills this command but Yahweh himself. What is impossible for man is made possible by God's sovereign grace.[59] Consequently, Merrill is exactly right to state that it is "only after the heart itself has been radically changed to a Godward direction" that sinners can love God with all their heart.

The same can be said of the apparent tension between Jeremiah 4:4 and 31:33/32:39–40. Notice, in 31:33 Yahweh says he will write his law on the people's hearts. Longman observes that this expression "intends to contrast with the Ten Commandments that were written on tablets of stone."[60] Longman's reference to the Law makes sense when one considers the command of Jeremiah 4:4. The people are to be in conformity with God's commands and therefore they are commanded to circumcise the foreskin of their hearts. And yet, as already seen, it is impossible for them to obey the command because of their slavery to sin. Jeremiah makes such a point in 17:9–10 where the heart is said to be "deceitful above all things" and "desperately sick." Therefore, the command given in Jeremiah 4:4 is fulfilled in 31:33 and 32:39–40. As Dearman observes, God promises in Jeremiah 24:7 to give sinners a "new heart," which assumes "the fatal fallibility of the 'old' one!"[61] Therefore, it is presupposed "that Israel must make a radical commitment to God but also that God's people will be unable to fulfill that commitment unless he acts decisively to renew and transform them."[62] Dearman rightly concludes that the command in Jeremiah 4:3–4 "does not assume that a mere act of the will on their part will make everything restored."[63] The law written on their heart is something they were commanded to do but could not do. Therefore, in fulfillment of his own command, Yahweh

---

59. J. G. McConville, *Deuteronomy*, AOTC (Downers Grove, IL: InterVarsity, 2002), 427.

60. Tremper Longman III, *Jeremiah, Lamentations*, NIBC (Peabody, MA: Hendrickson, 2008), 211.

61. Dearman, *Jeremiah*, 85.

62. Ibid.

63. Ibid.

himself must write it on their hearts. Augustine's prayer then is most appropriate, "Give what you command, and command what you will."[64]

Thus, it is far better to interpret these passages in a way similar to that in which other passages are interpreted that speak of a gospel call to all people. As previously discussed, all throughout Scripture a gospel call is given to all people and with it comes the invitation as well as the *command* to turn from sin and trust in God. However, it does not follow that because the command to repent and trust in Christ is given, man has the ability to do so. In fact, he does not, as already seen. The same is true of Deuteronomy 10:16 and Jeremiah 4:4. The command in Deuteronomy 10:16, Ezekiel 18:31, and Jeremiah 4:4 is given, but the text says nothing concerning man's ability or inability to obey such a command. Two conclusions result.

First, by interpreting these passages in light of texts which support man's total depravity and spiritual inability, we must conclude that though man is commanded to change, he is not able to do so. Yahweh makes man's inability especially evident in Jeremiah 13:33 when he asks, "Can the Ethiopian change his skin or the leopard his spots? Then also you can do good who are accustomed to do evil."

Second, in light of the texts above (Deut. 30:6, Jer. 31:33, Ezek. 11:19–21 and 36:26–27), it is clear that God must be the one to execute the spiritual change within the dead sinner. So, though the command is given, only God can fulfill such a command on the sinner's behalf. Therefore, James Hamilton is right when he explains, "Although in Deut. 10:16 the people are commanded to circumcise their hearts, in Deut. 29:4 they are told that Yahweh has not given them hearts to understand, eyes to see, or ears to hear. Then in 30:6 they learn that Yahweh will circumcise their hearts. Like Paul's command to be filled with the Spirit in Eph. 5:18, the command for spiritual circumcision is a call to cry out to God to do for us what we cannot do for ourselves."[65]

---

64. Augustine, *The Confessions*, trans. Maria Boulding, part 1, vol. 1 of *The Works of Saint Augustine: A Translation for the Twenty-first Century*, ed. Boniface Ramsey (New York: New City, 1997), 10.29, 40.

65. Hamilton also makes the interesting point that though the phrase "circumcise yourselves" (ESV, HCSB, NIV, NRSV) is usually translated as a reflexive, it could be translated as a passive, namely, "be circumcised." Hamilton, *God's Indwelling Presence*, 46n82.

THE NEW BIRTH

John 3:3–8

The Context of John 3. Perhaps one of the most well known and important texts on the new birth or regeneration is the account of Jesus' encounter with Nicodemus.

> Jesus answered him, "Truly, truly, I say to you, unless one is born again he cannot see the kingdom of God." Nicodemus said to him, "How can a man be born when he is old? Can he enter a second time into his mother's womb and be born?" Jesus answered, "Truly, truly, I say to you, unless one is born of water and the Spirit, he cannot enter the kingdom of God. That which is born of the flesh is flesh, and that which is born of the Spirit is spirit. Do not marvel that I said to you, 'You must be born again.' The wind blows where it wishes, and you hear its sound, but you do not know where it comes from or where it goes. So it is with everyone who is born of the Spirit." (John 3:3–8)

In order to understand John 3 we must begin with the context of the passage. In John 2 Jesus cleanses the Temple, showing his righteous anger at the defilement of God's house. Such an incident demonstrates the wickedness of the religious leaders, that though they appeared righteous externally, inwardly they were corrupt, leading the people astray. After the cleansing of the Temple, the narrative moves to the Passover Feast in Jerusalem (John 2:23–25). John states that "many believed in his name when they saw the signs that he was doing" (John 2:23). However, what appeared to be belief was mere superficiality. They "believed" because they saw the miracles, but John reveals that Jesus knew what was within them, namely, unbelief and wickedness. Jesus refused to entrust himself to the people because "he knew all people and needed no one to bear witness about man, for he himself knew what was in man" (John 2:25).[66] As John 3 will show, it was not only what was in man (unbelief and wickedness) that troubled Jesus but also what was *not* within man,

---

66. Andreas J. Köstenberger, *John*, BECNT (Grand Rapids: Baker, 2004), 117. Also see Leon Morris, *The Gospel according to John*, NICNT (Grand Rapids: Eerdmans, 1971), 183.

145

namely, a new spirit. In John 3 Jesus will get right to the point with Nicodemus: there is a lack of regeneration by the Spirit.[67]

In John 3:1–2 we first learn that Nicodemus is a Pharisee and a ruler of the Jews who comes to Jesus at night. "Night" is not an insignificant word for John and elsewhere is symbolic for the spiritual darkness in the world (cf. John 9:4; 11:10; 13:30; 21:3). While Nicodemus comes to Jesus at night to find privacy with Jesus, probably trying to avoid the crowds and perhaps even the ridicule of his fellow Pharisees, it is also possible that John may be conveying a spiritual reality by the term, namely, that Nicodemus comes to Jesus (the light of the world) as one who is in spiritual darkness. Such an interpretation fits with John's use of "night" in John 3:2; 9:4; 11:10; and 13:30, where it is meant "metaphorically for moral and spiritual darkness, or, if it refers to the nighttime hours, it bears the same moral and spiritual symbolism."[68] Paul uses "light" and "darkness" as well to convey the miracle of new birth: "For God, who said, 'Let light shine out of darkness,' has shone in our hearts to give the light of the knowledge of the glory of God in the face of Jesus Christ" (2 Cor. 4:6).

Born from Above. Nicodemus begins the dialogue by stating, "Rabbi, we know that you are a teacher come from God, for no one can do these signs that you do unless God is with him" (John 3:2). It may appear that Jesus avoids answering the assertion made by Nicodemus when he responds, "Truly truly, I say to you, unless one is born again he cannot see the kingdom of God" (John 3:3). However, Jesus is simply getting to the heart of the matter, directing Nicodemus's attention to how it is one can know God in a saving way. Nicodemus seems to ask his question wanting an answer, namely, who are you Jesus? The answer Jesus gives shows that the only way one can truly know who God is (and therefore who Jesus is) is by being born again. In other words, Nicodemus will never believe that Jesus is from God (let alone that Jesus is the Son of

---

67. Köstenberger, *John*, 117.
68. D. A. Carson, *The Gospel according to John*, PNTC (Grand Rapids: Eerdmans, 1991), 186.

God) unless he first receives the new birth from the Spirit. Therefore, rather than Jesus telling Nicodemus, "Yes, I am from God," he responds by saying that unless one is born by the Spirit he will never understand who Jesus is in a saving way. As Morris and Carson note, it is not by human reasoning but by spiritual rebirth that one comes to understand Jesus.[69]

The phrase "born again" (γεννηθῇ ἄνωθεν) can also be rendered "born from above."[70] Either translation seems to be textually possible in Greek and conveys the message Jesus is communicating. To render the phrase "from above" indicates where this new birth comes from. The second birth is not one of the earth or of the flesh but rather must come from heaven. Nicodemus took the phrase as "born again," or born a second time, as evidenced in how he is perplexed, wondering how a man can enter a second time into his mother's womb (John 3:4). Therefore, translating the phrase "born again" is appropriate, though "born from above" seems to demonstrate the point that Nicodemus misses: this is not a second natural birth, but rather a supernatural birth which must be accomplished by God and God alone.

Born of the Spirit. Jesus is insistent that if Nicodemus is not born again he will not enter the kingdom of God.[71] In theological language, Jesus is teaching the necessity of the new birth, which leads him also to explain in John 3:5–6 exactly what it means to be born again: "Truly, truly, I say to you, unless one is born of water and the Spirit, he cannot enter the kingdom of God. That which is born of the flesh is flesh, and that which is born of the Spirit is spirit." Jesus says that the birth he speaks of is not one of flesh but of the Spirit (v. 6). If one is born of the Spirit he is spirit. John's use of flesh (*sarx*) here is not the same as Paul's use of

69. Morris, *John*, 189; Carson, *John*, 187–88. The way Jesus answers Nicodemus has huge implications for how we understand the order of salvation. Unless one is first born again he cannot know or believe in Jesus in a saving way.

70. Literally top to bottom. See Köstenberger, *John*, 123.

71. Notice, in 3:3 Jesus says unless a man is born again he cannot "see" the kingdom of God, while in 3:5 Jesus answers that a man cannot "enter" the kingdom of God. Seeing and entering are therefore synonymous.

it to mean the sinful, enslaved nature. Rather, John is referring to flesh as physical flesh. In other words, the contrast is not between sinful flesh and spiritual new life, but between physical birth and spiritual birth or new life.[72] Hence, Nicodemus misunderstands Jesus' words as referring to physical birth. Jesus must clarify for Nicodemus: I am not talking about an earthly birth of human flesh, but of a spiritual birth from above.

Furthermore, this second birth is of "water and the Spirit" (John 3:5). There has been considerable debate over what Jesus means by "water."

(1) Some have argued that water refers to physical birth and would therefore interpret Jesus as saying that not only does one need to be born physically, but one also needs to be born spiritually. However, such an interpretation of water finds little support, and natural birth is not usually designated by the phrase "from water."[73] Moreover, such an interpretation seems to contradict the point Jesus is trying to make, namely, that the birth he speaks of is not physical but spiritual.

(2) Others have argued that Jesus is referring to water baptism.[74] Such a view argues that one is born by the Spirit through the waters of baptism. This view also looks to the sacramental language of John 6 to buttress a sacramental reading in John 3. However, such a view results in baptismal regeneration, which contradicts 1 Peter 3:21. Moreover, if Jesus is referring to water baptism as that which the Spirit uses to effect regeneration, it is very surprising that nowhere else in John's Gospel is the phrase used again. Also, this view contradicts what Jesus says about the Spirit acting like the wind, blowing wherever it wishes. A sacramental reading of water and Spirit, which ties regeneration to water, seems to restrict the Spirit to elements rather than affirm the sovereignty of the Spirit in the new birth. Last, many have doubted that John even has the sacraments in mind in John 6, which, if true, undercuts the baptismal regeneration view altogether.[75]

72. Hoekema, *Saved by Grace*, 98; Morris, *John*, 219.

73. Carson, *John*, 191.

74. Raymond E. Brown, *The Gospel according to John I–XII*, AB, vol. 29 (New York: Doubleday, 1966), 141–44.

75. Carson, *John*, 192.

(3) The best interpretation of "water" is one that identifies it symbolically as that which cleanses the believer.[76] Water is used to represent the spiritual washing that must take place for one to be regenerated.[77] Such an association of water with cleansing is supported in the Old Testament. As already seen, Yahweh promises in Ezekiel 36:25–27, "I will sprinkle clean water on you, and you shall be clean from all your uncleannesses, and from all your idols I will cleanse you. And I will give you a new heart, and a new spirit I will put within you. And I will remove the heart of stone from your flesh and give you a heart of flesh. And I will put my Spirit within you, and cause you to walk in my statutes and be careful to obey my rules" (cf. Exod. 30:20–21; 40:12; Lev. 14:8–9; 15:5–27; Num. 19; 2 Kings 5:10; Ps. 51:2–3; Isa. 1:16; 32:15–20; 44:3–5; Jer. 33:8; Ezek. 11:10–20; 39:29; Zech. 13:1; 14:8; Joel 2:28). Ferguson explains,

> The reference to water is, however, best interpreted in the light of the probable background to this section of Jesus' teaching in the new covenant promise of Ezekiel 36:25–27. . . . In the rest of the passage, Jesus speaks of only one birth, the birth from above (3:3, 6–7). "Water and Spirit" probably refers to the two-fold work of the Spirit in regeneration: he simultaneously gives new life and cleanses the heart.[78]

Water then is coordinate with Spirit, demonstrating, as in Ezekiel 36, the cleansing, purifying nature of the Spirit in regeneration. Such a washing or cleansing is at the very essence of what it means to be born by the Spirit. Schreiner observes,

> The word "rebirth" points to God's creative work in which a person is radically changed, and the word "renewal" signifies the beginning of the new life and the end of the old. The washing is one that signifies new birth and new life. Both the new life and the new birth signified

---

76. Murray, *Redemption Accomplished and Applied*, 98.

77. Ibid., 121–22; Bavinck, *Reformed Dogmatics*, 4:21; Hoekema, *Saved by Grace*, 94.

78. Ferguson, *The Holy Spirit*, 122. Also see Thomas R. Schreiner, *New Testament Theology: Magnifying God in Christ* (Grand Rapids: Baker, 2008), 462–63; Köstenberger, *John*, 123–24.

by the washing come from the Holy Spirit. He is the one who grants new life to believers and cleanses them from sin. Believers are born by the Spirit (Gal. 4:29), so their new life is a miraculous spiritual work.[79]

As Schreiner states, water is used to show the cleansing nature of the Spirit.[80]

Additionally, Jesus places emphasis (as will the rest of the New Testament writers) on the role of the Spirit in new birth. He who is "born of the Spirit is spirit" (John 3:6). In other words, those whom the Holy Spirit regenerates are made spiritual.[81] "Spirit" here must refer to the Holy Spirit (John 3:8; cf. John 1:13; 1 John 2:29; 3:9; 4:7; 5:1, 4, 18), demonstrating that it is a birth of "divine and supernatural character."[82] Such an emphasis on the Spirit does not begin in the New Testament but rather in the promises of the Old Testament. In the context of redemptive history, Yahweh had covenanted with his chosen people Israel. However, unlike Yahweh, Israel was unfaithful, disobeying the law he put in place (Exod. 20) and pursuing the gods of the surrounding nations (Judg. 2:11–15). While all of Israel was God's covenant people, not all within Israel believed. As Paul states, not all Israel is Israel (Rom. 9:6). Therefore, God made a new covenant in which he promised to give his people a new heart and a new spirit so that all of his people will walk in his ways. Unlike the old covenant, in the new covenant Yahweh will regenerate *all* of those with whom he covenants so that all of them will keep his statutes and rules and obey him (Ezek. 11:20). Yahweh declares that he will put his law within them and will write it on their hearts (Jer. 31:33). He will circumcise their hearts so that they will love the Lord with all of their heart and soul and live (Deut. 30:6; cf. Col. 2:11–14). He will give them one heart and put "a new spirit" within them, removing their heart of stone and giving them a heart of flesh (Ezek. 11:19–20).

---

79. Schreiner, *New Testament Theology*, 462–63.

80. It is not uncommon for Jesus in John's Gospel to use water and Spirit interchangeably. Consider John 7:37–39 where Jesus draws from the Old Testament (cf. Isa. 44:3; Ezek. 36:25–27).

81. "That is to say, the person born of the Holy Spirit is indwelt and directed by the Holy Spirit." Murray, *Redemption Accomplished and Applied*, 104.

82. Ibid., 98.

Moreover, he will sprinkle them with clean water, cleansing his people from all their uncleanness, causing them to turn from idols and follow the true and living God (Ezek. 36:25).

Birth Is Monergistic. Before moving into John 3:7–8, it is essential to observe that the language of "birth" in John 3:3–7 precludes the possibility of synergism. The miracle of human birth is a unilateral activity. There is nothing the infant does to be born. The infant does not birth itself. Nor is it the case that birth is conditioned upon the infant's will to accept it or not.

Likewise, the same is true with spiritual birth. Man is dead in his sins and spiritually in bondage to sin. His only hope is the new birth, and yet such a birth is a unilateral, monergistic act of God. Man plays no role whatsoever in the spiritual birthing event. Rather, God acts alone to awaken new life, as demonstrated in the use of the *passive voice*, which tells the reader that the recipient of this new birth is absolutely inactive. Carson writes, "Jesus' reply is not framed in terms of what Nicodemus must do to see the kingdom, but in terms of what must happen to him. The point is made both by the nature of the demanded transformation (a man neither begets nor bears himself) and by the passive mood of the verb."[83] Edwin Palmer explains the birth metaphor,

> In birth a baby is completely helpless. He does not make himself. He is made. He is born. There is complete passivity on his part. Obviously a baby could not have said to his parents before he was born, "I determine that I shall now be born." And so it is in the case of a spiritual birth. That which is not yet born cannot say, "I will to be born." That which is dead spiritually cannot say, "I will to live." And that which has not yet been created can never say, "I will to be created." These are manifest impossibilities. Rather, as in the case of a baby, or creation yet to be, or a dead man, spiritual birth, creation, or life comes wholly at the discretion of the Holy Spirit. It is he who does the deciding, and not man. Man is entirely passive. The Holy

83. D. A. Carson, *Divine Sovereignty and Human Responsibility* (Eugene, OR: Wipf and Stock, 1994), 180. Also see Hoekema, *Saved by Grace*, 97.

Spirit is entirely sovereign, regenerating exactly whom he wills. Consequently, John could say that the children of God are "born not of natural descent, nor of human decision or a husband's will, but born of God" (John 1:13).[84]

John Murray is just as insightful,

We are as dependent upon the Holy Spirit as we are upon the action of our parents in connection with our natural birth. We were not begotten by our father because we decided to be. And we were not born of our mother because we decided to be. We were simply begotten and we were born. We did not decide to be born. This is the simple but too frequently overlooked truth which our Lord here teaches us. We do not have spiritual perception of the kingdom of God nor do we enter into it because we will to or decided to. If this privilege is ours it is because the Holy Spirit willed it and here all rests upon the Holy Spirit's decision and action. He begets or bears when and where he pleases. Is this not the burden of verse 8? Jesus there compares the action of the Spirit to the action of the wind. The wind blows—this serves to illustrate the factuality, the certainty, the efficacy of the Spirit's action. The wind blows where it wills—this enforces the sovereignty of the Spirit's action. The wind is not at our beck and call; neither is the regenerate operation of the Spirit. "Thou canst not tell whence it cometh, and whither it goeth"—the Spirit's work is mysterious. All points up the sovereignty, efficacy, and inscrutability of the Holy Spirit's work in regeneration.[85]

In John 3:3–7 there is not a hint of indication that the new birth has anything to do with the human will. To the contrary, Jesus is emphasiz-

84. Edwin H. Palmer, *The Person and Ministry of the Holy Spirit: The Traditional Calvinistic Perspective* (Grand Rapids: Baker, 1974), 82–83. Also see Boettner, *Reformed Doctrine of Predestination*, 165–66; Owen, *A Display of Arminianism*, 10:136–37; Turretin, *Institutes*, 2:544; Van Mastricht, *Regeneration*, 37; John Murray, "Regeneration," in *Collected Writings of John Murray* (Edinburgh: Banner of Truth, 1976), 2:167–201; Ferguson, *The Holy Spirit*, 123; Schreiner, *New Testament Theology*, 463; Köstenberger, *John*, 124–25; J. I. Packer, "Regeneration," in *Evangelical Dictionary of Theology*, ed. Walter A. Elwell (Grand Rapids: Baker, 2001), 925.

85. Murray, *Redemption Accomplished and Applied*, 99. Also see John M. Frame, *Salvation Belongs to the Lord* (Phillipsburg, NJ: P&R Publishing, 2006), 186.

ing, through the image of birth, the passivity and inability of the sinner and the autonomy of God in creating new life. As Packer states, "Infants do not induce, or cooperate in, their own procreation and birth; no more can those who are 'dead in trespasses and sins' prompt the quickening operation of God's Spirit within them (see Eph. 2:1–10)."[86] This same principle of monergism is again taught by Jesus as he further explains the role of the Spirit in John 3:7–8.

The Sovereignty of the Spirit. In John 3:7–8 Jesus turns to the sovereignty of the Spirit in regeneration. Already Jesus has indicated that one must be born of water and Spirit (John 3:5), demonstrating that the new birth is effected by the power of the Spirit.[87] Two points demonstrate the sovereignty of the Spirit.

First, in 3:1–8 the new birth is described in the passive voice and it is justified to conclude that here we see examples of the divine passive being used. Hamilton explains that "this new birth is not something that people do to or for themselves. Each time the verb *gennaō* appears in John 3:3–8 it is passive (3:3, 4 [2x], 5, 6 [2x], 7, 8). John 1:13 ('born of God') provides clear warrant for seeing these as divine passives. God causes people to experience the new birth from above by the Spirit."[88] Hamilton continues, "The need for new birth is connected to another clear feature in this passage: the stress on human inability to experience God's kingdom apart from this new birth. The word *dunamai* appears five times in 3:2–5 and again in verse 9. The new birth is brought about by God, and without it people are unable to see/enter the kingdom of God."[89] In summary, the sovereignty of the Spirit is demonstrated by both the presence of the divine passive and the emphasis Jesus places on human inability.

Second, the sovereignty of the Spirit is manifested in how Jesus compares the Spirit to the wind. Jesus states, "Do not marvel that I said

---

86. J. I. Packer, "Regeneration," 925. Also see idem, "Call, Called, Calling," in *Baker's Dictionary of Theology*, ed. Everett F. Harrison (Grand Rapids: Baker, 1973), 184.

87. Hoekema, *Saved by Grace*, 97–98.

88. Hamilton, *God's Indwelling Presence*, 130.

89. Ibid.

to you, 'You *[plural]* must be born again.' The wind [spirit] blows where it wishes, and you hear its sound, but you do not know where it comes from or where it goes. So it is with everyone who is born of the Spirit." In the Greek the word for Spirit (πνεῦμα) is also wind and likewise the word for wind is also spirit. Jesus is drawing a clear parallel here between wind and Spirit (as made obvious by John 3:8), so that when he speaks of one he is speaking of the other.[90] He is comparing the effects of the wind to the effects of the Spirit. It is very important to note that the phrase the "wind blows where it wishes" conveys the sovereignty of the Spirit. The Spirit is not controlled by the human will but works as God pleases to bring about new life. As Hoekema states, "The action of the Spirit in regenerating people is as sovereign as the wind which blows wherever it pleases."[91] Therefore, a regeneration dependent upon man's will to believe or a regeneration where God and man cooperate is ruled out by this text.

As Schreiner says, the Spirit's role in the new birth is sovereign because, like the wind, he works apart from human control (John 3:8). "The Spirit grants new life sovereignly and unexpectedly, producing new life where humans least expect it to occur. New life comes not from human effort or human accomplishment but from the miraculous work of God's Spirit."[92] Berkhof also puts the matter acutely,

> The only adequate view is that of the Church of all ages, that the Holy Spirit is the efficient cause of regeneration. This means that the Holy Spirit works directly on the heart of man and changes its spiritual condition. There is no co-operation of the sinner in this work whatsoever. It is the work of the Holy Spirit directly and exclusively, Ezek. 11:19; John 1:13; Acts 16:14; Rom. 9:16; Phil. 2:13. Regeneration, then, is to be conceived monergistically. God alone works, and the sinner has no part in it whatsoever.[93]

90. Herman Ridderbos, *The Gospel according to John*, trans. J. Vriend (Grand Rapids: Eerdmans, 1997), 129.

91. Hoekema, *Saved by Grace*, 98.

92. Schreiner, *New Testament Theology*, 463. Also see Palmer, *Holy Spirit*, 82–83.

93. Berkhof, *Systematic Theology*, 473.

Likewise, Ferguson states,

> The New Testament's statements on regeneration emphasize the sovereign, monergistic, activity of the Spirit. The metaphor of birth itself implies not only a radical new beginning, but one which is never autonomous. The divine monergism behind it is spelled out elsewhere in antitheses: we are born, not of our own will, but of God's decision (John 1:12); from above, not from below; of the Spirit, not of the flesh (John 3:3, 5–6); of God, not of man (1 John 2:29; 3:9; 4:7; 5:1, 4, 18); by God's choice, not our own; through his word, not out of the energies of an autonomous will (James 1:18). The priority here is accorded to God, not to man. The reason for this is that man is "flesh."[94]

Similarly, Hamilton also explains how the Spirit's will, not man's will, is decisive:

> The new birth from above is a "second birth" (see 3:4–5). The stress on ability (five uses of *dunamai* in vv. 2–5) suggests that the new birth brings a new ability. Regeneration, then, involves the Spirit *enabling* people to believe. Being "born of God" (1:13) and being "born of the Spirit" (3:6) in John's Gospel are equivalent. As in John 1:11–13, the new birth in John 3 is for those who "receive" what Jesus says (3:11) and "believe" Him (3:12). No one is able to believe Jesus, however, unless God draws that person to Jesus (6:44, 65), and the Spirit is like the wind, which "blows where it wishes" (3:8). Those to whom the Spirit is pleased to give new birth (3:6) are those whom the Father draws to Jesus (6:44), and they believe Him not because of human will, but because they have been born of God (1:12–13).[95]

Berkhof, Schreiner, Ferguson, and Hamilton all agree: Jesus emphasizes the sovereignty of the Spirit in producing the new birth apart from the will of man. As we will later see, the rest of the New Testament also

---

94. Ferguson, *The Holy Spirit*, 119.

95. Hamilton, *God's Indwelling Presence*, 131. On being "born of God" (1:13) and being "born of the Spirit" (3:6) as being equivalent, see J. H. Bernard, *The Gospel according to St. John*, ICC (Edinburgh: T&T Clark, 1928), 1:105; Carson, *John*, 189.

testifies to the sovereignty of God in the new birth. Old and New Testament authors alike use many other biblical analogies to demonstrate the sovereignty of the Spirit, including: circumcising the heart (Deut. 30:6; Jer. 31:31–34); writing the law on the heart (Jer. 31:31–34); removing the heart of stone and replacing it with a heart of flesh (Ezek. 11:19; 36:26; cf. Jer. 24:7); breathing new life into dead dry bones (Ezek. 37); shining light out of darkness and the very act of creation itself (2 Cor. 4:6 and 5:17); creating man anew (2 Cor. 5:17); the resurrection of a spiritually dead corpse (Rom. 6:4; Eph. 2:1; 1 Peter 1:3); and washing and renewing (Titus 3:4–7).[96] Turretin observes that all of these "imply the invincible and supreme power of God."[97] Therefore, to conclude that man in some way cooperates with God in regeneration (synergism) or that man's will (*liberum arbitrium*) in the act of faith is the cause of regeneration, so that conversion causally precedes regeneration, is an assault on the sovereignty of the Holy Spirit and furthermore denies the proper meaning of the biblical images used to speak of the Spirit's work in regeneration.[98] Murray states, "It should be specially noted that even faith that Jesus is the Christ is the effect of regeneration. This is, of course, a clear implication of John 3:3–8. . . . We are not born again by faith or repentance or conversion; we repent and believe because we have been regenerated."[99] Reymond agrees: "Regeneration is essential to faith as the latter's causal prius."[100]

To conclude our discussion of John 3, we should say that to reject what Jesus is teaching in these verses about man's passivity and God's sovereignty is no light matter. John Murray appropriately warns of the seriousness of interpreting Jesus wrongly here:

> It has often been said that we are passive in regeneration. This is a
> true and proper statement. For it is simply the precipitate of what

96. John M. Frame, *The Doctrine of God*, A Theology of Lordship (Phillipsburg, NJ: P&R Publishing, 2002), 75.

97. Turretin, *Institutes*, 2:532.

98. Murray, "Regeneration," 183–84; Douglas F. Kelly, *Systematic Theology*, vol. 1, *Grounded in Holy Scripture and Understood in Light of the Church* (Fearn, Ross-shire, Great Britain: Christian Focus, 2008), 1:340ff.

99. Murray, *Redemption Accomplished and Applied*, 103.

100. Reymond, *New Systematic Theology*, 709.

156

our Lord has taught us here. We may not like it. We may recoil against it. It may not fit into our way of thinking and it may not accord with the time-worn expressions which are the coin of our evangelism. But if we recoil against it, we do well to remember that this recoil is recoil against Christ. And what shall we answer when we appear before him whose truth we rejected and with whose gospel we tampered? But blessed be God that the gospel of Christ is one of sovereign, efficacious, irresistible regeneration. If it were not the case that in regeneration we are passive, the subjects of an action of which God alone is the agent, there would be no gospel at all. For unless God by sovereign, operative grace had turned our enmity to love and our disbelief to faith we would never yield the response of faith and love.[101]

John 1:12–13 and 1 John 2:29; 3:9; 4:7; 5:1, 4, 18

1 John 5:1. Just as the gospel of John teaches that the grace that regenerates is monergistic, preceding man's faith, so also in John's first epistle is the same truth evident. Consider the following, with special attention to the grammatical construction:

> If you know that he is righteous, you may be sure that everyone who practices righteousness *has been* born of him. (1 John 2:29)

> No one born of God makes a practice of sinning, for God's seed abides in him, and he cannot keep on sinning because he *has been* born of God. (1 John 3:9)

> Beloved, let us love one another, for love is from God, and whoever loves *has been* born of God and knows God. (1 John 4:7)

> Everyone who believes that Jesus is the Christ *has been* born of God, and everyone who loves the Father loves whoever has been born of him. (1 John 5:1)

101. Murray, *Redemption Accomplished and Applied*, 99.

For everyone who *has been* born of God overcomes the world. And
this is the victory that has overcome the world—our faith. Who is
it that overcomes the world except the one who believes that Jesus is
the Son of God? (1 John 5:4)

We know that everyone who *has been* born of God does not keep on
sinning, but he who was born of God protects him and the evil one
does not touch him. (1 John 5:18)

The grammar in each of these passages is absolutely essential. Beginning
with 1 John 5:1, which Piper calls "the clearest text in the New Testament
on the relationship between faith and the new birth,"[102] the Greek reads,
Πᾶς ὁ πιστεύων ὅτι Ἰησοῦς ἐστιν ὁ Χριστὸς ἐκ τοῦ θεοῦ γεγέννηται, καὶ
πᾶς ὁ ἀγαπῶν τὸν γεννήσαντα ἀγαπᾷ [καὶ] τὸν γεγεννημένον ἐξ αὐτοῦ.
Notice, "believes" (πιστεύων) in the phrase "Everyone who believes" (or
"Everyone believing") is a present active participle in the nominative
case, indicating ongoing faith.[103] In contrast, when John says all those
believing "*have been* born of him," "have been born" (θεοῦ γεγέννηται)
is in the perfect passive indicative, meaning that it is an action that has
already taken place in the past (it is completed) and has ongoing effects
in the present. As Daniel Wallace explains, the perfect speaks "of an
event accomplished in the past (in the indicative mood, that is) with
results existing afterwards—the perfect speaking of results existing in
the present."[104] In 1 John 5:1, the action in the perfect passive indica-

102. John Piper, *Finally Alive* (Fearn, Ross-shire, Great Britain: Christian Focus, 2009), 118;
also see 138–39. It could be objected from the outset that the logical priority of regeneration to
faith in 1 John is unfounded because John never had this debate over the *ordo salutis* in mind.
As Burdick writes, "This verse is not written to prove either the Calvinistic or the Arminian
ordo salutis." Donald W. Burdick, *Letters of John the Apostle* (Chicago: Moody, 1985), 358.
However, as Snoeberger comments, "Admittedly, the present argument was probably not filling
John's mind as he penned these words; however, it does not follow that he is indifferent toward
the issue. Two factors, namely, the syntax and the purpose for writing, militate against such
a conclusion." Snoeberger, "Logical Priority of Regeneration," 82.
103. On the use of the participle, see Daniel B. Wallace, *Greek Grammar: An Exegetical
Syntax of the New Testament* (Grand Rapids: Zondervan, 1996), 613ff.
104. See Wallace, *Greek Grammar*, 572–73; M. Zerwick, *Biblical Greek Illustrated by
Examples* (Rome: Pontificii Instituti Biblici, 1963), 96; William D. Mounce, *Basics of Biblical
Greek Grammar* (Grand Rapids: Zondervan, 2003), 225. John is not using the perfect tense

tive (regeneration) precedes and causes the action in the present active participle (faith). The result is clear: God's act of regeneration precedes belief.[105] As John Stott explains,

> The combination of the present tense (believes) and perfect tense [has been born] is important. It shows clearly that believing is the consequence, not the cause, of the new birth. Our present, continuing activity of believing is the result, and therefore, the evidence, of our past experience of new birth by which we became and remain God's children.[106]

The implication, therefore, is that it is God's act of regeneration that creates the faith man needs to believe. Peterson and Williams similarly conclude,

> The perfect-tense verb in 1 John 5:1, "has been born," indicates that the new birth is the cause of faith in Christ, even as the new birth is the cause of godliness and love in the passages cited above [1 John 2:29; 3:9; 4:7; 5:18]. As a result of God's grace in regeneration, all those who have been born of God believe savingly in the Son of God.[107]

Likewise, Robert Yarbrough states, "In Johannine theology, spiritual rebirth seems to precede and ultimately create faith: those who believe do so not so much as the result of human volition as of prior divine intention (cf. John 1:12–13)."[108]

---

randomly or without intention. As Moulton observes, the perfect tense is "the most important, exegetically, of all the Greek Tenses," and as Wallace observes, "when it is used, there is usually a deliberate choice on the part of the writer." J. H. Moulton, *A Grammar of New Testament Greek*, 2 vols. (Edinburgh: T&T Clark, 1908), 1:140.

105. Bruce A. Ware, "Divine Election to Salvation," in *Perspectives on Election: Five Views*, ed. Chad Owen Brand (Nashville: B&H Publishing Group, 2006), 20.

106. John Stott, *The Letters of John* (Grand Rapids: Eerdmans, 1988), 175. Also see White on this issue in Dave Hunt and James White, *Debating Calvinism: Five Points, Two Views* (Sisters, OR: Multnomah, 2004), 198–201.

107. Robert A. Peterson and Michael D. Williams, *Why I Am Not an Arminian* (Downers Grove, IL: InterVarsity, 2004), 189. Also see Hoekema, *Saved by Grace*, 100–101.

108. Robert W. Yarbrough, *1–3 John*, BECNT (Grand Rapids: Baker, 2008), 270.

It should be noted that in regard to 1 John 5:1, the New International Version (NIV) should not be followed. The English Standard Version (ESV) correctly translates the perfect verb as a perfect, but the NIV translates the perfect as if it were a present tense verb.[109] "Everyone who believes that Jesus is the Christ *is born* of God," could be taken to mean that one's faith produces or results in regeneration. Strangely, the NIV translates the same perfect in 1 John 2:29; 3:9; 4:7; and 5:4 as a perfect tense verb ("*has been* born").[110] Why the NIV is inconsistent when it comes to 1 John 5:1 is unclear, but it gives the impression that faith precedes regeneration when that is not in fact the case.

1 John 2:29. As seen above, the use of the perfect in 1 John 5:1 can also be found in 1 John 2:29; 3:9; 4:7; and 5:4. In 1 John 2:29 the Greek reads, ἐὰν εἰδῆτε ὅτι δίκαιός ἐστιν, γινώσκετε ὅτι καὶ πᾶς ὁ ποιῶν τὴν δικαιοσύνην ἐξ αὐτοῦ γεγέννηται. Those who are doing righteousness *have been born of God* (γεγέννηται). The grammar here is parallel to 1 John 5:1. The phrase "*have been* born of him" is a perfect passive indicative (from γεννάω, to beget or bring forth), while the phrase "everyone who practices righteousness" (πᾶς ὁ ποιῶν τὴν δικαιοσύνην) is a present active participle. Again, the perfect here refers to the new birth, an act that has been completed in the past and has continuing results in the present. Practicing righteous (present tense) is what results from the new birth. Or as Stott says, "A person's righteousness is thus the evidence of his new birth, not the cause or condition of it."[111] Similarly, Murray states, "In 2:29, we must infer, that the reason why the person in view does righteousness is that he is begotten of God."[112] To interpret 1 John 2:29 as if regeneration came after faith would mean that one's own righteousness

---

109. Peterson and Williams, *Why I Am Not an Arminian*, 188.

110. Unfortunately, the New American Standard Bible (NASB) makes the same mistake as the NIV in 1 John 5:1. However, unlike the NIV the NASB continues to make this mistake not only with 5:1 but with 2:29; 3:9; 4:7; and 5:4; as well. Again, the ESV is far superior at this point.

111. Stott, *Letters of John*, 122. Also see Gary M. Burge, *The Letters of John*, NIVAC (Grand Rapids: Zondervan, 1996), 145.

112. Murray, *Redemption Accomplished and Applied*, 102. Also see Frame, *Salvation Belongs to the Lord*, 186.

would precede regeneration. This interpretation would evidently teach works righteousness. Ware explains,

> The perfect tense normally indicates past action that continues into the present. So John is saying that the person who has been and is born again is like this: he does what is right. That is, being born again accounts for doing right. This surely means that the new birth precedes a righteous life; otherwise John would be teaching works-righteousness (i.e., doing "what is right" accounting for being born again)! No, rather, regeneration accounts for the "right" sort of actions and behavior of which John speaks.[113]

We must observe that Arminians find themselves faced with a number of contradictions at this point. For example, concerning 1 John 2:29 I. Howard Marshall agrees that practicing righteousness is the result of the new birth and not the other way around. "What John is trying to stress is that doing what is right is the consequence of spiritual birth; hence if a person does what is right, this is a sign of spiritual birth." And again, "True righteousness (the kind shown by Jesus) is possible only on the basis of spiritual birth."[114] When Marshall comes to 1 John 5:1 he begins as he did in 2:29 by saying, "Faith is thus a sign of the new birth, just as love (4:7) and doing what is right (2:29; 3:9) are also indications that a person has been born of God."[115] Marshall sounds like a Calvinist. It is obvious even to Marshall that in 1 John 2:29; 3:9; and 4:7 doing righteousness, avoiding sin, and loving are all the result of the new birth. One would then expect Marshall to say the same about 1 John 5:1. After all, 5:1 has the same grammatical structure as 2:29; 3:9; and 4:7. Moreover, Marshall begins his commentary on 5:1 in this direction when he says, "Faith is thus a sign of the new birth," just like love and doing righteousness. However, Marshall immediately qualifies such a statement by saying,

113. Ware, "Divine Election to Salvation," 19.
114. I. Howard Marshall, *The Epistles of John*, NICNT (Grand Rapids: Eerdmans, 1978), 169.
115. Ibid., 226.

> At the same time, however, faith is a condition of the new birth: "to all who received him, to those who believed in his name, he gave the right to become children of God" (John 1:12). Here, however, John is not trying to show how a person experiences the new birth; his aim is rather to indicate the evidence which shows that a person stands in the continuing relationship of a child to God his Father: that evidence is that he holds to the true faith about Jesus.[116]

Marshall's logic seems to contradict itself. He begins by saying that faith is a sign of the new birth, but then he says that faith is a condition of the new birth. It is clear that for Marshall, saying faith is a sign of the new birth is not the same as saying that faith is caused by the new birth and only the result of the new birth. For Marshall, regeneration cannot occur without man having faith first. Consequent to regeneration, faith continues, and so Marshall can simultaneously say that faith is the condition of the new birth and yet faith is the sign of the new birth, as shown in 1 John 5:1.[117] Two responses are in order.

First, Marshall would never apply his exegesis of 1 John 5:1 to 2:29 ("everyone who practices righteousness has been born of him"). Why not? Because it would imply works righteousness! If Marshall were to be consistent he would have to apply the same hermeneutic to 1 John 2:29 that he does in 5:1 and it would sound like this:

> Righteousness is thus a sign of the new birth, just as love (4:7) and doing what is right (3:9f.) are also indications that a person has been born of God. At the same time, however, righteousness is a condition of the new birth . . .

Notice how closely this parallels his comment on 5:1,

> Faith is thus a sign of the new birth, just as love (4:7) and doing what is right (2:29; 3:9f) are also indications that a person has

---

116. Ibid.

117. Smalley makes the same move that Marshall does. Stephen S. Smalley, *1, 2, 3 John*, WBC, vol. 51 (Dallas: Word, 1984), 266–67.

been born of God. At the same time, however, faith is a condition of the new birth . . .[118]

It is astonishing that it can be so obvious to Marshall that in 1 John 2:29 righteousness could never be the condition of regeneration, but in 1 John 5:1, a verse with the same grammatical structure, faith can be the condition of regeneration. In the end, Marshall refuses to apply the same method of exegesis he uses in 2:29; 3:9; and 4:7 to 5:1. Why? Evidently because to do so would mean that faith precedes regeneration and is caused by regeneration, a conclusion unacceptable to an Arminian like Marshall. Therefore, instead, Marshall has allowed his Arminian presuppositions to alter the plain meaning of the text.

Second, Marshall not only is inconsistent in his exegesis, but he also completely ignores the grammar of the text in 1 John 5:1. Marshall's statements in 2:29; 3:9; and 4:7 seem to demonstrate (though he never says it explicitly) that he has knowledge of the fact that a perfect passive is being used in the phrase "have been born of God." However, when Marshall comes to 5:1 he ignores the grammar altogether and actually interprets 5:1 as saying that faith is the condition of regeneration, which is the exact opposite of what the text says grammatically—that is, that regeneration (perfect passive indicative) results in faith (present active participle). This negligence of the grammatical structure is poor exegesis on Marshall's part.

John 1:12–13. Marshall, however, not only misconstrues the meaning of 1 John 5:1, but he does so by jumping over the plain meaning of 5:1 in order to appeal to John 1:12. John 1:12–13 reads, "But to all who did receive him, who believed in his name, he gave the right to become children of God, who were born, not of blood nor of the will of the flesh nor of the will of man, but of God." It must be observed that such a move gives the reader the impression that Marshall does not want to deal with what 1 John 5:1 actually says on its own terms, but rather that he wants to allow *his* interpretation of

118. Marshall, *The Epistles of John*, 226.

John 1:12 to be the key factor in providing an alternative interpretation to 1 John 5:1.[119]

Furthermore, Marshall's appeal to John 1:12 is unfounded precisely because John 1:12–13 actually proves the opposite of what Marshall wants it to say. Marshall believes that John 1:12 proves that faith is the condition of regeneration, for the text says that to all who received Jesus, who believed in him (had faith), God gave the right to become children of God.[120] There are several problems with Marshall's interpretation here.

First, Marshall assumes that the phrase "become children of God" is synonymous with "new birth."[121] However, Marshall never shows evidence that this is the case. Why should the reader assume that the phrase "become children of God" is synonymous with the new birth? Why not interpret becoming a child of God as the result of the new birth? Why not interpret the phrase as referring to adoption, which is produced by the new birth? Indeed, for several reasons I would argue that the phrase "become children of God" is referring to adoption, not regeneration.

(1) The phrase "children of God" in John 1:12 is also used by Paul in Romans 8:15–16 to refer to adoption, not regeneration. Paul writes, "For you did not receive the spirit of slavery to fall back into fear, but you have received the Spirit of adoption as sons, by whom we cry, 'Abba! Father!' The Spirit himself bears witness with our spirit that we are children of God" (Rom. 8:15–16; cf. Eph. 1:5). Paul's language

119. To clarify, I am not saying that it is unjustified to appeal to other texts (especially by the same author in this case) in order to interpret properly. This would be to deny the analogy of Scripture, which I do not. However, in Marshall's case, it seems as if his appeal to John 1:12 is so that he does not have to interpret 5:1 as he already did interpret 2:29, 3:9, and 4:7. Moreover, as will be seen above, even in Marshall's appeal to John 1:12 his bias becomes evident when he only quotes verse 12 and ignores verse 13, which has much to say concerning his interpretation. On appealing to the gospel of John to interpret 1 John see Colin G. Kruse, *The Letters of John*, PNTC (Grand Rapids: Eerdmans, 2000), 157.

120. Also Barrett, "This birth is conditional upon receiving Christ and believing on his name." C. K. Barrett, *The Gospel according to St. John* (Philadelphia: Westminster, 1978), 137. Contra H. J. Holtzmann, *Lehrbuch der neutestamentlichen Theologie* (Tübingen: n.p., 1911), 2:534; Morris, *John*, 101; Barnabas Lindars, "The Fourth Gospel an Act of Contemplation," in *Studies in the Fourth Gospel*, ed. F. L. Cross (London: A. R. Mowbray, 1957), 27.

121. Likewise Kruse, *The Letters of John*, 124.

of adoption is again reiterated when he says in Galatians 3:26, "For in Christ Jesus you are all sons of God, through faith" (cf. Gal. 4:5). As a consequence to believing (John 1:12) or having faith (Gal. 3:26), one is adopted into God's family as a son.[122]

(2) Adoption, as Snoeberger observes, is emptied of meaning "if the regeneration has already placed the believer into the family of God and given him all the privileges of heirs."[123]

(3) Many scholars agree that the phrase "become children of God" in John 1:12 is a reference to adoption, not regeneration.[124]

Second, in order to argue that the phrase "become children of God" is referring to the new birth or regeneration,[125] one must take a leap that is not warranted by the text and assume that the text reads that one becomes a child of God because he believes. However, the text of John 1:12 does not make such a causal correlation. As Ware explains,

> Notice that John does not say, "He gave them the right to be children of God because they believed in His name." Rather, he merely notes that these two things both happen: they are given the right to be children of God, and they believe in his name. What he does not say in verse 12 is that becoming children of God results from their faith.[126]

Michaels makes a similar observation between "believing" in verse 12 and being born again in verse 13.

122. It is also important to keep in mind that while those who believe are adopted by God here and now, adoption is also a future hope and reality, something which cannot also be said of regeneration, which is a one-time event at initiation. Paul states in Rom. 8:23 that we who have the firstfruits of the Spirit groan inwardly as "we wait eagerly for adoption as sons, the redemption of our bodies." See Thomas R. Schreiner and Ardel B. Caneday, *The Race Set Before Us: A Biblical Theology of Perseverance and Assurance* (Downers Grove, IL: InterVarsity, 2001), 68.

123. Snoeberger, "Regeneration," 77–78.

124. Ibid., 78. Also see Carson, *John*, 126; Ridderbos, *John*, 45; John Calvin, *The Gospel according to St. John*, trans. T. H. L. Parker (Grand Rapids: Eerdmans, 1959), 1:17; Murray, *Redemption Accomplished and Applied*, 81, 87, 132–34; Hoekema, *Saved by Grace*, 96, 185–87; Wayne Grudem, *Systematic Theology* (Grand Rapids: Zondervan, 1994), 738; Reymond, *New Systematic Theology*, 759.

125. Ridderbos, *John*, 45–46.

126. Ware, "Divine Election to Salvation," 20. Also see J. Ramsey Michaels, *The Gospel of John*, NICNT (Grand Rapids: Eerdmans, 2010), 69.

It is important to notice here what is *not* said. The text defines no temporal or causal relationship between "believing" and being "born of God," either to the effect that individuals are born of God *because* they believe [contra Bultmann], or that they believe because they are *already* born of God.[127]

In fact, causal language does not come into view until verse 13, which actually prohibits the new birth being conditioned on man's free will.

Third, we cannot ignore verse 13, which reads, "who were born, not of blood nor of the will of the flesh nor of the will of man, but of God." Why does Marshall not quote verse 13? Could it be that verse 13 actually would prohibit his interpretation of verse 12? Anthony Hoekema exposes such a textual bias:

> Arminian theologians often quote verse 12 to prove that faith must precede regeneration: "To those who believed in his name he gave the right to become children of God." But we must not separate verse 12 from verse 13. The latter verse tells us that being children of God is not the result of natural descent or human decision, but of divine activity alone. It is, of course, true that those who believed in Christ did receive the right to become children of God—but behind their faith was the miraculous deed of God whereby they were spiritually reborn. They were born not of man but of God.[128]

Verse 13 actually clarifies and qualifies verse 12, stating, "who were born, not of blood nor of the will of the flesh nor of the will of man, but of God." In other words, being born is in no way due to the "will of man." Since the will of man is involved in faith, there is no way that faith could precede being born again.[129]

Thus, John makes it clear that the new birth is *not* conditioned upon man's will, but is completely and only the act of God. Ware is right when

127. Michaels, *John*, 71.
128. Hoekema, *Saved by Grace*, 96.
129. Snoeberger, "Logical Priority of Regeneration," 80, expresses this point in the following syllogism: A: No act of the human will can inaugurate regeneration. B: Faith is an act of human will. C: Therefore, faith cannot inaugurate regeneration.

he states, "What accounts for them having the right to be God's children, and what accounts for their believing in Christ's name, is that they had been born of God."[130] Robert Reymond also comments on John 1:13,

> By this particular reference to God's "begetting" activity John refers to regeneration, and clearly suggests by his statement that, while faith is the instrumental precondition to justification and adoption, regeneration is the necessary precondition and efficient cause of faith in Jesus Christ. In short, regeneration causally precedes faith.[131]

Herman Ridderbos is just as adamant,

> However, against this [the interpretation of John 1:12–13 which views faith as preceding regeneration] it has to be asserted that the concluding statement in v. 13 traces the entire gift of being a child of God, including the manner in which it is effected, to its deepest ground: "procreation" by God. The idea that faith as a human choice should precede that birth and therefore that in some sense a person should have this rebirth of God at his or her disposal not only seems absurd but is also at variance with statements like this in 1 John 5:1: "Everyone who believes . . . is born of God." By saying this one does not in any way detract from the call and invitation to believe so emphatically issued in John's Gospel, a call addressed to all without distinction.[132]

Therefore, when Marshall concludes from verse 12 that regeneration is conditioned upon man's faith, he does so in direct conflict with the rest of the sentence in verse 13, where John is clear that the new birth is in no way conditioned upon man.[133]

1 John 3:9. The same grammar and logic that appear in 1 John 2:29 also apply to 1 John 3:9: "No one born of God [Πᾶς ὁ γεγεννημένος

130. Ware, "Divine Election to Salvation," 20. Also see Snoeberger, "Logical Priority of Regeneration," 80.
131. Reymond, *New Systematic Theology*, 708.
132. Ridderbos, *John*, 47.
133. See Carson, *Divine Sovereignty*, 182.

ἐκ τοῦ θεοῦ; perfect passive participle] makes a practice of sinning, for God's seed abides in him, and he cannot keep on sinning [οὐ δύναται ἁμαρτάνειν; present active infinitive] because he *has been* born of God [θεοῦ γεγέννηται; perfect passive indicative]." 1 John 3:9 is very similar to 1 John 5:18: "We know that everyone who has been born of God does not keep on sinning, but he who was born of God protects him, and the evil one does not touch him." If the Arminian view of 1 John 3:9 and 5:18 is affirmed, the sinner would be expected to not make a practice of sinning so that he may be born again. The text, however, never warrants this. Instead, the believer is not to make a practice of sinning because he *has been born of God* and consequently "God's seed abides in him."

Once again, as in 1 John 5:1 and 2:29, we see the same grammatical structure. The perfect verb (has been born of God) is what grounds and results in the present active infinitive (makes a practice of sinning). The point then is that it is *because* one has been born again that he does not make a practice of sinning. As John Murray concludes, "He does not sin because God's seed abides in him. Now this abiding seed alludes clearly to the divine impartation which took place in the divine begetting. It is this divine begetting with its abiding consequence that is the *cause* of not doing sin. Hence regeneration is logically and causally prior to the not doing sin."[134]

1 John 4:7. In 1 John 4:7 we also see the priority of the new birth: "Beloved, let us love one another, for love is from God, and whoever loves *has been* born of God and knows God" (Ἀγαπητοί, ἀγαπῶμεν ἀλλήλους, ὅτι ἡ ἀγάπη ἐκ τοῦ θεοῦ ἐστιν, καὶ πᾶς ὁ ἀγαπῶν ἐκ τοῦ θεοῦ γεγέννηται καὶ γινώσκει τὸν θεόν.). Loving (ὁ ἀγαπῶν; present active participle) is the result of having been born of God (θεοῦ γεγέννηται; perfect passive indicative).[135] Love is from God and until God regenerates the dead heart, the sinner cannot love God or neighbor. Therefore, "Whoever loves has been born of God and knows God" (4:7). As John states in 1 John 4:19, "We love because he first loved us." John does not say, "He

134. Murray, *Redemption Accomplished and Applied*, 101.
135. Burge, *The Letters of John*, 186; Smalley, *1, 2, 3 John*, 238.

loves us because we first loved him." Rather, it is God's love that precedes the sinner's, and it is God's love which enables and produces the sinner's faith, evidenced in love for God and neighbor.[136]

This same truth is affirmed in 1 John 5:1 where John states that not only is belief in Jesus the result of being born of God, but so also is love for the Father, who has sent his only Son. Again, love for the Father and the Son is caused by the new birth. But notice, 1 John 4:7 not only says that regeneration precedes love, but also that it precedes saving knowledge of God. John states that "whoever loves has been born of God and *knows God*." "Knows" is not referring to pure cognitive, factual data of God's existence and acts in the world. Rather, "knows," like love, is tied to saving faith. To have saving faith in God is to know God personally. To know God is to have saving faith in God. Again, we must conclude that saving knowledge of God is the result of God regenerating the believer, not the other way around.

1 John 5:4, 18. This is another text that supports the Reformed view. John states, "For everyone who has been born of God [γεγεννημένον ἐκ τοῦ θεοῦ; perfect passive participle] overcomes the world [νικᾷ τὸν κόσμον; present active indicative]. And this is the victory that has overcome the world—our faith." What is John referring to when he says that we overcome the world? John is clear in the very next sentence: "And this is the victory that has overcome the world—our faith." So it is faith that overcomes the world, and John goes on to say that such faith that overcomes is faith that "believes that Jesus is the Son of God." Again, saving faith is the result of being born of God. Just as righteousness, rejecting sin, and loving God are the result of being born of God, so also is having faith which overcomes the world. To reverse this order, as Arminians so often do, is to teach works righteousness. How unorthodox it would be to say that being righteous (1 John 2:29), resisting sin (1 John 3:9), loving God and neighbor (1 John 4:7), having saving knowledge of God (1 John 4:7 and 5:1), possessing a faith that overcomes the world (1 John 5:4), and abstaining from sin (1 John 5:18) all result in

136. Ware, "Divine Election to Salvation," 19.

regeneration. Though Arminians would never say such a thing, their reading of the text (that faith precedes regeneration) inevitably ends up moving in such a direction. In contrast, it is the Calvinist who is exegeting the text according to its proper grammatical structure. All of these benefits, faith included, come from the fountain of regeneration, not the other way around.[137]

The same principle is evident in 1 John 5:18: "We know that everyone who has been born of God [γεγεννημένος ἐκ τοῦ θεοῦ; perfect passive participle] does not keep on sinning [οὐχ ἁμαρτάνει; present active indicative], but he who was born of God protects him, and the evil one does not touch him." The reason one does not keep on sinning (which is surely a faith-involved deed) is because one has already been born again. Reymond states, "Though [John] does not say so in so many words, it is surely appropriate, because of his earlier pattern of speech in 1 John 3:9, to understand him to mean that the cause behind one's not sinning is God's regenerating activity." Therefore, John's "established pattern of speech would suggest that he intended to say that God's regenerating activity is the *cause* of one's believing that Jesus is the Christ, and conversely that such faith is the effect of that regenerating work."[138]

Thus, these passages teach that regeneration precedes and brings about the believer's faith. Schreiner makes two relevant observations:

> First, in every instance the verb "born" (*gennaô*) is in the perfect tense, denoting an action that precedes the human actions of practicing righteousness, avoiding sin, loving, or believing. Second, no evangelical would say that before we are born again we must practice righteousness, for such a view would teach works-righteousness. Nor would we say that first we avoid sinning, and then are born of God, for such a view would suggest that human works cause us to be born of God. Nor would we say that first we show great love for God, and then he causes us to be born again. No, it is clear that practicing righteousness, avoiding sin, and loving are all the consequences or results of the new birth. But if this is the case, then we must interpret

137. Murray, *Redemption Accomplished and Applied*, 102.
138. Reymond, *New Systematic Theology*, 709.

1 John 5:1 in the same way, for the structure of the verse is the same as we find in the texts about practicing righteousness (1 John 2:29), avoiding sin (1 John 3:9), and loving God (1 John 4:7). It follows, then, that 1 John 5:1 teaches that first God grants us new life and then we believe Jesus is the Christ.[139]

Concerning these passages in 1 John, John Murray also concludes,

> It should be specially noted that even faith that Jesus is the Christ is the effect of regeneration. This is, of course, a clear implication of John 3:3–8. But John the apostle here takes pains to make that plain. Regeneration is the beginning of all saving grace *in us*, and all saving grace in exercise on our part proceeds from the fountain of regeneration. We are not born again by faith or repentance or conversion; we repent and believe because we have been regenerated. No one can say in truth that Jesus is the Christ except by regeneration of the Spirit and that is one of the ways by which the Holy Spirit glorifies Christ. The embrace of Christ in faith is the first evidence of regeneration and only thus may we know that we have been regenerated.[140]

Schreiner and Murray are exactly right and consequently these texts not only support the Calvinist position regarding the *ordo salutis*, but also exclude the Arminian position.

BROUGHT FORTH BY GOD'S WILL: JAMES 1:18

James also has much to say concerning regeneration. Speaking of what God has done in and to the believer, James states, "Of his own will he brought us forth by the word of truth, that we should be a kind of firstfruits of his creatures." It is important to note two things in this passage. First, "brought us forth" (ἀπεκύησεν) refers to regeneration, as it is a metaphor for spiritual rebirth. As seen with John 3, just as a baby is

---

139. Thomas R. Schreiner, "Does Regeneration Necessarily Precede Conversion?" available online from 9Marks at http://www.9marks.org/ejournal/does-regeneration-necessarily-precede -conversion; accessed July 6, 2008.
140. Murray, *Redemption Accomplished and Applied*, 103.

brought forth or birthed from the womb, so the sinner is brought forth or birthed by the power of God. Some, such as Elliott-Binns, have argued that the language of bringing forth is not soteriological or redemptive in nature but rather refers to creation itself.[141] The phrase "Father of lights" (v. 17) draws the reader back to Genesis where Adam is brought forth by God's word as a firstfruits of the human race to come. However, as Moo and McCartney have observed, the language in James 1:18 is similar to Romans 8:18–25 in which redemption is promised.[142] Moreover, the context of James 1:18 has to do with suffering, sin, temptation, and faith (1:2–17), all of which demonstrate that it is salvation which is in view and not strictly creation. Also, the "word of truth" is a clear reference to the gospel (cf. 2 Cor. 6:7; Eph. 1:13; Col. 1:5; 2 Tim. 2:15), again demonstrating that redemption and not creation is the focus.[143] The phrase "Father of lights" does indeed refer to God as creator and giver of all good gifts to men, but the point is that it is this same Father who brought forth the heavenly lights who also, by his will and the power of his Word, brings forth sinners from spiritual death to new life.[144] Similar to what happened in creation, James saw his hearers who were trusting in Christ as the firstfruits of the harvest to come.

Second, God brought us forth of "his own will" (βουληθεὶς). The emphatic "his" highlights both the gracious benevolence of God in begetting new life to sinners and the omnipotence of God in doing so by "his own will."[145] James's language here is very similar to Peter's when Peter says that according to God's mercy "he has caused us to be born again" (1 Peter 1:3). James also shares similarities with John, who states that those who believe are born not of the will of man but of God (John 1:12–13). It is not man's will or man's cooperation with God's will that effects this new birth. Rather, it is by God's own will that he brings us

---

141. L. Elliott-Binns, "James 1.18: Creation or Redemption?" *New Testament Studies* 3 (1955): 148–61. For a critique, see James B. Adamson, *The Epistle of James*, NICNT (Grand Rapids: Baker, 1976), 76–77; Davids, *The Epistle of James*, 90.

142. Moo, *The Letter of James*, 79; McCartney, *James*, 113.

143. Moo, *The Letter of James*, 79.

144. McCartney, *James*, 110.

145. Adamson, *The Epistle of James*, 75–76.

forth. As Peter Toon states, "James is teaching what John taught: God takes the initiative and causes new life to begin in the soul."[146] Again, no mention is made of man's cooperation with God's grace, nor is there any hint by James that God's work of bringing us forth is conditioned upon man's will to believe. To the contrary, James places all of the emphasis on God. It is God's will, not man's, which brings the sinner into new life in order that he should be the firstfruits of God's creatures. Therefore, it is "by his doing you are in Christ Jesus" (1 Cor. 1:30).

CAUSED TO BE BORN AGAIN: 1 PETER 1:3–5

Peter also places emphasis on God's sovereignty in the new birth.

Blessed be the God and Father of our Lord Jesus Christ! *According to his great mercy, he has caused us to be born again* [ἀναγεννήσας] to a living hope through the resurrection of Jesus Christ from the dead, to an inheritance that is imperishable, undefiled, and unfading, kept in heaven for you, who by God's power are being guarded through faith for a salvation ready to be revealed in the last time. (1 Peter 1:3–5)

Peter uses the language of causation to describe God's merciful yet powerful act of new birth. Several observations are necessary. First, the reason Peter gives as to why God is to be praised is that in his great mercy God caused us to be born again.[147] Peter will use the language of spiritual begetting again in 1 Peter 1:23 where he says that believers "have been born again, not of perishable seed but of imperishable, through the living and abiding word of God." Here Peter shows that God the Father takes the initiative in producing spiritual children by his Word. Second, Peter says that this new birth is according to God's great mercy. By definition mercy precludes any possibility of human works or contribution. Prior to the new birth, those who will believe are dead in sin and only deserving of God's judgment and wrath. However, as will be

146. Toon, *Born Again*, 40.
147. Schreiner, *1, 2 Peter, Jude*, 60.

seen in Ephesians 2:4–5, God granted mercy to those who have rebelled against him.

Third, Peter here uses the image of birth and, as with John 3:5–6, this image precludes any human contribution. As Schreiner states, "The focus therefore is on God's initiative in producing new life. No one takes any credit for being born. It is something that happens to us."[148] Schreiner's point is demonstrated when Peter states that out of this great mercy God *caused* us to be born again. God causes, creates, brings about, and produces the new birth, not on the basis of anything we have done, but purely on the basis of his great mercy.

MADE ALIVE WITH CHRIST

Ephesians 2:1–7

While Jesus and Peter explain regeneration through the imagery of birth, Paul explains regeneration through the imagery of resurrection from the dead. As Hoekema states, for Paul "regeneration is the fruit of the Spirit's purifying and renewing activity, that it is equivalent to making dead persons alive, that it takes place in union with Christ, and that it means that we now become part of God's wondrous new creation."[149] Paul speaks of God making dead persons alive in Ephesians 2:

> And you were dead in the trespasses and sins in which you once walked, following the course of this world, following the prince of the power of the air, the spirit that is now at work in the sons of disobedience—among whom we all once lived in the passions of our flesh, carrying out the desires of the body and the mind, and were by nature children of wrath, like the rest of mankind. But God, being rich in mercy, because of the great love with which he loved us, even when we were dead in our trespasses, made us alive [συνεζωοποίησεν] together with Christ—by grace you have been saved— and raised us up with him and seated us with him in the heavenly places in Christ

148. Ibid., 61.
149. Hoekema, *Saved by Grace*, 99.

Jesus, so that in the coming ages he might show the immeasurable riches of his grace in kindness toward us in Christ Jesus. (Eph. 2:1–7)

In Ephesians 2 we see a powerful picture of what takes place in regeneration. The sinner is dead but God makes him alive. The sinner is in the grave but God resurrects him from the dead. Notice that, contrary to Arminianism, there is no contingency or intermediate stage here (see chapter 5) in which God begins to make a sinner alive but the outcome of that act is dependent upon the sinner's decision. Rather, the transition is immediate, instantaneous, and unilateral as the sinner is at one moment dead and the next moment alive (Eph. 2:10). The situation is comparable with the resurrection of Christ. Christ was dead but God in great power resurrected him bodily from the grave (Eph. 1:19–20).[150] Or consider Lazarus, who was dead, rotting in the tomb for days, and suddenly, at the command of Christ, was resurrected and walked out of the tomb alive (John 11).[151] Reymond observes, "The conclusion cannot be avoided that God's regenerating work must causally precede a man's faith response to God's summons to faith."[152]

Moreover, the sinner who is "made alive" is in a situation not only comparable to Christ's, but also receives new life that is actually found in and with Christ. Paul states that God made us alive *together with Christ* and seated us with Christ in the heavenly places (Eph. 2:6), so that in the coming ages we would know the immeasurable riches of his grace in kindness toward us *in Christ Jesus* (Eph. 2:7). Peter O'Brien explains,

Paul's readers have come to life with Christ, who was dead and rose again; their new life, then, is a sharing in the new life which he received when he rose from the dead. It is only in union with him that death is vanquished and new life, an integral part of God's new creation, received. Because the believer's previous condition has been spoken

150. Frank Thielman, *Ephesians*, BECNT (Grand Rapids: Baker, 2010), 134.

151. Boettner, *Reformed Doctrine of Predestination*, 166; Piper, *Finally Alive*, 68, 79, 84; Sinclair Ferguson, *The Christian Life: A Doctrinal Introduction* (Edinburgh: Banner of Truth, 1981), 34–35; Bryan Chapell, *Ephesians*, REC (Phillipsburg, NJ: P&R Publishing, 2009), 80–81.

152. Reymond, *New Systematic Theology*, 709.

of as a state of death (vv. 1, 5), there is no direct reference to Christ's death or to the believer's participation in it. Instead, the sharp contrast between our former condition outside of Christ and being made alive with him is presented.[153]

O'Brien is right in identifying being made alive with the resurrection of Christ. As Ferguson states, "Regeneration is causally rooted in the resurrection of Christ (1 Peter 1:3). Like produces like; our regeneration is the fruit of Christ's resurrection."[154] It is Christ's resurrection which is the very basis of the sinner's coming to life with Christ, as is further demonstrated in Ephesians 2:6 where the sinner is raised up and seated in Christ. Our spiritual resurrection to new life is made explicit by what Paul contrasts it to, namely, deadness in trespasses and sins and bondage to the world ("following the course of this world," Eph. 2:2), Satan ("following the prince of the power of the air," Eph. 2:2), and the flesh ("once lived in the passions of our flesh, carrying out the desires of the body and the mind," Eph. 2:3). Like the rest of mankind we were "by nature children of wrath" (Eph. 2:3). Therefore, being made alive, as O'Brien states, implies not only forgiveness, but also "liberation from these tyrannical forces."[155] Paul's words here in Ephesians 2 closely parallel his words in Colossians: "And you, who were dead in your trespasses and the uncircumcision of your flesh, God made alive together with him, having forgiven us all our trespasses" (Col. 2:13; cf. Rom. 6:11).

Finally, Paul also states that being made alive together with Christ is by grace ("by grace you have been saved"). O'Brien comments, "He draws attention to a mighty rescue which arose out of God's gracious initiative, which had already been accomplished in Christ, and which has abiding consequences for them: *it is by grace you have been saved*."[156] As seen throughout Paul's epistles, grace stands opposed to merit or any contribution on the part of man (Eph. 2:8–10). Grace is God's

---

153. Peter T. O'Brien, *The Letter to the Ephesians*, PNTC (Grand Rapids, Eerdmans, 1999), 167.
154. Ferguson, *Holy Spirit*, 119.
155. Ibid.
156. Ibid., 168.

favor toward sinners in spite of what they deserve (Rom. 3:21–26; 4:4; 5:15). The word "save" ("by grace you have been saved") can and is many times used to refer to an eschatological reality (as will be seen in chapter 7), the deliverance from God's wrath and final judgment.[157] As Thielman observes, in some passages Paul can "describe it [saved] as an ongoing event in the present (1 Cor. 1:18; 15:2; 2 Cor. 2:15) and say, 'Now is the day of salvation' (2 Cor. 6:2; cf. Isa. 39:8; Best 1998:602)." But Paul "normally refers to it as something believers will experience in the future, presumably at the final day (1 Thess. 2:16; 1 Cor. 3:15; 5:5; 10:33; Rom. 5:9–10; 9:27; 10:9; 11:26)."[158] However, as O'Brien explains, the case differs in Ephesians 2, for "saved" refers specifically to what "has already been accomplished and experienced." It describes a "rescue from death, wrath, and bondage and a transfer into the new dominion with its manifold blessings. The periphrastic perfect construction draws attention to the resulting state of salvation."[159] Paul is referring to salvation as something that is "emphatically present for believers" even though the "use of the perfect tense in Eph. 2:5, 8 for salvation is unusual."[160] Paul does draw our attention to the future eschatological consequences of this salvation in verse 7 (being seated with Christ in the coming age). However, in verses 5–6 Paul shows that being saved by grace means that God making us alive together with Christ is also by grace. Therefore, being made alive or regenerated is neither an act that is accomplished by man's works righteousness nor an act conditioned upon man's willful cooperation. Rather, being made alive is *by grace and by grace alone*, meaning that it is purely by God's initiative, prerogative, and power that the sinner is resurrected from spiritual death.

> Grace is not merely unmerited favor in the sense that one may choose to receive or reject a gift. Grace is the impartation of new life. Grace is a power that raises someone from the dead, that lifts those in the grave into new life. Grace is not merely an undeserved gift, though

157. Ibid., 169.
158. Thielman, *Ephesians*, 135.
159. O'Brien, *The Letter to the Ephesians*, 169. Also see Thielman, *Ephesians*, 135.
160. Thielman, *Ephesians*, 135.

it is such; it is also a transforming power. Grace imparted life when we were dead, and grace also raises us and seats us with Christ in the heavenlies. (Eph. 2:6)[161]

Therefore, it will not do to say with the Arminian that God's grace is a gift to be accepted or resisted. Yes, God's grace is a gift, but more than that it is a powerful gift that actually and effectually accomplishes new life as God intends.

Colossians 2:11–14

Another passage of Scripture which is a powerful example in support of monergistic regeneration is Colossians 2:11–14, where Paul writes to the Colossians,

> In him [Christ] also you were circumcised with a circumcision made without [human] hands, by putting off the body of the flesh by the circumcision of Christ, having been buried with him in baptism, in which you were also raised with him through faith in the powerful working of God, who raised him from the dead. And you, who were dead in your trespasses and the uncircumcision of your flesh, God made alive [συνεζωοποίησεν] together with him, having forgiven us all our trespasses, by canceling the record of debt that stood against us with its legal demands. This he set aside, nailing it to the cross.

In verse 11 Paul presents the metaphor of circumcision, a clear reference to the Old Testament, where Moses and the prophets Jeremiah and Ezekiel call for a "circumcision of the heart" (Deut. 10:16; 30:6; Jer. 4:4; Ezek. 44:7; cf. Rom. 2:17). As Moo states, "Paul takes up this concept, claiming that it is the circumcision of the heart, performed by the Spirit—not physical circumcision as such—that marks a person as belonging to the people of God (Rom. 2:28–29). It is this nonphysical circumcision that Paul has in mind here, as the qualification 'not performed by human

161. Thomas Schreiner, *Paul: Apostle of God's Glory in Christ* (Downers Grove, IL: InterVarsity, 2001), 246.

hands' suggests."[162] The contrast is not a circumcision by human hands but a circumcision by the Spirit on the heart as that which is needed for a person to experience new life in Christ.[163]

As already noted in our commentary on Deuteronomy and Jeremiah, the metaphor of circumcision itself communicates the monergistic work of God. Spiritual circumcision is an act performed upon the recipient by God, apart from the sinner's cooperation. God and God alone circumcises the heart and then and only then can the sinner trust in Christ. As a result of being circumcised spiritually, "No longer are we dominated by those 'powers' of the old era, sin, death, and the flesh; we are now ruled by righteousness, life, grace, and the Spirit (see esp. Rom. 5:12–8:17; 12:1–2; Gal. 1:4; 5:14–6:2)."[164] It is only when spiritual circumcision takes place that the sinner is set free from the flesh. As Paul states in verse 12, we have been "raised with him through faith in the powerful working of God, who raised him from the dead." Paul transitions from the metaphor of circumcision to the metaphor of resurrection. Notice the parallel Paul makes in verses 12–13 between God raising Christ from the dead and God spiritually raising the sinner from the dead. Paul calls this act the "powerful work of God," and rightly so, for just as God takes a dead corpse and brings it to life, so also does he take a dead soul and breath new spiritual life into it. As O'Brien notes, the giving of this new life is an "act of pure grace" and is in no way conditioned on man.[165]

THE WASHING OF REGENERATION: TITUS 3:3-7

Paul's words in Colossians show many similarities to his words in Titus:

162. Douglas J. Moo, *The Letters to the Colossians and to Philemon*, PNTC (Grand Rapids: Eerdmans, 2008), 197.

163. Ibid., 198–200; Peter T. O'Brien, *Colossians, Philemon*, WBC, vol. 44 (Dallas: Word, 1982), 123.

164. Moo, *Colossians and Philemon*, 201. Likewise, see F. F. Bruce, *The Epistles to the Colossians, to Philemon, and to the Ephesians*, NICNT (Grand Rapids, Baker, 1989), 108.

165. O'Brien, *Colossians, Philemon*, 123. Also see Richard R. Melick Jr., *Philippians, Colossians, Philemon*, NAC, vol. 32 (Nashville: B&H Publishing Group, 1991), 262.

For we ourselves were once foolish, disobedient, led astray, slaves to various passions and pleasures, passing our days in malice and envy, hated by others and hating one another. But when the goodness and loving kindness of God our Savior appeared, he saved us, not because of works done by us in righteousness, but according to his own mercy, by the washing of regeneration [λουτροῦ παλιγγενεσίας] and renewal of the Holy Spirit, whom he poured out on us richly through Jesus Christ our Savior, so that being justified by his grace we might become heirs according to the hope of eternal life. (Titus 3:3–7)

As in Ephesians 2 and Colossians 2, Paul begins in Titus 3 with man's depravity and slavery to sin, once again emphasizing man's deadness in sin and his spiritual inability. Prior to the washing of regeneration, man was a slave to evil desires (cf. Titus 2:12; 1 Tim. 6:9), spending his time in malice, envy, and hatred. However, out of his love and goodness, "God our Savior" saved us. How exactly did he save us? Not by our own works of righteousness but purely according to his "own mercy." Therefore, according to Paul, salvation is unconditional. Such mercy is made effective by the power of the Holy Spirit, who washes the sinner clean, as Paul says, "by the washing of regeneration [λουτροῦ παλιγγενεσίας] and renewal of the Holy Spirit" (Titus 3:5; cf. 2:14). The very purpose of Christ's redeeming work is for the Spirit to purify a people unto God.[166]

Two observations can be made. First, Paul's two prepositional phrases provide the basis for God's redemption of sinners, the first of which dismisses any "contribution on our part" and the second of which is an "equally strong affirmation that salvation is solely based on God's mercy."[167] Therefore, Paul clearly eliminates works righteousness, or works plus faith (Rom. 3:21–28; 4:2–6; 9:11; Gal. 2:16; Eph. 2:8–9; Phil. 3:9; 2 Tim. 1:9; cf. Exod. 34:6–7; Pss. 78:38; 86:15).[168]

166. Mounce, *Pastoral Epistles*, 448.
167. Knight, *The Pastoral Epistles*, 340.
168. Ibid., 341; Mounce, *Pastoral Epistles*, 447; Philip H. Towner, *The Letters to Timothy and Titus*, NICNT (Grand Rapids: Baker, 2006), 779–80; Thomas D. Lea and Hayne P. Griffin, *1, 2 Timothy, Titus*, NAC, vol. 23 (Nashville: B&H Publishing Group, 1992), 322.

Second, one cannot escape the unconditionality of this passage by arguing that while one is saved by faith alone, not works, one must cooperate with God's grace in order to receive the washing of regeneration. This is the Arminian argument, and it still contradicts the point Paul is making, namely, that man can contribute absolutely nothing whatsoever to God's work, including the washing of regeneration. To the contrary, man is passive in the washing of regeneration. This point is further proven by the language Paul uses for regeneration. Paul refers to regeneration as a "washing" which is accomplished by the Spirit who renews. Paul's language here parallels 1 Corinthians 6:11, where Paul, much as he does in Titus 3:3–7, begins with a long list of the types of depravity in which the believer once walked, but then says that such were some of his readers, "But you were washed, you were sanctified, you were justified in the name of the Lord Jesus Christ and by the Spirit of our God." Notice that not only does Paul use the same metaphor of being "washed" to refer to the change and inner renewal or cleansing that must take place, but he also once again ties the washing of regeneration to the agency of the Spirit. Paul's union of regeneration and Spirit, both in Titus 3:3–7 and 1 Corinthians 6:11, utilizes the Old Testament language of Ezekiel 36:25–27 (also used by Jesus in John 3:5): "I will sprinkle clean water on you, and you shall be clean from all your uncleannesses, and from all your idols I will cleanse you" (Ezek. 36:25).[169] God, through Ezekiel, goes on to say in verses 26–27 that he will give his people a new heart, putting his Spirit within, and cause them to walk in his ways. As Towner recognizes, the Spirit-enabled doing of the law in Ezekiel cannot be far from Paul's mind in Titus 3.[170] Paul, like Ezekiel, is emphasizing the power of the Spirit to wash or regenerate the sinner, causing him to walk in obedience and new life.

As already demonstrated, Ezekiel 36 and John 3 both attribute to the Spirit the sovereign work of regeneration, which is always monergistic. Paul is no different. As demonstrated already in Ephesians 2:5

---

169. Knight, *The Pastoral Epistles*, 343–44; Murray, *Redemption Accomplished and Applied*, 100.

170. Towner, *Timothy and Titus*, 774.

and Colossians 2:11–14, so also in Titus 3, Paul connects the washing of regeneration with the Spirit, who blows wherever he wills, quickening sinners from death to new life. The difference in Titus 3 is that the metaphor has changed slightly from regeneration as birth (John 3:5) or the resurrection from death to new life (Eph. 2:5; Col. 2:13) or circumcision (Col. 2:14–15), to the washing of the dirty and stained sinner.[171] Yet, though the metaphor shifts, the message remains the same.[172]

LET LIGHT SHINE OUT OF DARKNESS:
2 CORINTHIANS 4:3–6

Another passage which serves to complement what has been seen so far is 2 Corinthians 4:3–6, in which we read that God has shone in the hearts of sinners "to give the light of the knowledge of the glory of God in the face of Jesus Christ." Here we see an example of the revealing of the Son to those who are veiled and blinded. However, it is not a mere revelation that takes place; the knowledge Paul speaks of is actually a "light" that pierces into the heart and like creation brings into existence a heart that has been radically changed.[173] To understand this miracle we need to look at the entire passage,

> And even if our gospel is veiled, it is veiled only to those who are perishing. In their case the god of this world has blinded the minds of the unbelievers, to keep them from seeing the light of the gospel of the glory of Christ, who is the image of God. For what we proclaim is not ourselves, but Jesus Christ as Lord, with ourselves as your servants for Jesus' sake. For God, who said, "Let light shine out of darkness,"

171. Marshall seems to miss this point when he argues that since the metaphor of washing is totally different than the metaphor of new birth, therefore, "It is hard to see how washing can convey new birth." The problem, however, is that washing is connected to new birth because both metaphors share the substance and reality of "regeneration." In other words, the doctrine of regeneration is present in both John 3 and Titus 3 but with different metaphors. See Marshall, *Pastoral Epistles*, 318.

172. Lea and Griffin, *1, 2 Timothy, Titus*, 322.

173. See Jonathan Edwards, "A Divine and Supernatural Light Immediately Imparted to the Soul by the Spirit of God, Shown to be Both a Scriptural and Rational Doctrine," in *The Works of Jonathan Edwards* (Peabody, MA: Hendrickson, 2004), 2:12–17.

has shone in our hearts to give the light of the knowledge of the glory
of God in the face of Jesus Christ. (2 Cor. 4:3–6)

The unbeliever is veiled to the truth of the gospel, blinded by the god of
the world so that he cannot see "the light" of the gospel of the glory of
Christ. As one who is blind, the sinner is in darkness, unable to see, and
without the spiritual light that comes from beholding Christ in faith.[174]

Notice that Paul does not say here that, while man is blinded and
veiled, he is not so blinded and veiled that he cannot see or come to the
light of Christ (Semi-Pelagianism). Schreiner explains, "Unbelievers are
not portrayed as neutral, having ability to pursue or reject God. Rather,
they are held in captivity under the devil's power, prevented by him from
seeing the glory of Christ."[175] Nor is it the case that man was blinded
and veiled but that God provided a prevenient grace so that every man
can, if he wills to, cooperate and come to the light (classic Arminianism).
Neither of these options is present in the text. To the contrary, God acts
in a direct, unilateral, unconditional, monergistic manner, creating sight
where there was *only* blindness.

As Paul says in verse 6, "For God, who said, 'Let light shine out
of darkness,' has shone in our hearts to give the light of the knowledge
of the glory of God in the face of Jesus Christ." Hafemann explains
that "this shining in the heart most naturally refers to God's work of
changing the moral disposition and spiritual condition of his people."[176]
Paul is referring to Genesis 1:3 where God creates light when "darkness
was over the face of the deep" (Gen. 1:2). Though darkness was over
the face of the deep, so did the Spirit hover over the face of the waters
(Gen. 1:2b), so that at the very word of God light would be created.
As Genesis 1:3–4 states, "And God said, 'Let there be light,' and there
was light. And God saw that the light was good. And God separated

---

174. David E. Garland, *2 Corinthians*, NAC, vol. 29 (Nashville: B&H Publishing Group,
1999), 211; Paul Barnett, *The Second Epistle to the Corinthians*, NICNT (Grand Rapids: Baker,
1997), 218–20.

175. Schreiner, *Paul*, 138.

176. Scott J. Hafemann, *2 Corinthians*, NIVAC (Nashville: B&H Publishing Group,
2000), 180.

the light from the darkness." Paul, speaking from personal experience, uses this language and miraculous event to describe, in parallel fashion, what takes place when God transforms a sinner. Just as God calls light into being where there is only darkness, so also God calls spiritual light (the light of the glory of his own Son) into being where there is only spiritual darkness.[177]

The language of calling light out of darkness resembles the biblical language of regeneration as an act that brings about a new creation (2 Cor. 5:17; Gal. 6:15). Frame explains, "Similarly with new creation. Creation is 'out of nothing,' as we saw. Before creation, there was nothing. Nothing can't produce anything. Reality all comes by the creative act of God. The same is true of resurrection. Before resurrection there is death. Death can't produce life. Only God can. So, in the new birth we are passive."[178] Such a divine fiat is not the light of prevenient grace, as the Arminian would have it, because (1) the light shines directly into the heart and (2) immediately moves the sinner from darkness to light (salvation) without any conditionality or cooperation. The state described here is not an "intermediate state" in which man has been enlightened by prevenient grace and it is now up to him to believe, resulting in final regeneration. To the contrary, Paul says that man is in darkness, and when God shines light into the heart it is the light of the knowledge of the glory of God in the face of Jesus Christ. In other words, the light results in a saving knowledge of Christ in the very heart of man, something that is not true of all people everywhere who receive prevenient grace.

STRUCK DOWN BY GRACE AND AN OPENED HEART

Struck Down by Grace: Acts 9:1–20

Most passages on regeneration are didactic in nature. However, there are others that occur within the narrative portions of Scripture. Two in particular can be found in the book of Acts.

---

177. Murray J. Harris, *The Second Epistle to the Corinthians*, NIGTC (Grand Rapids: Eerdmans, 2005), 335.
178. Frame, *Salvation Belongs to the Lord*, 186.

As will be seen in the next chapter, Arminians often complain and object to the Calvinist doctrine of monergism because, they say, such a view of grace does not respect man's libertarian freedom to choose to believe but works in a way that irresistibly overpowers man. Essentially, the Arminian has compromised the power and efficacy of God's grace for the sake of man's free will. However, there is perhaps no text which more demonstrates how erroneous the Arminian view is than Acts 9.[179] Luke tells us in Acts 8 of Saul, a Hebrew of Hebrews, and as to the law, a Pharisee (see Phil. 3:5), who was ravaging the church of Jesus Christ, persecuting believers of the Way. Saul was "breathing threats and murder against the disciples of the Lord" (Acts 9:1) and after going to the high priest, Saul received permission to arrest those in Damascus who belonged to the Way and bring them back to Jerusalem (Acts 9:2). Luke explains what happened next,

> Now as he went on his way, he approached Damascus, and suddenly a light from heaven flashed around him. And falling to the ground he heard a voice saying to him, "Saul, Saul, why are you persecuting me?" And he said, "Who are you, Lord?" And he said, "I am Jesus, whom you are persecuting. But rise and enter the city, and you will be told what you are to do." The men who were traveling with him stood speechless, hearing the voice but seeing no one. Saul rose from the ground, and although his eyes were opened, he saw nothing. So they led him by the hand and brought him into Damascus. And for three days he was without sight, and neither ate nor drank.
>
> Now there was a disciple at Damascus named Ananias. The Lord said to him in a vision, "Ananias." And he said, "Here I am, Lord." And the Lord said to him, "Rise and go to the street called Straight, and at the house of Judas look for a man of Tarsus named Saul, for behold, he is praying, and he has seen in a vision a man named Ananias come in and lay his hands on him so that he might regain his sight." But Ananias answered, "Lord, I have heard from many about this man, how much evil he has done to your saints at Jerusalem. And here he has authority from the chief

179. Hodge, *Systematic Theology*, 2:707–8.

priests to bind all who call on your name." But the Lord said to him, "Go, for he is a chosen instrument of mine to carry my name before the Gentiles and kings and the children of Israel. For I will show him how much he must suffer for the sake of my name." So Ananias departed and entered the house. And laying his hands on him he said, "Brother Saul, the Lord Jesus who appeared to you on the road by which you came has sent me so that you may regain your sight and be filled with the Holy Spirit." And immediately something like scales fell from his eyes, and he regained his sight. Then he rose and was baptized; and taking food, he was strengthened. (Acts 9:3–19)

Why is it that Saul changed from a murderer of God's people and a hater of Christ to a man who suddenly believed in the very Christ he was persecuting? For Arminianism to be consistent, it would have to say that ultimately it was Saul's will to believe that resulted in a changed heart. However, Luke's explanation of what took place on the Damascus road is the exact opposite. Paul was struck down by the Lord himself and the light of Christ pierced the very center of Saul's being, asking him why he continued to persecute those who belonged to the living Savior.[180] This encounter with the resurrected Christ turned Saul's heart of stone into a heart of flesh.

Moreover, Luke goes on to explain that the Lord appeared to Ananias in a dream telling him to go to Paul. Ananias, naturally afraid of Saul, reminds the Lord that this is the man who has done much evil to the saints in Jerusalem (Acts 9:13–14). Notice how the Lord responds: "Go, for he is a chosen instrument of mine to carry my name before the Gentiles and kings and the children of Israel. For I will show him how much he must suffer for the sake of my name" (Acts 9:15–16). Saul, prior to the Damascus road experience, was already chosen by God. In other words, just as we saw in Acts 13:48, so it is the case here that God's sovereign choice resulted in Saul's regeneration to new life. Saul was determined by God to believe, and when it came time, God struck Saul down violently, radically changing his understanding of Christ.

180. Peterson, *Acts*, 303.

Finally, lest one conclude that the role of effectual grace was unique in Paul's conversion, we should take heed of the fact that Paul saw his effectual calling and regeneration to be paradigmatic for all believers in Christ (Gal. 1:15–16). Before Paul was born God determined to call him at the proper time (Gal. 1:15). When that time came, God effectively revealed his Son to Paul. As Schreiner comments,

> Paul's call was completely and utterly the work of God. The three accounts of Paul's conversion and call in Acts (Acts 9:1–19; 22:1–16; 26:1–18) match the account in Galatians. Paul was summoned into ministry by a powerful hand. And despite the exceptional nature of Paul's apostolic ministry, he viewed his call as paradigmatic of the conversion of all believers, maintaining that "Christ Jesus showed all his patience to me, the foremost, as an example of those who were about to believe in him for eternal life." (1 Tim. 1:16)[181]

In other words, the sovereign grace seen in Paul's calling and regeneration were only a foretaste of the work God was about to do in other elect sinners as well.

An Opened Heart: Acts 16:13–15

A second passage which also reveals the monergistic nature of regeneration is Acts 16:13–15, in which Paul, Silas, and Timothy are traveling to encourage the churches. Suddenly, Paul receives a vision at night in which a man calls him to Macedonia (Acts 16:9). Paul concludes that God is calling him to preach the gospel to those in Macedonia who need help (Acts 16:10). Luke explains what took place next:

> And on the Sabbath day we went outside the gate to the riverside, where we supposed there was a place of prayer, and we sat down and spoke to the women who had come together. One who heard us was a woman named Lydia, from the city of Thyatira, a seller of purple goods, who was a worshiper of God. The Lord opened her heart to pay attention to what was said by Paul. And after she was baptized,

181. Schreiner, *Paul*, 241–42.

and her household as well, she urged us, saying, "If you have judged me to be faithful to the Lord, come to my house and stay." And she prevailed upon us. (Acts 16:13–15)

Why is it that Lydia believed and was baptized? Answer: The Lord opened her heart.[182] Again, the order in the text is telling. The Lord does not open Lydia's heart because she believed, as the Arminian view must have it. Rather, the text says the exact opposite: Lydia believed the gospel message because the Lord opened her heart. Once again, as in other passages we have examined, Lydia is a clear example of the Lord's monergistic way of opening a sinner's heart to believe.

FINAL NOTE ON THE NEW BIRTH

It has been a common practice among evangelical traditions to say, "You must be born again," in such a way that it is equivalent to the command to repent and trust in Christ.[183] However, as Ferguson explains, these evangelicals wrongly assume that the new birth "is something we must do." "But in the New Testament new birth is something God gives. The point of the metaphor lies in the fact that the new birth is *not* something we can do."[184] As seen above, the new birth is not a work conditioned on our will; rather, any spiritual activity by our will is conditioned upon God's sovereign decision to grant us new life by the Spirit.

REGENERATION AND THE LIBERATION OF THE WILL

In the previous chapter we used the work of Jonathan Edwards to better understand exactly how the will is involved in total depravity. We argued that though man's slavery to sin is necessitated by his corrupt

182. Turretin, *Institutes*, 2:534; Peterson, *Acts*, 461; John Stott, *The Message of Acts* (Downers Grove, IL: InterVarsity, 1990), 263.

183. Billy Graham, *How to Be Born Again* (Waco, TX: Word, 1977), 150, 152, 158, 168. Also see idem, *The World Aflame* (Minneapolis: Billy Graham Evangelistic Association, 1967), 134. For a critique, see John H. Gerstner, *Wrongly Dividing the Word of Truth* (Brentwood, TN: Wolgemuth & Hyatt, 1991), 132–41.

184. Ferguson, *Christian Life*, 49. Also see Frame, *Salvation Belongs to the Lord*, 186.

nature, nevertheless, this slavery is a willful slavery because sin is what he most wants to do (i.e., freedom of inclination). The same understanding of the will must now be brought into our discussion of grace. Prior to effectual calling and regeneration, the will of man is in bondage to sin. Therefore, the will is not active, but passive, that is, passive toward the things of God. If it were active, then synergism would follow. However, in monergism, the will is completely and totally passive, having no bearing on God's sovereign choice. The will only becomes active *as a result of* and *consequence of* regeneration. As Paul makes clear in Romans 6, we once were enslaved to sin, but God made us alive (Rom. 6:11). Though we were enslaved, we died with Christ and have been "set free from sin" (Rom. 6:7, 18, 22). Therefore, the liberation of the will is freedom *from* sin. However, liberation is not only freedom *from* sin; it is also a freedom *to* trust in Christ.[185]

What this means is that in regeneration God reorients the will so that man is able to repent and believe, something the will in no way could do before. Therefore, God's regenerating miracle always precedes any activity by the will. God is the cause and the active will is the effect. This truth is argued by William Perkins:

> Everie cause is before his effect, if not in time, yet in prioritie of nature. The will converted, so soone as God hath begunne to renew it, wils to be renewed: and it could not will the conversion of it selfe, unlesse it had formerly tasted the goodnesse thereof. . . . Will in the act of working, effecting, producing of our conversion or regeneration, is not cause at all, but in it selfe considered, a meere patient or subject to receive the grace of covnersion wrought and given by God.[186]

---

185. Calvin, *Institutes*, 3.19.1–9; Anthony A. Hoekema, *Created in God's Image* (Grand Rapids: Eerdmans, 1986), 237–43.

186. William Perkins, *Treatise of God's Free Grace and Man's Free Will*, in *Works of William Perkins*, 1:715.2D, 716.1B, as quoted in Richard Muller, "Grace, Election, and Contingent Choice: Arminius's Gambit and the Reformed Response," in vol. 2 of *The Grace of God, the Bondage of the Will: Historical and Theological Perspectives on Calvinism*, ed. Thomas R. Schreiner and Bruce A. Ware (Grand Rapids: Baker, 1995), 276. Also see Michael Horton, *Putting Amazing Back into Grace* (Grand Rapids: Baker, 2002), 61–62.

Muller astutely observes, "As Perkins's comments indicate . . . grace does not wrench or force the will; it regenerates and reforms the will in order that it might freely choose to believe."[187] Therefore, the Arminian charge that in the Calvinist stance God coerces the sinner is unjustified. Rather, God "reforms" the will so that it now *wants* to choose Christ.[188] As slavery to sin was free because what man wanted most was to sin, so also is choosing Christ free because now Christ is what the will wants most, thanks to God's prior work of effectual calling and regeneration. Man is not coerced to choose Christ, but necessitated to choose Christ. Yet, such a divinely ordained necessity is perfectly consistent with genuine freedom because though God acts effectually and irresistibly to save, after being regenerated it is now the case that choosing Christ is what man now wants more than anything else.[189]

Here is yet another reason why it is imperative that regeneration precede faith in the *ordo salutis*. God must reorient, renew, and reform the will so that in conversion man will repent and trust in Christ. If regeneration does not come first, then man will continue to only want sin. However, if God first regenerates, then man will want Christ above all things, repent of his sins, and trust in Christ. Once again, freedom of inclination (compatibilist freedom) helps make sense of man's faith and repentance. Whereas before man was willfully enslaved to sin, now, due to God's prior work in effectual calling and regeneration, man is enabled to repent willfully and trust in Jesus for eternal life. Nevertheless, unlike in Arminianism, this enabling is not one that may or may not result in faith. Rather, as Sproul states, after a dead

187. Muller, "Grace, Election, and Contingent Choice," 277. Also see idem, "Perkins' A Golden Chaine: Predestinarian System or Schematized Ordo Salutis?" *Sixteenth Century Journal* 9, 1 (April 1978): 69–81.

188. Wollebius, *Compendium Theologiae Christianae*, 28.1.propositions 11; Greg Welty, "Election and Calling: A Biblical Theological Study," in *Calvinism: A Southern Baptist Dialogue*, ed. E. Ray Clendenen and Brad J. Waggoner (Nashville: B&H Publishing Group, 2008), 241.

189. See Ludovicus Crocius, *Syntagma Sacrae Theologiae* (Bremen: n.p., 1636), 918; as quoted in Heinrich Heppe, *Reformed Dogmatics: Set Out and Illustrated from the Sources*, ed. Ernst Bizer, trans. G. T. Thomson (Eugene, OR: Wipf & Stock, 1950), 520. Also see Michael Horton, *For Calvinism* (Grand Rapids: Zondervan, 2011), 105–10.

corpse is resurrected to new life, "Not only *can* it respond then, it most certainly *will* respond."[190]

THE EFFECTUAL GIFTS OF FAITH AND REPENTANCE

Are faith and repentance gifts from God, or are they something the sinner does by his own free will? Arminian Roger Olson believes the answer is simple: "Evangelicals in the Lutheran and Reformed traditions tend to treat faith as gift, while those in the Arminian-Wesleyan traditions tend to treat it as human response to prevenient grace." He continues,

> Lutheran and Reformed evangelicals argue that if faith is salvation's instrumental cause and a human response, it is a meritorious work, and in that case salvation is not sheer gift of grace; they see Protestantism itself as at stake in saying faith is a gift. Arminian-Wesleyan evangelicals regard faith not as a work but as reception of gift; it is not meritorious work but only an acknowledgement of sin and need of grace. They argue that if faith is a gift and not a free human response to the initiative of prevenient and resistible grace, the urgency of evangelism (especially as solicitation of faith) is undermined. Evangelical activism hangs on belief that repentance and faith are grace-enabled but free responses of hearers of the gospel.[191]

Olson makes a significant observation: in the Reformed understanding faith is the work of God, while in the Arminian understanding prevenient grace is the work of God and faith is man's work in response. The gift, for the Arminian, is only effective *if* man chooses to act upon it.[192]

This same point is made by Jan Rohls as he comments on what the Remonstrants believed:

190. R. C. Sproul, *What Is Reformed Theology?* (Grand Rapids: Baker, 1997), 184 (cf. 186).

191. Roger E. Olson, "Faith," in *The Westminster Handbook to Evangelical Theology* (Louisville: Westminster John Knox, 2004), 184.

192. William Gene Witt, "Creation, Redemption and Grace in the Theology of Jacob Arminius" (PhD diss., University of Notre Dame, 1993), 2:632.

Indeed, the Remonstrants stressed that human beings did not have faith through their own free will, but rather were dependent for it on prevenient, posterior and co-operative grace. However, this in no way meant that all effort to gain salvation was in vain. Rather, it was serviceable to hear the Word of God, repent of one's sins and pray for God's grace; God would then work on the will in such a way that He would grant it the capacity to have faith, even though human beings could then reject that faith.[193]

Not so for the Dortian Calvinist,

In contrast, that view is rejected according to which God had willed to save all through Christ, as also is the view that some do not attain salvation because of their own actions. Rather, the fact that fallen individuals convert is not attributable to their free will but to their election by God, who calls them efficaciously and grants them faith and contrition. To this end God not only allows them to hear His Gospel externally, but illuminates them through the Holy Spirit and thus effects their regeneration and recreation. Regeneration, therefore, does not happen through a process of moral persuasion, so that it is up to human beings whether to convert or not, but rather through God's influence. As a result, that view is rejected according to which human beings have not totally lost their free will to seek the good through sin and faith is not merely a gift of grace infused into the individual by God.[194]

For the Arminian, God stands, hands stretched out, and offers the gifts of faith and repentance, but it is up to the sinner whether or not he will take them.[195] As Rolhs explains, there is an "effort to gain salvation" that must

193. Jan Rohls, "Calvinism, Arminianism and Socinianism in the Netherlands until the Synod of Dort," in *Socinianism and Arminianism: Antitrinitarians, Calvinists, and Cultural Exchange in Seventeenth-Century Europe*, ed. Martin Mulsow and Jan Rohls, Brill Studies in Intellectual History, vol. 134 (Leiden: Brill, 2005), 40.

194. Ibid., 42.

195. Elsewhere Olson denies the following: "A popular evangelical illustration— rejected by evangelical theologians—is that God casts a vote for the sinner and Satan casts a vote against him or her and salvation depends on how the sinner votes. Evangelical theologians reject

be present if faith is to be accepted. The Arminian view of faith is evident in Witt's description of Arminius: "The gift of faith is not an omnipotent force which overwhelms the human being and irresistibly causes him or her to believe." Instead, "the mode by which grace works is persuasion."[196]

Repentance, for the Arminian, works the same way. Summarizing Arminius, Clarke explains, "Repentance is man's act as distinct from regeneration, which is God's act."[197] While the efficient cause of repentance is God, the proximate but subsidiary cause is man, who converts himself by God's grace.[198] Olson elaborates,

> Evangelicals of the Arminian persuasion agree that true repentance, like true faith, is a gift of God, but they also believe it is resistible and that its reception necessarily involves a cooperation by the person who repents. By his prevenient (going before) grace God calls, convicts, enlightens, and enables the sinner to repent and believe; the sinner then must respond to the Spirit's work by allowing it to change his or her life, and that change takes the aspect of repentance and faith. These are not works that merit salvation (contrary to some Reformed anti-Arminian polemics), but simply what it means to accept the gift of salvation. Both Reformed and Arminian evangelicals equally regard repentance as a work of God that manifests itself in the sinner's contrition, confession, and life amendment; the difference lies in whether or not the sinner called by God could resist so that repentance and faith are aborted.[199]

---

such semi-Pelagian analogies for salvation and insist that even the *initium fidei*—beginning of faith—is made possible by God, whose prevenient grace calls, convicts, enlightens, and enables sinners who hear the gospel message to repent and believe." Olson, "Salvation," in *The Westminster Handbook*, 261–62. However, even if it is granted that prevenient grace enables faith, still, such faith is conditioned on the sinner's choice. Olson himself admits that it is the human choice which is decisive. Therefore, the analogy is not far off since God stands there, dependent upon the sinner to cast the decisive vote in favor of grace.

196. Witt, "Creation, Redemption and Grace," 2:633. See James Arminius, "Examination of a treatise concerning the Order and Mode of Predestination, and the Amplitude of Divine Grace, by William Perkins," in *The Writings of James Arminius*, 3 vols., trans. James Nichols and William Nichols (Reprint, Grand Rapids: Baker, 1956), 3:315.

197. F. Stuart Clarke, *The Ground of Election: Jacob Arminius' Doctrine of the Work and Person of Christ* (Waynesboro, GA: Paternoster, 2006), 93.

198. Ibid. See James Arminius, "Seventy-Nine Private Disputations," in *Writings*, 2:238–40.

199. Olson, "Repentance," in *The Westminster Handbook*, 251.

Olson's recognition of man's determinative role in salvation is also emphasized by William Cannon who agrees with how Wesley explained the
matter.

> In conclusion, therefore, we cannot say that the "Wesleyan doctrine
> of saving faith . . . is a complete renewal of the Luther-Calvin thesis
> that in the thought of salvation God is everything, man is nothing."
> Quite the contrary seems actually to be the case—not, of course, in
> the sense that man is everything and God is nothing; not in the sense
> that Wesley believed man could in any degree save himself by moral
> and ecclesiastical works or by any inherit goodness; but simply in
> this sense, and in this sense alone, that man is the sole determinative
> factor in the decision of his own justification. Faith as the condition
> of justification is offered unto him as a free gift by a gracious God,
> but then he must actively respond to that offer and reach out with
> the arms of true repentance to receive the gift.[200]

Cannon's honesty is enlightening. For Wesley, "Man is the sole determinative factor in the decision of his own justification." Therefore, not only is
regeneration conditioned upon man's free will choice, but also faith and
repentance are first and foremost the act of man's will, not God's. Here
is exactly where the Arminian and the Calvinist differ. For the Calvinist
God actually works faith within his elect in an efficacious manner so
that those whom he has effectually called and monergistically regenerated *necessarily* repent and believe. No conditionality is involved. Not
so for the Arminian. Since faith precedes regeneration in the *ordo salutis*
it is not the case that faith is worked efficaciously within the sinner by
God. Rather, God offers faith but it is up to the sinner (granted, a sinner
enabled by prevenient grace) to decide by his own free will whether or
not he will cooperate. If he cooperates, repentance and faith result and
regeneration follows. However, man's will is the ultimate decider in the

---

200. William R. Cannon, *The Theology of John Wesley: With Special Reference to the Doctrine
of Justification* (New York: University Press of America, 1974), 117. Also see Thomas Oden,
John Wesley's Scriptural Christianity: A Plain Exposition of His Teaching on Christian Doctrine
(Grand Rapids: Zondervan, 1994), 246.

matter, making conversion primarily the work of man, not God. Boyd and Eddy explain their Arminian view,

> God graciously makes it *possible* for people to believe, but he does not make it *necessary* for them to believe. It is one thing to claim that without the Holy Spirit we *cannot* believe and quite another to say that with the work of the Holy Spirit we *must* believe. Scripture affirms the former but not the latter. In any event, this demonstrates that Arminianism does not undermine the truth that God is to receive all the glory for salvation.[201]

But do Arminians like Olson, Boyd, and Eddy get it right? Does such a view fit with what Scripture says? Can such a view avoid robbing God of the credit and glory?

Contrary to the Arminian view, Scripture reveals that faith and repentance are the work of God first and foremost, necessarily resulting from God's work in effectual calling and regeneration. While man does play a role—he must trust in Christ (faith) and be penitent for his sin (repent)—such activities are not only gifts from God's hand but also gifts that God works effectually within his elect. As Turretin put it, "God is said to give not only the power of believing, but the belief (*to pisteuein*) or the act itself (Phil. 1:29)."[202] Turretin draws the comparison to the healing of a blind man. God not only gives the blind man the power to open his eyes, but God himself also actually opens the man's eyes and makes him see. Therefore, Sproul correctly states, "God himself creates the faith in the believer's heart."[203] As the Canons of Dort state, God produces not only the *velle credere* (the will to believe), but also the *actum credenda* (the act of believing).[204] Or as John Owen writes,

---

201. Gregory A. Boyd and Paul R. Eddy, *Across the Spectrum: Understanding Issues in Evangelical Theology*, 2nd ed. (Grand Rapids: Baker, 2009), 159.

202. Turretin, *Institutes*, 2:523 (cf. 552).

203. Sproul, *What Is Reformed Theology?*, 156. Also see John R. W. Stott, *God's New Society* (Downers Grove, IL: InterVarsity, 1982).

204. See chapter 2 of *Reclaiming Monergism*, e-book. Also see Wollebius, *Compendium Theologiae Christianae*, 28.1.propositions 9; Owen, *A Display of Arminianism*, 10:104–6; idem, *Holy Spirit*, 3:308–9.

"The Scripture says not that God gives us ability or power to believe only,—namely, such a power as we may make use of if we will, or do otherwise; but faith, repentance, and conversion themselves are said to be the work and effect of God."[205]

Faith

The first passage we will examine in this regard is Acts 13:48. Chapter 13 begins with Paul and Barnabas being sent off by the Holy Spirit, to arrive eventually at Antioch in Pisidia. On the Sabbath Paul is invited to speak. Paul, drawing from the storyline of the Old Testament, reminds his listeners of God's faithfulness to his people Israel as they wandered through the wilderness, fought wars with other nations in the land of Canaan, and were governed first by judges, then by the prophet Samuel, who was followed by King Saul, and finally by David, the son of Jesse, who was a man after God's own heart, accomplishing God's will (Acts 13:18–22). It is from the offspring of David that God, as he had promised, brought to Israel a Savior in Jesus (Acts 13:23–27), who was unrecognized and condemned to death though no guilt was found in him. Yet, God raised him from the dead (Acts 13:30–33), and it is in Jesus that "forgiveness of sins is proclaimed to you" (Acts 13:38) so that "everyone who believes is freed from everything from which you could not be freed by the law of Moses" (Acts 13:39). Afterward, Paul is invited back for the next Sabbath, during which almost the whole city gathers to hear him. However, many Jews are filled with jealousy, reviling him. Paul and Barnabas respond boldly, saying, "It was necessary that the word of God be spoken first to you. Since you thrust it aside and judge yourselves unworthy of eternal life, behold, we are turning to the Gentiles" (Acts 13:46). While the Jews heard Paul and reviled him, the Gentiles also heard Paul and began rejoicing. Luke explains the scenario,

> And when the Gentiles heard this, they began rejoicing and glorifying the word of the Lord, and as many as were appointed to eternal life

205. Owen, *Holy Spirit*, 3:320 (cf. 3:323–24).

believed. And the word of the Lord was spreading throughout the whole region. But the Jews incited the devout women of high standing and the leading men of the city, stirred up persecution against Paul and Barnabas, and drove them out of their district. (Acts 13:48–50)

What is to account for the Jews rejecting the gospel message Paul presented, while many Gentiles, hearing the same message, believe? One could assume, as many Arminians do, that it is the will of man. God tried to save them through the gospel presentation of Paul, but only those who exercised their will to believe were saved. However, such an assumption is foreign to the text. Rather, Luke explains that the reason the Gentiles believed while the Jews did not was because "as many as were appointed to eternal life believed" (Acts 13:48).[206] Notice, Luke does not say "as many as believed were appointed to eternal life," as the Arminian synergist would have it. To the contrary, Luke says that God's appointment (ordination; cf. Acts 15:2; 22:10; 28:23; Matt. 28:16–17; Luke 7:8; Rom. 13:1; 1 Cor. 16:15–16) or election to eternal life is what determined who would and would not believe.[207] Ware appropriately comments,

> So it is not ultimately a matter of human choice that determines who rejects and who accepts the gospel. Although human choice (i.e., belief in Christ) is necessary for any to be saved, what stands prior—both temporally prior and logically prior—to this human choice is the choice of God, which divine choosing is causally linked to and hence accounts for the human choice to believe. In short, these Gentiles believed the gospel, while Jews rejected the same saving message because God had chosen these very Gentiles to believe.[208]

Here again we see that it is God's choice, not man's, which determines whether or not a sinner will receive new life and consequently believe in

---

206. *The 1599 Geneva Bible* (White Hall, WV: Tolle Lege, 2008), 1113.

207. "The passive voice indicates that God does the assigning. It is as strong a passage on God's sovereignty as anywhere in Luke-Acts and has OT roots." Darrell L. Bock, *Acts*, BECNT (Grand Rapids: Baker, 2007), 465. Also see Barrett, *Acts 1–14*, 658; Richard N. Longenecker, *The Acts of the Apostles*, EBC, vol. 9 (Grand Rapids: Zondervan, 1981), 430.

208. Ware, "Divine Election to Salvation," 9.

Christ. Until God pierces through the sinner's heart he cannot respond in faith and repentance (cf. Acts 2:37). As Peterson states, "God must open hearts, to enable people to listen and respond with faith (cf. [Acts] 16:14; 18:10)."[209] God's choice, not man's, is the determining factor in salvation.

A second passage where we see God's sovereignty in granting faith is Ephesians 2:8–10. Here Paul says, "For by grace you have been saved through faith. And this is not your own doing; it is the gift of God, not a result of works, so that no one may boast. For we are his workmanship, created in Christ Jesus for good works, which God prepared beforehand, that we should walk in them." Or, as the NASB translates, "For by grace you have been saved through faith; and that not of yourselves, it is the gift of God." The debate here is over the meaning of the phrases "*this* is not your own doing" and "*it* is the *gift* of God." What do "this" and "it" refer to? Arminians will argue that the Greek does not warrant the gift being understood as faith. "Faith" is feminine while the pronoun "that" is neuter. Therefore, if Paul had wanted to say faith is a gift, he could have used the feminine form of the pronoun instead. The same applies to the word "grace" since it also is feminine in gender.

However, many Calvinists grant such a grammatical point, which is the consensus view today.[210] Even Calvin himself says, "His [Paul's] meaning is, not that faith is the gift of God, but that salvation is given to us by God, or, that we obtain it by the gift of God."[211] Schreiner elaborates when he affirms that the demonstrative pronoun *this* (*touto*) is neuter and "thus cannot be the specific antecedent to *grace* or *faith* since the words *grace* (*charity*) and *faith* (*pisteōs*) are both feminine. Nor can it refer specifically back to *saved*, for the participle *saved* (*sesōmenoi*) is masculine."[212] Nevertheless, the question remains, what in Paul's mind

---

209. Peterson, *Acts*, 399.

210. There have been exceptions such as Charles Hodge, *Ephesians*, ed. Alister McGrath and J. I. Packer (Wheaton, IL: Crossway, 1994), 118–19; William G. T. Shedd, *Dogmatic Theology*, 3rd ed. Alan W. Gomes (Phillipsburg, NJ: P&R Publishing, 2003), 744, 754, 796.

211. John Calvin, *Commentaries on the Epistles of Paul to the Galatians and Ephesians*, trans. William Pringle (Grand Rapids: Eerdmans, 1948), 228–29.

212. Schreiner, *Paul*, 246–47.

is the antecedent of "that" ("this" in the ESV) in Ephesians 2:8? Answer: The gift is salvation in its totality.[213] As Schreiner says,

> Paul wanted to communicate that everything said in Ephesians 2:8 is God's gift. That is, if he had used the masculine or feminine form of the pronoun, some might have concluded that some of the elements contained in this verse were not part of God's gift. By using the neuter he emphasizes that the whole is God's gift.[214]

All and every aspect of salvation, says Paul, is by grace alone. As Sam Storms explains, "From beginning to end, from its inception to its consummation, salvation is a gift of God to his elect."[215] What then does this mean for "faith" itself? Storms continues, "Consequently, that faith by which we come into experiential possession of what God in grace has provided is as much a gift as any and every other aspect of salvation. One can no more deny that faith is wrapped up in God's gift to us than he can deny it of God's grace."[216] Storms is exactly right. While the "gift" refers to salvation in its totality, salvation is all of grace and, as Paul says in Ephesians 2:8, it is "by grace you have been saved through faith." Therefore, if salvation is "not your own doing" but is a "gift of God," so also must it be the case that faith is also by grace and a gift of God. O'Brien states,

> The point being made, then, is that the response of faith does not come from any human source but is God's gift. . . . God's magnificent rescue from death, wrath, and bondage is all of grace. It neither originates in nor is effected by the readers. Instead, it is God's own gift, a point which Paul goes out of his way to emphasize by changing the normal word order and contrasting "God's" with "yours."[217]

213. Samuel C. Storms, *Chosen for Life* (Wheaton, IL: Crossway, 2007), 71; Clinton E. Arnold, *Ephesians*, ZECNT (Grand Rapids: Zondervan, 2010), 139.
214. Schreiner, *Paul*, 246.
215. Storms, *Chosen for Life*, 71.
216. Ibid.
217. O'Brien, *Ephesians*, 175–76.

Contrary to Arminianism, faith is not effected by the sinner nor does it originate in the sinner. Thielman observes that faith cannot be a synergism which brings about divine grace. "In Paul's thinking, faith is not something that people offer to God and with which God's grace then cooperates to save them. Rather, faith is aligned with grace, and both faith and grace stand over against anything that human beings can offer God: it is neither a work deserving payment nor a ground for boasting (Rom. 4:2–5, 16)."[218]

Before moving to a third passage, it is essential to recognize here that all boasting is excluded by Paul. Grace precludes works, which include any "human effort in general." Salvation "is not based on human performance or on any effort to win God's approval."[219] How could human effort be included when Paul previously made it obvious that man is dead in trespasses and sins (Eph. 2:1–3)? Therefore, as O'Brien states, "It was impossible for the readers to turn to their previous behaviour as the basis for achieving salvation."[220] Boasting is excluded since mankind is "in no position to claim even the slightest credit for their acceptance with God (note Paul's argument in Rom. 4:1–8). . . . Men and women have nothing which they can bring as their own to the living God."[221] Can the Arminian escape bringing something of his own to God? It seems unlikely since he insists that while faith is a gift it is one that man can reject, and even when it is accepted it is seen as the work of man primarily. Though the Arminian denies it, it is difficult to see how boasting is excluded, especially when someone like Wesley rejected Calvin's thesis that in salvation God is everything and man is nothing and instead argued that "man is the sole determinative factor in the decision of his own justification."[222] Surely this is a serious threat to the glory of God and the gratuity of God's sovereign grace.

A third passage relevant to this discussion is Philippians 1:29–30, in which Paul says, "For it has been *granted* to you that for the sake of

218. Thielman, *Ephesians*, 143.
219. O'Brien, *Ephesians*, 177.
220. Ibid.
221. Ibid., 177–78.
222. Cannon, *The Theology of John Wesley*, 117.

Christ you should not only *believe* in him but also suffer for his sake, engaged in the same conflict that you saw I had and now hear that I still have." Paul explains that not only is suffering a gift from God's sovereign hand, but so also is belief (faith) in Christ.[223] But notice, Paul specifically says "it [belief] has been granted." The word "granted" here (*echaristhē*) should not be understood, as it sometimes is in English, as a reluctance or mere permission on God's part.[224] Rather, in Greek, "granted" means to give graciously and freely. It is the same word from which *grace* is derived.[225] Out of love, God grants to his elect faith or belief in his Son. Belief in Christ is not something the sinner produces, but rather is something that God gives. If God does not grant it, then belief does not result. As in Ephesians 2:8–10, so in Philippians 1:29–30 we again see that faith is something which God produces in us, not something we do by our own free will.

A fourth passage that also exemplifies God's sovereign work of faith is 2 Peter 1:1, which reads, "Simeon Peter, a servant and apostle of Jesus Christ, To those who have obtained a faith of equal standing with ours by the righteousness of our God and Savior Jesus Christ." Is Peter saying that it is by man's will that faith is obtained? Not at all, for obtaining faith here refers to the reception of a gift that is given by God's choice. Storms explains, "What is of paramount importance here is the word translated 'have obtained' or 'have received.' It is related to a verb that means 'to obtain by lot' (see Luke 1:9; John 19:24; Acts 1:17). Thus, faith is removed from the realm of human free will and placed in its proper perspective as having originated in the sovereign and altogether gracious will of God."[226] Therefore, while faith is an act of believing (*fides qua creditor*), this act is not a human but a divine work.[227] As Calvin states, "Faith is something merely passive, bringing nothing of ours to the recovering of God's favor but receiving from Christ that which we

---

223. Moisés Silva, *Philippians*, 2nd ed., BECNT (Grand Rapids: Baker, 2005), 84.
224. Storms, *Chosen for Life*, 71.
225. Schreiner, *Paul*, 247.
226. Storms, *Chosen for Life*, 72.
227. Calvin, *Institutes*, 3.1.4. Cf. Barbara Pitkin, "Faith and Justification," in *The Calvin Handbook*, ed. Herman J. Selderhuis (Grand Rapids: Eerdmans, 2008), 290.

lack."[228] It is no wonder then that Calvinists like Packer see Arminianism as such a threat since it makes "man's salvation dependent ultimately on man himself, saving faith being viewed throughout as man's own work and, because his own, not God's in him."[229]

Repentance

Faith is surely a gift that is granted and effectually applied by God's sovereign will, but so also is repentance. As Bavinck states, "True repentance according to Scripture, does not arise from the natural 'man' but from the new life that was planted in a person by regeneration."[230] Therefore, "Faith and repentance both arise from regeneration."[231] It is essential to keep in mind then that faith and repentance are "ultimately inseparable."[232] Since we have already seen that faith is a gift (Matt. 11:25–27; 16:17; John 1:12–13; 6:44; 1 Cor. 12:3; Gal. 1:16; Eph. 1:11; 2:8; Phil. 1:29; 2:13), it should not be surprising that we would find texts that indicate that repentance also is a gift.

Notice how Paul writes to Timothy: "And the Lord's servant must not be quarrelsome but kind to everyone, able to teach, patiently enduring evil, correcting his opponents with gentleness. God may perhaps grant them repentance leading to a knowledge of the truth, and they may come to their senses and escape from the snare of the devil, after being captured by him to do his will" (2 Tim. 2:24–26). The opponents Paul refers to are unbelievers, as is evident by the fact that they are opposing the Lord's servant (2 Tim. 2:24), are in need of repentance and knowledge of the truth (2 Tim. 2:25), and are in "the snare of the devil." The sinner cannot repent nor does he want to. Rather, he loves sin and therefore shows himself to be a slave of the devil, doing his will. Paul explains that the only way the sinner can be liberated from such a slavery is by God granting repentance.

---

228. Calvin, *Institutes*, 3.13.5. Also see Turretin, *Institutes*, 2:523.

229. J. I. Packer, *A Quest for Godliness: The Puritan Vision of the Christian Life* (Wheaton, IL: Crossway, 1990), 128.

230. Bavinck, *Reformed Dogmatics*, 4:163.

231. Ibid., 4:152.

232. Schreiner, *Paul*, 247.

If God does not grant repentance, then the sinner is left to his sinful captivity. As Storms states,

> If a person is to repent, he or she must be enabled by God to do so. He must be "granted" repentance as a gift. Whether or not a person repents, says Paul, is ultimately up to God. It rests with him and his sovereign good pleasure to give or to withhold that which leads to "a knowledge of the truth." That God does not bestow this gift universally is self-evident.[233]

Likewise, Schreiner states,

> Such repentance can only come from God, for human beings are anesthetized by the devil; and only God can provide the power to "sober them up" (*ananēpsōsin*, 2 Tim. 2:26). No hope for the transformation of human beings lies in the human will. God must grant repentance and the necessary sobriety. Human beings are snared in the devil's trap and are held captive (*ezōgrēmenoi*) by him, so that they always do the devil's will.[234]

Furthermore, the fact that a sinner cannot repent unless God decides he will grant it also reveals the truth that repentance is not given universally but only to the elect. As Storms explains, "Were repentance something God gives to all, Paul would hardly have said that 'perhaps' God may grant repentance. Clearly he envisions the real possibility that God may *not* so grant."[235] Consequently, the Arminian view that God tries through prevenient grace to work repentance on all people, with the success of his act being dependent upon the will of man, is contrary to passages like 2 Timothy 2:24–26. God, not man, determines whether or not repentance will be given and made effective.[236]

233. Storms, *Chosen for Life*, 72–73.
234. Schreiner, *Paul*, 247–48.
235. Storms, *Chosen for Life*, 72–73.
236. Ibid., 73. Moreover, contrary to what the Arminian says, God's sovereignty in applying salvation efficaciously and selectively does not lead to a laxness in evangelism. Notice that Paul tells Timothy to go to great lengths to not be quarrelsome but kind, teaching and patiently

Two other significant texts concerning repentance are Acts 5:31 and 11:18. Acts 5:31 reads, "God exalted him [Jesus] at his right hand as Leader and Savior, to give repentance to Israel and forgiveness of sins." Acts 11:18 explains how God not only grants repentance to Israel but to Gentiles as well: "When they heard these things they fell silent. And they glorified God, saying, 'Then to the Gentiles also God has granted repentance that leads to life.'" Peter recognized that not only had God intended to grant repentance to Jews (Acts 5:31), but to Gentiles as well. Seeing such a miracle take place, Peter draws the conclusion not that these sinners exercised their free will, but rather that God, in his sovereignty, decided to grant them repentance. Storms argues, "Peter would not need to have drawn such a conclusion if repentance were a universal gift that all receive. . . . If everyone, even those who persist in unbelief, are granted repentance, Peter could not and would not have reasoned as he did."[237] A universal granting of repentance by God is not in view. Quite the contrary; God and God alone decides to whom he will grant repentance (cf. Acts 2:47) and nothing in man makes such an act by God conditional or contingent. Passages like Acts 5:31 and 11:18 only serve to complement those we have already examined (see the sections on Acts 13:48 and Acts 16:14 above).

CONCLUSION: MONERGISM PRESERVES GOD'S GLORY

As we have seen, the exegetical evidence for monergistic regeneration preceding faith is overwhelming. Yet, because Scripture places the emphasis on God's sovereignty, some readers will undoubtedly find themselves uncomfortable. Piper explains,

> [T]he new birth is unsettling because it refers to something that is done to us, not something we do. . . . God causes the new birth; we don't. . . . Any spiritually good thing we do is a result of the

---

enduring evil, even correcting opponents with gentleness because God may perhaps grant Timothy's opponents repentance. Therefore, sovereign grace, here evident in the granting of repentance, is not a barrier to evangelism and the preaching of the gospel to all but is perfectly compatible and consistent with it.

237. Ibid.

new birth, not a cause of the new birth. This means that the new birth is taken out of our hands. It is not in our control. And so it confronts us with our helplessness and our absolute dependence on Someone outside ourselves. This is unsettling. We are told that we won't see the kingdom of God if we're not born again. And we're told that we can't make ourselves to be born again. . . . Therefore, if we are going to be born again, it will rely decisively and ultimately on God. His decision to make us alive will not be a response to what we as spiritual corpses do, but what we do will be a response to his making us alive.[238]

Despite how unsettling monergism makes one feel, the fact is that the doctrine is found everywhere in Scripture. Moreover, if such a biblical doctrine is compromised, we surrender that which is ultimately at stake in such a debate, namely, the glory of God. As Ware explains, the biblical view is of "one who reigns supreme over all, whose purposes are accomplished without fail, and who directs the course of human affairs, including the central drama of saving a people for the honor of his name, all with perfect holiness and matchless grace."[239] Key in such a statement is that God accomplishes his purposes without fail. For the Calvinist, God's effectual grace is not dependent on the will of man as it is for the Arminian. Only the former can truly give God *all* of the glory in regeneration. Herman Kuiper explains,

> It is a distinguishing mark of Reformed theologians that they always champion the glory of God over against all tendencies to exalt man. And it is especially in its doctrine of the Ordo Salutis that Reformed Theology magnifies God as the Sole Author of our salvation. It traces back the application of salvation to the sovereign and gracious will of God. Whether or not a man is to become a partaker of salvation, does not in the last analysis rest with man. It rests on the eternal decree of election, which God Himself effectually realizes in the course of history.[240]

238. Piper, *Finally Alive*, 26–27.
239. Ware, "Divine Election to Salvation," 9.
240. Kuiper, *By Grace Alone*, 36.

Like Kuiper, James M. Boice and Philip Ryken explain the dividing line,

> Having a high view of God means something more than giving glory to God, however; it means giving glory to God *alone*. This is the difference between Calvinism and Arminianism. While the former declares that God alone saves sinners, the latter gives the impression that God enables sinners to have some part in saving themselves. Calvinism presents salvation as the work of the triune God—election by the Father, redemption in the Son, calling by the Spirit. Furthermore, each of these saving acts is directed toward the elect, thereby infallibly securing their salvation. By contrast, Arminianism views salvation as something that God makes possible but that man makes actual. This is because the saving acts of God are directed toward *different* persons: the Son's redemption is for humanity in general; the Spirit's calling is only for those who hear the gospel; narrower still, the Father's election is only for those who believe the gospel. Yet in none of these cases (redemption, calling, or election) does God *actually* secure the salvation of even one single sinner! The inevitable result is that rather than depending exclusively on divine grace, salvation depends partly on a human response. So although Arminianism is willing to give God the glory, when it comes to salvation, it is unwilling to give him *all* the glory. It divides the glory between heaven and earth, for if what ultimately makes the difference between being saved and being lost is man's ability to choose God, then to just that extent God is robbed of his glory. Yet God himself has said, "I will not yield my glory to another" (Isa. 48:11).[241]

God's glory is wrapped up in the doctrine of monergistic regeneration and is compromised when the focus is placed on man's autonomy.[242]

---

241. Boice and Ryken, *The Doctrines of Grace*, 34–35.
242. Owen, *Holy Spirit*, 3:308.

ARMINIAN SYNERGISM IN THEOLOGICAL PERSPECTIVE

Jacob Arminius (1559–1609) once said in his *Sentiments*,

> In his lapsed and sinful state, man is not capable, of and by himself, either to think, to will, or to do that which is really good; but it is necessary for him to be regenerated and renewed in his intellect, affections or will, and in all his powers, by God in Christ through the Holy Spirit, that he may be qualified rightly to understand, esteem, consider, will, and perform whatever is truly good.[1]

Perhaps for many Calvinists, such an affirmation of spiritual inability by Arminius is surprising. However, though there are notable exceptions, many Arminians and Wesleyans who followed Arminius would likewise affirm total depravity and the necessity of God's grace to precede the will of man. Why then does such a chasm exist between Calvinism and Arminianism if both camps agree on a doctrine as vital as man's depravity and bondage to sin? The divide exists because, as William Cannon observes, though Calvinists and Arminians come so close together, in reality they are worlds

---

1. James Arminius, "A Declaration of the Sentiments of Arminius," in *The Writings of James Arminius*, 3 vols., trans. James Nichols and William Nichols (Reprint, Grand Rapids: Baker, 1956), 1:252 (hereafter referred to as *Writings*). Also see F. Stuart Clarke, *The Ground of Election: Jacob Arminius' Doctrine of the Work and Person of Christ* (Waynesboro, GA: Paternoster, 2006), 74; Carl Bangs, *Arminius: A Study of the Dutch Reformation* (Grand Rapids: Zondervan, 1985), 338. For a more in-depth treatment of Arminianism, see *Reclaiming Monergism*, e-book.

apart due to the doctrine of prevenient grace.[2] One could ask, for example, how it is that the Arminian can, on the one hand, affirm total depravity and spiritual inability, and yet, at the same time—and while avoiding Pelagian and Semi-Pelagian notions of cooperation—affirm that man's free will is able to accept or resist God's grace (synergism).[3] For the Arminian, the answer lies in the doctrine of prevenient grace because it is here that a free will ability to cooperate with or resist subsequent grace is restored to man.[4] The idea is that God provides a *gratia praeveniens* which mitigates depravity and enables man to either resist or cooperate with the Spirit. Therefore, while the Calvinist views God's grace as effectual, the Arminian disagrees, arguing that while grace must be the initiator, nevertheless, the efficacy of grace is ultimately conditioned upon man's free will and is therefore synergistic. Consequently, prevenient grace is no small doctrine, but the very hinge of an Arminian and Wesleyan soteriology which diverges so drastically from Calvinism.[5] As Robert Chiles confesses, "Without it, the Calvinist logic is irrefutable."[6] And Thomas Schreiner suitably concludes that "if prevenient grace is not taught in Scripture, then the credibility of Wesleyan theology is seriously undermined."[7] In this chapter our goal is to represent Arminianism accurately, then to offer a critique of synergism in chapter 6.

ARMINIANS AND TOTAL DEPRAVITY

Before examining Arminian synergism, it is necessary and essential to recognize where Arminians stand on original sin. As discussed in

2. William R. Cannon, *The Theology of John Wesley: With Special Reference to the Doctrine of Justification* (New York: University Press of America, 1974), 102.

3. Herbert Boyd McGonigle, *Sufficient Saving Grace: John Wesley's Evangelical Arminiansim* (Milton Keynes: Paternoster, 2001), 319.

4. Robert E. Picirilli, *Grace, Faith, Free Will—Contrasting Views of Salvation: Calvinism and Arminianism* (Nashville: Randall House, 2002), 149.

5. Thomas R. Schreiner, "Does Scripture Teach Prevenient Grace in the Wesleyan Sense?" in *Still Sovereign: Contemporary Perspectives on Election, Foreknowledge, and Grace*, ed. Thomas R. Schreiner and Bruce A. Ware (Grand Rapids: Baker, 2000), 234.

6. Robert Chiles, *Theological Transition in American Methodism: 1790–1935* (Nashville: Abingdon, 1965), 50.

7. Schreiner, "Does Scripture Teach Prevenient Grace?," 234. Likewise, see Picirilli, *Grace, Faith, Free Will*, 149.

chapter 2, original sin is comprised of two aspects: guilt (*reatus*) and corruption (*vitium*), the latter of which is sometimes referred to as pollution or depravity.[8] Regarding the former, Calvinists and Arminians have disagreed on the imputation of guilt from original sin. While most in the Reformed tradition have argued that *both* guilt and corruption (pollution) are imputed to Adam's posterity, many in the Arminian tradition have affirmed the imputation of corruption but have denied the imputation of guilt.[9] But even within the Arminian tradition there has been disagreement over exactly *why* it is that mankind does not inherit Adam's guilt.[10] For instance, John Miley argued that original sin does not include guilt or condemnation. Though there is "native depravity," there is not "native demerit."[11] The reason why guilt is not imputed is because no guilt actually exists to be imputed. It is impossible for mankind to be held guilty or culpable for a sin it did not commit. However, not all Arminians agree or explain the absence of original guilt as Miley does. John Wesley, John Fletcher, Richard Watson, William Pope, and Thomas Summers have argued that the guilt of original sin does exist but is set aside, abrogated, and mitigated by the atoning work of Christ, which provides prevenient grace to all sinners.[12] This

8. Anthony A. Hoekema, *Created in God's Image* (Grand Rapids: Eerdmans, 1986), 143–50.

9. Wayne Grudem, *Systematic Theology* (Grand Rapids: Zondervan, 1994), 496; Roger E. Olson, "Sin/Original Sin," in *The Westminster Handbook to Evangelical Theology*, ed. Roger E. Olson (Louisville: Westminster John Knox, 2004), 268–69.

10. Roger E. Olson, *Arminian Theology: Myths and Realities* (Downers Grove, IL: InterVarsity, 2006), 153. It should, however, be qualified that some Arminians do affirm original guilt. See Picirilli, *Grace, Faith, Free Will*, 152–53; James Arminius, "Epistolary Discussion, concerning Predestination, between James Arminius, D. D., and Francis Junius, D. D.," in *Writings*, 3:178.

11. John Miley, *Systematic Theology*, 3 vols. (Peabody Clarke, MA: Hendrickson, 1989), 1:509.

12. John Wesley, "The Doctrine of Original Sin, according to Scripture, Reason, and Experience," in *The Works of John Wesley*, ed. T. Jackson (Grand Rapids: Baker, 1978), 9:191–464; citations from this edition hereafter referred to as *Works* (Jackson). Randy L. Maddox, *Responsible Grace: John Wesley's Practical Theology* (Nashville: Kingswood, 1994), 87; Barry E. Bryant, "Original Sin," in *The Oxford Handbook of Methodist Studies*, eds. William J. Abraham and James E. Kirby (Oxford: Oxford University Press, 2009), 522, 537; Marjorie Suchocki, "Wesleyan Grace," in *The Oxford Handbook of Methodist Studies*, 547; McGonigle, *Sufficient Saving Grace*, 158–59; Olson, *Arminian Theology*, 148–53; Kenneth J. Collins, *Wesley on Salvation: A Study of the Standard Sermons* (Grand Rapids: Zondervan, 1989), 20–22; idem, *The Scripture Way of Salvation: The Heart of John Wesley's Theology* (Nashville: Abingdon, 1997), 31–45; Cannon, *The Theology of John Wesley*, 198–200.

view seems to be the most faithful to Arminius himself,[13] who, contrary to the Reformed tradition, preferred to speak of the result of Adam's sin in terms of "privation" rather than "depravation."[14] Despite this disagreement between Calvinists and Arminians over the imputation of guilt, most agree on the inheritance of corruption, a discussion to which we now turn.

Jacob Arminius

According to Arminius, man is dead in sin and the severity of sin has penetrated every aspect of man's being due to the corruption inherited from Adam.[15] For Arminius, man's will is in bondage to sin, unable to accomplish anything spiritually good toward God.[16] Arminius is very clear that every aspect of man must be renewed since he is infected by sin.[17] Arminius is not content with saying, as the Semi-Pelagians do, that man's will is merely wounded, maimed, infirmed, bent, and weakened.[18] Rather, he goes farther, describing man's will as imprisoned, destroyed, and lost. Apart from grace the will is debilitated and useless.[19]

Arminius denied the charges of Pelagianism and Semi-Pelagianism, accusing both groups of ignorance in spiritual matters,[20] and argued that "what they attributed to natural free will, his theology attributes

13. Arminius, "Twenty-Five Public Disputations," in *Writings*, 1:479–86. See Olson, *Arminian Theology*, 145n26; Bangs, *Arminius*, 339. Episcopius advocates a similar view. See Shedd's quotations of and comments on Episcopius's *Apology for the Remonstrants* in W. G. T. Shedd, *A History of Christian Doctrine* (Vestavia Hills, AL: Solid Ground Christian, 2006), 2:181–83. Also see D. C. Shipley, "Methodist Arminianism in the Theology of John Fletcher," (PhD diss., Yale University, 1942), 195–96, who argues that Episcopius and the Remonstrance repudiated any affirmation of guilt in original sin.

14. Arminius, "Seventy-Nine Private Disputations," in *Writings*, 2:77–79. See Clarke, *The Ground of Election*, 74; Bangs, *Arminius*, 338.

15. For example, see Arminius, "Twenty-Five Public Disputations," in *Writings*, 1:485.

16. Arminius, "A Declaration of the Sentiments of Arminius," in *Writings*, 1:252. Also see Arminius, "Twenty-Five Public Disputations," in *Writings*, 1:526.

17. Arminius, "Twenty-Five Public Disputations," in *Writings*, 1:526.

18. William Gene Witt, "Creation, Redemption and Grace in the Theology of James Arminius" (PhD diss., University of Notre Dame, 1993), 2:608.

19. Bangs, *Arminius*, 341.

20. Arminius, "Examination of a Treatise Concerning the Order and Mode of Predestination, and the Amplitude of Divine Grace, by William Perkins," in *Writings*, 3:289.

to divine grace."[21] Medieval Semi-Pelagianism argued that "God will not deny his grace to any one who does what is in him." Arminius called such a saying "absurdity," unworthy of "sacred matters,"[22] and instead modified the medieval slogan, saying: "To him who does what he can *by the primary grace already conferred upon him*, God will bestow further grace upon him who profitably uses that which is primary."[23] Arminius taught that due to man's radical corruption and bondage of the will, it is God, not man, who must initiate salvation (see Private Disputation 44). Until God provides prevenient ("preventing") grace man can in no way cooperate with God.[24] Therefore, while Arminius does affirm synergism, it is a God-initiated and God-enabled synergism.[25]

The Arminian Remonstrants

Arminius was not lacking followers who sought to be true to his doctrine, as is evident in the Arminian Articles of 1610 (see especially Article III).[26] And when the Synod of Dort called upon the Remonstrants to more fully articulate their beliefs, the Remonstrants, led by Simon Episcopius, would in the *Sententiae Remonstrantium* again affirm man's pervasive depravity, corruption, and inability.[27] Though these *Sententiae* were condemned by Dort, Episcopius would again reiterate

21. Witt, "Arminius," 2:629.

22. Arminius, "Apology Against Thirty-One Defamatory Articles," in *Writings* 1:328–29.

23. Ibid., 1:329, emphasis added. For Arminius's denial of Pelagianism and Semi-Pelagianism, see Keith D. Stanglin and Thomas H. McCall, *Jacob Arminius: Theologian of Grace* (Oxford: Oxford University Press, 2012), 142–51; William den Boer, *God's Twofold Love: The Theology of Jacob Arminius (1559–1609)*, trans. Albert Gootjes, vol. 14 in Reformed Historical Theology, ed. Herman J. Selderhuis (Göttingen: Vandenhoeck & Ruprecht, 2010), 187–94.

24. Bangs, *Arminius*, 341; D. E. Eaton, "Arminianism in the Theology of John Wesley" (PhD diss., Duke University, 1988), 75.

25. James Arminius, "A Letter Addressed to Hippolytus A .Collibus," in *Writings*, 2:472–73. Also see idem, "A Declaration of the Sentiments of Arminius," in *Writings*, 1:253–54.

26. Philip Schaff, *The Evangelical Protestant Creeds*, vol. 3 of *The Creeds of Christendom* (Grand Rapids: Baker, 1997), 546–47.

27. See articles 1–4 in "Appendix H: The Opinions of the Remonstrants," in *Crisis in the Reformed Churches: Essays in Commemoration of the Great Synod of Dort, 1618–1619*, ed. Peter Y. De Jong (Grand Rapids: Reformed Fellowship, 1968), 225–26.

the Remonstrance articles in his 1621 confession, clearly affirming man's inability apart from grace.[28]

However, not all Remonstrants would agree. Philip Limborch (1633–1712), whom Olson describes as one who "defected from Arminius's theology," upheld an "optimistic anthropology" as opposed to Arminius's "pessimistic anthropology."[29] While Arminius argued that man's will is in bondage to sin apart from God's grace, Limborch denied the total bondage of man's will. Influenced by the Enlightenment and the development of seventeenth-century Socinianism, Limborch argued that Adam's sin merely resulted in a "universal misery." This universal misery or "inherited misfortune" does not put man in bondage to sin but merely inclines people toward sin. Therefore, Limborch denied not only inherited guilt but inherited depravity.[30] Moreover, when Limborch did affirm special grace, he made prevenient grace (i.e., that which excites man's free will) synonymous with common grace, thereby relinquishing prevenient grace of its supernatural nature. Limborch is an example of the tendency of some Arminians to adopt Semi-Pelagianism.[31] Despite Limborch, however, later Arminians would repudiate this stance, siding instead with Arminius.

John Wesley and Wesleyan-Arminianism

John Wesley (1703–91) wrote more than two hundred pages defending the doctrine of original sin against John Taylor, who denied the doctrine.[32] Though Wesley did not affirm the imputation of the guilt of

28. See chapter 7, article 10 of Simon Episcopius, *The Confession of Faith of Those Called Arminians, or, A Declaration of the Opinions and Doctrines of the Ministers and Pastors, Which in the United Provinces are Known by the Name of Remonstrants Concerning the Chief Points of the Christian Religion* (London: n.p., 1684), 68–69, 107.

29. Olson, *Arminian Theology*, 147.

30. Ibid. See Philip Limborch, *A Complete System, or, Body of Divinity*, trans. William Jones (London: John Darby, 1713), 192, 409. However, as Olson observes, Limborch was inconsistent because at times it sounded as if he was affirming inherited original sin.

31. John M. Hicks, "The Theology of Grace in the Thought of James Arminius and Philip van Limborch" (PhD diss., Westminster Theological Seminary, 1985), 3. Also see Olson, *Arminian Theology*, 148.

32. Wesley, "The Doctrine of Original Sin," in *Works* (Jackson) 9:191–464; John Taylor, *The Scripture-Doctrine of Original Sin, Exposed to Free and Candid Examination* (London: n.p.,

original sin, he did affirm the corruption of original sin.[33] Man is dead in sin until God supernaturally calls him to new life.[34] Wesley even equated human nature as it was in his own time with man's sinful nature at the time of the flood. "In his natural state every man born into the world is a rank idolater."[35] Man has inherited from Adam a corrupt nature so that "every one descended from him comes into the world spiritually dead, dead to God, wholly dead in sin; entirely void of the life of God; void of the image of God, of all that righteousness and holiness wherein Adam was created." Consequently, "Every man born into the world now bears the image of the devil in pride and self-will; the image of the beast, in sensual appetites and desires."[36] To deny man's total corruption, says Wesley, is to show that "you are but a heathen still."[37] Moreover, not only did Wesley affirm man's inherited and pervasive corruption, but he also asserted the bondage of man's will. After the fall, "no child of man has a natural power to choose anything that is truly good."[38]

1740); David Steers, "Arminianism amongst Protestant Dissenters in England and Ireland in the Eighteenth Century," in *Arminius, Arminianism, and Europe: Jacob Arminius (1559/60–1609)*, ed. Marius van Leeuwen, Keith D. Sranglin, and Marijke Tolsma, Brill's Series in Church History, vol. 39 (Leiden: E. J. Brill, 2010), 195.

33. Maddox, *Responsible Grace*, 74–83; Jason Vickers, "Wesley's Theological Emphasis," in *The Cambridge Companion to John Wesley*, ed. Randy L. Maddox and Jason E. Vickers (Cambridge: Cambridge University Press, 2010), 195; Albert C. Outler, "The Wesleyan Quadrilateral in John Wesley," in *The Wesleyan Theological Heritage: Essays of Albert C. Outler*, ed. Thomas C. Oden and Leicester R. Longden (Grand Rapids: Zondervan), 88 (cf. 55–96, 189–209); B. E. Bryant, "John Wesley's Doctrine of Sin" (PhD diss., University of London, 1992), 178.

34. See Wesley, "On Working Out Our Own Salvation," in *Works* (Jackson), 6:506–13; idem, "The New Birth," in *Works* (Jackson), 6:65–77; idem, "On the Deceitfulness of the Human Heart," in *Works* (Jackson), 7:340. Also see idem, "On Original Sin," in *Works* (Jackson), 6:54–64; "On the Fall of Man," in *Works* (Jackson), 6:215–24; "God's Love to Fallen Man," in *Works* (Jackson), 6:231–40; Collins, *The Scripture Way of Salvation*, 26–45.

35. John Wesley, "On Original Sin," in *Works* (Jackson), 6:59. Also see Bryant, "Original Sin," 533.

36. Wesley, "The New Birth," in *Works* (Jackson), 6:68.

37. John Wesley, "On Original Sin," in *Works* (Jackson), 6:63 (cf. 6:59).

38. John Wesley, "Some Remarks on 'A Defense of the Preface to the Edinburgh Edition of Aspasio Vindicated,'" in *Works* (Jackson), 10:350. Also see idem, "The Spirit of Bondage and of Adoption," in *Works* (Jackson), 5:104; idem, *Wesley's Standard Sermons*, ed. Edward H. Sugden (London: Epworth, 1955–56), 1:181–82; Charles A. Rogers, "The Concept of Prevenient Grace in the Theology of John Wesley" (PhD diss., Duke University, 1967), 109, 111.

Wesleyans in the eighteenth, nineteenth, and twentieth centuries have likewise affirmed Wesley's doctrine of man's pervasive corruption and inability apart from grace.[39] Perhaps no one is as clear as Richard Watson (1781–1833), who said, "The true Arminian, as fully as the Calvinist, admits the doctrine of the total depravity of human nature in consequence of the fall of our first parents." Watson concludes, "Man is so totally overwhelmed, as with a deluge, that no part is free from sin, and therefore whatever proceeds from him is accounted sin."[40] William Pope (1822–1903), Thomas Summers (1812–82), John Miley (1813–95), H. Orton Wiley (1877–1961), and even Wesleyans of our own time, such as Thomas Oden, all agree.[41]

Nevertheless, despite such affirmations of total depravity, today a number of prominent Arminian theologians still deny the doctrine in order to preserve the libertarian freedom of man. Arminians like Jack Cottrell, Bruce Reichenbach, and Clark Pinnock argue that though the fall has devastating effects, some degree of libertarian freedom remains afterward. There is no need, they say, to turn to a doctrine like total depravity when such a doctrine cannot be found in Scripture and only serves to destroy libertarian freedom, which is essential to Arminian synergism.[42] Reichenbach, Cottrell, and Pinnock demonstrate that Semi-

39. Olson, *Arminian Theology*, 151–56. John Fletcher also affirmed total depravity. See Shipley, "Methodist Arminianism in the Theology of John Fletcher," 198, esp. 152–202.

40. Richard Watson, *Theological Institutes* (New York: Lane & Scott, 1851), 2:48. Also see Olson, *Arminian Theology*, 151.

41. William Burton Pope, *A Compendium of Christian Theology* (New York: Phillips & Hunt, n.d.), 2:80; Thomas O. Summers, *Systematic Theology: A Complete Body of Wesleyan Arminian Divinity*, 2 vols. (Nashville: Methodist Episcopal Church, South, 1888), 1:34, 2:68–69; Miley, *Systematic Theology*, 1:509; H. Orton Wiley, *Christian Theology*, 2 vols. (Kansas City, MO: Beacon Hill, 1952), 2:98, 129; Thomas C. Oden, *John Wesley's Scriptural Christianity: A Plain Exposition of His Teaching on Christian Doctrine* (Grand Rapids: Zondervan, 1994), 161. Also consider *The Articles of Religion of the Methodist Church*; J. Kenneth Grider, *A Wesleyan-Holiness Theology* (Kansas City, MO: Beacon Hill, 1994), 230–96; H. Ray Dunning, *Grace, Faith, and Holiness: A Wesleyan Systematic Theology* (Kansas City, MO: Beacon Hill, 1988), 1988), 275–301.

42. Clark Pinnock, "Responsible Freedom and the Flow of Biblical History," in *Grace Unlimited*, ed. Clark Pinnock (Eugene, OR: Wipf and Stock, 1999), 104–5; idem, "From Augustine to Arminius: A Pilgrimage in Theology," in *The Grace of God and the Will of Man*, ed. Clark H. Pinnock (Minneapolis: Bethany House, 1989), 21–22; Jack Cottrell, "Conditional Election," in *Grace Unlimited*, 68; Reichenbach, "Freedom, Justice, and Moral Responsibility," in *The Grace of God and the Will of Man*, 286.

Pelagianism continues to have a strong influence within Arminianism today.[43]

To summarize, man's radical, inherited depravity is a matter of debate within Arminianism. While a majority of Arminians clearly affirm total depravity, others do not. For those who do, such an affirmation seems to provide common ground between Calvinists and Arminians.[44] Indeed, in a letter to John Newton, dated May 14, 1765, John Wesley states that there is not a hair's breadth separating his own position from that of John Calvin.[45] Nevertheless, the hair's breadth is the doctrine of prevenient grace.[46] Such commonality on total depravity is quickly forgotten by the introduction of prevenient grace into the Arminian and Wesleyan traditions.

ARMINIAN VIEWS ON GRACE AND FREE WILL

The Nature of Prevenient Grace

The Source of Prevenient Grace. The term "prevenient grace" can be easily misunderstood, for the term gives the impression that something or someone must be prevented. To the contrary, the word is used by Arminians to describe a grace that comes before salvation. The word "prevent" is derived from the Latin *venio*, meaning "to come."[47] The word "pre" is a prefix meaning "before." "Pre-venient" grace is a grace that "comes before" salvation (*prevenire*).[48] Thomas Summers explains

43. E.g., consider: "A Statement of the Traditional Southern Baptist Understanding of Salvation," signed by Paige Patterson, Jerry Vines, Chuck Kelley, among other SBC leaders.

44. Schreiner, "Does Scripture Teach Prevenient Grace?," 233. Likewise, see Melvin E. Dieter, "The Wesleyan Perspective," in *Five Views on Sanctification*, ed. Melvin E. Dieter (Grand Rapids: Zondervan, 1987), 21–23; M. Elton Hendricks, "John Wesley and Natural Theology," *Wesley Theological Journal* 18 (1983): 9; J. Weldon Smith III, "Some Notes on Wesley's Doctrine of Prevenient Grace," *Religion in Life* 34 (1964–65): 70–74.

45. See Wesley, "The Question, 'What Is an Arminian?' Answered. By a Love of Free Grace," in *Works* (Jackson), 10:359. Also see Bryant, "Original Sin," 534

46. Bryant, "John Wesley's Doctrine of Sin," 241; Dunning, *Grace, Faith, and Holiness*, 49; Cannon, *The Theology of John Wesley*, 93, 102; Collins, *The Scripture Way of Salvation*, 38–39.

47. R. C. Sproul, *Willing to Believe: The Controversy Over Free Will* (Grand Rapids: Baker, 1997), 129.

48. Ibid.

that prevenient grace is that influence which "precedes our action, and gives us the capacity to will and to do right, enlightening the intellect, and exciting the sensibility."[49] The question that inevitably follows is what event in the history of redemption is the source for prevenient grace? For Arminians and Wesleyans, the source is in the atonement of Christ.[50] As John 12:32 states, it is when Christ is lifted up (on the cross) that he draws all men to himself. Leo Cox explains, "Rather than holding that the good found in man apart from salvation is a goodness left over from the fall of man, Wesleyan-Arminianism has always taught that God has supernaturally restored to all men a measure of His Spirit through the grace that flows from Calvary."[51]

The Recipients of Prevenient Grace. If the atonement of Christ is the source of prevenient grace, who is the recipient of it? Do all people receive prevenient grace, or only some? There is disagreement between those in the Arminian and Wesleyan traditions over the scope or extent of prevenient grace. Though the point has been debated, Arminius himself viewed prevenient grace as being restricted to where the gospel is preached.[52] Prevenient grace for Episcopius is restricted to the evangelized as well. However, many Wesleyan-Arminians, such as John Wesley, John Fletcher, and later Wesleyans like John Miley, have argued that prevenient grace is universal in scope, common to all mankind.[53] The universality of prevenient grace is directly tied to the universality of Christ's atonement. Because the extent of Christ's atoning

---

49. Summers, *Systematic Theology*, 2:77. Also see Bryant, "Original Sin," 534.

50. Arminius, "Certain Articles to be Diligently Examined and Weighed," in *Writings*, 2:494–95; Richard P. Heitzenrater, "God with Us: Grace and the Spiritual Senses in John Wesley's Theology," in *Grace Upon Grace: Essays in Honor of Thomas A. Langford*, ed. Robert K. Johnston, L. Gregory Jones, and Jonathan R. Wilson (Nashville: Abingdon, 1999), 94.

51. Cox, "Prevenient Grace," 145.

52. Arminius, "Examination of Dr. Perkins's Pamphlet on Predestination," in *Writings*, 3:525. See Olson, *Arminian Theology*, 167; Eaton, "Arminianism in the Theology of John Wesley," 72.

53. Shipley, "Methodist Arminianism in the Theology of John Fletcher," 21–22; Roger Olson, "The Classical Free Will Theist Model of God," in *Perspectives on the Doctrine of God: Four Views*, ed. Chad O. Brand (Nashville: B&H Publishing Group, 2008), 169; Cannon, *The Theology of John Wesley*, 102.

work is universal rather than particular, it follows that prevenient grace is universal rather than particular.[54] Why would Christ die for all people, but his grace be given only to some? All must have the opportunity to be saved, to choose or reject God's grace through Christ. As Grant Osborne explains, "God is an 'equal opportunity' convictor who, in drawing all to himself, makes it possible to make a true decision to accept or reject Jesus."[55] Therefore, the extent of Christ's atonement and the extent of prevenient grace are universal in scope.

Those who view prevenient grace as universal find textual support in a number of places. John 12:32 says, "But I, when I am lifted up from the earth, will draw all men to myself." Commenting on this passage Thiessen states, "There issues a power from the cross of Christ that goes out to all men, though many continue to resist that power."[56] When Jesus states that he will draw "all people" to himself, he means all men without exception. Osborne states, "All people are equally drawn to the Father."[57] He not only dies for all men, but then also applies the grace from his atoning work to all men. He draws them to himself, but such a drawing is not an irresistible drawing as the Calvinist affirms; rather, it is a drawing that can be resisted. Therefore, such a drawing of all men in no way secures or guarantees salvation, but rather provides the opportunity for man to be saved if he should so choose to cooperate.

Also consider John 1:9, "The true light that gives light to every man was coming into the world." Jesus is this true light and the light he gives to every person is the light of prevenient grace. John

---

54. Rogers, "Prevenient Grace," 159–61. Also see McGonigle, *Sufficient Saving Grace*, 327; A. Skevington Wood, "The Contribution of John Wesley to the Theology of Grace," in *Grace Unlimited*, 216; Theodore Runyon, *The New Creation: John Wesley's Theology Today* (Nashville: Abingdon, 1998), 33–41; Cannon, *The Theology of John Wesley*, 100–102; Collins, *The Scripture Way of Salvation*, 39–40; idem, *A Faithful Witness: John Wesley's Homiletical Theology* (Wilmore, KY: Wesley Heritage, 1993), 63–66; Steve Harper, "Cross Purposes: Wesley's View of the Atonement," in *Basic United Methodist Beliefs: An Evangelical View*, ed. James V. Heidinger II (Wilmore, KY: Good News, 1986), 42–43.

55. Grant R. Osborne, "Soteriology in the Gospel of John," in *The Grace of God and the Will of Man*, 257.

56. Henry C. Thiessen, *Lectures in Systematic Theology* (Grand Rapids: Eerdmans, 1979), 261.

57. Osborne, "Soteriology in the Gospel of John," 256.

continues by stating that some rejected the light, not receiving the Christ (John 1:11), but others responded to Christ (the light) by receiving him (John 1:12).[58] To the surprise of many Calvinists who appeal to John 6 in support of effectual calling and grace, Arminians like Thomas Oden also appeal to such a passage in support of prevenient grace. Jesus states, "No one can come to me unless the Father who sent me draws him. And I will raise him up on the last day" (John 6:44; cf. 6:65). Oden concludes that such a "drawing and enabling is precisely what is meant by prevenient grace."[59]

Arminians also believe that prevenient grace is supported by Titus 2:11, which states that "the grace of God has appeared, bringing salvation for all people." Paul seems to be saying that God's grace is universal, coming to all men so that they may be saved.[60] Oden concludes from Titus 2:11, "To no one, not even the recalcitrant unfaithful, does God deny grace sufficient for salvation. Prevening grace precedes each discrete human act."[61]

Finally, Arminians also appeal to Philippians 2:12–13, a text which Oden, following Wesley, says is the "most important homily that touches upon prevenient grace."[62] Paul states, "Work out your own salvation with fear and trembling, for it is God who works in you, both to will and to work for his good pleasure."[63] Oden interprets Paul as saying, "God working in us enables our working and co-working with God."[64] Since God works in us by giving us prevenient grace, it is now on us to cooperate with all subsequent grace, for the "chief function of prevenient grace

---

58. Wesley, "Predestination Calmly Considered," in *Works* (Jackson), 10:230; 7:188; Lindstrom, *Wesley and Sanctification*, 45.

59. Thomas Oden, *The Transforming Power of Grace* (Nashville: Abingdon, 1993), 120.

60. Miley, *Systematic Theology*, 2:247; Wiley, *Christian Theology*, 2:353; Adam Clarke, *Christian Theology* (New York: Eaton and Mains, 1835), 117; Thomas A. Langford, *Practical Divinity*, 2 vols. (Nashville: Abingdon, 1998–99), 34; Lindstrom, *Wesley and Sanctification*, 49; Dunning, *Grace, Faith, and Holiness*, 339.

61. Oden, *The Transforming Power of Grace*, 48.

62. Oden, *John Wesley's Scriptural Christianity*, 244.

63. Wesley, "On Working Out Our Own Salvation," in *Works* (Jackson), 6:509; idem, "Predestination Calmly Considered," in *Works* (Jackson), 10:230–32; Oden, *John Wesley's Scriptural Christianity*, 246.

64. Oden, *John Wesley's Scriptural Christianity*, 244.

is to bring the person to a state of nonresistance to subsequent forms of grace."[65] Stated otherwise, "Prevenient grace is that grace that goes before us to prepare us for more grace, the grace that makes it possible for persons to take the first steps toward saving grace."[66] Taking these first steps, however, requires that we must do something to arouse the grace within us. "All are called to be ready to stir up whatever grace is in them that more grace will be given."[67]

The Content of Prevenient Grace. If, at least for some, the extent of prevenient grace is universal (common even among those who have never heard of Christ, rather than restricted to the preaching of the gospel), the content of prevenient grace can be defined by several characteristics. First, Wesleyans argue on the basis of texts like Romans 1:19 that a general, basic knowledge of God is given to all of mankind due to prevenient grace.[68] Second, not only is a basic knowledge of God distributed through prevenient grace, but so also is the moral law, as it is written on the human heart. Even after the fall, Wesley says, God reinscribed the law on the sinner's heart via prevenient grace.[69] Third, not only the law but the human conscience also is imprinted with God.[70] Fourth, prevenient grace's universal scope also results in the restraining of sin worldwide. As Collins states, prevenient grace places a "check on human perversity."[71] These four characteristics demonstrate that universal prevenient grace

65. Ibid., 247. Also see idem, *The Transforming Power of Grace*, 53.

66. Oden, *John Wesley's Scriptural Christianity*, 247.

67. Ibid., 244 (cf. 245, 250–51).

68. Collins, *The Scripture Way of Salvation*, 41; Oden, *John Wesley's Scriptural Christianity*, 251. For many, inclusivism follows. See Runyon, *The New Creation*, 34–35; Randy L. Maddox, "Wesley and the Question of Truth or Salvation Through Other Religions," *Wesleyan Theological Journal* 27 (1992): 14–18.

69. Wesley, "Predestination Calmly Considered," in *Works* (Jackson), 10:233. Also see Collins, *The Scripture Way of Salvation*, 41.

70. Wesley, "Heavenly Treasure in Earthen Vessels," in vol. 4 of *The Works of John Wesley*, ed. Albert C. Outler (Nashville: Abingdon, 1986), 4:169 (citations from this edition hereafter referred to as *Works* [Outler]); Wesley, "Thoughts upon Necessity," in *Works* (Jackson), 10:473; Oden, *John Wesley's Scriptural Christianity*, 251–52; Collins, *The Scripture Way of Salvation*, 41–42.

71. Collins, *The Scripture Way of Salvation*, 42–43. Also see Oden, *The Transforming Power of Grace*, 63–76.

shares many similarities with the doctrine of common grace, though many Wesleyans insist that these two loci remain distinct.[72]

The Purpose of Prevenient Grace

The Mitigation of Original Sin and Restoration of the Will. As already discussed, for the Arminian the guilt of original sin is either (1) not imputed to Adam's posterity (John Miley) or (2) is mitigated by the atoning work of Christ so that no man actually inherits Adam's guilt (Wesley, Fletcher).[73] While some contemporary Arminians (such as Bruce R. Reichenbach[74]) accept the first view, many Arminians accept the second view and go further to argue that not only is the *guilt* mitigated by Christ's atonement, but so also is the *corruption* of Adam's sin.[75] Olson explains that the

> Arminian doctrine of universal prevenient grace means that because of Jesus Christ and the Holy Spirit *no human being is actually in a state of absolute darkness and depravity.* Because of original sin, helplessness to do good is the natural state of humanity, but because of the work of Christ and the operation of the Holy Spirit universally *no human being actually exists in that natural state.*[76]

Olson's statement is revealing. For the Arminian, due to prevenient grace, no person actually exists in a state of total depravity. Collins traces such a view of the mitigation of depravity back to Wesley

72. Cox, "Prevenient Grace," 144–45. Also see Shipley, "Methodist Arminianism in the Theology of John Fletcher," 216. Again, Wesleyans may differ slightly on the relationship between common and prevenient grace. While Cox seems to sharply distinguish between the two, Oden seems to see more affinity and synonymy. Oden, *John Wesley's Scriptural Christianity*, 249–51.

73. Cox, "Prevenient Grace," 146; idem, "John Wesley's Concept of Sin," *JETS* 7, 3 (1966): 19–20; Eldon R. Fuhrman, "The Wesleyan Doctrine of Grace," in *The Word and Doctrine*, ed. Kenneth E. Geiger (Kansas City: Beacon Hill, 1965), 143–44.

74. Reichenbach, "Freedom, Justice, and Moral Responsibility," 277–79, 286–87.

75. Maddox, *Responsible Grace*, 87; Bryant, "Original Sin," 522, 537; Suchocki, "Wesleyan Grace," 547; McGonigle, *Sufficient Saving Grace*, 158–59; Olson, *Arminian Theology*, 145n26; Oden, *The Transforming Power of Grace*, 45.

76. Olson, *Arminian Theology*, 154, emphasis added.

himself.[77] And it is evident that Wesleyan-Arminians today agree with Wesley.[78]

Furthermore, Wesley's belief that prevenient grace abrogates depravity, so that no man is in such a state, is crucial for human responsibility. Wesley is seriously concerned that men might excuse themselves by arguing that there is nothing they can do since it is God who regenerates and they are depraved and unable to regenerate themselves.[79] However, the fact that all men are dead by nature excuses no one, says Wesley, because "there is no man that is in a state of mere nature."[80] Wesley then brings in prevenient grace, showing that man has been lifted from a state of depravity in order to choose for God if he so desires. Since everyone "has some measure of that light" it is the case that "no man sins because he has not grace, but because he does not use the grace which he hath."[81] As Wesley states in his "Some Remarks on Mr. Hill's 'Review of All the Doctrines Taught by John Wesley'" (1772), "We [Wesley and Fletcher] both steadily assert that the will of man is by nature free only to evil. Yet we both believe that every man has a measure of free-will restored to him by grace."[82] Wesley will not tolerate the Calvinist logic which ultimately attributes belief and unbelief to whether or not God decides to give sinners grace. If man is not saved it is because he did not exercise his free will to do so.[83]

To summarize, prevenient grace (1) mitigates total depravity so that no man is in a state of mere nature and (2) restores to every man a measure of free will so that he can cooperate or resist God's plea to be saved.[84]

77. Collins, *Scripture Way of Salvation*, 38–39. See Wesley, "On Working Out Our Own Salvation," 6:512.

78. Umphrey Lee, *John Wesley and Modern Religion* (Nashville: Cokesbury, 1936), 124–25; Collins, *Scripture Way of Salvation*, 39; Oden, *The Transforming Power of Grace*, 45; Wilbur Tillett, *Personal Salvation* (Nashville: Barbee and Smith, 1902), 117, 120.

79. Wesley, "On Working Out Our Own Salvation," in *Works* (Jackson), 6:512.

80. Ibid.

81. Ibid.; Cox, "John Wesley's Concept of Sin," 17.

82. Wesley, "Some Remarks on Mr. Hill's 'Review of All the Doctrines Taught by John Wesley,'" in *Works* (Jackson), 10:392. Also see idem, "Thoughts upon God's Sovereignty," in *Works* (Jackson), 10:362. See Collins, *The Scripture Way of Salvation*, 42.

83. Collins, *The Scripture Way of Salvation*, 42.

84. Oden, *The Transforming Power of Grace*, 47.

The "Intermediate State." Prevenient grace, by mitigating total depravity, also places sinners in an "intermediate state," where, according to Arminians like Olson, the process of regeneration has begun due to the application of prevenient grace, but is incomplete because regeneration is still contingent upon whether or not man will cooperate with God.[85] Therefore, the sinner in this stage is neither unregenerate nor regenerate. Olson, claiming that Arminius himself taught this intermediate state, explains,

> The intermediate stage is when the human being is not so much free to respond to the gospel (as the semi-Pelagians claimed) but is freed to respond to the good news of redemption in Christ. Arminius thus believes not so much in free will but in a freed will, one which, though initially bound by sin, has been brought by the prevenient grace of the Spirit of Christ to a point where it can respond freely to the divine call. *The intermediate stage is neither unregenerate nor regenerate, but perhaps post-unregenerate and pre-regenerate.* The soul of the sinner is being regenerated but the sinner is able to resist and spurn the prevenient grace of God by denying the gospel. All that is required for full salvation is a relaxation of the resistant will under the influence of God's grace so that the person lets go of sin and self-righteousness and allows Christ's death to become the only foundation for spiritual life.[86]

The sinner is not unregenerate because regeneration has already been initiated by prevenient grace.[87] However, since the sinner is able to resist

---

85. Since regeneration has begun due to prevenient grace but is incomplete, many Wesleyan-Arminians, including Wesley himself, must argue that grace is gradual rather than instantaneous, progressive rather than immediate. See Maddox, *Responsible Grace*, 87; Iain H. Murray, *John Wesley and the Men Who Followed* (Edinburgh: Banner of Truth, 2003), 77.

86. Olson, *Arminian Theology*, 164–65, emphasis added. Also see Olson, "The Classical Free Will Theist Model of God," 167–68; idem, *Against Calvinism* (Grand Rapids: Zondervan, 2011), 171; Witt, "Arminius," 2:636–64.

87. Olson, therefore, even says that because of this intermediate stage the Arminian can say that regeneration precedes conversion. "That is, God begins the renewal of the soul that is often called being 'born again' before the human person exercises repentance and faith." However, this affirmation as made by the Arminian is very different (if not radically different) from that made by the Calvinist because for the Calvinist regeneration is actually complete, causing conversion. However, for Olson and Arminianism, this cannot be the case because

God (i.e. *gratia resistibilis*), the finality of regeneration is pending. It is not until the sinner decides to cooperate that he moves from this intermediate status, where he is neither unregenerate nor regenerate, to a regenerated status.[88]

Prevenient Grace Irresistible, Cooperating Grace Resistible

Is grace, for the Arminian, resistible or irresistible? Depending on what stage of grace is being referred to, the answer is both. Grace in its first coming or arrival as "prevenient" is irresistible. God bestows *prevenient* grace on sinners independent of whether they want it or not. However, once prevenient grace has been given by God, *subsequent* or *cooperating* grace can then be resisted.[89] Such a distinction is crucial to understanding the Arminian view correctly. The Arminian and Calvinist differ on exactly where grace is irresistible in the *via salutis*.[90] For the Arminian, God bestows a prevenient grace which, in its first stage, is irresistible, in order to enable man's faculties to cooperate. However, in the second stage, now that man is enabled to cooperate, he can accept or resist this subsequent grace (synergism). Not so for the Calvinist. Special, saving grace is always irresistible and, in one instantaneous act, God works monergistically not only to call but also to regenerate the sinner completely.

This two-stage process, the first irresistible and the second resistible, is also affirmed by Arminius.[91] While prevenient grace, says

---

of the "intermediate state." Regeneration is not complete but is contingent upon what man will do in this intermediate state. If man does decide to cooperate with grace, then man will come out of this intermediate state to be finally and completely regenerated. Olson, *Arminian Theology*, 164. Most Arminian theologies do not talk about an intermediate state; rather, when they organize the *ordo salutis*, they place faith, repentance, and justification before regeneration. Therefore, Olson's affirmation that regeneration precedes conversion is potentially misleading because he does not mean that regeneration in its entirety precedes conversion, otherwise the intermediate state would be negated.

88. Not all Arminians would agree with Olson that prevenient grace is applied in such a way that regeneration has begun but is incomplete. For example, see Picirilli, *Grace, Faith, Free Will*, 153, 156.

89. Oden, *The Transforming Power of Grace*, 47; Thomas C. Oden, *Systematic Theology*, 3 vols. (Peabody, MA: Hendrickson, 2006), 2:78; Collins, *The Scripture Way of Salvation*, 43–44.

90. Collins, *The Scripture Way of Salvation*, 44.

91. Arminius, "An Examination of the Treatise of William Perkins Concerning the Order and Mode of Predestination," in *Writings*, 3:470. Also see idem, "Certain Articles to be

Arminius, is given to man whether he desires it or not, once it is given it is up to him to decide whether or not he will give or withhold his assent to it. Eighteenth- and nineteenth-century Arminians would follow Arminius in this distinction, as is evident in Wesley and Fletcher.[92] Richard Watson, in his *Theological Institutes*, would say the same.[93] Such a distinction is apparent in contemporary Arminians also.[94] Thomas Oden distinguishes between prevenient grace and saving grace, stating, "*Prevenient* grace is the grace that begins to enable one to choose further to cooperate with *saving* grace. By offering the will the restored capacity to respond to grace, the person then may freely and increasingly become an active, willing participant in receiving the conditions for justification."[95] What Oden calls "saving" grace is also referred to as "cooperating" grace (*gratia cooperans*).[96] Therefore, God initiates prevenient grace, and once it is given man must decide of his own free will whether he will cooperate "with ever-fresh new offerings of grace."[97]

Prevenient Grace, Total Depravity, and Libertarian Freedom

Disagreement and Agreement. As with the debate over the scope of prevenient grace, disagreement continues among Arminians over the nature of free will in relation to prevenient grace and total deprav-

Diligently Examined and Weighed," in *Writings*, 2:498; Bangs, *Arminius*, 216; Witt, "Arminius," 2:655. Francis Turretin, *Institutes of Elenctic Theology*, ed. James T. Dennison Jr., trans. George Musgrave Giger, 3 vols. (Phillipsburg, NJ: P&R Publishing, 1992–97), 2:547–48, had this same reading of Arminius. See Sproul, *Willing to Believe*, 131–32. More recently, see Stanglin and McCall, *Jacob Arminius*, 151–64; den Boer, *God's Twofold Love*, 179–84.

92. Rogers, "Prevenient Grace," 162; Collins, *Wesley on Salvation*, 24. See John Fletcher, "Fourth Check," in *The Works of the Reverend John Fletcher* (New York: John Wilson and Daniel Hitt, 1809), 3:442–43, as quoted in Shipley, "Methodist Arminianism in the Theology of John Fletcher," 187.

93. Watson, *Theological Institutes*, 2:77; Olson, *Arminian Theology*, 171.

94. Cox, "Prevenient Grace," 147–48.

95. Oden, *John Wesley's Scriptural Christianity*, 243. Also see McGonigle, *Sufficient Saving Grace*, 5. Contra George Croft Cell, *The Rediscovery of John Wesley* (New York: H. Holt, 1935), 244–70.

96. Oden, *John Wesley's Scriptural Christianity*, 243; Oden, *The Transforming Power of Grace*, 51.

97. Oden, *John Wesley's Scriptural Christianity*, 244.

ity. As already discussed, while some Arminians deny total depravity, others believe man is totally depraved but, due to the gift of prevenient grace, total depravity is mitigated and a measure of man's free will is restored.[98] Arminians like Cottrell, Reichenbach, and Pinnock fall into the camp that denies man's total depravity, affirming that some degree of free will remains after the fall. Cottrell states, "The fact is, however, that the Bible does not picture man as totally depraved."[99] However, other Arminians disagree, arguing instead that man is totally depraved and utterly powerless in his will, though, due to the gift of prevenient grace, no man actually exists in such a state, but is born with an ability to cooperate with or resist God.[100]

Either way, Cottrell is right in concluding that both views believe that, at the moment of salvation, man's will is able to resist or cooperate with God's grace. Indeed, "the final decision belongs to each individual."[101] Whether or not the sinner is partially depraved and retains free will, or is depraved but with his depravity mitigated due to prevenient grace so that his will is made capable of cooperating, at the moment of the gospel call, it is still, as Arminius himself explains, in the power of man's will to choose or reject the grace of God.[102] What matters most, explains Cottrell, is that when the gospel message reaches the sinner, "he is *not* in a state of unremedied total depravity and thus of total inability" but "able to make his own decision of whether to believe or not."[103] It is this issue of man's final, determinative say in salvation that divides the Arminian from the Calvinist. Since, in the Arminian system, the final decision rests with the individual, the *type* of freedom man possesses is of critical importance.

98. Jack W. Cottrell, "The Classical Arminian View of Election," in *Perspectives on Election: Five Views*, ed. Chad O. Brand (Nashville: B&H Publishing Group, 2006), 120–21.

99. Cottrell, "Conditional Election," 68. Also see Reichenbach, "Freedom, Justice, and Moral Responsibility," 286; Pinnock, "From Augustine to Arminius," 21–22; idem, "Responsible Freedom and the Flow of Biblical History," 104–5.

100. Wesley, "Predestination Calmly Considered," in *Works* (Jackson), 10:229–30.

101. Cottrell, "The Classical Arminian View of Election," 121.

102. Arminius, "Certain Articles to be Diligently Examined and Weighed," in *Writings*, 2:497.

103. Cottrell, "The Classical Arminian View of Election," 121.

Defining Freedom as Libertarian. According to the Arminian, man's free will must be a *libertarian* freedom or a freedom of *contrary choice.* Libertarian freedom is an independence from necessity or determination, either external or internal to the choosing agent. As Arminius explains, "It is also a freedom from necessity, whether this proceeds from an external cause compelling, or from a nature inwardly determining absolutely to one thing."[104] According to Arminius, freedom from necessity "always pertains to him because it exists naturally in the will, as its proper attribute, so that there cannot be any will if it be not free."[105] Similarly, Wesley defines liberty as "a power of choosing for himself, a self-determining principle."[106] If I do not have a liberty of self-determination then I cannot trust all my "outward" and "inward" senses which tell me I can act to the contrary and that my choice "depends on me, and no other being."[107] Moreover, without such a liberty "man is under a moral necessity to accept grace because he is elect, or reject it because he is non-elect," an idea "repugnant to the notion of human liberty."[108] Consequently, as McGonigle explains, in Wesley's pneumatology there was absolutely "no place for a doctrine of irresistible grace."[109] Man must have a freedom of contrary choice where he can decide for himself whether he will or will not choose life. As John Fletcher states, "The error of rigid Calvinists centers in the denial of that evangelical liberty, whereby all men, under various dispensations of grace, may *without necessity* choose life."[110]

The description of libertarian freedom by Arminius, Wesley, and Fletcher is not only carried on by eighteenth-, nineteenth-, and twentieth-century Arminians like Clarke, Watson, Summers, Pope, Ralston, Raymond, Miley, and Wiley, but is also developed today by contemporary advocates of libertarian freedom such as Oden, Olson, Walls,

---

104. Arminius, "Twenty-Five Public Disputations," in *Writings*, 1:524; Bangs, *Arminius*, 341.

105. Arminius, "Twenty-Five Public Disputations," in *Writings*, 1:524. Also see Arminius, "Seventy-Nine Private Disputations," in *Writings*, 2:74, 75–76.

106. Wesley, "Thoughts upon Necessity," in *Works* (Jackson), 10:468 (cf. 10:467).

107. Ibid., 10:471. Also see Wesley, "Predestination Calmly Considered," 10:224.

108. Here McGonigle is summarizing Wesley. McGonigle, *Sufficient Saving Grace*, 307.

109. Ibid., 308.

110. John Fletcher, "On Reconciliation," in *Checks to Antinomianism* (New York: J. Collard, 1837), 2:333–34, quoted in Langford, *Practical Divinity*, 53.

Dongell, Reichenbach, Pinnock, and many others.[111] For example, J. P. Moreland and William Lane Craig define libertarian freedom as follows:

> Real freedom requires a type of control over one's actions—and, more importantly, over one's will—such that, given a choice to do *A* (raise one's hand and vote) or *B* (refrain from voting, leave the room), nothing determines that either choice is made. Rather the agent himself must simply exercise his own causal powers and will to do one alternative, say *A*. When an agent wills *A*, he also could have chosen *B* without anything else being different inside or outside of his being. He is the absolute originator of his own actions. . . . When an agent acts freely, he is a first or unmoved mover; no event causes him to act. His desires, beliefs and so on may influence his choice, but free acts are not caused by prior states in the agent; rather, they are spontaneously done by the agent himself acting as a first mover.[112]

There are several significant factors to consider here. First, libertarian freedom means that man can equally choose one alternative or another (*A* or *B*). If he did not choose *A* he could have chosen *B*.[113] Second, for man to be able to choose *A* or *B* he cannot be determined in any way. In other words, man is under no casual necessity or determination to

111. Oden, *John Wesley's Scriptural Christianity*, 248; Roger Olson, "Freedom/Free Will," in *The Westminster Handbook*, 187; idem, "Grace," in *The Westminster Handbook*, 194–95; Reichenbach, "Freedom, Justice, and Moral Responsibility," 285; idem, "God Limits His Power," in *Predestination and Free Will: Four Views of Divine Sovereignty and Human Freedom*, ed. David Basinger and Randall Basinger (Downers Grove, IL: InterVarsity, 1986), 102–4; Jerry L. Walls and Joseph R. Dongell, *Why I am Not a Calvinist* (Downers Grove, IL: InterVarsity, 2004), 103; Clark Pinnock, *Most Moved Mover: A Theology of God's Openness* (Grand Rapids: Baker Academic, 2001), 127. Similarly see John Sanders, *The God Who Risks: A Theology of Providence* (Downers Grove, IL: InterVarsity, 1998), 221; David Basinger, "Middle Knowledge and Classical Christian Thought," *Religious Studies* 22 (1986): 416; Gregory A. Boyd, *Satan and the Problem of Evil* (Downers Grove, IL: InterVarsity, 2001), 60; William Hasker, "A Philosophical Perspective," in *The Openness of God: A Biblical Challenge to the Traditional Understanding of God*, by Clark H. Pinnock, Richard Rice, John Sanders, William Hasker, and David Basinger (Downers Grove, IL: InterVarsity, 1994), 136–37.

112. J. P. Moreland and William Lane Craig, *Philosophical Foundations for a Christian Worldview* (Downers Grove, IL: InterVarsity, 2003), 270.

113. Jack Cottrell, *What the Bible Says about God the Ruler*, vol. 2 of *The Doctrine of God* (Eugene, OR: Wipf and Stock, 1984), 192.

choose either *A* or *B*.[114] Third, when man chooses, he could have chosen otherwise "without anything else being different inside or outside of his being." The factors that would influence one to choose *A* have not changed if one would have chosen *B*. For something to be different inside or outside of man's being would mean that man is not the "absolute originator of his own actions." Man must be, in order to act freely, the "first or unmoved mover" in any particular choice, for "no event causes him to act." If man is not his own unmoved mover, then some event has caused him to act, and therefore he is not truly free in the libertarian sense. However, Moreland and Craig make a qualification: if man is an unmoved mover, that does not mean that he is not influenced by his own desires or beliefs or by the influences of external sources (other people, his environment, or God). Rather, what it does mean is that even though man's choice is influenced, no choice can ever be caused by an influence or by "prior states in the agent." As Moreland and Craig state, "An agent must be the absolute, originating source of his own actions to be in control."[115] Or as Gregory Boyd puts it, man must be the "ultimate cause and explanation."[116]

Libertarian Freedom and Synergism. The doctrine of libertarian freedom is what guarantees synergism for the Arminian. While there can be many *internal* influences in man, no prior state in him can necessitate his choice at the present. What "internal influences in man" could the Arminian possibly be worried about? The answer must be man's own corrupt nature. If man is pervasively corrupt, then the will is indeed influenced in a causal way to choose one thing (sin) over another (God). Therefore, the Arminian has two options: (1) deny total depravity or (2) affirm total depravity but argue that no person ever exists in such

114. See Episcopius, *The Confession of Faith of Those Called Arminians*, 64. Episcopius is reiterating Arminius, "Certain Articles to be Diligently Examined and Weighed," in *Writings*, 2:491. See Eaton, "Arminianism in the Theology of John Wesley," 67.

115. See Moreland and Craig, *Philosophical Foundations*, 271–72.

116. Boyd, *Satan and the Problem of Evil*, 375. Consequently, libertarian freedom is incompatible with divine determinism. If God determines man's actions, especially in salvation, then man does not possess the power of contrary choice but rather is necessitated to choose one thing over another. Therefore, those who affirm libertarianism also embrace indeterminism.

a state due to prevenient grace. Reichenbach, for example, opts for the former in order to preserve libertarian freedom.[117] However, either option removes the causal nature of depravity and corruption so that at the moment of decision man has no internal factor that would necessitate him choosing sin instead of God.[118] Rather, man has the ability of contrary choice and he is able to choose God or reject God, cooperate with grace or resist grace, and nothing internal to man causes him to do one rather than the other.

Moreover, not only can no prior state *in man* necessitate his present choice, but neither can a prior state *outside of man* necessitate his present choice. As Reichenbach explains, in order for man to be free, he must be able to say that "he was not compelled by causes either internal to himself (genetic structure or irresistible drives) or external (other persons, God) to act as he did."[119] The key word used by Reichenbach is "God." God himself is one of the "external" influences that cannot sway man to such a degree that he *must* choose A instead of B. "Though certain causal conditions are present and indeed are necessary for persons to choose or act, if they are free *these causal conditions are not sufficient to cause them to choose or act. The individual is the sufficient condition for the course of action chosen.*"[120] Therefore, God, being one of these external "causal conditions," can seek to influence man to choose A instead of B, but cannot act in such a way that man would necessarily have to choose A instead of B. It is man's choice which must be the "sufficient condition for the course of action chosen," not God's.

117. Also see Reichenbach, "Freedom, Justice, and Moral Responsibility," 286.
118. This does not mean, however, that without prevenient grace men do not possess libertarian freedom due to the bondage of depravity. For the Arminian who affirms total depravity, even in the hypothetically depraved state, the sinner would still possesses libertarian freedom. However, such libertarian freedom is not an absolute or unrestricted freedom. In other words, the depraved sinner has a libertarian choice between various options of evil, so that he can choose one evil or another equally. However, due to depravity, the will does not have the option of choosing God. Therefore, even libertarian freedom is a limited freedom. However, once prevenient grace is in effect, the options are expanded so that choosing God is now possible. See Reichenbach, "God Limits His Power,"102–4.
119. Ibid. Also see Reichenbach, "Freedom, Justice, and Moral Responsibility," 286.
120. Reichenbach, "God Limits His Power,"102–4.

What this means then is that God's grace must be resistible. If God's saving grace is irresistible or necessarily effectual, then man's libertarian freedom is violated and it is not man who is the "sufficient condition for the course of action chosen" but God. Cottrell clearly understands such an implication; that is why he says, "All Arminians believe that at the time of the hearing of the general gospel call, every sinner has the free will either to accept or to reject it."[121]

Synergism, then, is grounded in the adoption of libertarian freedom. Regardless of how the Arminian gets there (whether through a denial of total depravity or an affirmation of prevenient grace), at the moment of salvation the sinner has a libertarian will that is capable to choose *A* (God's grace) or to choose *B* (reject God's grace), and such a choice, if it is to remain undetermined and therefore libertarian, cannot in any way be necessitated or caused by God. God can woo, pursue, and lure man to himself, but never in such a way that his drawing of man is necessary and determined.[122]

Biblical Support for Libertarian Freedom. Now that we have a definition of libertarian freedom and its role in relation to synergism, we must examine the reasons Arminians give from Scripture to show why such a notion is biblical. For the Arminian and Wesleyan, the power of contrary choice must be granted by God because God has issued *commands, invitations, and promises* in Scripture that imply that man possesses the ability to obey.[123] For example, God has issued many *invitations* to come to him and believe (Joel 2:32; Matt. 7:24; 10:32–33; 11:6, 28; 12:50; 16:24–25; Mark 16:15–16; John 1:7, 9; 3:15–16; 4:13–14; 6:40, 51; 7:17, 37; 8:51; 11:26; 12:46; Acts 2:21, 37, 40; 8:36–37; 10:32, 43; 16:30–31; Rom. 9:33; 10:9–13; 1 John 2:23; 4:15; Rev. 3:20; 22:17).

121. Cottrell, "The Classical Arminian View of Election," 120–21.
122. Keith D. Stanglin, *Arminius on the Assurance of Salvation* (Leiden: E. J. Brill, 2007), 79–80.
123. Reichenbach, "God Limits His Power," 104. Also see Pope, *Christian Theology*, 2:344–45; Clarke, *Christian Theology*, 130–32; Miley, *Systematic Theology*, 2:245–46; Thiessen, *Lectures in Systematic Theology*, 106; Gregory A. Boyd and Paul R. Eddy, *Across the Spectrum: Understanding Issues in Evangelical Theology*, 2nd ed. (Grand Rapids: Baker, 2009), 155.

Arminians like Steve Lemke have called these the "All-Inclusive Invitations in Scripture,"[124] and he believes they disprove irresistible grace because in them God not only invites but also *commands* all people to repent and believe in Christ, *promising* that if they do they will inherit eternal life (Josh. 24:15; 1 Chron. 16:11; 2 Chron. 7:14; Pss. 9:10; 34:10; Matt. 16:24; Acts 2:38; 13:26; 16:31; Eph. 5:14; Rev. 3:20).[125] God would not command, invite, warn, and even give promises of reward if he had not provided man, via prevenient grace, with the ability to do so.[126] For example, Romans 2:4 states, "Or do you show contempt for the riches of his kindness, tolerance and patience, not realizing that God's kindness leads you toward repentance?" (NIV). God, in his kindness is waiting for the sinner to repent. Why would God command the sinner to repent and then wait for the sinner to repent if he had not already granted to the sinner the ability to do so? If it is not the case that we are able to come, then God's sincerity in such invitations and promises is without credibility.[127]

Synergism and the Arminian Appeal to Scripture

Prevenient grace does not *guarantee* that the sinner will choose to believe, but merely provides the *opportunity* for the sinner to exercise his libertarian freedom to believe.[128] Therefore, due to man's power of contrary choice, while prevenient grace is *necessary*, it is not *sufficient*, since man can ultimately veto divine grace.[129] Arminians believe that several biblical passages demonstrate the resistibility of grace (Prov. 1:23–25;

124. Steve W. Lemke, "A Biblical and Theological Critique of Irresistible Grace," in *Whosoever Will: A Biblical-Theological Critique of Five-Point Calvinism*, ed. David L. Allen and Steve W. Lemke (Nashville: B&H Publishing Group, 2010), 122–27.

125. Ibid., 157–59. Also see Witt, "Arminius," 2:619.

126. Wesley, "Thoughts upon God's Sovereignty," in *Works* (Jackson), 10:362.

127. Wesley, "Predestination Calmly Considered," in *Works* (Jackson), 10:226–27.
Furthermore, argues the Arminian, not only is libertarian freedom assumed in Scripture, but also human culpability and responsibility only make sense if man is free in a libertarian way. See Wesley, "On Predestination," in *Works* (Jackson), 6:227.

128. Collins, *Wesley on Salvation*, 23; Boyd, *Satan and the Problem of Evil*, 83.

129. Greg Welty, "Election and Calling: A Biblical Theological Study," in *Calvinism: A Southern Baptist Dialogue*, ed. E. Ray Clendenen and Brad J. Waggoner (Nashville: B&H Academic, 2008), 234.

Hos. 11:1–9; Pss. 78:10; 81:11–13; 95:7–8; Jer. 17:23; 32:33; Isa. 5:4; Zech. 1:3; Matt. 22:3; 23:37; Luke 13:34; Mark 6:5–6; Luke 7:29–30; John 6:63; Acts 7:51; Heb. 3:7–12).[130] Consider, for example, Matthew 23:37, where Jesus cries out, longing to gather Israel to himself as his children, but they would not let him! Or Acts 7:51, where Stephen states that the Jews "always resist the Holy Spirit" just as their fathers did. Based on passages such as these, Arminians believe that while it is God who initiates the free gift of prevenient grace, it is man who has the ultimate determinative choice as to whether he will or will not be saved.[131] He is able of his own free will to resist the Spirit and thwart God's saving purpose.[132]

However, Arminians believe not only that Scripture contains texts where the sinner *resists* grace, but that it also contains texts where the sinner *cooperates with* grace. Thomas Summers (1812–82), for example, provides a thorough presentation of synergism from Scripture by beginning with the Old Testament.[133] First, he appeals to Deuteronomy 30:15–20 (cf. Jer. 21:8), where Yahweh says he has set before Israel life and death and it is up to the people to choose for themselves which of the two they will have. Summers then turns to Ezekiel 18:31, in which Yahweh commands Israel to repent and turn from their transgressions. Yahweh states that the sinner is to make for himself a new heart. These passages, says Summers, are clear examples of man's ability to cooperate. Summers also sees Ezekiel 36:25–26, a text to which Calvinists often appeal, as a passage where "we have divine and human agencies, preventing and co-operating grace."[134] He sees the same type of cooperation in Jeremiah

---

130. Many of these texts can be found listed as support by Wesley in "Predestination Calmly Considered," in *Works* (Jackson), 10:254–55; Lemke, "Critique of Irresistible Grace," 117–20; Oden, *The Power of Transforming Grace*, 49, 114.

131. Robert V. Rakeshaw, "John Wesley as a Theologian of Grace," *JETS* 27 (1984): 199.

132. Lemke, "Critique of Irresistible Grace," 129.

133. Most Arminians only appeal to those texts above where man resists grace. Very few, if any, Arminians today interact with Scripture to show that man cooperates with grace. Consequently, I have chosen to interact with Summers because he actually tries to argue for synergism from the text. I will be using the translations of Scripture that Summers quotes. Summers, *Systematic Theology*, 85–90.

134. Summers, *Systematic Theology*, 85.

31:33 and Hebrews 8:10 and 10:15–17. Jeremiah 31:18 is so explicit that God says, "Turn thou me, and I shall be turned." Summers concludes, "What a striking case of co-operation is here!"[135] Similarly, he believes Psalm 25:8–9 teaches that "those who with docility yield to his gracious influence will be sure to be led into the way of life."[136]

Yet, synergism is not limited to the Old Testament but can be found also in the New. In John 6:44–46, a Calvinist proof text, the "*giving* here is the same as the *drawing* in ver. 44, and implies willingness, docility, and concurrence on the part of those thus given or drawn."[137] Therefore, John 6 does not support irresistible grace, says Summers, but synergism and the dependency of grace upon man's will. Such dependency and conditionality of God upon man's will is again proven from Matthew 11:28–30 where Christ tells sinners to come to him and take his yoke. If we come to him, he will come to us. As John 7:17 says, "If any man will do his will, he shall know of the doctrine, whether it be of God." Summers interprets, "Here the verb 'will' is not a sign of the future tense, but it denotes volition—'will to do'—not if any man should do it, but if any man is disposed to do it—resolves to comply with God's will. This is a rule of universal application."[138]

Perhaps one of the most quoted passages in support of synergism, though, is Revelation 3:20: "Behold I stand at the door and knock: if any man hear my voice, and open the door, I will come in to him, and will sup with him, and he with me." Summers elaborates, "The standing and knocking and calling . . . sets forth preventing and co-operating grace."[139] God knocks on the door of our heart but waits upon us to open that door and let him in. Summers believes this is the case with Lydia (Acts 16:14) and Cornelius (Acts 10). Is God's opening of Lydia's heart a monergistic act? No, for "she opened it herself; for she availed herself of the opportunity to hear the gospel,

---

135. Ibid. Also see Pope, *Christian Theology*, 2:365.
136. Summers, *Systematic Theology*, 85.
137. Ibid., 85–86.
138. Ibid., 87.
139. Ibid.

listened attentively to it, yielded with ingenuousness and docility to the gracious influence thus brought to bear upon her, and promptly espoused the cause of Christ."[140] The same is true of Cornelius and Saul of Tarsus, who respond to the divine call with "Lord, what wilt thou have me to do?" Here, Summers insists, are further examples of "co-operation with divine grace."[141]

Synergism is again evident with the Bereans (Acts 17:11–12) and the Gentiles in Antioch (Acts 13:45–48), who turned to God for life.[142] The ability to turn and come to Christ is also demonstrated in Hebrews 11:6: "He that cometh to God must believe that he is, and that he is a rewarder of them that diligently seek him." Promising a reward makes no sense if there is not something to reward, namely, man's part in cooperating with grace. Summers also argues that "Peter sets forth the same synergistic doctrine" in 1 Peter 1:22–23. "They purified themselves, but it was through the Spirit; they were to love the brethren, but then they were to be born again in order that they might fulfill the injunction."[143] Or consider "that wonderful synergistic passage," Romans 8:26, in which Paul says that the Spirit helps sinners pray. Yet, we "cannot employ the Holy Spirit as our proxy to do our praying for us, and, on the other hand, we cannot pray for ourselves without his assistance."[144]

Summers shows that for the Arminian all of these passages give ample proof of synergism in conversion. William Pope (1822–1903) agrees: "We find it [synergism], literally, in all those passages which declare that believers themselves voluntarily receive the Word of God or of Christ or of grace."[145]

Having seen what Scriptures Arminians appeal to, let us now try to understand exactly how Arminians believe synergism works itself out in practice.

140. Ibid.
141. Ibid., 88.
142. Ibid., 88.
143. Ibid., 89.
144. Ibid., 90.
145. Pope lists 1 Thess. 1:6; 2:13; Col. 1:6; 2 Cor. 6:1. Pope, *Christian Theology*, 2:366.

The Complexity of Synergism in the Arminian Tradition

Synergism according to Arminius and the Remonstrants. For Arminius, if libertarian freedom is restored in greater measure by prevenient grace so that man can now choose whether or not he will cooperate with God's subsequent grace, then such a grace must be resistible. Such resistibility presupposes a synergistic relationship (*synergismus*) between the sinner and God.[146] Rather than God working alone, or monergistically, to effectually call and regenerate the sinner by a grace that is irresistible, God's grace is successful if, and only if, man chooses to cooperate (*cooperatio*) with it.[147] God woos and persuades (Arminius's word) the sinner, but God does not overpower, overwhelm, or irresistibly change the sinner.

The resistibility of grace parallels the resistibility of God's call.[148] The call of God can excite, draw, and assist through grace, but man always has the ability to resist and refuse to assent.[149] Arminius even goes so far as to say that man may be passive, simply receiving the grace bestowed, as long as he still reserves the freedom to either give or withhold his assent when he feels grace affecting and inclining his mind and heart.[150] Arminius did not accept the Calvinistic distinction between an effectual call and an ineffectual call, as articulated by Calvin himself in

146. Witt, "Arminius," 2:661.

147. Arminius, "Declaration of Sentiments," in *Writings*, 1:253–54, emphasis added; idem, "Certain Articles to be Diligently Examined and Weighed," in *Writings*, 2:497–98; Also see Witt, "Arminius," 2:639–45. On the synergism of Arminius made evident in his dialogue with Adrianus Smetius, see Bangs, *Arminius*, 324–25; Witt, "Arminius," 2:657–59; Eric H. Cossee, "Arminius and Rome," in Leeuwen, Stanglin, and Tolsma, *Arminius, Arminianism, and Europe,* 73–88.

148. Stanglin, *Arminius on the Assurance of Salvation,* 94; Richard A. Muller, "Grace, Election, and Contingent Choice: Arminius's Gambit and the Reformed Response," in *The Grace of God, the Bondage of the Will: Historical and Theological Perspectives on Calvinism*, ed. Thomas R. Schreiner and Bruce A. Ware (Grand Rapids: Baker, 1995), 260.

149. Arminius, "Certain Articles to be Diligently Examined and Weighed," in *Writings*, 2:498. See Witt, "Arminius," 2:633; Bangs, *Arminius*, 343; Richard Muller, *God, Creation, and Providence in the Thought of James Arminius: Sources and Directions of Scholastic Protestantism in the Era of Early Orthodoxy* (Grand Rapids: Baker, 1991), 308; Clarke, *The Ground of Election*, 76–77.

150. Arminius, "Certain Articles to be Diligently Examined and Weighed," in *Writings*, 2:498–99, emphasis added.

his *Institutes*.[151] Muller explains that "The 'efficacy' of calling, according to Arminius, results from the concurrence of the external calling of the preached Word with the internal calling of the Spirit, but this is an efficacy that may be rejected by the hearer of the Word who may resist the divine counsel and the work of the Spirit."[152] Muller rightly concludes that Arminius's doctrine carries a "synergistic emphasis" because man can reject God's call.[153] Such an emphasis is a concession to the medieval maxim, made famous by William of Ockham and Gabriel Biel, that *facienti quod in se est* (God will deny his grace to no one who does what is in himself). As Arminius states, "For if the expression be understood in this sense, to the one who does what he can (*potest*) by the first grace already conferred on him, then there is no absurdity in saying God will bestow further grace on him who profitably uses what is first."[154]

The synergism of Arminius takes on further meaning when he states that when the sinner rejects God's grace and call (that is, the universal call or *vocatio catholica*), such a rejection is in no way intended by God himself. Arminius writes, "The accidental result of vocation, and that which is not of itself intended by God, is the rejection of the word of grace, the contemning of the divine counsel, the resistance offered to the Holy Spirit."[155] Such a rejection and resistance is not willed by God but is in its entirety due to the "malice and hardness of the human heart."[156] Here we see that for Arminius the resistance to the divine call

---

151. John Calvin, *Institutes of the Christian Religion*, ed. John T. McNeil, trans. Ford Lewis Battles, LCC, vols. 20–21 (Philadelphia: Westminster John Knox, 1960), 3.24.8. Also see Bangs, *Arminius*, 213, 343.

152. Muller, "Grace, Election, and Contingent Choice," 261.

153. Arminius, "A Letter to Hippolytus A Collibus," in *Writings*, 2:470–73. See Muller, "Grace, Election, and Contingent Choice," 260–61; idem, "The Priority of the Intellect in the Soteriology of James Arminius," *WTJ* 55 (1993): 55–72; idem, "Arminius and the Scholastic Tradition," *CTJ* 24 (1989): 269; idem, *God, Creation, and Providence*, 78ff.

154. Arminius, "Apology Against Thirty-one Theological Articles," in *Writings*, 1:329. Muller argues that even though Arminius affirms prevenient grace, there may still be hints of Semi-Pelagianism because his modification of the maxim is slight. Muller, "Grace, Election, and Contingent Choice," 261, 277. On Arminius and this medieval maxim also see Stanglin, *Arminius on the Assurance of Salvation*, 82–83.

155. Arminius, "Twenty-Five Public Disputations," in *Writings*, 1:574. Also see Arminius, "Seventy-Nine Private Disputations," in *Writings*, 2:106.

156. Muller, "Grace, Election, and Contingent Choice," 262.

is "accidental" and unintended by God.[157] Does such an accident render God frustrated and impotent since the sinner successfully thwarts God's will? Arminius does not think so since "the ultimate end of God's designs is not the life of this human being and the death of that, but the illustration of the divine goodness, justice, wisdom, and power—which he always obtains."[158]

To conclude, the synergism of Arminius is a *major* tenet of his overall system of conditioning God's saving efforts on the will of man. As Aza Gouldriaan states, "According to Arminius, it is up to the human being to decide whether to use free choice well and to accept grace in order to be saved. Those who deliberately refuse grace will not be saved."[159] Therefore, the synergism of Arminius, as Muller observes, was considered "inimical to the Pauline and Augustinian foundation of Reformed Protestantism."[160]

This synergism was again highlighted by the Remonstrants at the Synod of Dort, who were led by Episcopius. As already discussed, the *Five Articles* originally presented by the Remonstrants were brief, so Dort called upon them to present a fuller description of their views, which resulted in the *Sententiae Remonstrantium*. Synergism is readily apparent throughout the document as the Remonstrants explicitly reject irresistible and effectual grace. Though the Spirit confers the strength to believe, nevertheless, "man is able of himself to despise that grace and not to believe, and therefore to perish through his own fault."[161]

Synergism in the *Sententiae Remonstrantium* is again reiterated by Episcopius in the *Arminian Confession* of 1621. There is perhaps no other statement which so clearly articulates both a rejection of monergism and an affirmation of synergism.[162] It is very evident

---

157. Clarke, *The Ground of Election*, 93; Witt, "Arminius," 2:642.

158. Arminius, "Examination of Dr. Perkins's Pamphlet on Predestination," in *Writings*, 3:478; Witt, "Arminius," 2:642–43.

159. Aza Goudriaan, " 'Augustine Asleep' or 'Augustine Awake'? James Arminius's Reception of Augustine," in Leeuwen, Stanglin, and Tolsma, *Arminius, Arminianism, and Europe*, 69.

160. Muller, "Grace, Election, and Contingent Choice," 277.

161. As quoted in "Appendix H: The Opinions of the Remonstrants," 226.

162. Episcopius, *The Confession of Faith of Those Called Arminians*, 106–10. On the synergism of Episcopius, see Jan Rohls, "Calvinism, Arminianism and Socinianism in the Netherlands

that for Arminians like Episcopius, God's intention to save can be resisted and thwarted, and unless man cooperates with God's grace it is left ineffective.[163] Muller writes concerning such a synergism that it was not only inimical "to the Reformed, Augustinian, and Pauline doctrine of predestination but also to the fundamental teaching of the Reformation that salvation is by grace alone."[164] As the Reformed saw things, the Remonstrant synergism was an apparent threat to *sola gratia* because it added human contribution to salvation, even if that salvation was initiated by God. Eric Cossee brings out this point when he states that the Remonstrants were seeking to preserve free will. "Following Arminius, the Remonstrants made a powerful plea for acknowledgment of *a human contribution to the implementation of God's intention towards man.* God's greatness must not preclude the recognition of people as responsible beings."[165] Likewise, David Eaton, commenting on Arminius, observes the same, "Synergistic methodologies . . . require the imposition of prevenient grace but postulate a sufficient human ability to accept and cooperate with prevenient grace. . . . This seems to be a *human work be it ever so slight. Yet not so slight since one has power to accept or reject* God's acceptance, love, and mercy."[166]

Synergism according to Wesley and Wesleyanism. Such synergism is evident in the writings of Wesley and Wesleyanism as well. Wesley was a staunch defender of Arminian synergism against the "horrible blasphemies" and "mischievous doctrine" of Calvinism, as represented in particular by George Whitefield (1714–70) and Augustus Toplady (1740–78), who argued that Wesley seriously erred in teaching that

until the Synod of Dort," in *Socinianism and Arminianism: Antitrinitarians, Calvinists, and Cultural Exchange in Seventeenth-Century Europe*, ed. Marin Mulsow and Jan Rohls (Leiden: E. J. Brill, 2005), 34.

163. For a summary of the Remonstrant view of synergism, see Oden, *The Transforming Power of Grace*, 153–54.

164. Muller, "Grace, Election, and Contingent Choice," 262–63.

165. Eric Cossee, "Our Liberal Protestant Heritage, A European Perspective," *The Non-Subscribing Presbyterian* 15 (1997), 1088 (cf. 99).

166. Eaton, "Arminianism in the Theology of John Wesley," 76, emphasis added.

God granted to all men the ability to freely come to or resist Christ.[167] As founder of the *Arminian Magazine* (which argued that Calvinism is "very shocking, and ought utterly to be abhorred"), Wesley rejected irresistible grace, arguing that if God acts irresistibly then man is no longer a moral agent.[168] Wesley preached (cf. "Free Grace," "Predestination Calmly Considered") that though prevenient grace enables, making a willful response possible, it is not necessary or determined.[169] Therefore, synergism is characterized first by a divine initiative but ultimately by a human freedom which determines the success of divine grace.[170]

Despite the uniformity in affirming synergism seen so far, differences evolved as to how strong or soft this synergism is.[171] Langford identifies three views, which I have labeled as follows:

(1) *Strong synergism*, which credits man with the initiative (affirmed by Rupert Davies and Umphrey Lee[172]).

(2) *Semi-strong synergism*, where man does not initiate but merely responds (affirmed by William Cannon, Harald Lindstrom, and Colin Williams[173]).

167. Wesley, "Free Grace," in *Works* (Jackson), 7:381. Also see McGonigle, *Sufficient Saving Grace*, 6, 316.

168. Wesley, "The General Spread of the Gospel," in *Works* (Jackson), 2:488–89; Wesley, "Free Grace," in *Works* (Jackson), 7:383–84; idem, "On Predestination," in *Works* (Jackson), 6:225–30; idem, "Predestination Calmly Considered," in *Works* (Jackson), 10:204–58; idem, "A Dialogue between a Predestinarian and His Friend," in *Works* (Jackson), 10:259–65; idem, "The Question, 'What Is an Arminian?,'" in *Works* (Jackson), 10:358–60; idem, "Thoughts upon God's Sovereignty," in *Works* (Jackson), 10:361–63; idem, "Thoughts upon Necessity," in *Works* (Jackson), 10:457–79. Also see McGonigle, *Sufficient Saving Grace*, 305; Maddox, *Responsible Grace*, 86. To qualify, Wesley is inconsistent in his rejection of irresistible grace, as he leaves room for possible exceptions. See Wesley, "Predestination Calmly Considered," 10:254–55; McGonigle, *Sufficient Saving Grace*, 154–55, 281.

169. Suchocki, "Wesleyan Grace," 541.

170. Maddox, *Responsible Grace*, 66–67; Suchocki, "Wesleyan Grace," 541–42; Runyon, *The New Creation*, 30–31; Langford, *Practical Divinity*, 33–34; John C. English, "References to St. Augustine in the Works of John Wesley," *ATJ* 60, 2 (2005): 5–24; Runyon, *The New Creation*, 30–31.

171. Langford, *Practical Divinity*, 33.

172. Rupert E. Davies, "The People Called Methodist: 'Our Doctrines,'" in *History of Methodist Church in Great Britain*, ed. Rupert Davies, George A. Raymond, and Rupp Gordon (London: Epworth, 1965), 1:158; Lee, *John Wesley and Modern Religion*, 110.

173. Cannon, *The Theology of John Wesley*, 113; Lindstrom, *Wesley and Sanctification*, 46; Williams, *John Wesley's Theology Today*, 42–43.

(3) *Soft synergism*, where grace works invincibly unless man resists proactively (promoted by Robert Cushman[174]).

William Cannon argues that without a doubt Wesley went beyond Arminius in affirming a strong synergism.[175] Nevertheless, argues Cannon, Wesley's strong synergism is more consistent than Arminius's view of *mere resistance*. For Wesley, Cannon notes, man is able not just to resist but to actively kill divine grace. He thwarts the power of the gospel and "is the absolute master of his fate and the captain of his own salvation." Once man is made the deciding factor, says Cannon, you lift him out of a state "of mere passivity into one of activity and of co-operation or non-operation with the grace of God."[176] Thus, man has a *major role* in his own salvation. This being the case, Cannon is comfortable affirming that there is not only a divine initiative with a human response but also a "human initiative" that brings about the "divine response."[177]

Nevertheless, for other Arminians, synergism does not mean that God and man are *equal* in cooperating with one another. Rather, God is the initiator and man the enabled responder.[178] Describing the synergism of Arminius, Roger Olson comments,

> Was Arminius's soteriology then synergistic? Yes, but not in the way that is often understood. Calvinists tend to regard synergism as equal cooperation between God and a human in salvation; thus the human is contributing something crucial and efficacious to salvation. But this is not Arminius's synergism. Rather, this is an evangelical synergism that reserves all the power, ability and efficacy in salvation to grace, but allows humans the God-granted ability to resist or not resist it. The only "contribution" humans make is non-resistance to grace.[179]

174. Robert E. Cushman, "Salvation for All," in *Methodism*, ed. William Anderson (Nashville/New York: Abingdon/Cokesbury, 1947), 105–11.

175. Cannon, *The Theology of John Wesley*, 108.

176. Ibid., 114–15.

177. Ibid., 115.

178. See Shipley, "Methodist Arminianism in the Theology of John Fletcher," 222–23. Pope says the same in *Christian Theology*, 2:364–65.

179. Olson, *Arminian Theology*, 165. See Arminius, "Apology Against Thirty-One Defamatory Articles," in *Writings*, 1:365–66; Stanglin, *Arminius on the Assurance of Salvation*,

Olson is reacting to Philip Limborch who elevated man's will to such a height that the sinner's role in synergism is equal with God's. According to Limborch, prevenient grace is not so much restorative, renewing the enslaved will, as it is assisting, simply strengthening the natural ability that is already there.[180] To the dissatisfaction of Arminians like Olson, Limborch's doctrine was resurrected by Nathaniel Taylor (1786–1858) and nineteenth-century revivalist Charles Finney (1792–1875), who argued that man has a natural ability to repent and obey God's law.[181] Semi-Pelagianism, however, came into conflict with the *Christian Theology* of Adam Clarke (1760–1832) and the *Christian Institutes* (1823) of British Methodist Richard Watson (1781–1833).[182] Watson, though, made sure to preserve man's free will, arguing that God's qualities of justice and goodness must be expressed "not through irresistible grace, but through a grace that both creates and relies upon human responsibility."[183] For prevenient grace to be successful, man must cooperate with it or "improve upon" it.[184] The same can be said for Thomas Summers (1812–82), William B. Pope (1822–1903), and Thomas N. Ralston (1806–91).[185] Summers' *Systematic Theology: A Complete Body of Wesleyan Arminian Divinity*, for example, also sought to rescue Arminian synergism from Pelagianism and Semi-Pelagianism.[186] Specifically, he rejected Limborch, Taylor, and Whitby, "who pass under the name of Arminians, by a misnomer."[187] Summers also rejected New England's eighteenth-century

---

98; Peter White, *Predestination, Policy, and Polemic: Conflict and Consensus in the English Church from the Reformation to the Civil War* (Cambridge: Cambridge University Press, 1992), 33–34.

180. Hicks, "The Theology of Grace," 177, 286; Olson, *Arminian Theology*, 167–68.

181. Charles Finney, *Finney's Systematic Theology*, ed. J. H. Fairchild (Minneapolis: Bethany Fellowship, 1976), 199–278.

182. See Adam Clarke, *Christian Theology* (New York: Eaton and Mains, 1835).

183. Langford, *Practical Divinity*, 64. Also see McGonigle, *Sufficient Saving Grace*, 4.

184. Watson, *Theological Institutes*, 2:77. Also see Olson, *Arminian Theology*, 171.

185. Summers, *Systematic Theology*, 2:19–92; Pope, *A Compendium of Christian Theology*, 2:3–84, 319–451; Thomas Ralston, *Elements of Divinity* (Louisville: Morton and Griswald, 1847), 238–57.

186. Summers, *Systematic Theology*, 2:81, 2:34. Also see 2:54–56, 62–63, 68–69. This same approach is taken by Pope, *Christian Theology*, 2:390.

187. Summers, *Systematic Theology*, 2:34–35. Summers instead seeks to uphold the Arminianism of Wilbur Fisk, Miner Raymond, J. O. A. Clarke, William Pope, Watson, and others.

"New Divinity," which is "essentially Pelagian, as it denies that sin is in the nature of man, but only in his voluntary actions, and affirms that man has the natural ability to do what God requires."[188]

However, as seen with Summers, the emphasis on prevenient grace was never at the expense of highlighting man's determinative say in salvation. For example, while Pope's *A Compendium of Christian Theology* (1874) argues that prevenient grace "is free in all, to all, and for all,"[189] it also argues that the divine operation "acts in such a manner as not to interfere with the natural freedom of the will." Though it is because of divine grace, ultimately "man determines himself."[190] The same emphasis becomes evident in the systematic theologies of Miner Raymond (1877) and John Miley (1892–94).[191] Miley, for example, made "free personal agency the foundation principle of his work"[192] and his "Ethical Arminianism" brought him into conflict with Princetonian Benjamin B. Warfield (1851–1921), a Calvinist in the tradition of Charles Hodge (1797–1878).[193]

Despite these efforts to avoid Semi-Pelagianism, Nazarene scholar H. Orton Wiley (1877–1961) would show much sympathy with Limborch's theology, arguing that man's free will was not destroyed by Adam's fall but retains the power of volition so he can cooperate with grace.[194] Such inconsistency plagues pockets of Arminianism in which Semi-Pelagianism still finds a home.

Synergism according to Contemporary Arminians. In the twentieth century a number of Arminian and Wesleyan scholars have come to the

---

188. Ibid., 2:63.

189. Langford, *Practical Divinity*, 69. Also see McGonigle, *Sufficient Saving Grace*, 4–5.

190. Pope, *Christian Theology*, 2:367. Also see Wiley, *Christian Theology*, 2:355.

191. Miner Raymond, *Systematic Theology*, 3 vols. (New York, Phillips & Hunt, 1877–79), 2:7–406.

192. Langford, *Wesleyan Theology*, 127. Also see idem, *Practical Divinity*, 114; Olson, *Arminian Theology*, 261; Chiles, *Theological Transition in American Methodism*, 60.

193. For Warfield's review of Miley see Benjamin B. Warfield, "Review of John Miley's *Systematic Theology*," in *Selected Shorter Writings*, ed. John E. Meeter (Phillipsburg, NJ: Presbyterian and Reformed, 1980), 2:308.

194. Olson, *Arminian Theology*, 175. See Wiley, *Christian Theology*, 2:352, 354, 356–57.

defense of synergism. For example, New Testament scholar I. Howard Marshall argues that, "The effect of the call of God is to place man in a position where he can say 'Yes' or 'No' (which he could not do before God called him; till then he was in a continuous attitude of 'No')."[195] Similarly, Cox argues that salvation "is dependent upon man's response" and concludes that while prevenient grace does not actually save the sinner (for the sinner must cooperate), it "lifts all men to a salvable point."[196] "He can by this grace choose more grace leading on to salvation, or he may reject the grace."[197] In other words, while God initiates, ultimately the choice is man's. We are once again reminded of Cannon's words: "man is the absolute master of his fate and the captain of his own salvation."[198] Such a sentiment is also expressed by Barry Callen, who says, "Saving grace is not received irresistibly." Quoting John Sanders, Callen states, "The crux of the debate is 'whether God ever *responds* to us and does things *because* of us (not merely through us).' "[199] For Sanders and Callen, the answer is yes; God responds to our libertarian choice and if God regenerates us it is "because of us."

Thomas Oden also advocates synergism when he says, "God prepares the will and coworks with the prepared will."[200] Oden argues that even though it is God who provides "sufficient grace to every soul," only those who "cooperate with sufficient grace" are then given the means to make it *efficax*.[201] By *efficax*, however, Oden does not mean, as the Calvinists do, that grace is irresistible. Rather, efficacious grace is a "further refinement of the idea of cooperating grace," which may be willfully resisted.[202] Rejecting the monergism of Dort as well as the

---

195. I. Howard Marshall, "Predestination in the New Testament," in *Grace Unlimited*, 140.

196. Cox, "Prevenient Grace," 147 (cf. 148).

197. Ibid., 149.

198. Cannon, *The Theology of John Wesley*, 114–15.

199. Barry L. Callen, "A Mutuality Model of Conversion," in *Conversion in the Wesleyan Tradition*, ed. Kenneth J. Collins and John H. Tyson (Nashville: Abingdon, 2001), 147 (cf. 152). Also see Sanders, *The God Who Risks*, 244.

200. Oden, *The Transforming Power of Grace*, 49 (cf. 47). Also see Olson, *Arminian Theology*, 177.

201. Oden, *The Transforming Power of Grace*, 47. For Oden's synergistic twist to "efficacious grace" and "effectual calling," see pp.113–15, 194–205.

202. Ibid., 114.

affirmation of irresistible grace by the Jansenists of 1653, Oden, citing the synergism of Melanchthon and the Council of Trent in support, states, "Grace is not the simply, direct, omnicausal will of God that nothing can resist, but rather a gift in which God condescends to cooperate with human freedom, and where responsive freedom is enabled to cooperate freely with grace."[203] Following Oden, Roger Olson also affirms synergism when he argues that "grace is resistible" and therefore "the human response is crucial and determinative." In other words, "Grace is not effectual but enabling; only with free human consent does it become effectual."[204] Thus, "regeneration does not precede repentance and faith; it follows from them."[205]

Synergism and the *Ordo Salutis*

The synergism of Arminianism becomes even more explicit in the arrangement of the *ordo salutis*. For the Arminian, synergism entails the belief that God's power to regenerate is causally conditioned upon man's will to believe. What this means for the *ordo salutis* is that conversion logically and causally precedes regeneration. Wesley makes such a point in his sermon "The New Birth" by comparing justification (God's work "for us") to regeneration (God's work "in us"). In time, Wesley says, both occur simultaneously. However, in the order of thinking, "justification precedes the new birth." "We first conceive his wrath to be turned away, and then his Spirit to work in our hearts."[206] Therefore, as Langford concludes, "justification results in regeneration."[207]

A glance at Wesleyan systematic theologies will reveal that Wesleyans have taken this same view, as their systematics first treat conversion (faith and repentance) and justification and then turn to regeneration. This *ordo salutis* gives faith logical priority over regeneration so that the new birth is always contingent upon man's faith-response. As Wiley and

203. Ibid., 112 (cf. 114–15).
204. Roger Olson, "Conversion," in *The Westminster Handbook*, 162. Also see Olson, *Against Calvinism*, 169–74.
205. Ibid.
206. Wesley, "The New Birth," in *Works* (Jackson), 6:65–66.
207. Langford, *Practical Divinity*, 35.

Raymond recognize, such conditionality is in direct contrast to monergism.[208] Notice, Arminians like Wiley and Raymond want to affirm that regeneration is God's act alone. However, God's regenerate act is conditioned and contingent upon man's will to repent and believe (i.e., the "antecedent conditions").[209] Therefore, the *ordo* is organized as follows:

Arminianism/Wesleyanism	Calvinism
1. Prevenient Grace/Calling	1. Effectual Calling/Regeneration
2. Conversion	2. Conversion
3. Justification	3. Justification
4. Regeneration	4. Sanctification
5. Sanctification	

Such an *ordo* shows us that faith must be defined differently for the Arminian. If conversion, which includes not only repentance but also faith, precedes regeneration, then prevenient grace cannot make faith *necessary* but only a *possibility*. As Picirilli explains, prevenient grace cannot by itself "guarantee the conversion of the sinner."[210] While the Calvinist affirms a chain of salvation (unconditional election, effectual calling, regeneration, conversion, etc.) in which the first step necessarily and effectually leads to the next, the Arminian affirms a chain of salvation in which the first step in the application of salvation (prevenient grace) in no way guarantees the next (conversion) but is conditioned upon man's free will.

CONCLUSION

Now that we have examined the Arminian view(s) carefully in order to get an accurate picture of its complexity rather than constructing unfair and misleading caricatures, we can proceed to look critically at this position in light of the biblical witness.

208. Wiley, *Christian Theology*, 416–21 (cf. 378); Raymond, *Systematic Theology*, 2:356–57.
209. Wiley, *Christian Theology*, 419–21.
210. Picirilli, *Grace, Faith, Free Will*, 156.

245

6

THE INADEQUACY OF
ARMINIAN SYNERGISM

Jonathan Edwards, in his treatise on *Original Sin*, claimed that if Arminianism is correct in its affirmation of libertarian freedom, then "they [Arminians] have an impregnable castle, to which they may repair, and remain invincible, in all the controversies they have with the reformed divines, concerning original sin, the sovereignty of grace, election, redemption, conversion, the efficacious operation of the Holy Spirit, the nature of saving faith, the perseverance of the saints, and other principles of the like kind."[1] Edwards went on to argue that Arminianism possesses no such invincibility or "impregnable castle" because their definition of free will is inherently faulty and at odds with Scripture itself. As seen in chapter 5, besides libertarian freedom, a second doctrine that is indispensable for the Arminian is the doctrine of prevenient grace. Arminian Robert Chiles has admitted that if the Arminian and Wesleyan doctrine of prevenient grace is wrong, the Calvinist logic is irrefutable.[2] This chapter will argue that these two doctrines—libertarian freedom and prevenient grace—are unbiblical in nature and consequently rob God of his glory in salvation by resorting to a synergistic view of grace that exalts the will of man over the will of

---

1. Jonathan Edwards, *Original Sin*, ed. Clyde A. Holbrook, vol. 3 of *The Works of Jonathan Edwards* (New Haven, CT: Yale University Press, 1970), 376.

2. Robert E. Chiles, *Theological Transition in American Methodism: 1790–1935* (Nashville: Abingdon, 1965), 50.

God. Thus, since these two doctrines cannot be supported by Scripture, Arminianism possesses no "impregnable castle" and the Calvinist logic does indeed remain irrefutable.

A CRITIQUE OF PREVENIENT GRACE

Man *Is* Totally Depraved

As discussed in chapter 5, while Arminians like Pinnock, Reichenbach, and Cottrell deny total depravity and spiritual inability, others, such as Wesley, affirm total depravity and spiritual inability but argue that, because of prevenient grace, corruption is mitigated, meaning that no person actually exists in a state of total depravity and spiritual inability.[3] Consequently, man is able to resist or cooperate with the Spirit's moral persuasion.

However, both of these views are erroneous. The first group of Arminians who reject total depravity do so in the face of the entire scope of Scripture. As chapter 2 demonstrated, the doctrine of total depravity is affirmed in both the Old Testament (Gen. 6:5; 8:21; Job 14:1–3; Pss. 14:2–3; 51:5; 58:3–5; Prov. 20:9; Eccl. 7:20; Jer. 17:9; Ezek. 36:26; Hos. 6:7) and the New Testament (Rom. 1:21–32; 3:10–18; 8:5–8; Gal. 4:3; Eph. 2:1–3; Eph. 4:17–19; Col. 2:13; Titus 3:3). This is exactly why other Arminians, including Arminius himself and the Remonstrants at Dort, affirm the doctrine as biblical. Man is not merely weakened by the fall, but is spiritually dead and unable to do anything to receive eternal life. Man's total deadness in sin is exactly why analogies like that of Arminian Steve Lemke utterly fail.[4] Lemke compares salvation to a man who is drowning in the middle of the ocean. God comes by in a rescue ship and throws a life buoy to him. It is then up to the man to grab the buoy so he can be pulled out of the water. Lemke goes on to say that perhaps the man is even too weak to grab the buoy.

3. Bruce Demarest, *The Cross and Salvation: The Doctrine of Salvation* (Wheaton, IL: Crossway, 1997), 208.

4. Steve W. Lemke, "A Biblical and Theological Critique of Irresistible Grace," in *Whosoever Will: A Biblical-Theological Critique of Five-Point Calvinism*, ed. David L. Allen and Steve W. Lemke (Nashville: B&H Publishing Group, 2010), 160.

Instead, he needs a helicopter to come down and pick him out of the water. Yet, even here, what is required is his assent and cooperation. He can refuse to do so. At the very least, in order to be saved he must choose to not resist being rescued. The reason such an analogy fails is that according to passages like Ephesians 2:1–3, man is not drowning, struggling for breath at the surface of the water; rather, he has already drowned and is dead at the bottom of the ocean. Man does not need God to throw him a buoy, but to do a miracle by raising him from the dead (Rom. 6:4), as Jesus did to Lazarus (John 11:43).[5] Analogies like Lemke's reveal a Semi-Pelagianism that continues to pervade certain Arminian circles and fails to heed Anselm's warning, "You have not yet considered how great your sin is."[6]

Regarding the second group of Arminians (classical Arminians)—who argue that prevenient grace negates total depravity so that no person *actually exists* in such a state—they also are without biblical warrant because Scripture not only affirms total depravity in principle, but also states explicitly that men are indeed in such a state presently. To take but one example, Paul states that *before man was saved* he actually walked according to the flesh, setting his mind on the things of the flesh (Rom. 8:5–8). Before salvation man was actually hostile toward God, unable and unwilling to submit to God's law (Rom. 8:7). Man was in the flesh. and the "flesh cannot please God" (Rom. 8:8). Scripture does not speak of man's depravity as that which is negated by prevenient grace or as that in which no man actually ever exists; rather, it speaks of depravity as that state of man in which he currently exists and in which he will die unless an effectual work of grace is accomplished (Gen. 6:5; 8:21; 11:1–9; 18–19; Deut. 12:8; Judg. 17:6; 21:25; Job 14:1, 3; 15:16; Pss. 10:7; 14:1–3; 36:1; 51:5; 53:3; 58:3–5; 140:3; 143:2; Prov. 1:16; 20:9; Eccl. 7:20; 9:3; Isa. 53:6; 59:7–8; Jer. 5:16; 17:9; Ezek. 36:26; Mark 7:18–23; John 5:42–44;

5. See George Whitefield's commentary on John 11:43 as quoted in John H. Gerstner, *A Predestination Primer* (Winona Lake, IN: Alpha, 1979), 20.

6. As quoted in Michael S. Horton, "The *Sola*'s of the Reformation," in *Here We Stand! A Call from Confessing Evangelicals for a Modern Reformation*, ed. James Montgomery Boice and Benjamin E. Sasse (Phillipsburg, NJ: P&R Publishing, 1996), 119.

Rom. 1:21–32; 3:10–18; 5:12; 8:5–8; Gal. 4:3; Eph. 2:1–3; 4:17–19; Col. 1:13; 2:13; Titus 1:15–16; 3:3).

Moreover, to affirm total depravity in name and then to deny its functionality, as some Arminians do, is to rob the doctrine of its meaning and effect. The doctrine thus becomes purely hypothetical. Gordon Lewis and Bruce Demarest explain the issue precisely:

> These Wesleyan hypotheses amount to a universal restoration of spiritual and moral ability in unrepentant sinners—proposals difficult to reconcile with scriptural teaching concerning pre-Christians' blindness, enmity, and alienation. The spiritually enslaved conditions of fallen humans (vol. 2, chap. 4) appear in Scripture *as actual conditions of people encountered by prophets, Christ, and apostles, not merely as hypothetical conditions.* The human depravity the biblical writers taught in such strong language *has an actual referent in actual persons.* It does not apply only to a *hypothetical condition* from which all have been delivered. Such a prevenient grace hypothesis does not fit the facts of Scripture or the general experience of pastors and counselors.[7]

Therefore, as Peterson and Williams argue, the Arminian affirmation of total depravity in light of prevenient grace is simply misleading.[8] What good is it to affirm the doctrine of total depravity when no person exists in that state? What effect can total depravity have if it is of no consequence to man in the moment of salvation? However, Olson disagrees, arguing that the Arminian affirmation of total depravity is not purely hypothetical or vacuous. Simply because "no human being is actually in a state of absolute darkness and depravity" does not mean that affirming the doctrine is unjustified.[9] Olson believes Peterson and Williams are disingenuous because "they know very well that Arminians do affirm total depravity as the natural state of human

7. Gordon R. Lewis and Bruce A. Demarest, *Integrative Theology*, 3 vols. (Grand Rapids: Zondervan, 1994), 3:60, emphasis added.

8. Robert A. Peterson and Michael D. Williams, *Why I Am Not an Arminian* (Downers Grove, IL: InterVarsity, 2004), 165, 175, emphasis added.

9. Roger E. Olson, *Arminian Theology* (Downers Grove, IL: InterVarsity, 2006), 154.

beings."[10] However, Olson misses the point Peterson and Williams are trying to make.

Peterson and Williams do not deny that Arminians affirm total depravity—indeed, they actually correct other Calvinists who misrepresent Arminians on this point—but instead argue that such an affirmation is without warrant if, as some Arminians claim, no person actually exists in a state of total depravity, but humanity instead enjoys the power of contrary choice due to the arrival of prevenient grace. Nevertheless, Olson does not find such an accusation persuasive. Olson tries to counter this by saying, "The inability to will the good is not merely hypothetical; it is the state of nature in which every person (except Jesus Christ) lives. But no person is left by God entirely in that state of nature without some measure of grace to rise above it if he or she cooperates with grace by not resisting it."[11] Ultimately, however, Olson's affirmation of total

---

10. Ibid.

11. Olson uses several analogies and parables, which he thinks prove his point. "What would they think of a person who said of a man who is legally blind but with special glasses can see a little bit that he is only 'hypothetically blind'? Or what would they think of a person who said of a woman who is deaf but with special hearing aids can hear a little that she is only 'hypothetically deaf'? What would they think of a Roman Catholic who accused all Protestants of believing in a mere hypothetical unrighteousness of regenerate and justified believers because of the Reformation doctrine of imputed righteousness? The doctrine of *simul justus et peccator* lies at the heart of the Protestant Reformation. It says that Christians are always at best simultaneously sinners and righteous because their righteousness is Christ's imputed to their account. To Catholic eyes this appears a subterfuge, but to Protestant eyes it is the very heart of the gospel! Surely these two Reformed authors would reject any claim that they believe in a purely hypothetical unrighteousness of believers. In classical protestant theology neither sinfulness nor righteousness is a fiction." Ibid., 154–55.

Olson's analogies suffer serious flaws. (1) The blind man: This analogy does not work because even if the blind man receives the special glasses, the reality remains that before he receives those glasses he really was blind. This is not the case with prevenient grace. In reality, no person actually is depraved (like the blind man is blind) because no person ever exists in such a state. (2) The deaf woman: the same argument applies here as with the blind man. (3) Hypothetical unrighteousness: Olson's error here is significant. Against Rome's charge that the Reformers were affirming an imputed righteousness that is mere subterfuge, the Reformers argued that it is not because there actually is a change in status. Unlike a state of depravity in which nobody ever exists due to prevenient grace, justified sinners actually did exist in a guilty status prior to being justified. In other words, once they actually were "guilty," but due to Christ's imputed righteousness they have been declared "not guilty." This is not so with prevenient grace. As chapter 6 showed, Arminians argue that no person is ever in a depraved state. Therefore, the analogy fails in comparison.

depravity in light of prevenient grace is unsuccessful and unconvincing. Even an Arminian like Jack Cottrell exposes fellow Arminians (with whom he disagrees) for such a maneuver. Ironically, Cottrell levels the same accusation that Lewis, Demarest, and Peterson and Williams do. Cottrell argues that such a view "in effect negates the main consequences of total depravity" as it no longer is "total." Cottrell states that it is "confusing and misleading" to retain the term while denying the heart of the doctrine.[12]

Thus, Calvinists can agree with Cottrell on this point. On biblical evidence, the Calvinist must conclude, "We are *actually* (not merely hypothetically) unable to rescue ourselves and thus need sovereign grace if we are to be saved. And this is exactly what our heavenly Father provides—unconquerable, invincible, irresistible grace."[13]

Finally, it should be noted that Arminians who believe that prevenient grace has negated total depravity so that no man actually exists in such a state provide no biblical evidence to support such a negation. As Schreiner observes, "Wesleyans contend that prevenient grace counteracts the inability of humanity due to Adam's sin, but firm biblical evidence seems to be lacking. One can be pardoned, then, for wondering whether this theory is based on scriptural exegesis."[14] This lack of scriptural exegesis and support is especially demonstrated when Olson has to create a third category—an "intermediate state"—for all of those who have prevenient grace but have not yet chosen to believe. As we will see, Olson offers no scriptural warrant for such a claim. In fact, nowhere does Scripture ever recognize a sinner as being neither unregenerate nor regenerate but simply in an intermediate stage.

12. Jack E. Cottrell, "The Classical Arminian View of Election," in *Perspectives on Election: Five Views*, ed. Chad O. Brand (Nashville: B&H Publishing Group, 2006), 121–22. Culver also analyzes how prevenient grace annuls total depravity. Robert Duncan Culver, *Systematic Theology: Biblical and Historical* (Fearn, Ross-shire, Great Britain: Christian Focus, 2005), 359.

13. Peterson and Williams, *Why I Am Not an Arminian*, 191.

14. Thomas R. Schreiner, "Does Scripture Teach Prevenient Grace in the Wesleyan Sense?" in *Still Sovereign: Contemporary Perspectives on Election, Foreknowledge, and Grace*, ed. Thomas R. Schreiner and Bruce A. Ware (Grand Rapids: Baker, 2000), 246. To prove Schreiner's point, consider Roger Olson, *Against Calvinism* (Grand Rapids: Zondervan, 2011), 173, where the only text Olson offers in support of prevenient grace is Phil. 2:12–13.

Prevenient Grace Is Exegetically Fallacious

John 1:9. This verse reads: "The true light, which gives light to everyone, was coming into the world." The argument from this text is that the phrase "gives light to everyone" refers to universal prevenient grace. John Wesley appealed to John 1:9 more than any other verse to argue for universal prevenient grace.[15] However, the verse can be understood in at least three other ways than this:

(1) Enlightenment refers to universal general revelation, not prevenient grace, and this illumination is grounded in creation.[16] Such a view is improbable because the context of the passage concerns Christ, the Son of God, who has come into the world, not an enlightenment at creation.[17]

(2) Enlightenment refers to the inner conviction and illumination that results in faith and repentance.[18] Such a view argues that John uses "all" in the sense that all without distinction rather than all without exception are enlightened.[19] In other words, not just Jews but also Gentiles are enlightened by Christ's advent in the world (see John 10:16; 11:51–52). However, the immediate context does not seem to imply such a distinction.

(3) As Schreiner, says, "The word *enlighten* (*photizo*) refers not to inward illumination but to the exposure that comes when light is shed upon something. Some are shown to be evil because they did not know or receive Jesus (John 1:10–11), while others are revealed to be righteous because they have received Jesus and have been born of God (John 1:12–13)."[20] This interpretation of John 1:9–13 is the best because it fits the context of John 3:19–21 which says,

15. Thomas C. Oden, *John Wesley's Scriptural Christianity* (Grand Rapids: Zondervan, 1994), 250.

16. Leon Morris, *The Gospel according to John*, NICNT (Grand Rapids: Eerdmans, 1971), 94–95.

17. D. A. Carson, *The Gospel according to John*, PNTC (Grand Rapids: Eerdmans, 1991), 123.

18. Köstenberger seems to adopt this interpretation though he says the illumination is external rather than internal. Andreas J. Köstenberger, *John*, BECNT (Grand Rapids: Baker, 2004), 35–36.

19. Carson, *John*, 123; Schreiner, "Does Scripture Teach Prevenient Grace?," 240.

20. Schreiner, "Does Scripture Teach Prevenient Grace?," 240–41.

And this is the judgment: the light has come into the world, and people loved the darkness rather than the light because their works are evil. For everyone who does wicked things hates the light and does not come to the light, lest his works should be exposed. But whoever does what is true comes to the light so that it may be clearly seen that his works have been carried out by God.

When John speaks of the light which enlightens all men, he is not speaking of a light which bestows universal prevenient grace, nor of a light which conveys general revelation through creation to all of humanity, nor of a light which inwardly illumines every man, but rather of a light which "exposes and reveals the moral and spiritual state of one's heart."[21] D. A. Carson explains,

> The verb *photizei* may have its primary lexical meaning "to shed light upon," i.e., "to make visible," "to bring to light." Inner illumination is then not in view (whether of general revelation or of the special light that attends salvation). What is at stake, rather is the objective revelation, the "light," that comes into the world with the incarnation of the Word, the invasion of the "true light." It shines on every man, and divides the race: those who hate the light respond as the world does (1:10): they flee lest their deeds should be exposed by this light (3:19–21). But some receive this revelation (1:12–13), and thereby testify that their deeds have been done through God (3:21). In John's Gospel it is repeatedly the case that the light shines on all, and forces a distinction (e.g., 3:19–21; 8:12; 9:39–41).[22]

Therefore, the text does not teach that Christ gives prevenient grace to all of humanity, enabling man to cooperate with God's grace, but rather that the light of Christ reveals the true condition of men as being either desperately wicked or trusting in God.

John 12:32. The verse reads, "And I, when I am lifted up from the earth, will draw all people to myself." As seen in chapter 5, Arminians

21. Ibid.
22. Carson, *John*, 124.

254

argue that when Jesus says here that when he is lifted up he will draw (ἐλκύσω) all men to himself, he refers to the universal drawing of humanity whereby, through prevenient grace, all men can come, if they choose, to Christ. However, such a reading misunderstands the words of Jesus as well as the context in which he spoke.

First, such a reading would contradict what Jesus said earlier in John 6:37: "All that the Father gives me will come to me, and whoever comes to me I will never drive away." And again in John 6:44: "No one can come to me unless the Father who sent me draws him." The word "draw" (ἐλκύσῃ) here is the same exact word Jesus uses in John 12:32 (ἐλκω). If all whom the Father gives to Jesus come to Jesus, and there are some in the world who do not come to Jesus, then there are some who do not come to Jesus because they are not drawn. Therefore, not all are drawn by the Father to Jesus (see chapter 3). Why would Jesus say that only some will be drawn by the Father, then later say that all men will be drawn to the Son? This would result in a contradiction on Jesus' part. Rather, as Carson states, "The combination of v. 37a and v. 44 prove that this 'drawing' activity of the Father cannot be reduced to what theologians sometimes call 'prevenient grace' dispensed to every individual, for this 'drawing' is selective, or else the negative note of v. 44 is meaningless."[23] Schreiner concludes, "The Johannine conception of drawing is not that it makes salvation possible, but that it makes salvation effectual. Those who are drawn will come to Jesus and believe in him."[24] Therefore, the Wesleyan reading fails on two accounts: (1) drawing is particular, not universal, and (2) drawing is effectual not resistible.

Furthermore, if the reader pays close attention to the context of John 12:32, the meaning is clear. Just before Jesus says all men will be drawn, he also interacts with a dispute that occurs over the arrival of some Greeks who want to speak with him (John 12:20–26). Jesus seems to ignore these Greeks and instead says that the Son of Man must fall to the ground like a grain of wheat so that much fruit will result (speaking of his death). However, Jesus is not ignoring the Greeks, but explaining

23. Ibid., 293.
24. Schreiner, "Does Scripture Teach Prevenient Grace?," 242.

in parabolic fashion how it is that the Greeks will be saved, that is, by his death. It is through the death of the Son of Man that not only Jews but Gentiles also can receive eternal life, as demonstrated in John 10:16 and 11:51–52.[25] Jesus is explaining to his disciples the basis for which Greeks also will be drawn to the Son by the Father. Therefore, as Morris, Schreiner, Mounce, and Carson observe, when Jesus says he will draw all people to himself, he is not referring to all *without exception*, but rather to all *without distinction*, Jew and Greek alike.[26]

Romans 2:4. Paul here says, "Or do you presume on the riches of his kindness and forbearance and patience, not knowing that God's kindness is meant to lead you to repentance?" Grider quotes Romans 2:4 as proof that God's kindness in leading man to repent is evidenced in prevenient grace.[27] However, Paul says nothing about a *universal* grace that is provided to all people, *enabling* them to repent. Such a detailed description of grace is not included in this passage. Rather, the present tense verb "leads" (ἄγει) in verse 4 simply indicates that it is God's *desire* that sinners repent.[28] How exactly God goes about executing such a desire is not specified in this text.[29] What is specified is that God, in his kindness, withheld his judgment temporarily, showing his patience with

25. Köstenberger, *John*, 384–85.

26. Morris, *John*, 598–99; Schreiner, "Does Scripture Teach Prevenient Grace?," 242; Robert H. Mounce, *John*, Expositor's Bible Commentary, vol. 10 (Grand Rapids: Zondervan, 2007), 538; Carson, *John*, 242.

27. Kenneth J. Grider, *A Wesleyan-Holiness Theology* (Kansas City, MO: Beacon Hill, 1994), 353.

28. Anders Nygren, *Commentary on Romans* (Philadelphia: Fortress, 1972), 117; Peterson and Williams, *Why I Am Not an Arminian*, 178; Thomas R. Schreiner, *Romans*, BECNT (Grand Rapids: Baker, 1998), 108; H. C. G. Moule, *The Epistle to the Romans*, The Expositor's Bible (New York: Armstrong & Son, 1894), 8; James D. G. Dunn, *Romans 1–8*, WBC, vol. 38A (Dallas, Word, 1988), 91; John Murray, *The Epistle to the Romans*, NICNT (Grand Rapids: Eerdmans, 1959), 60; Leon Morris, *Epistle to the Romans*, PNTC (Grand Rapids: Eerdmans, 1988), 113n30; Douglas J. Moo, *The Epistle to the Romans*, NICNT (Grand Rapids: Eerdmans, 1996), 125–35.

29. Indeed, it is rather the assumption of the Arminian—that if God desires all to be saved he must provide salvation to all—that leads the Arminian to interpret Paul in this way. Such an assumption not only reads too much into the text but fails to do justice to the complexity of God's desires. For example, God can simultaneously love Jacob and hate Esau (Rom. 9:13).

sinners who persisted in ungodliness. Such forbearance and patience is generous to say the least, and sinners would be wise not to take it for granted, but to repent, lest tomorrow God should unleash his judgment. To repeat, there is nothing here that indicates a doctrine of universal prevenient grace. What is being described is not a *giving* of universal grace but rather the *withholding* of God's judgment for a period of time. This is reinforced in the very next verse: "But because of your hard and impenitent heart you are storing up wrath for yourself on the day of wrath when God's righteous judgment will be revealed" (Rom. 2:5).

Furthermore, the context of the passage demonstrates that Paul is arguing that the wrath of God is coming not only on Gentiles but also on Jews. As Peterson and Williams state, "But a closer examination of the verse reveals that Paul is making not a universal statement but a particular one showing that the Jews are condemned along with the Gentiles."[30] This is why Paul states that "in passing judgment on another you condemn yourself, because you, the judge, practice the very same things" (Rom. 2:1). In other words, God's kindness should have alerted the Jews to repent, but instead they looked upon the Gentiles with condemnation and contempt. All the while they themselves practiced the same sins. Israel only heaped judgment on themselves by showing contempt for God's tolerance and patience. Therefore, the passage has nothing to do with a universal prevenient grace, but rather speaks of the judgment that awaits Israel for her rejection of God's kindness (Rom. 2:5).

Philippians 2:12–13. Arminians also appeal to Philippians 2:12–13, in which Paul exhorts, "Work out your own salvation with fear and trembling, for it is God who works in you, both to will and to work for his good pleasure." Wesley believes Paul teaches here the doctrine of prevenient grace, as do contemporary Wesleyan-Arminians like Oden.[31] Oden interprets Paul as saying, "God working in us enables

30. Peterson and Williams, *Why I Am Not an Arminian*, 178.

31. John Wesley, "On Working Out Our Own Salvation," in *The Works of John Wesley*, ed. T. Jackson, 14 vols. (Reprint, Grand Rapids: Baker, 1978), 6:509; citations from this edition hereafter referred to as *Works* (Jackson). Also see Oden, *John Wesley's Scriptural Christianity*, 246.

our working and co-working with God."[32] Since God works in us by giving us prevenient grace, Oden says, it is now on us to cooperate with subsequent grace, for the "chief function of prevenient grace is to bring the person to a state of nonresistance to subsequent forms of grace."[33] Therefore, "Prevenient grace is that grace that goes before us to prepare us for more grace, the grace that makes it possible for persons to take the first steps toward saving grace."[34] Roger Olson also cites Philippians 2:12–13 as a proof text for prevenient grace: "The directive to 'work out your own salvation' refers to receiving the gift of saving grace through repentance and faith; 'God who is working in you' refers to prevenient and assisting grace that goes before and makes possible free human reception of the grace of God."[35]

However, Philippians 2:12–13 has nothing to do with prevenient grace, calling, or regeneration because Paul is talking here about *the Christian* (not the unbeliever) who is commanded to work out his salvation in *sanctification*. As Moisés Silva states, "Paul here points to our conscious activity in sanctification."[36] Likewise, Peter O'Brien says Paul is referring to the "outworking of the gospel in their [the Philippians'] day-to-day living" as they await "the approaching day of Christ when their salvation will be complete (cf. Rom. 13:11)."[37] Two contextual and exegetical points bear this out.

(1) Paul and Timothy open the letter by addressing those who are "saints in Christ Jesus" at Philippi, not those who are unbelievers being instructed on how to be converted (Phil. 1:1). Paul rejoices because these believers partnered with him "in the gospel from the first day until now" (Phil. 2:5). Moreover, Philippians 2:12–13 is parallel in language

---

32. Oden, *John Wesley's Scriptural Christianity*, 244.

33. Ibid., 247. Also see idem, *The Transforming Power of Grace* (Nashville: Abingdon, 1993), 53.

34. Oden, *John Wesley's Scriptural Christianity*, 247.

35. Roger Olson, "The Classical Free Will Theists Model of God," in *Perspectives on the Doctrine of God: Four Views*, ed. Bruce A. Ware (Nashville: B&H Publishing Group, 2008), 169.

36. Moisés Silva, *Philippians*, 2nd ed., BECNT (Grand Rapids: Baker, 2005), 122.

37. Peter T. O'Brien, *The Epistle to the Philippians*, NIGTC (Grand Rapids: Eerdmans, 1991), 273–74. Also see Gordon D. Fee, *Paul's Letter to the Philippians*, NICNT (Grand Rapids: Eerdmans, 1995), 235.

to Philippians 1:6: "And I am sure of this, that he who began a good work in you will bring it to completion at the day of Jesus Christ." Here we see Paul addressing those who are already believers, giving them confidence that God, who began such a work in them, will finish it. So also in Philippians 2:12–13 Paul is again addressing believers ("my beloved," 2:12), exhorting them to persevere in the faith, and reminding them once again that God is at work in them and will finish what he started.[38] This is evident by the fact that Paul then addresses them as those who are "children of God" who are to be blameless, innocent, without blemish, and lights in the world (Phil. 2:14–16).

(2) The word "salvation" is not always used by Paul, as we tend to use it today in evangelical circles, to refer only to the first instance of new life. Rather, this word can refer broadly to the entire process of conversion, sanctification, and glorification (a point to which we will return in chapter 7). Silva insightfully explains the matter,

> It is conceded by all parties in the discussion that the term salvation (or its cognate verb) need not be restricted, as it normally is in contemporary evangelical language, to the initial act of conversion ("Have you been saved?") or to the status of being in a right relationship with God ("Are you saved?"). . . . But the biblical concept of salvation is not thus restricted to justification; more commonly what is in view includes God's redemptive work in its totality. Thus, while in a very important sense we have already been saved (Eph. 2:5, 8; Titus 3:5), in another sense we are yet to be saved (Rom. 5:9–10; 1 Cor. 3:15; 5:5; 2 Tim. 4:18). Calvin rightly claims "that salvation is taken to mean the entire course of our calling, and that this term includes all things by which God accomplishes that perfection, to which He has determined us by His free election."[39]

In other words, "salvation" for Paul can refer to the *total* process rather than only to the initial event. Therefore, to conclude that such a passage

38. John Murray, *Redemption Accomplished and Applied* (Edinburgh: Banner of Truth, 1961), 148–49.
39. Silva, *Philippians*, 121.

refers specifically to the initial act of prevenient grace or, worse yet, to synergism, because God instructs the unbeliever to "work out" his salvation, does violence to the proper meaning of the text.

Titus 2:11. A final text that Wesleyan-Arminians appeal to for prevenient grace is Titus 2:11, which says, "For the grace of God has appeared, bringing salvation for all people." Should "all people" be interpreted as all without exception? Schreiner helpfully shows that even if the text were referring to a potential salvation of all people, Titus 2:11 "is a far cry from saying through the atonement God has counteracted the effects of Adam's sin so that all people have the opportunity to accept or reject him."[40] To argue from this verse that the grace it speaks of negates total depravity and enables man to cooperate or resist is simply reading into the text more than is there. The text does not say as much as the Wesleyan wants it to say. Furthermore, one must pay attention to the context of the passage. Wesleyans like to interpret this passage as teaching *universal* prevenient grace. However, in the previous ten verses Paul lists all different types of people that make up the kingdom of God: elderly men, elderly women, young women, young men, slaves, and masters. Paul then says that salvation has come for all people. In light of the previous ten verses, "all people" in Titus 2:11 refers to all *kinds* of people, not to all people without exception. The universality of grace is one of kind and class.[41]

In light of all this, it is very surprising, as both Schreiner and Erickson recognize, that Arminians and Wesleyans continue to defend the doctrine of prevenient grace when there is so little scriptural evidence for it.[42] Roger Olson, for example, has to say that prevenient grace is not explicitly named or stated in Scripture; one must find it, he says,

---

40. Schreiner, "Does Scripture Teach Prevenient Grace?," 241.

41. Donald Guthrie, *The Pastoral Epistles* (Leicester, England: Inter-Varsity Press, 1990), 210; George W. Knight III, *The Pastoral Epistles: A Commentary on the Greek Text*, NIGTC (Grand Rapids: Eerdmans, 1992), 319.

42. Schreiner, "Does Scripture Teach Prevenient Grace?," 246; Millard J. Erickson, *Christian Theology*, 2nd ed. (Grand Rapids: Baker, 1985), 925.

"between the lines."[43] Even Asbury Theological Seminary professor Ben Witherington III shockingly confesses that "Wesley's concept of prevenient grace is frankly weakly grounded if we are talking about proof texts from the Bible." He goes on to say that arguments from the text are simply a "stretch."[44] Witherington concludes by admitting that though he thinks prevenient grace is consistent with God's gracious character, "one should not hang one's entire theology about what sinners can do by free choice on such an exegetically weakly supported notion."[45] This is no small confession from one who is himself within the Wesleyan-Arminian tradition. Surely Arminians do seek to ground their arguments on Scripture, but the scriptural support offered is not only mistakenly interpreted, but also meager, for they lack texts to bolster their claim.[46] Therefore, other doctrines must be brought into play, such as that of libertarian freedom.

PROBLEMS WITH LIBERTARIAN FREEDOM

Besides the doctrines of prevenient grace and the universal love of God, there is no doctrine as important to the Arminian system as that of libertarian freedom. Whether the Arminian affirms the use of libertarian freedom through *nature* (i.e., man is not totally depraved) or by *grace* (i.e., prevenient grace enables full use of free will), at the moment of decision it is the will of man which must choose to cooperate with (synergism) or resist God's grace. However, such a choice is libertarian in nature, meaning that man can always do otherwise than what he chose to do. As seen in chapter 5, no single factor, external or internal, can cause or necessitate man to choose one thing rather than another.[47]

43. Olson, "The Classical Free Will Theist Model of God," 168.

44. Ben Witherington III, *The Problem with Evangelical Theology: Testing the Exegetical Foundations of Calvinism, Dispensationalism, and Wesleyanism* (Waco, TX: Baylor University Press, 2005), 207–8.

45. Earlier Witherington states that such a doctrine "is not revealed in the NT." Ibid., 209.

46. Herman Bavinck, *Reformed Dogmatics*, ed. John Bolt, trans. John Vriend, 4 vols. (Grand Rapids: Baker, 2008), 4:86.

47. Bruce R. Reichenbach, "Freedom, Justice, and Moral Responsibility," in *The Grace of God and the Will of Man: A Case for Arminianism*, ed. Clark H. Pinnock (Minneapolis: Bethany House, 1989), 285; J. P. Moreland and William Lane Craig, *Philosophical Foundations for a*

Man is his own uncaused mover or *causa sui* (cause of oneself), possessing self-determination of the will. Consequently, as Burson and Walls argue, at the moment of salvation man can equally choose to accept or reject divine grace.[48] While prevenient grace is necessary (for most Arminians at least), it is not sufficient because the will of man is the final determiner, equally able to accept or reject the gospel. Though God can seek to persuade and influence man's choice, he can never necessitate man to choose one way rather than another. As Cottrell states, "For Arminians the final decision belongs to each individual."[49]

While our aim here is not to provide an extensive critique of libertarianism (as others have done quite adequately[50]), nevertheless, we must discuss several major problems with the libertarian view, particularly as it has reference to salvation. For example, John Frame has listed eighteen devastating reasons why libertarianism is faulty.[51] Frame's eighteen points are overwhelming for a libertarian view, especially the first, which argues that Scripture always displays God as the one who determines and controls all things, including man's will (Exod. 3:21–22; 11:2–3; 12:35–36; Isa. 10; Acts 2:23; 4:27–28; 2 Peter 1:20–21). God's exhaustive and meticulous control is simply incompatible with a libertarian view; thus, Arminians have tremendous difficulty explaining such biblical texts in light of libertarian freedom.

Though we could mention still other problems with libertarian freedom,[52] we should note that there is one significant point Frame has

---

Christian Worldview (Downers Grove, IL: InterVarsity, 2003), 270; Jack Cottrell, *What the Bible Says about God the Ruler*, vol. 2 of *The Doctrine of God* (Eugene, OR: Wipf and Stock, 1984), 192.

48. Scott R. Burson and Jerry L. Walls, *C. S. Lewis and Francis Schaeffer* (Downers Grove, IL: InterVarsity, 1998), 91.

49. Cottrell, "The Classical Arminian View of Election," 121. Also see Burson and Walls, *C. S. Lewis and Francis Schaeffer*, 67–68; Clark H. Pinnock, *Most Moved Mover: A Theology of God's Openness* (Grand Rapids: Baker, 2001), 127.

50. For example, see John S. Feinberg, *No One Like Him: The Doctrine of God*, Foundations of Evangelical Theology, vol. 3 (Wheaton, IL: Crossway, 2001), 625–734; R. K. McGregor Wright, *No Place for Sovereignty: What's Wrong with Freewill Theism* (Downers Grove, IL: InterVarsity, 1996), 43–78; Bruce A. Ware, *God's Greater Glory: The Exalted God of Scripture and the Christian Faith* (Wheaton, IL: Crossway, 2004), 61–95.

51. John Frame, *The Doctrine of God*, A Theology of Lordship (Phillipsburg, NJ: P&R Publishing, 2002), 139–45.

52. See Jonathan Edwards, *Freedom of the Will*, ed. Paul Ramsey, vol. 1 of *Works of Jonathan Edwards* (New Haven: Yale University Press, 1966), 164, 191, 197, 270–73; Stephen

left out, namely, the arbitrariness of choices made in a libertarian model, sometimes evident in the title "liberty of *indifference*." Ware explains the philosophical dilemma, originally observed by Jonathan Edwards himself,

> The philosophical problem comes here: if at the moment that an agent chooses A, with all things being just what they are when the choice is made, he could have chosen B, or not-A, then it follows that any reason or set of reasons for why the agent chooses A would be the *identical reason or set of reasons* for why instead the agent might have chosen B, or not-A. That is, since at the moment of choice, all factors contributing to why a choice is made are present and true regardless of which choice is made (i.e., recall that the agent has the power of contrary choice), this means that the factors that lead to one choice being made must, by necessity, also be able to lead just as well to the opposite choice. But the effect of this is to say that there can be *no choice-specific reason or set of reasons* for why the agent chose A *instead* of B, or not-A. It rather is the case, according to libertarian freedom, that every reason or set of reasons must be *equally explanatory* for why the agent might choose A, *or* B, *or* not-A. As a result, our choosing reduces, strictly speaking, to arbitrariness. We can give no reason or set of reasons for why we make the choices we make that wouldn't be the identical reason or set of reasons we would invoke had we made the opposite choice! Hence, our choosing A over its opposite is arbitrary.[53]

What happens if Ware's (or Edwards's) critique is applied to the issue of man's will in salvation? If man has libertarian freedom, and if man's reason for selecting *A* is the "identical reason or set of reasons" for choosing *B*, then in the moment of salvation, man's reason for choosing *A* (assenting to God's grace) is the "identical reason or set of reasons" for choosing *B* (resisting God's grace). Consequently, if man possesses

---

J. Wellum, "The Importance of Nature of Divine Sovereignty for Our View of Scripture," *SBJT* 4, 2 (2000): 76–90.

53. Ware, *God's Greater Glory*, 86. For Edwards's statement of the same issue, see Edwards, *Freedom of the Will*, 207. Also see John S. Feinberg, "God, Freedom, and Evil in Calvinist Thinking," in *The Grace of God, the Bondage of the Will: Historical and Theological Perspectives on Calvinism*, ed. Thomas R. Schreiner and Bruce A. Ware (Grand Rapids: Baker, 1995), 2:469.

libertarian freedom, then man's choice in salvation is arbitrary. Because there can be "no choice-specific reason or set of reasons" for choosing *A* instead of *B*, and because man's reason(s) for choosing *A* must be "equally explanatory" for why he chose *B* instead, man's choice of accepting God or rejecting God is arbitrary. Man can ultimately give no reason as to why he chose God's grace instead of rejecting God's grace.

Such a problem has two effects. First, if man chooses God, his arbitrary choice of God is disrespectful and dishonoring, for man cannot give any unique reason or set of reasons for why he chose God instead of choosing sin. Second, if man chooses sin instead of God, man cannot be held responsible for his sinful action of rejecting God's grace because his reason or set of reasons for choosing sin would be the same reason or set of reasons why he would have chosen God. As Ware explains, "There is no accounting, then, for human moral choice, and our actions become fully inexplicable." In other words, there is no "choice-specific explanation" or sufficient reason for why man chooses to cooperate with God's grace (synergism) rather than reject God's grace. If there is not a *sufficient* reason, then the choice is arbitrary, and if the choice is arbitrary, particularly the choice to resist and reject God's grace, then man cannot be held morally accountable for doing so.[54] Moreover, neither has there been a choice in any meaningful sense of the term.[55] We must, therefore, conclude that the Arminian attempt to explain freedom in a libertarian manner is an utter failure.

However, Arminians remain unconvinced and pose a further objection, namely, that the commands in Scripture for man to repent and believe demonstrate that man must be able to do so. In other words, it would be unfair of God to require man to do something that he is unable to do. It is to such an objection that Edwards's distinction between natural and moral ability or inability is crucial.[56] Man possesses the natural ability to obey God's commands. It is not as if God is commanding man to do something he physically cannot do, such as fly or

54. Ware, *God's Greater Glory*, 86.
55. Unlike freedom of inclination. See Ware, *God's Greater Glory*, 87ff.; Edwards, *Freedom of the Will*, 137–470.
56. Edwards, *Freedom of the Will*, 159.

walk on water. Man can physically obey God's commands if he desires to. However, man is morally incapable of obeying God's commands. The sinner does not desire to obey God's commands (Rom. 1:18–3:20; Gal. 3:10). Therefore, though God commands men everywhere to obey him, no sinner is morally able to do so due to the corruption caused by sin. However, even though men are slaves to sin, Jesus still commands sinners to keep the commandments (Mark 1:15), knowing full well that they will inevitably sin instead (John 8:34).[57] The commands are not physically impossible to keep, but due to the corruption of man's nature, it is morally impossible for man to keep them (cf. Rom. 8:6–8; 14:23; Heb. 11:6).[58] Moreover, this is not unfair to man because man's spiritual refusal to keep God's commands is exactly what he most wants to do (i.e., freedom of inclination). Therefore, he is morally culpable. As Ware states,

> So, while unbelievers do not have libertarian freedom (they cannot obey the command of God), they nonetheless do exactly what they, by nature, want to do upon hearing the gospel or being faced with the command of God. And since they act out of their natures in disbelief, doing exactly what they most want, they are free in this rejection of the gospel and they rightly are held accountable.[59]

Schreiner and Ware are exactly right, and once again we see that the Arminian view has no biblical or rational foundation on which to stand.

THE LEAVEN OF SYNERGISM

Along with prevenient grace and libertarian freedom, one of the most important pieces of the Arminian system is the nature of synergistic grace. If man possesses libertarian free will, then he is able to reject God's grace no matter how hard God tries to persuade the sinner to do otherwise. Consequently, for the Arminian, God can never work

---

57. Schreiner, "Does Scripture Teach Prevenient Grace?," 243.
58. Ibid.
59. Ware, *God's Greater Glory*, 93.

in an effectual, monergistic, or irresistible manner to save the sinner. As seen in chapter 5, there are two implications to such a view: (1) God only has one call by which he seeks to persuade and draw sinners, and this call is universal and always resistible. (2) Since man is able to resist God's cooperating grace, regeneration is conditioned upon man's choice to believe. As MacDonald states, "God cannot and—to say the same thing—will not regenerate a heart that will not admit him."[60] Therefore, for the Arminian, conversion causally precedes regeneration in the *ordo salutis*.[61]

Resistible Grace

In chapter 5 we saw that Arminians appeal to several scriptural passages in order to say that man can resist God's saving efforts (Prov. 1:23–25; Hos. 11:1–9; Pss. 78:10; 81:11–13; 95:7–8; Jer. 17:23; 32:33; Isa. 5:4; Matt. 22:3; 23:37; Mark 6:5–6; Luke 7:29–30; John 6:63; Heb. 3:7–12). The passage most commonly referenced is Acts 7:51, in which Stephen rebukes the Jewish leaders because they "always resist (ἀντιπίπτετε) the Holy Spirit." The Arminian Remonstrants comment, "But as respect the mode of the operation of this [prevenient] grace, it is not irresistible, inasmuch as it is written concerning many, that they have resisted the Holy Ghost. Acts vii., and elsewhere in many places."[62] For the Arminian, besides those passages examined above as proof texts for prevenient grace, the case for synergism rests on these passages.

However, the Arminian, in arguing that God's calling and grace can *always* be resisted, fails to understand the complexity of Scripture when it describes God's work of grace. As already proven in chapter 3, God works in a general way (*vocatio externa*) through a gospel call

---

60. William G. MacDonald, "The Spirit of Grace," in *Grace Unlimited*, ed. Clark H. Pinnock (Eugene, OR: Wipf and Stock, 1999), 85–87. Also see Clark H. Pinnock, "Responsible Freedom and the Flow of Biblical History," in *Grace Unlimited*, 106; Grant Osborne, "Exegetical Notes on Calvinist Texts," in *Grace Unlimited*, 171, 184–85; A. Skevington Wood, "The Contribution of John Wesley to the Theology of Grace," in *Grace Unlimited*, 218.

61. MacDonald, "The Spirit of Grace," 86.

62. "The Five Arminian Articles, 1610," in *The Evangelical Protestant Creeds*, vol. 3 of *The Creeds of Christendom*, ed. Philip Schaff, rev. David S. Schaff (Reprint, Grand Rapids: Baker, 1997), 547.

(*vocatio verbalis*; cf. Matt. 11:28–30; 28:18–20; Acts 1:6–8; 26:16–23; Rom. 10:8–15; 1 Cor. 15:1–8), but God also works in a special way, effectually calling (*vocatio interna*) his elect to himself (John 6:44, 65; Rom. 8:28–30; 1 Cor. 1:9, 22–24; 2 Thess. 2:14). The Calvinist does *not* deny that there are passages in Scripture, such as Acts 7:51, which depict the Spirit as being resisted (Eph. 4:30; 1 Thess. 5:19). In fact, a passage like Acts 7:51 actually supports the Calvinist position, which argues that man's will is in bondage to sin.

Certainly God is resisted by rebellious sinners all throughout Scripture. However, such resistance does not encapsulate the *totality* of how God works. Rather, while God may be and is often resisted, when *God so chooses* to work in a special, saving manner to call and regenerate a sinner, he does so irresistibly and effectually (cf. John 6:22–65; Acts 16:14; Rom. 8:28–30; 1 Cor. 1:18–31; 2 Cor. 4:4–6; 2 Tim. 2:25). As Ware explains, "When Calvinists refer to irresistible grace, they mean to say that the Holy Spirit is able, *when he so chooses*, to overcome all human resistance and so cause his gracious work to be utterly effective and ultimately irresistible."[63] The key words are "when he so chooses." A sinner can resist God his entire life, but when God so chooses to intervene in order to save this sinner, God will ineffably and successfully overcome this sinner's resistance.[64] Consequently, when someone does resist God until the end, the fact is that God never intended, nor did he ever try, to *effectually* call that person to himself. If he had, then, in the Arminian view, he would have failed.

Chapter 5 additionally showed that Arminians like Thomas Summers also appeal to passages where man cooperates with grace (Deut. 30:15–20; Ps. 25:8–9; Ezek. 18:31; 36:25–26; Jer. 31:18; John 6:44; 7:17; Acts 13:45–48; 17:11–12; Rom. 8:26; Heb. 8:10; 10:15–17; 11:6; 1 Peter 1:22–23; Rev. 3:20). Chapter 4 already addressed Deuteronomy 30:15–20, Jeremiah 31:18, and Ezekiel 18:31, showing that these passages do not affirm synergism but a gospel call to all people; thus, we will

63. Ware, "Effectual Calling and Grace," in *Still Sovereign*, 211.
64. See Rejection 8 in "Canons of Dort," in *Reformed Confessions Harmonized*, eds. Joel R. Beeke and Sinclair B. Ferguson (Grand Rapids: Baker, 1999), 93.

not readdress them here. Likewise, there is no need to discuss Ezekiel 36:25–26, John 6:44, Acts 16:14, Hebrews 8:10, or 10:15–17 as chapters 3 and 4 demonstrated that these are strong proof texts for monergism (not for synergism as Summers thinks). But what about other passages that Summers claims support synergism? A close look shows that none of these passages are what Summers makes them to be.

For example, while it is true that in Acts 13:45–48 the Jews resist and revile Paul and Barnabas, thrusting aside God's word, Summers ignores verse 48, which says "as many as were appointed to eternal life believed." As we saw in chapters 3–4, this verse supports monergism, showing that it is God's choice that determines who will believe. Strangely, Summers also appeals to Acts 17:11–12, where we read that the Bereans "received the word with all eagerness, examining the Scriptures daily to see if these things were so." But Luke says nothing here about the Bereans cooperating with grace. In fact, the specifics of grace operating on the soul are not given here at all. We are only told that the Bereans received God's Word with eagerness and many of them "believed" (Acts 17:12). Summers also tries to read synergism into Romans 8:26. However, commentators are in agreement that this text is not referring to unbelievers or the initial moment of faith, but rather, is addressed to *believers* in regard to their perseverance in holiness throughout the Christian life.[65]

Summers attempts the same kind of argument with Revelation 3:20, which reads, "Behold, I stand at the door and knock. If anyone hears my voice and opens the door, I will come in to him and eat with him, and he with me." However, as Gregory Beale states, "This is an invitation not for the readers to be converted but to renew themselves in a relationship with Christ that has already begun, as is apparent from v 19."[66] Even Arminian Grant Osborne admits such a point: "This verse has all too often been misunderstood as an evangelistic call (linked with Holman Hunt's famous picture, 'the Light of the World') to the unsaved

---

65. Schreiner, *Romans*, 442–47; Moo, *Romans*, 522–26; Morris, *Romans*, 326–28.

66. Beale even shows how if it is referring to unbelievers it is simply a gospel call to confess Christ. G. K. Beale, *The Book of Revelation*, NIGTC (Grand Rapids: Eerdmans, 1999), 308.

to become Christians. However, that does not fit the context. Rather, it is a call to a weak church to repent (as in 3:19)."[67] Therefore, Christ is calling his bride to renew her relationship with him in repentance (Rev. 3:19). Synergism at conversion is nowhere in view.

Two other texts to which Summers appeals are 1 Peter 1:22 and Hebrews 11:6. First Peter 1:22–23 says, "Having purified your souls by your obedience to the truth for a sincere brotherly love, love one another earnestly from a pure heart, since you have been born again, not of perishable seed but of imperishable, through the living and abiding word of God." Does purification in verse 22 refer to conversion or sanctification? While some Calvinists argue that sanctification is in view, there are significant textual reasons to believe that Peter has conversion in mind.[68] But, as Schreiner argues, even in the latter view "no idea of synergism is involved, nor was Peter suggesting that believers are the ultimate agent of their salvation."[69] Thus, it would be wrong to conclude that synergism is in view here simply because Peter is referring to conversion. Peter is speaking to the issue of initial faith and repentance. As seen in chapter 4, faith and repentance involve man's participation and yet they are a sovereign gift from God which he works effectually in his elect. Therefore, as Schreiner states, synergism is not involved.

Finally, Summers appeals to Hebrews 11:6, "And without faith it is impossible to please him, for whoever would draw near to God must believe that he exists and that he rewards those who seek him." Summers assumes that being rewarded for one's faith is evidence of synergism. There are several problems with such a reading.

(1) Hebrews 11:6 may have the believer in mind, not the unbeliever, as is indicated in the reference to divine rewards yet to be received. The believer exercises faith in God, drawing near to him,

---

67. Grant R. Osborne, *Revelation*, BECNT (Grand Rapids: Baker, 2002), 212. Also see Robert H. Mounce, *The Book of Revelation*, NICNT (Grand Rapids: Baker, 1977), 113.

68. For the case for sanctification, see Wayne A. Grudem, *The First Epistle of Peter*, TNTC (Downers Grove, IL: InterVarsity, 1988), 87–88. For the case for conversion, see Thomas R. Schreiner, *1, 2 Peter, Jude*, NAC, vol. 37 (Nashville: B&H Publishing Group, 2003), 93; Peter H. Davids, *The First Epistle of Peter*, NICNT (Grand Rapids: Eerdmans, 1990), 76.

69. Schreiner, *1, 2 Peter, Jude*, 93.

with the expectation that one day he will receive his reward. If this view is correct, then Hebrews is much like the Psalms where, as O'Brien notes, seeking the Lord is a common expression "to refer to those who rely firmly on God, trust that his promises will be fulfilled, and find in him the source of their deepest satisfaction."[70] The reward then would refer not to the unbeliever receiving regeneration but to the Christian who looks forward (like Moses did; Heb. 11:26) to his future heavenly reward and the consummation of his salvation. As O'Brien states, "For believers who persevere, full life in God's presence has already been anticipated in our access to him here and now (4:16; 6:19–20; 10:22)."[71]

(2) Even if Hebrews 11:6 does refer to the unbeliever, it is unwarranted to read synergism into this verse. The text would simply be explaining that if a sinner repents, God will be faithful to his promise by rewarding the believer with eternal life. The text does not say the believer is to cooperate with grace, nor does it say that belief is the condition of regeneration. All the text says is that if the sinner believes, God will reward him in the end, as was the case with Abel (Heb. 11:4), Enoch (Heb. 11:5), Noah (Heb. 11:7), and Abraham (Heb. 11:8).

Before moving on, it is essential to note that Arminians like Olson try to soften the man-centeredness of synergism by arguing that the success of synergism simply means "non-resistance" on man's part (chapter 5). All man does is "relax" while God applies grace.[72] However, such language is not new, but is reincarnated from Philip Melanchthon's conflict with his teacher, Martin Luther. Melanchthon argued that though a sinner does not contribute anything to his salvation, it is still necessary that he not resist God's grace.[73] Man must simply be "non-resistant" while grace acts. Therefore, God is the grand initiator and man's part is slight. Luther, however, saw such a

70. Peter T. O'Brien, *The Letter to the Hebrews*, PNTC (Grand Rapids: Eerdmans, 2010), 406. See Pss. 14:2; 22:27; 34:4, 10; 33:5, 11; 68:33; 69:32; Deut. 4:29; Amos 9:12; Acts 15:17.
71. Ibid.
72. Olson, *Against Calvinism*, 171–72.
73. Philip Melanchthon, *Loci Communes 1543*, trans. J. A. O. Preus (St. Louis: Concordia, 1992), Locus 3, 4, 5, 8, 14.

slight role as more dangerous than the large role the Pelagians gave to man.[74] As Boice explains,

> What made it dangerous was its subtlety. After all, what was the harm in adding just a little bit of human effort to the work of God? But Luther recognized that this was tantamount to the error of Roman Catholicism, which insisted that the will of man is the decisive factor in salvation. He also recognized that the leaven of synergism eventually works its way through the entire loaf of soteriology.[75]

Arminians like Olson do not escape Melanchthon's problem. Softening the blow of synergism by saying it is merely "non-resistance" or a relaxing on man's part merely makes the poison more discrete. Synergism is there nonetheless, and the Arminian still does not avoid the problem of attributing the final and ultimate say in salvation to man, rather than to God.[76] Calvin reveals the toxin in such a view when he says, "Any mixture of the power of free will that men strive to mingle with God's grace is nothing but a corruption of grace. It is just as if one were to dilute wine with muddy, bitter water."[77] Abraham Kuyper is just as acute, "Every effort to claim for the sinner the *minutest co-operation* in this first grace destroys the gospel, severs the artery of the Christian confession and is anti-scriptural in the highest degree."[78]

The Speculation of an Intermediate Stage

Arminianism is insistent that free choice must precede regeneration. However, one would not know this given the way Wesley

---

74. See James Montgomery Boice and Philip Graham Ryken, *The Doctrines of Grace: Rediscovering the Evangelical Gospel* (Wheaton, IL: Crossway, 2002), 37; Arthur C. Custance, *The Sovereignty of Grace* (Brockville, ON: Doorway, 1979), 363–64.

75. Boice and Ryken, *The Doctrines of Grace*, 37.

76. Ibid., 88.

77. John Calvin, *Institutes of the Christian Religion*, ed. John T. McNeill, trans. Ford Lewis Battles, LCC, vols. 20–21 (Philadelphia: Westminster John Knox, 1960), 1.25.15.

78. Abraham Kuyper, *The Work of the Holy Spirit*, trans. Henri De Vries (Reprint, Grand Rapids: Eerdmans, 1941), 2:338.

describes the new birth.[79] In many places Wesley sounds remarkably like a Calvinist. He is clear that man goes from death to new life and that before there is new life there is only death. So what place is there then for a willful cooperation which causes and brings about the new birth?[80] If the transition is direct—from no life to new life—where does an active, willful choice prior to regeneration fit in? It would seem, given Wesley's statements on the new birth, that there is no place whatsoever for the will prior to regeneration. Indeed, "It is then only when a man is born, that we say he begins to live," says Wesley.[81] But Wesleyans do make room for the will prior to regeneration, and this is where their inconsistency lies. They simultaneously want to affirm that prior to rebirth there is only death, and that the new birth is conditioned upon faith, man's willful choice to believe. Does prevenient grace solve this contradiction? No, it cannot. While prevenient grace mitigates death and depravity, enabling man's will to believe, man still is not born again until he accepts God's grace and chooses to believe (see chapter 5). So even with prevenient grace there is still a point prior to regeneration where man's will is active. The same question remains: Granting that prevenient grace lifts man out of his depravity, enabling him to choose, how can man choose if he is not yet regenerate?

This contradiction and tension is what causes Arminians like Roger Olson to affirm an "intermediate state" in which regeneration has already begun but in which its finality is conditioned upon man's willful choice (see chapter 5). In other words, prevenient grace begins regeneration and will bring it to completion unless man resists. What this means is that the sinner can be partially regenerate but not completely regenerate because the sinner has not yet chosen to believe. As John Girardeau observes, the Arminian argues that "a degree of spiritual life is imparted to him to enable him to embrace salvation offered to him" and therefore "the sinner is neither wholly dead nor wholly alive: he is partly dead and

---

79. E.g., Wesley, "The New Birth," in *Works* (Jackson), 6:69–70.

80. Such a problem becomes even more evident when we look at how Wesley actually defines the new birth. See ibid., 6:71.

81. Ibid., 6:69–70.

partly alive."[82] But where is this concept in Scripture? Where in John 3 do we see Jesus teaching Nicodemus about an "intermediate state" in which regeneration has begun but during which, if man chooses to resist, regeneration can be aborted and revoked? There is no hint of this in John 3 or in the entire New Testament. Rather, what we see is exactly what Wesley writes of above, namely, an instantaneous and immediate transition from death to new life. There is no contingency or conditionality but pure resurrection from death to life by the Spirit who blows like the wind wherever he pleases. It is evident that Arminians like Olson are looking to extrabiblical concepts to solve the irresolvable tension within the Arminian system. Clearly, prevenient grace does not solve this tension, and since the intermediate state Olson asserts is nowhere found, or even inferred, in Scripture, we must conclude once again that the doctrine of prevenient grace and the affirmation of synergism are deeply erroneous and unbiblical in nature.[83]

Prevenient Grace Irresistible?

The Arminian speculation of an "intermediate stage" raises yet another problem. As already seen, two pillars of Arminianism are prevenient grace and libertarian freedom. Prevenient grace, Arminians say, is given to all regardless of whether or not one wants it. In a real sense it is irresistible. Prevenient grace has initiated the regeneration process, but whether or not that process will be finalized depends on man's libertarian freedom to cooperate with subsequent grace. So while prevenient grace is irresistible, subsequent grace is resistible due to libertarian freedom. However, Bavinck explains the serious problem the Arminian has created for himself:

> If humans have to receive the power to accept or reject the gospel in advance by the prevenient grace conferred in baptism or calling, then

82. John L. Girardeau, *Calvinism and Evangelical Arminianism: Compared as to Election, Reprobation, Justification, and Related Doctrines* (1890; repr., Harrisonburg, VA: Sprinkle, 1984), 321.

83. Abraham Kuyper understood the danger of adopting this "intermediate state" view in the Netherlands during the late nineteenth-century. See Kuyper, *Holy Spirit*, 2:290.

here too a kind of *irresistible grace precedes believing, for preparatory grace is granted to all without their knowledge or consent.* Then regeneration actually does occur before the decision of the human will, for "functioning follows being" (*operari sequitur esse*). The act follows the ability to act. The will enabling persons to accept the gospel, according to the Gospel of John, is a renewed and regenerate will existing prior to the act of acceptance. In that case, however, *it is impossible to understand how, after all this, a "free" act of volition is still possible.* The will, after all, thanks to the good power conferred on it without its consent, has already been determined for good and is so determined precisely in the same measure as it received the power to make a good choice. The more one construes the will as being weakened by sin, the more power one accords to it in prevenient grace, the more, and to the same degree, its indifferent freedom ceases to exist. In addition, it is unfathomable why such an act of free will is still necessary. For if God has to renew human beings beforehand and irresistibly to the extent that they can choose for the gospel, what purpose does the maintenance of the indifferent freedom of the will still serve other than again to frustrate God's grace, to render his covenant of grace as shaky and unstable as the covenant of works was before the fall, and to picture Christ as being even more powerless and loveless than Adam? For he has accomplished and acquired everything, but when he wants to apply it, his power and his love bounce off the human will, a will, mind you, that has even been endowed with new energies! Merely to rescue a pseudofreedom attributed to humans, God is deprived of his sovereignty, the covenant of grace of its firmness, and Christ of his royal power.[84]

Bavinck's insight is significant. What the Arminian denies to the Calvinist (irresistible grace) he finds appropriate to use in his own system with prevenient grace. But how can the irresistible nature of prevenient grace fit with the Arminian's insistence upon libertarian freedom? As Bavinck pointed out, prevenient grace is thrown upon man without his consent. Therefore, not only do we see inconsistency in the fact that the Arminian denies to the Calvinist what he himself appropriates in prevenient

84. Bavinck, *Reformed Dogmatics*, 4:84–85, 86, emphasis added.

grace, but also inconsistency in the fact that the thing appropriated is against the very nature of libertarian freedom. Bluntly put, the Arminian is trying to have his cake and eat it too, and, as Bavinck observes, all at the expense of God being deprived of his sovereignty.

Re Infecta: Synergism Strips God of His Omnipotence

Perhaps one of the most serious problems with synergism is how it minimizes the power of God to save. Loraine Boettner, quoting Augustus Toplady, explains,

> If, as Arminians say, God is earnestly trying to convert every person, He is making a great failure of His work; for among the adult population of the world up to the present time, where He has succeeded in saving one He has let perhaps twenty-five fall into hell. Such a view sheds little glory on the Divine Majesty. Concerning the Arminian doctrine of resistible grace Toplady says that it is "a doctrine which represents Omnipotence itself as wishing and trying and striving to no purpose. According to this tenet, God, in endeavoring (for it seems that it is only an endeavor) to convert sinners, may, by sinners, be foiled, defeated, and disappointed; He may lay close and long siege to the soul, and that soul can, from the citadel of impregnable free will, hang out a flag of defiance to God Himself, and by a continued obstinacy of defense, and a few vigorous sallies of free will compel Him to raise the siege. In a word, the Holy Spirit, after having for years perhaps, danced attendance on the free will of man, may at length, like a discomfited general, or an unsuccessful politician, be either put to ignominious flight, or contemptuously dismissed, *re infecta*, without accomplishing the end for which He was sent."[85]

Boettner and Toplady could not state the issue better. In synergism man's will is the decider even over God himself. Therefore, God's power is defeatable, his omnipotence made weak. As John Owen states, for the Arminian "God may fail in his purposes, come short

---

85. Loraine Boettner, *The Reformed Doctrine of Predestination* (Philadelphia: Presbyterian and Reformed, 1932), 170.

of what he earnestly intendeth, or be frustrated of his aim and end."[86] God does not decide for himself whom he will save, but man decides for him.

Not so for the Calvinist, who upholds the omnipotence of God by affirming that God alone saves in regeneration. As Hodge explains, "Regeneration is not only an act of God, but also an act of his almighty power. . . . If an act of omnipotence, it is certainly efficacious, for nothing can resist almighty power."[87] Likewise, Kuyper states, in Scripture the "omnipotence of divine grace is unlimited."[88] And as à Brakel writes, "God cannot fail to achieve His objective."[89] Scripture states that nothing is too hard for the Lord (Gen. 18:14: Jer. 32:17, 27). He does whatever his will pleases and no one can say to him, "What have you done?" or stay his hand, not even the will of man (Dan. 4:35; cf. Rom. 9:19). How contrary these scriptural statements are to the Arminian view, where God must say, "I will that all men should be saved; nevertheless, it must finally be, not as I will but as they will."[90]

Salvation Is *of Us*, Not of the Lord: Synergism Robs God of His Glory in Salvation

It is necessary at this point to outline several unbiblical consequences of a synergistic view. First, synergism means God is dependent upon man's free will for his success in salvation. As Muller states, "In the Arminian view, the will is the effective ground of salvation."[91] Muller's assertion is demonstrated when Arminians like Pinnock write, "God makes the initial move by saying yes to us. Then it is our turn

86. John Owen, *A Display of Arminianism*, in *The Works of John Owen* (Edinburgh: Banner of Truth, 2000), 10:49.

87. Hodge, *Systematic Theology*, 3:31.

88. Kuyper, *Holy Spirit*, 2:290. Also see Owen, *A Display of Arminianism*, 10:20–21; Peter Van Mastricht, *A Treatise on Regeneration*, ed. Brandon Withrow (Morgan, PA: Soli Deo Gloria, 2002), 43; Francis Turretin, *Institutes of Elenctic Theology*, ed. James T. Dennison Jr., trans. George Musgrave Giger, 3 vols. (Phillipsburg, NJ: P&R Publishing, 1992–97), 2:506.

89. Wilhelmus à Brakel, *The Christian's Reasonable Service*, ed. Joel R. Beeke, trans. Bartel Elshout, 4 vols. (Grand Rapids: Reformation Heritage, 1992–95), 2:205 (cf. 2:206).

90. Boettner, *The Reformed Doctrine of Predestination*, 171.

91. Richard Muller, "Synergismus," in *Dictionary of Latin and Greek Theological Terms: Drawn Principally from Protestant Scholastic Theology* (Grand Rapids: Baker, 2004), 294.

to respond with a yes or a no."[92] Or as Wood says, man "has in himself the casting voice."[93] In other words, it is our answer, not God's, which determines salvation. As Boettner observes, this means that "man proudly seizes the helm and proclaims himself the master of his destiny" and allows man to boast over those who are lost. "He can point the finger of scorn and say, 'You had as good a chance as I had. I accepted and you rejected the offer.'"[94]

Second, synergism means that God can be defeated in his saving purposes. God tries to save, but ultimately he is dependent upon man's free will as to whether man will believe or not. How sobering this is when one realizes that, the majority of the time, God is thwarted and defeated in his saving purpose.

Third, if faith precedes regeneration, even if it be a faith enabled by prevenient grace, then regeneration is not so much a sovereign act of grace as it is a reward for man's cooperation.[95]

Fourth, and most importantly, synergism robs God of *all* of his glory in salvation, a natural consequent of points one, two, and three. Arminians like Olson argue that their view does give God all the glory because it is God and not man who initiates salvation through prevenient grace.

> Arminians point to a beggar who is on the verge of starvation and receives a gift of food or money that saves life. Can that person boast of accepting the life-saving gift? Hardly. So it is with salvation; even though the person being saved must freely accept and not reject grace, he or she has no ground for boasting because all of the ability came from God.[96]

92. Clark H. Pinnock, "Divine Election as Corporate, Open, and Vocational," in *Perspectives on Election*, 304. Also see Boettner, *The Reformed Doctrine of Predestination*, 175.

93. Wood, "The Contribution of John Wesley to the Theology of Grace," 218. Also see Wesley, "The General Spread of the Gospel," in *Works* (Jackson), 6:281.

94. Boettner, *The Reformed Doctrine of Predestination*, 175. Also see Turretin, *Institutes*, 2:553.

95. R. C. Sproul, *What Is Reformed Theology?* (Grand Rapids: Baker, 1997), 187.

96. Olson, "The Classical Free Will Theist Model of God," in *Perspectives on the Doctrine of God*, 168. Likewise see H. Orton Wiley, *Christian Theology*, 2 vols. (Kansas City, MO: Beacon Hill, 1952), 2:356; Oden, *John Wesley's Scriptural Christianity*, 269.

However, what Olson fails to recognize is that even if synergism is enabled by God's prevenient grace, the fact still remains that man, not God, is the determinative factor as to whether or not grace will be effective. As long as man determines God's success, there is grounding for man to boast. Stated otherwise, if Arminius and recent Arminians like Cottrell are right when they say that it is man, not God, who has the *final* say and determination in salvation, then God cannot receive all of the glory when a sinner believes.[97] Rather, man's will plays not a minor role but a *major* role in determining whether or not grace will be effective.[98] As Pinnock states, while God tries his hardest to "win our consent," the final decision and "right of refusal, he has vested in us."[99]

Therefore, while God may initiate salvation, man ultimately receives credit in his own salvation because it is man's will, not God's, which makes the final choice. James M. Boice rightly concludes, "For Arminianism, human decision making holds a central place in salvation. This results in a theology that is not exclusively God-centered but is distorted in the direction of self."[100] Such a view robs God of his glory in salvation, providing a ground for man to boast. Sam Storms' words are sharp but accurate,

> Those who embrace the gospel would be deserving of some credit for finding within themselves what others do not find within themselves. Arminians object. They are quick to point out that if anyone does believe in the gospel it is only because of prevenient grace, something that they didn't deserve. Yes, but whereas it is *only* because of prevenient grace that they believe it is *ultimately* because of what they, as over against others, choose to do with the power God has thereby

97. James Arminius, "Certain Articles to be Diligently Examined and Weighed," in *The Writings of James Arminius*, 3 vols., trans. James Nichols and William Nichols (Reprint, Grand Rapids: Baker, 1956), 2:497.

98. E. Earle Ellis, *The Sovereignty of God in Salvation* (New York: T&T Clark, 2009), 8.

99. Pinnock, *Most Moved Mover*, 163. To see how such a view undermines our prayers in asking God to save the unconverted, see Samuel C. Storms, *Chosen for Life: The Case for Divine Election* (Wheaton, IL: Crossway, 2007), 206–11.

100. Boice and Ryken, *The Doctrines of Grace*, 28.

restored to them. Prevenient grace only makes saving faith possible. The individual himself makes saving faith actual. So we must still ask, "Who *ultimately* accounts for why one comes to faith and another does not?" In the Arminian system, the answer is the person himself, not God.[101]

Likewise, G. C. Berkouwer exposes the man-centeredness of synergism,

> In no form of synergism is it possible to escape the conclusion that man owes his salvation not solely to God but also to himself. Still more accurately, he may thank himself—by virtue of his decision to believe—that salvation actually and effectively becomes his in time and eternity. To be sure, synergism is constantly seeking to avoid this conclusion, and it is seldom expressed in so many words that salvation really depends partly on man. Nevertheless, this conclusion cannot in the long run be avoided and it is clear that we actually are confronted here with the real problem of synergism as it results in a certain amount of human self-conceit.[102]

Berkouwer's point is that synergism inevitably makes salvation depend partly upon man, and the part that does depend upon man is the *most important* part, namely, the *final* part where man's will has the last stop en route to salvation or damnation. As Ware observes, in such a view "God does all that he can do, but the choice, in the end, *is up to us*." Therefore, man's will is "ultimately decisive in personal salvation" and thus "at its most crucial moment (the moment of belief or disbelief), salvation is *of us*, not of the Lord."[103]

Ware's last sentence is the dividing line and the breaking point in the debate. As he explains, in the Arminian view it is man, not God, who is the person to credit in salvation. Therefore, while the Arminian may claim that in his system it is God and not man who saves, the

---

101. Storms, *Chosen for Life*, 31.

102. G. C. Berkouwer, *Divine Election*, trans. Hugo Bekker (Grand Rapids, MI: Eerdmans, 1960), 42.

103. Bruce A. Ware, "Divine Election to Salvation," in *Perspectives on Election*, 5, emphasis added.

Arminian still admits that whether or not man is saved is determined not by God but by man's free will. This, for the Calvinist, inevitably robs God of his glory and gives man something to boast about. The Arminian view could not be in more direct conflict with Paul when he says, "So then it depends not on human will or exertion, but on God, who has mercy" (Rom. 9:16).[104] Indeed, for the Arminian, it does depend on human will and exertion!

CONCLUSION

This chapter has shown that the Arminian and Wesleyan doctrines of prevenient grace and libertarian freedom are not only logically inconsistent but also, and most importantly, contrary to what Scripture says. Therefore, the chasm between Calvinism and Arminianism remains. No one describes this divide with such clarity as Cottrell when he says,

> Thus, for Calvinists, the universal presence of total depravity means that the only gospel call which anyone can answer must be selective and irresistible. For Arminians the universal absence of total depravity (whether by nature or by grace) means that the only gospel call God issues is universal and resistible. For Calvinists total depravity dictates that the final decision of who is saved and who is not must be made by God. For Arminians the final decision belongs to each individual.[105]

What is most troubling to the Calvinist here is that man and not God has the "final decision." A. Skevington Wood, quoting John Wesley, makes it absolutely clear that man is the authority in his own salvation and God's success is totally dependent upon man's will.

> I am persuaded that there are no men living that have not many times "resisted the Holy Ghost," and made void "the counsel of God against themselves." Yes, I am persuaded, every child of God has, at

104. Boice and Ryken, *The Doctrines of Grace*, 33.
105. Cottrell, "The Classical Arminian View of Election," 121.

some time, "life and death set before him," eternal life and eternal death; and has in himself the casting voice.[106]

What a horrific attack upon the majesty of God and, as John Owen states, an exaltation of the idol of free will.[107] Or as Dort says, "This is nothing less than the denial of all the efficiency of God's grace in our conversion, and the subjecting of the working of the Almighty God to the will of man, which is contrary to the apostles."[108] Likewise, Turretin observes,

> If grace always works resistibly in us so that it depends upon the free will of man to either use this or resist that, it will follow that in conversion more is to be ascribed to the will of man than to God and that he who uses grace rightly makes himself to differ from others (contrary to Paul, 1 Cor. 4:7) and has some cause for glorying. For if after all the operations of grace, the will of man is left in equilibrium, it necessarily follows that not God through grace, but man through free will is the principal cause of faith and conversion; he contributes what is the greater, God contributing the lesser. Again, if the will is left doubtful in order that it may determine itself, who does not see that man is properly the cause of his own distinction, since grace which is held to be common and resistible could not accomplish this? And since suasion acts only objectively, it cannot be considered the efficient cause, but man must be.[109]

Therefore, John R. de Witt is right on target when he states, "Arminianism essentially represents an attack upon the majesty of God, and puts in place of it the exaltation of man."[110]

106. Wood, "The Contribution of John Wesley to the Theology of Grace," 218. Wood is quoting John Wesley, "The General Spread of the Gospel," in *Works* (Jackson), 6:281.

107. Owen, *A Display of Arminianism*, 10:14.

108. "Canons of Dort," in *Reformed Confessions Harmonized*, 93.

109. Turretin, *Institutes*, 2:553. John Owen says almost exactly the same thing in *A Discourse Concerning the Holy Spirit,* in *Works*, 3:334. Also see Owen, *A Display of Arminianism*, 10:36–37, 114–37; Girardeau, *Calvinism and Evangelical Arminianism*, 141.

110. John R. de Witt, "The Arminian Conflict," in *Puritan Papers*, vol. 5, *1968–1969*, ed. J. I. Packer (Phillipsburg, NJ: P&R Publishing, 2000), 23. Likewise see J. I. Packer, "Arminianisms," in *Puritan Papers*, 5:39; Michael Horton, *Putting Amazing Back into Grace* (Grand Rapids: Baker, 2002), 126.

THE FAILURE OF RECENT ATTEMPTS
AT A MIDDLE WAY

This project has shown that the Reformed tradition has consistently argued that effectual calling and regeneration causally precede conversion.[1] Though there is minor disagreement among the Reformed on the precise relationship between effectual calling and regeneration,[2] Reformed theologians agree that conversion cannot precede regeneration unless one adopts the view of synergistic Arminianism. However, in the latter half of the twentieth-century, a new proposal has surfaced, a *tertium quid* made popular by Millard Erickson, Gordon Lewis, and Bruce Demarest, which argues that while effectual calling precedes conversion (i.e., Calvinism), regeneration does not (i.e., Arminianism). Therefore, the proposed *ordo salutis* is: effectual calling, conversion, and *then* regeneration. Demarest is even so bold as to include his view within the "*Reformed* Evangelical" position, despite the fact that he freely confesses that his view borrows from Arminianism.[3] Such a claim deserves a fair evaluation.

Therefore, in this chapter we will analyze the modified view of Erickson, Lewis, and Demarest and argue that such a view not only stands outside of

1. Sinclair Ferguson, "Ordo Salutis," in *New Dictionary of Theology*, ed. S. B. Ferguson and D. F. Wright (Downers Grove, IL: InterVarsity, 1988), 480–81.
2. See Appendix 3 of *Reclaiming Monergism*, e-book.
3. Bruce Demarest, *The Cross and Salvation: The Doctrine of Salvation* (Wheaton: Crossway, 1997), 289–91, emphasis added.

Reformed soteriology, but also contradicts Scripture, which always identifies regeneration as logically and causally prior to conversion. We will then conclude by looking briefly at yet a second novel proposal, namely, that of Kenneth Keathley, who, while completely rejecting not only the Calvinist view but also the modified view of Erickson, Lewis, and Demarest, arguing instead for a view consistently in line with Arminianism, nevertheless adamantly claims that he can affirm "monergism." We will argue that Keathley's view is not new but simply Arminianism *incognito* and therefore his affirmation of "monergism" is ill-founded and should be dismissed.

THE VARIANTS OF REFORMED THEOLOGY

As we have already seen, historically Calvinism has emphasized the scriptural teaching of monergistic grace. God alone works efficaciously in the heart of the dead and depraved sinner to create new life. This work is not conditioned upon man's faith but precedes and causes faith (see chapters 3 and 4). More specifically, the Reformed tradition has identified two aspects of this monergistic work of God in calling and awakening sinners to new life: effectual calling and regeneration.

However, Calvinists have differed on the relationship between these two aspects.[4] For example, John Murray and, more recently, John Frame, distinguish between effectual calling and regeneration, placing the effectual call prior to regeneration in the *ordo salutis*.[5] On the other hand, Louis Berkhof differs, identifying regeneration preceding effectual calling.[6] Others, such as Anthony Hoekema and, more recently, Kevin Vanhoozer and Michael Horton, have argued that such bifurcations are erroneous and that a return to the view of the Westminster Confession, which includes regeneration in effectual calling, is needed.[7] Hoekema

4. For an overview, see A. T. B. McGowan, "Justification and the *Ordo Salutis*," in *Justification in Perspective*, ed. Bruce L. McCormack (Grand Rapids: Baker, 2006), 147–63.

5. John Murray, *Redemption Accomplished and Applied* (Grand Rapids: Eerdmans, 1955), 86–94; John Frame, *Salvation Belongs to the Lord* (Phillipsburg: P&R Publishing, 2006), 184–87.

6. Louis Berkhof, *Systematic Theology* (Edinburgh: Banner of Truth, 2003), 468–76.

7. Anthony A. Hoekema, *Saved by Grace* (Grand Rapids: Eerdmans, 1994), 106–10; Kevin J. Vanhoozer, "Effectual Call or Causal Effect? Summons, Sovereignty and Supervenient Grace,"

also argues that this was the view of the Synod of Dort as well.[8] Instead of separating regeneration from effectual calling, the two must be viewed as identical and synonymous. Effectual calling and regeneration are simply two ways of describing the same reality.

Despite these minor differences all Calvinists have agreed that regardless of the relationship between effectual calling and regeneration, Scripture teaches that conversion is always subsequent to, caused by, and conditioned upon effectual calling and/or regeneration. God does not respond to the sinner's cooperation (i.e., synergism), but rather, the sinner responds to God, who works alone to regenerate the unbelieving heart (i.e., monergism). Nevertheless, the traditional Reformed *ordo salutis* has been challenged by some contemporary theologians.

A NEW VIEW

Millard Erickson

In 1983 Millard Erickson wrote in his *Christian Theology*,

> Salvation consists of three steps: effectual calling, conversion, and regeneration. Through the Holy Spirit, God calls the unbeliever to salvation. The human response to that call involves turning from sin to faith in Christ. Faith also includes belief. God responds by regenerating the person to new life in Christ. We can only stand in awe of God's work of saving us and regenerating us as spiritual beings.[9]

Erickson's order of salvation does not consistently follow Calvinism or Arminianism but instead borrows from both. First, Erickson borrows from Calvinism. Man is depraved, lost in sin, spiritually blind, and unable to

---

Tyndale Bulletin 49, 2 (1998): 213–51; Michael S. Horton, *Covenant and Salvation: Union with Christ* (Louisville: Westminster John Knox, 2007), 216–41; "The Westminster Confession," in *The Evangelical Protestant Creeds*, vol. 3 of *The Creeds of Christendom*, ed. Philip Schaff, rev. David S. Schaff (Reprint, Grand Rapids: Baker, 1997), 624–25. Similarly, see William G. T. Shedd, *Dogmatic Theology*, ed. Alan W. Gomes, 3rd ed. (Phillipsburg, NJ: P&R Publishing, 2003), 761; Sinclair Ferguson, *The Holy Spirit* (Downers Grove, IL: InterVarsity, 1996), 117.

8. "The Canons of the Synod of Dort," in Schaff, *The Evangelical Protestant Creeds*, 587–92. Also see McGowan, "Justification and the *Ordo Salutis*," 151.

9. Millard J. Erickson, *Christian Theology*, 2nd ed. (Grand Rapids: Baker, 2004), 941.

believe. While God's gospel call goes out to all people, due to total depravity no one has the ability to believe. Therefore, God must intervene with a special call but, unlike the gospel call, the special call is efficacious and only for his elect. "Special calling means that God works in a particularly effective way with the elect, enabling them to respond in repentance and faith, and rendering it certain that they will."[10] What exactly occurs in special calling? According to Erickson, special calling is the Spirit's work of "illumination, enabling the recipient to understand the true meaning of the gospel."[11] This special call also includes the Spirit's work of conviction (John 16:8–10), which is necessary due to human depravity.

So far Erickson sounds like a Calvinist in placing the effectual call prior to conversion. However, he then borrows from Arminianism by placing regeneration subsequent to conversion. Erickson raises a question that is at the heart of the matter: "Is one converted because of God's work of regeneration within or does God regenerate *in response to and because of the person's repentance and belief*?"[12] Erickson admits that from a logical point of view the traditional Calvinist position (the sinner's response is caused by regeneration) makes the most sense. Because the sinner is radically depraved and his will is a slave to sin, God must first grant the sinner a new heart, enabling him to respond in repentance and belief.

> If we sinful humans are unable to believe and respond to God's gospel without some special working of his within us, how can anyone, even the elect, believe unless first rendered capable of belief through regeneration? To say that conversion is prior to regeneration would seem to be a denial of total depravity.[13]

Erickson, however, is not content with this logical consistency. He objects that the biblical evidence is to the contrary since it is the sinner's will to exercise faith and repentance that arouses in God the act of regeneration.

10. Ibid., 942–43.
11. Ibid.
12. Ibid., 944, emphasis added.
13. Ibid., 944–45.

Nonetheless, the biblical evidence favors the position that conversion is prior to regeneration. Various appeals to respond to the gospel imply that conversion results in regeneration. Among them is Paul's reply to the Philippian jailor (we are here assuming that regeneration is part of the process of being saved): "believe in the Lord Jesus, and you will be saved—you and your household" (Acts 16:31). Peter makes a similar statement in his Pentecost sermon: "Repent and be baptized, every one of you, in the name of Jesus Christ for the forgiveness of your sins. And you will receive the gift of the Holy Spirit" (Acts 2:38). This appears to be the pattern throughout the New Testament.[14]

According to Erickson, the gift of the Holy Spirit in Acts 2:38 refers to the act of regeneration. Therefore, the sinner's repentance is what brings about regeneration. Likewise, Erickson believes the phrase "you will be saved" in Acts 16:31 refers to regeneration. It then follows that it is the sinner's belief that brings about regeneration.

However, Erickson realizes there is a major problem with his position. How can conversion precede regeneration if the sinner is totally depraved and spiritually unable to act in faith and repentance? Isn't this inconsistent with total inability? Erickson believes he has a resolution to the problem.

There is a way out. That is to distinguish between God's special and effectual calling on the one hand, and regeneration on the other. Although no one is capable of responding to the general call of the gospel, in the case of the elect God works intensively through a special calling so that they do respond in repentance and faith. As a result of this conversion, God regenerates them. The special calling is simply an intensive and effectual working by the Holy Spirit. *It is not the complete transformation that constitutes regeneration*, but it does render the conversion of the individual both possible and certain. Thus the logical order of the initial aspects of salvation is special calling-conversion-regeneration.[15]

14. Ibid.
15. Ibid., emphasis added.

Erickson believes he has fixed the dilemma by modifying the special or effectual call. Notice how Erickson says that the effectual call is only partial. It cannot be the complete transformation of the sinner. If it were then Erickson would have to identify effectual calling with regeneration. However, by making the effectual call only partial, Erickson then has the freedom to separate the effectual call from regeneration and even to place conversion between the two. Erickson's understanding of the effectual call as partial is similar to the Arminian doctrine of prevenient grace. Like prevenient grace, the effectual call initiates grace but does not complete the total transformation of the sinner. The effectual call, however, differs from prevenient grace in that it is limited to the elect and guarantees a positive response from the sinner. Erickson explains,

> Special or effectual calling, then, involves an extraordinary presenta-
> tion of the message of salvation. It is sufficiently powerful to coun-
> teract the effects of sin and enable the person to believe. It is also so
> appealing that the person will believe. Special calling is in many ways
> similar to the prevenient grace of which Arminians speak. It differs
> from that concept, however, in two respects. It is bestowed only upon
> the elect, not upon all humans, and it leads infallibly or efficaciously
> to a positive response by the recipient.[16]

Two recent and adamant proponents of Erickson's view are Gordon R. Lewis and Bruce A. Demarest, to whom we now turn.

Gordon Lewis and Bruce Demarest

Lewis and Demarest acknowledge the traditional Calvinist position, but instead follow Erickson in a "modified Calvinistic hypothesis."[17] Lewis and Demarest appeal to John 3:15 in which Jesus says he must "be lifted up, that everyone who believes in him may have eternal life." Lewis and Demarest take the receiving of eternal life as regeneration. Therefore, it is not until one believes in Jesus that he has eternal life (regeneration).

16. Ibid., 944.
17. Gordon R. Lewis and Bruce A. Demarest, *Integrative Theology* (Grand Rapids: Zondervan, 1994), 3:57.

"Eternal life" in context can be shown to refer to the new birth more specifically than can the more general term "saved" in Acts 16:31. The teaching that regeneration must precede faith seems to contradict the teaching that we must believe in Christ to receive eternal life, justification, and adoption as children of God.[18]

Lewis and Demarest do admit that their view does agree with and borrow from Arminianism.

> This moderately Reformed scheme agrees with Arminianism in holding that human conversion precedes divine regeneration (Miley, Wiley) and disagrees with high Calvinism in its claim that the Spirit's regeneration takes logical precedence over conscious, human conversion (Strong, Berkhof, Murray).[19]

Lewis and Demarest are right when they say that they are borrowing from Arminianism. As was seen in chapter 5, Arminians like John Miley and H. Orton Wiley argue that conversion precedes regeneration. Contemporary Arminians do the same by appealing to many of the same passages as Lewis and Demarest. Take, for example, Arminians Steve Lemke and Kenneth Keathley. Similar to Erickson and Lewis and Demarest, Lemke and Keathley appeal to three types of passages.[20]

(1) There are a number of passages which state that if a sinner believes, he will receive "eternal life." For example, Jesus says to Nicodemus that "everyone who believes in him will not perish but have eternal life" (John 3:16). And again in John 3:36, Jesus states, "He who believes in the Son has eternal life," and also in verse 40, "You are unwilling to come to Me, that you may have life." Other passages say the same (John 6:51, 53–54, 57; 11:25; 20:31). Lemke and Keathley conclude from these

18. Ibid.
19. Ibid.
20. Steve W. Lemke, "A Biblical and Theological Critique of Irresistible Grace," in *Whosoever Will: A Biblical-Theological Critique of Five-Point Calvinism*, ed. David L. Allen and Steve W. Lemke (Nashville: B&H Publishing Group, 2010), 134–40; Kenneth Keathley, *Salvation and Sovereignty: A Molinist Approach* (Nashville: B&H Publishing Group, 2010), 119–23.

that to receive "life" or "eternal life" is to be regenerated, and since one must believe to receive eternal life (or regeneration), faith always precedes regeneration. Therefore, in each of these passages "faith and salvation clearly precede the new life in Christ."[21]

(2) Lemke and Keathley also enlist a number of passages that make receiving the Holy Spirit contingent upon man's initial faith. For example, in Acts 2:38 Peter states, "Repent, and let each of you be baptized in the name of Jesus Christ for the forgiveness of your sins; and you shall receive the gift of the Holy Spirit." And the apostle Paul states that "having also believed, you were sealed in him with the Holy Spirit of promise" (Eph. 1:13). Other passages also condition the reception of the Spirit on belief (John 7:38–39; Gal. 3:13; 4:6). As they do with eternal life, Arminians equate the reception of the Spirit with regeneration so that belief must precede regeneration whereby one receives the Spirit.[22]

(3) Finally, Lemke and Keathley enlist a host of passages which say that if one believes, he will be "saved" (Mark 16:15–16; John 1:12; 20:31; Acts 13:39; 16:31; 18:8; Rom. 1:16; 10:9–10; 1 Cor. 1:21; Heb. 11:6). For example, Acts 16:31 states, "Believe in the Lord Jesus, and you will be saved, you and your household." Romans 10:9 also states that "if you confess with your mouth that Jesus is Lord and believe in your heart that God raised him from the dead, you will be saved." "Saved" is equivalent with "regeneration" and therefore one is only saved or regenerated if he exercises belief.[23]

Arminians like Lemke and Keathley conclude from these three different types of passages that faith always precedes regeneration in the *ordo salutis*. Hence, Thomas Oden believes he is justified in arguing that "God does not desire to bring us into this new birth without our cooperation."[24] Indeed, "God does not will to save us without our will. God wills to save us with our will cooperating."[25]

21. Lemke, "Critique of Irresistible Grace," 137; Keathley, *Salvation*, 119–23.
22. Lemke, "Critique of Irresistible Grace," 137–38; Keathley, *Salvation*, 119–23.
23. Lemke, "Critique of Irresistible Grace," 138–39; Keathley, *Salvation*, 119–23.
24. Thomas C. Oden, *John Wesley's Scriptural Christianity* (Grand Rapids: Zondervan, 1994), 249.
25. Ibid. Also see 297.

Despite this fundamental agreement between Lewis and Demarest and Arminianism, Lewis and Demarest would not classify themselves as Arminians since their view (1) affirms a call that is effectual and (2) places this effectual call prior to conversion. As Lewis and Demarest state, "In contrast to Arminianism, however, the only sinners who convert to Christ are effectually called by the Spirit."[26] Nevertheless, Lewis and Demarest do not want to go as far as some Calvinists do in equating effectual calling with regeneration. Rather, effectual calling and regeneration are as distinct and separate as conception is from birth.

> The Spirit's effectual call provides fertile ground for the initial sowing of the seed of God's revealed truth. Those who conceive—as indicated by belief in the Gospel, repentance, and faith in Christ—are then reborn or regenerated. The internal call of the Spirit renews the sinner's abilities (mind, emotions, and will) and secures a positive response to the Gospel. The Spirit then brings about the new birth, permanently changing atrophied abilities and giving eternal life.[27]

Effectual calling and regeneration are different in that in the effectual call the Spirit renews the mind, emotions, and will, whereas in regeneration the Spirit permanently changes "atrophied abilities" and grants eternal life.

If conversion precedes regeneration can Lewis and Demarest say that their view is consistently monergistic? They believe they can: "While conversion is primarily a human act, regeneration is exclusively an act of God the Holy Spirit."[28] However, Lewis and Demarest recognize the difficulty when they ask, "Are we regenerated in order that we may convert? Or do we convert in order to be regenerated?"[29] While the traditional Calvinist argues the former, Lewis and Demarest argue the latter. They appeal to John's gospel (1:12–13; 3:16, 18, 36; 5:24) where "sinners convert in order to become children of God and receive

26. Lewis and Demarest, *Integrative Theology*, 3:57.
27. Ibid.
28. Ibid., 3:104.
29. Ibid.

eternal life."[30] It is by believing that the sinner has life (John 20:31). "So in our moderately Reformed *ordo salutis*, sinners who convert are regenerated. Spiritual conception (calling and conversion) precedes the spiritual birth of a child of God (1 Cor. 3:6)."[31]

YET ANOTHER "NEW" VIEW

Kenneth Keathley's Anti-Calvinism

As seen above, Erickson and Lewis and Demarest, in appealing to certain passages which they believe prove that regeneration comes subsequent to faith, freely admit that their view adopts elements of Arminianism, and they specifically mention Arminians of a previous generation, such as John Miley and H. Orton Wiley, in the process. The same Arminianism that Miley and Wiley advocated is also being propagated today by writers such as Steve Lemke and Kenneth Keathley, who also argue from the same passages used by Erickson and Lewis and Demarest that faith precedes regeneration. However, what sets Keathley apart is his novel attempt to affirm an Arminian view and simultaneously claim that he can affirm "monergism." There are two issues here that reveal the complexities of Keathley's position.

First, while Keathley's view (which he calls "Overcoming Grace")[32] is perfectly consistent with Arminianism, he insists that he is an anti-Calvinist, rejecting the label of Arminianism. Keathley's anti-Calvinism is obvious when he says concerning irresistible grace that it is a doctrine "shockingly weak" and therefore the "I" in the TULIP acronym "must go."[33] He says the same when it comes to the Calvinist distinction between a gospel call and an effectual call.[34] Effectual calling, says Keathley, is nowhere found in Scripture. But is it true that Keathley is not an Arminian when it comes to synergism? We saw above that Keathley is in agreement with Arminians that Scripture always teaches that faith

---

30. Ibid.
31. Ibid.
32. Keathley, *Salvation*, 104, 126.
33. Ibid., 2.
34. Ibid., 116–19.

precedes regeneration. Moreover, consider the following summary of points where Keathley lines up with Arminian synergism perfectly, even quoting Arminian authors.

> *Grace is always resistible*: "God's drawing grace should and would be efficacious for all. The only thing that could stop it is if, inexplicably, a person decides to refuse. As Robert Picirilli puts it, overcoming grace 'is so closely related to regeneration that it inevitably leads one to regeneration unless finally resisted.' . . . It is one thing to say that without the Holy Spirit's enabling we cannot believe, but it is another to say the Holy Spirit necessitates we believe. Simply put, the doctrine of irresistible grace renders incomprehensible major portions of the Bible. Scripture gives too many examples of persons successfully resisting God's grace."[35]

> *Conversion precedes regeneration*: "Salvation is by faith. Therefore, regeneration cannot precede conversion, for regeneration is the beginning of eternal life (i.e., salvation), and faith, along with repentance, is a component of conversion. When Calvinists such as Sproul Sr. argue that regeneration leads to conversion, they reverse what the Scriptures actually say."[36]

> *Grace is synergistic*: "By contrast [to Calvinism], the overcoming grace model understands God's grace to operate in terms of persuasion."[37]

> *Man is the ultimate determiner, not God*: "The overcoming grace model holds that the difference between those who believe and those who do not is found in *the unbelievers*."[38]

It is no wonder that Arminian Roger Olson declares his frustration with those (Keathley included) who contributed to the anti-Calvinist book *Whosoever Will*.

35. Ibid., 106, 124.
36. Ibid., 119.
37. Ibid., 107.
38. Ibid., 105.

In fact, as I will discuss more later, all of the authors are Arminians in the classical sense. I don't know why Vines and they run from the label. Perhaps because it has been so hijacked and misrepresented by Calvinists? But they don't seem to be afraid of Calvinists. So, why so much distance from Arminianism? I can only assume it is because Vines, and perhaps some of the other authors, have bought into the pejorative polemics against Arminianism by its Calvinist enemies.[39]

When Olson says "all" of the authors are classic Arminians, Keathley is not left out. The point here is obvious: even Arminian Roger Olson knows an Arminian when he sees one; he makes no exception in Keathley's case. Thus far we have not seen much novelty in Keathley's view as it is characteristic of many who, while rejecting Calvinism, will not adopt the Arminian label, despite evidence to the contrary.

The second issue which presents itself is that while Keathley's view is synergistic Arminianism in every way, nevertheless, he insists that he can affirm "monergism," which, according to Keathley, means "God is the only worker and accomplisher of our redemption."[40] In contrast to the first issue, here we do see novelty: an Arminian wanting to claim the term "monergism." Keathley is blunt: *"God's grace is both monergistic and resistible."*[41] Consider how Keathley says he can affirm both. First he says,

> *[T]he overcoming grace model is consistent with the gracious nature of salvation.* Here I nod to my Calvinist brethren: salvation is indeed a monergistic work of God. . . . So before anyone can be converted (i.e., repent and believe), God must graciously invade the darkness of a person's heart. God takes the initiative. Salvation is entirely a work of God.[42]

But then Keathley says,

39. Roger Olson, review of *Whosoever Will: A Biblical-Theological Critique of Five-Point Calvinism* (Nashville: B&H Publishing Group, 2010), ed. by David L. Allen and Steve W. Lemke, accessed November 1, 2010, http://www.baptisttheology.org/WhosoeverWill.com.

40. Keathley, *Salvation*, 11. Also see 103.

41. Ibid., 11. Also see 104, 125.

42. Ibid., 128–29.

[T]he overcoming grace model is consistent with the conditionality of salvation. Here I nod to my Arminian brethren: unbelief is the rejection of a Savior who was genuinely available. The convicting work of the Holy Spirit accompanies the preaching of the gospel and enables a response that a lost person does not intrinsically have the ability to give. This includes the ability to accept the gospel. At this point it is not a question of free will. In fact, the Bible uses a grander term than free will: it declares that the water of life is available to "whosoever will."[43]

In this way, Keathley believes that he can simultaneously affirm synergism and monergism.

Now that we have presented an overview of the modified view of Erickson and Lewis and Demarest, as well as the crypto-Arminian view of Keathley, we can examine these positions in greater detail.

BIBLICAL AND THEOLOGICAL PROBLEMS WITH A *TERTIUM QUID*

In Scripture Effectual Calling Is Not Partial Like Prevenient Grace

We begin with Erickson and Lewis and Demarest. Erickson claims that effectual calling is only partial (much like prevenient grace for Arminians) and that it is not until after the sinner is converted that regeneration completes what the effectual call began. Demarest agrees with Erickson: "Special calling stops short of effecting the complete transformation of life commonly represented by the term regeneration."[44] But if effectual calling is only partial, awaiting the conversion of the sinner and subsequently his regeneration, so also is regeneration incomplete and, strictly speaking, partial. Such a concept, however, is foreign to the Scriptures.

The Bible teaches that the sinner is called into fellowship with Christ (1 Cor. 1:9; John 6:44), called out of darkness into Christ's marvelous light (1 Peter 2:9), and called into Christ's kingdom and glory (1 Thess. 2:12; 2 Thess. 2:14; 1 Peter 5:10). One does not get the impression

43. Ibid., 129.
44. Demarest, *The Cross and Salvation*, 265.

from passages like these that calling is merely initial and partial, only to be completed by a regeneration that comes subsequent to man's will in conversion. Rather, as we saw in chapters 3 and 4, the effectual call both consists of and is followed by the regeneration of the sinner. Only then can the sinner respond with faith and repentance.

There is a second problem that arises from the definition of the effectual call that Lewis and Demarest propose. In the effectual call the Spirit internally renews "lost capacities for knowing, loving, and serving God because depraved sinners are persistently unable to respond to spiritual things."[45] Furthermore, the Spirit "persuades chosen sinners of the truth claims made in the verbal or external call."[46] In this supernatural influence, the sinner's capacities to know, love, and act upon the gospel are renewed. "The Spirit graciously enables the sinner's *mind* to apprehend the good, her *desires* to love the good, and her *will* to do the good."[47] Moreover, the "Spirit of grace helps sinners overcome their spiritual inabilities by an initial renewing of the depraved mind, desires, and will."[48] However, if this is how Lewis and Demarest define effectual calling, then what is left to take place in regeneration? In other words, Lewis and Demarest have already affirmed that in the effectual call the sinner's capacities are renewed, awakened, and made new in order to know, love, and choose Christ. No longer are they dead, but now they have restored desires, an awakened mind, and a will that is able to choose the good. Those capacities that were lost due to deadness in sin are now regained due to the effectual call. What then remains to be accomplished in regeneration?[49] Has not the sinner already been renewed and restored in all areas (mind, will, desires)? Has not the Spirit already made the

---

45. Lewis and Demarest, *Integrative Theology*, 3:54.
46. Ibid.
47. Ibid., 3:55.
48. Ibid.
49. Strangely enough Lewis and Demarest go on to say that in regeneration the person's "capacities to know, love, and serve God" are renewed. But previously they claimed that this occurred in effectual calling. Which is it? And if it is both then why would such "renewal" need to be repeated in regeneration? Perhaps this is why Lewis and Demarest must restrict their definition of regeneration to "eternal life." By making effectual calling the primary act

sinner conscious of sin, convicted of wrongdoing, and summoned to repentance and faith? Indeed, the sinner already has new life since he can respond in faith and repentance. Consequently, Lewis and Demarest have minimized and depleted regeneration of its full power to awaken the sinner. As a result, regeneration no longer is the first and primary event that brings new life into the dead sinner as Scripture affirms (Ezek. 36–37; John 3:5–8; Eph. 2:5; Titus 2:3–7; 1 Peter 1:23).

Scripture Does Not Teach That Conversion Precedes Regeneration

Erickson and Lewis and Demarest have conceded to the Arminian order of salvation by placing conversion prior to regeneration.[50] We must note that such a claim is in direct conflict with what we saw in chapter 4, namely, that in Scripture it is regeneration that causes and produces conversion. However, as mentioned already, their argumentation appeals to three types of passages which, in their view, are determinative for the priority of conversion to regeneration. These passages are summarized as follows:

1. Scripture teaches that if a sinner believes, then he will receive "eternal life" (John 3:16, 36; 5:24; 6:54, 57; 11:25; 20:31).
2. Scripture teaches that if one believes, then he will receive the Holy Spirit (John 7:38–39; Acts 2:38; Gal. 3:13; 4:6; Eph. 1:13).
3. Scripture teaches that if one believes, then he will be "saved" (Mark 16:16; Acts 16:31; Rom. 1:16; 10:9–10; 1 Cor. 1:21).

We will address each of these in turn. Because the argument of Erickson and Lewis and Demarest is the same as that used by Arminians like Lemke and Keathley, the following discussion will serve as a refutation of both the modified view and the Arminian view.

---

by which the sinner's capacities are renewed not much is left for regeneration. Therefore, regeneration is defined as receiving "the gift of eternal life." Ibid., 3:104–5.

50. Ibid., 3:57.

"Eternal Life." First, there are several passages where believing results in receiving "eternal life." Lewis and Demarest appeal to John 3:14–15, in which Jesus says that as the Son of Man he must be lifted up, so that whoever believes in him may have "eternal life." Lewis and Demarest take "eternal life" to mean "regeneration." Therefore, regeneration (eternal life) follows belief. Lemke and Keathley make the same argument with other passages as well (John 3:16, 36; 5:24; 6:54, 57; 11:25; 20:31). However, equating "eternal life" with regeneration is a case of eisegesis. Jesus is not describing the order of conversion and regeneration, but rather is comparing "perishing" with living eternally in the age to come as a consequence of faith in Christ here and now. Commenting on John 3:15, Leon Morris defines Jesus' use of eternal life as follows:

> The word rendered "eternal" (always used in this Gospel of life) basi-cally means "pertaining to an age." The Jews divided time into the present age and the age to come, but the adjective referred to life in the coming age, not the present one. "Eternal life" thus means "the life proper to the age to come." It is an eschatological conception (cf. 6:40, 54).[51]

Morris is right that eternal life is an eschatological concept. Jesus demonstrates this when he says in Mark 10:30 that it is "in the age to come" that one receives "eternal life." As Thomas Schreiner and Ardel Caneday demonstrate, the phrase "eternal life" is not only a present reality but also an eschatological reality and "by definition is life of the age to come."[52] In Scripture, eternal life is said not only to be received in the present (John 5:24; 6:47, 54; 1 John 5:11–13) but also to be received in the future (Mark 10:17, 29–30; Rom. 2:6–7; Gal. 6:8; 1 Tim. 6:19; Titus 1:2; 3:7; James 1:12; Rev. 2:10). In other words, unlike regeneration, which is a one-time instantaneous act that occurs at initiation,

---

51. Leon Morris, *The Gospel according to John*, NICNT (Grand Rapids: Eerdmans, 1971), 227. Also see Frank Thielman, *Theology of the New Testament* (Grand Rapids: Zondervan, 2005), 172.

52. Thomas R. Schreiner and Ardel B. Caneday, *The Race Set Before Us* (Downers Grove, IL: InterVarsity, 2001), 65, 66–67.

eternal life is an eschatological hope that pervades into the present but ultimately is received in the life to come. Therefore, Lewis and Demarest are simply in error to interpret eternal life as specifically referring to the act of regeneration.

Moreover, as Snoeberger observes, in many of the passages cited, life is said not only to follow belief but also justification (Titus 3:7), sanctification (Rom. 6:22), perseverance (Rom. 2:7; Jude 21), and even physical death (2 Cor. 5:4). "With this in view, the 'life' described in these passages cannot mean regeneration."[53] The point is made clear when one examines other passages (which Erickson, Lewis and Demarest, Lemke, and Keathley never mention) that use the phrase eternal life to refer to a gift to be received in the age to come (Mark 10:17, 29–30; Rom. 2:6–7, 23; Gal. 6:8; 1 Tim. 6:19; Titus 1:2; 3:7; James 1:12; Rev. 2:10). Notice how peculiar it sounds if we equate eternal life in these passages with regeneration. For example, Jesus, responding to the rich young ruler, would state, "Truly, I say to you, there is no one who has left house or brothers . . . for my sake and for the gospel, who will not receive a hundredfold now in this time . . . and in the age to come *regeneration* (eternal life)" (Mark 10:29–30). Likewise, Paul would state, "He will render to each one according to his works: to those who by patience in well-doing seek for glory and honor and immortality, he will give *regeneration* (eternal life)" (Rom. 2:6–7). Notice, if Erickson, Lewis and Demarest, Lemke, and Keathley are right in equating regeneration with eternal life, then in Romans 2:6–7 one must do works to be regenerated. The same would apply in passages like James 1:12 and Revelation 2:10. Surely Erickson, Lewis and Demarest, Lemke, and Keathley do not want to affirm works righteousness, but their logic, if applied consistently, inevitably leads to this.

Finally, the flaw in equating regeneration with eternal life is most evident in Titus 3:5–7: "He saved us, not because of works done by us in righteousness, but according to his own mercy, by the washing of regeneration and renewal of the Holy Spirit, whom he poured out on

---

53. Mark A. Snoeberger, "The Logical Priority of Regeneration to Saving Faith in a Theological *Ordo Salutis*," *DBSJ* 7 (2002): 64.

us richly through Jesus Christ our Savior, so that being justified by his grace we might become heirs according to the hope of eternal life." How can regeneration be equated with eternal life when in Titus 3:5 it is regeneration that is said to lead to the hope of eternal life? As Snoeberger writes, "Paul states unequivocally that regeneration must occur in order that (ἵνα) eternal life may result. It is obvious that this 'life' is not regeneration, but the eschatological experience of 'life that truly is life' (1 Tim. 6:19)."[54]

"Holy Spirit." Second, Erickson, Lewis and Demarest, Lemke, and Keathley also enlist a number of passages that make receiving the Holy Spirit contingent upon man's initial faith (John 7:38–39; Acts 2:38; Gal. 3:13; 4:6; Eph. 1:13). Like eternal life, the reception of the Spirit in these passages is equated with regeneration so that belief must precede regeneration. Erickson makes his case by arguing from Acts 2:38, in which Peter says, " 'Repent and be baptized every one of you in the name of Jesus Christ for the forgiveness of your sins, and you will receive the gift of the Holy Spirit.' " According to Erickson, the gift of the Holy Spirit in this passage refers to regeneration, and repentance must come before such a gift can be received. Lemke and Keathley make a similar argument. To take but one example, Jesus says in John 7:38, "Whoever believes in me, as the Scripture has said, 'Out of his heart will flow rivers of living water.' " John interprets, "Now this he said about the Spirit, whom those who believed in him were to receive, for as yet the Spirit had not been given, because Jesus was not yet glorified" (John 7:39). Lemke and Keathley conclude from passages like these that belief is the condition for the reception of the Spirit, a phrase which they believe is referring to regeneration.

However, as we saw with "eternal life," such an argument is reductionistic for two reasons. (1) No reason or explanation is given as to why one should equate the reception of the Spirit with regeneration. Why not interpret the reception of the Spirit as *the result of* regeneration? Or why should it refer to regeneration at all? Why

54. Ibid., 76–77.

not to conversion, adoption, justification, indwelling, or union with Christ? Or why not interpret the reception of the Spirit as distinct from all of them? (2) To the contrary, these passages are best interpreted as meaning that one receives the indwelling of the Spirit at conversion. As James Hamilton has demonstrated at great length, regeneration and indwelling by the Spirit are not to be equated nor are they identical but are distinct events.[55] If they are not distinct, then it is very difficult to make sense out of John 7:38–39, "Whoever believes in me, as the Scripture has said, 'Out of his heart will flow rivers of living water.' Now this he said about the Spirit, *whom those who believed in him were to receive, for as yet the Spirit had not been given*, because Jesus was not yet glorified." Working his way through John's gospel Hamilton explains:

> The Gospel of John has been clear to this point that no one is able to come to Jesus unless the Father draws him (6:44, 65), and that "everyone who does sin is a slave to sin" (8:34). If the disciples can love Jesus and keep His commandments, it is because they have been drawn to Jesus by the Father and freed from sin by the Son (8:36). Many assume that enabling an individual to believe is equivalent to an individual's reception of the indwelling Spirit. [See the stress on ability and inability in John 3:1–12. A form of the word "can" or "able" (δύναμαι) occurs six times there.] But John 7:39 speaks of people who had been enabled to believe in Jesus but had not yet received the Spirit. Similarly in this passage the disciples are assumed to be able to love and obey Jesus before they receive the Spirit. The grammatical connection between John 14:15 and 16 demonstrates the need to recognize that regeneration and indwelling are separate ministries of the Spirit. The disciples are able to love Jesus because they have been regenerated, though they are yet to receive the Spirit. If regeneration and indwelling are not separated, this text becomes very difficult to interpret because of its grammar.[56]

55. James M. Hamilton, Jr., *God's Indwelling Presence: The Holy Spirit in the Old and New Testaments* (Nashville: B&H Publishing Group, 2006), 127–59.

56. Ibid., 75.

Indeed, Hamilton makes a great point. A permanent reception or indwelling of the Spirit is a reality of the new covenant. In the old covenant God's presence indwelt the temple (1 Kings 8:10–11) and tabernacle (Exod. 40:34–38), while in the new covenant God indwells not only Jesus, who tabernacles among his people (John 1:14, 51), but also his Spirit comes and indwells every believer (John 14:17, 23; cf. John 4:21–24). Therefore, new covenant followers of Christ are called temples of the Holy Spirit (1 Cor. 6:19), in whom God's Spirit dwells (1 Cor. 3:16), something not said of old covenant believers. Therefore, while a sinner is regenerated by the Spirit regardless of where he is on the redemptive-historical timeline, receiving the Spirit or being permanently indwelt by the Spirit is only a reality after the glorification of Jesus.[57] Consequently, while regeneration and indwelling are both works of the Spirit, they are not the same but distinct.

For Erickson, Lewis and Demarest, Lemke, and Keathley, John 7:39 becomes not only difficult but impossible to interpret since they insist on making regeneration synonymous with reception of the Spirit or indwelling. However, if these terms are synonymous, then how could believers in the old covenant be regenerate since, as Jesus states in John 7:39, the Spirit had not yet been given? Given the view of Erickson, Lewis and Demarest, Lemke, and Keathley, it seems they would have to conclude that old covenant believers could not have been regenerate on the basis of John 7:39. Surely we would not want to say any such thing.

To the contrary, if we distinguish between regeneration and indwelling (on the basis of passages like John 7:39), then there is no problem. While the Spirit regenerated elect sinners in the old covenant, a *permanent* indwelling of *all* believers with the Spirit awaits the new covenant just as Jesus says.[58] For example, in John 3:5, as Hamilton shows, Jesus "speaks not of the Spirit *inhabiting* the one who is born again, but *causing*

---

57. Ibid., 143.

58. Please note that I am *not* saying that the Spirit did not have a role in regard to believers in the old covenant. Indeed, the Spirit did come upon certain leaders for certain tasks, though this may have been only for a limited time. However, it is not until the new covenant that *all* believers are indwelt and all are indwelt *permanently*. For a survey of the Old Testament on this issue see ibid., 25–56.

the new birth."[59] This interpretation is also consistent with John 7:39, which does not say, "the Spirit was not yet causing the new birth, but that He was about to be received by those who had *believed* in Jesus."[60] Moreover, in John 7:39 it is clear that the permanent reception of the Spirit will not be experienced until after the crucifixion, yet in John 3:5 Jesus does expect Nicodemus to understand the experience of the new birth, implying that it was a reality in the old covenant.[61] Therefore, Hamilton concludes,

> If John 3:6 is speaking of regeneration and not indwelling, then the door is open to an inward enablement by the Spirit (which the Old Testament calls "circumcision of the heart") prior to the cross. Since John 7:39 refers to believers who are yet to receive the Spirit, it would seem that prior to Jesus' glorification people could be enabled, i.e., regenerated, though they were not indwelt.[62]

Hamilton is correct given the fact that throughout the old covenant we see many examples (Noah, Abraham, David, etc.) of sinners being spiritually circumcised and regenerated (Pss. 87; 119:25; Isa. 55:3; Neh. 9:20, 30). As VanGemeren states, "The saints were those who were circumcised of heart, or 'regenerate.'"[63] Therefore, while "the New Testament explicitly states that the reception of the indwelling Spirit could not take place prior to the glorification of Jesus (John 7:39), it does not say that regeneration could not take place."[64]

Regrettably, Erickson, Lewis and Demarest, Lemke, and Keathley fail to address John 7:39 at all, nor do they address the larger issue of the textual evidence throughout both the Old and New Testaments which demonstrates that regeneration and indwelling are not the same. Moreover, since regeneration precedes conversion in the *ordo salutis*,

59. Ibid., 132.
60. Ibid.
61. Ibid., 134.
62. Ibid., 135.
63. Willem A. VanGemeren, *The Progress of Redemption: The Story of Redemption from Creation to the New Jerusalem* (Grand Rapids: Baker, 1988), 167.
64. Hamilton, *God's Indwelling Presence*, 141.

and since, after Jesus is glorified, it is *at conversion* that the sinner is indwelt by the Spirit (John 7:38–39; Acts 2:38; Gal. 3:13; 4:6; Eph. 1:13), the passages where belief is said to bring about reception of the Spirit present no problem for the Calvinist.[65] Notice that, in all of the texts that Lemke and Keathley put forward (John 7:38–39; Acts 2:38; Gal. 3:13; 4:6; Eph. 1:13), the Spirit is said to be received upon *faith*. None of these texts say anything about regeneration or new birth, which precedes and causes faith. What they do mention is an indwelling by the Spirit at conversion, which is not the same as regeneration but the *result* and *product* of regeneration. In essence, Erickson, Lewis and Demarest, Lemke, and Keathley fail to pay attention to the redemptive-historical timeline of Scripture and consequently they fall short of distinguishing, as Scripture does, between regeneration by the Spirit and indwelling by the Spirit.

"Saved." Third, the view of Erickson and Lewis and Demarest also agrees with Arminians like Lemke and Keathley by enlisting a host of passages which say that if one believes, he will be "saved" (Mark 16:16; Acts 16:31; Rom. 1:16; 10:9–10; 1 Cor. 1:21). To take one example, Erickson, Lemke, and Keathley appeal to Acts 16:31 where Paul and Silas say, "Believe in the Lord Jesus, and you will be saved, you and your household." Apparently "saved" (σωθήσῃ) in this passage refers to regeneration. Therefore, it is only after the sinner believes that he is saved (regenerated). However, such an interpretation of "you will be saved" is reductionistic since there is no contextual reason to read "saved" in such a narrow manner. Even Lewis and Demarest, who agree with Erickson's modified view, observe that Paul and Silas use the word "saved" in a general sense, not to refer specifically to the inward act of regeneration but to salvation holistically.[66]

65. One could make the objection that after Jesus is glorified believers receive the Spirit at conversion. Granted, this is true. However, almost all theologians recognize that there is a difference between regeneration and conversion (faith and repentance). Therefore, even if we say that after Jesus is glorified indwelling occurs at conversion, still it has not been shown that conversion or indwelling precedes regeneration. Ibid., 143.

66. Lewis and Demarest, *Integrative Theology*, 3:56.

Like the passages on "eternal life" and the "Holy Spirit," so also here we see "saved" equated erroneously with regeneration. Again, why should one interpret being saved in such a narrow manner? Why not interpret it as referring to adoption or justification? Or why not interpret it in a much broader sense as referring to the sinner's escape from hell and wrath in the age to come? Or, better yet, why not interpret being saved as a distinct metaphor in and of itself?[67] To interpret it as synonymous with regeneration is fallacious, as we can see when we look at how other passages would then have to be interpreted.

Consider Matthew 27:42, where Jesus is on the cross and his accusers mock him. According to the view of Lemke and Keathley, the mockers would be made to say, "He regenerated (saved) others; he cannot regenerate (save) himself." Clearly, such an interpretation is unwarranted. And again, 1 Corinthians 3:15 would then say, "If anyone's work is burned up, he will suffer loss, though he himself will be regenerated (saved), but only as through fire." According to Lemke and Keathley's understanding, Paul would be teaching that one is actually regenerated on the last day. The same point is made when we consider 1 Peter 1:4–5, in which Peter says God has caused us to be born again to a living hope and, in the interpretation of Lemke and Keathley, "an inheritance that is imperishable, undefiled, and unfading, kept in heaven for you, who by God's power are being guarded through faith for a regeneration (salvation) ready to be revealed in the last time." Again, if Erickson, Lewis and Demarest, Lemke, and Keathley are right that "salvation" refers to regeneration, then Peter would be saying that we are regenerated twice (born again and again), first in 1 Peter 1:3 at initiation and again in 1 Peter 1:5 in the "last time." To the contrary, "salvation" in 1 Peter 1:4–5 is used to refer to an inheritance we will one day receive in the "last time." Or consider Philippians 2:12b–13 as read through the lens we are studying: "Work out your own regeneration (salvation) with fear and trembling, for it is God who works in you, both to will and to work for his good pleasure." If "salvation" is to be equated with regeneration then Paul would be instructing the Philippians that they must work out their own regeneration.

67. Schreiner and Caneday, *The Race Set Before Us*, 46–86.

The meaning of "salvation" in Scripture is very different. The insightful comment of Silva, which we quoted previously in chapter 6, bears repeating here:

> It is conceded by all parties in the discussion that the term *salvation* (or its cognate verb) need *not be restricted, as it normally is in contemporary evangelical language, to the initial act of conversion* ("Have you been saved?") or to the status of being in a right relationship with God ("Are you saved?"). . . . [T]he biblical concept of salvation is not thus restricted to justification; more commonly what is in view includes God's redemptive work *in its totality*. Thus, while in a very important sense we have already been saved (Eph. 2:5, 8; Titus 3:5), in another sense we are yet to be saved (Rom. 5:9–10; 1 Cor. 3:15; 5:5; 2 Tim. 4:18). Calvin rightly claims "that salvation is taken to mean the entire course of our calling, and that this term includes all things by which God accomplishes that perfection, to which He has determined us by His free election."[68]

Silva is correct; while salvation can refer to the past (see Eph. 2:5, 8; Titus 3:5, two passages we have already seen that support monergism), many passages, including Philippians 2:12, refer to salvation in its totality or as a reality yet to come (Rom. 5:9–10; 1 Cor. 3:15; 5:5; 2 Tim. 4:18).

The same point is made by Schreiner, who observes that the language of salvation or deliverance is "fundamentally eschatological." Consider texts like Romans 2:3; 5:9; and 5:10 where one is said to be saved from God's wrath and saved by his life. Each of these texts uses the future tense, "constraining us as readers to think about future deliverance."[69] Therefore, these texts show us that salvation is not ours now but it is a "future gift, a hope that we will be spared from God's wrath on the day of the Lord."[70] Schreiner helpfully explains,

68. Moisés Silva, *Philippians*, 2nd ed., BECNT (Grand Rapids: Baker, 2005), 121, emphasis added.
69. Thomas R. Schreiner, *Paul: Apostle of God's Glory in Christ* (Downers Grove, IL: InterVarsity, 2001), 225. Cf. Schreiner and Caneday, *The Race Set Before Us*, 46–86.
70. Schreiner, *Paul*, 225–26.

When Paul speaks of the gospel "which results in salvation" (Rom. 1:16), he has in mind eschatological salvation that will be our possession in the coming age. Similarly, the salvation that belongs to those who confess Jesus as Lord and believe on him in their hearts (Rom. 10:9–10; cf. Rom. 10:13) is fundamentally eschatological. The future tenses refer to the coming age. . . . The eschatological character of salvation is strikingly confirmed in Romans 13:11, where salvation is said "to be nearer than when we first believed." Paul does not speak here of salvation as something obtained at the moment we first believed but as a gift to be given at the last day.[71]

While salvation is fundamentally eschatological, it does have reference to both the past and the present. It would be incorrect, in other words, to restrict salvation to the eschaton since some texts do indeed speak of salvation in the past tense. Take Ephesians 2:5, 8, in which Paul says, "By grace you have been saved," or Colossians 1:13, where God "rescued us from the authority of darkness and transferred us into the kingdom of his Son." Likewise 2 Timothy 2:9 says God saved us. In Titus 3:5 Paul writes that God saved us through the washing of regeneration and the renewal from the Holy Spirit. Paul again says in Romans 8:24, "For in hope we have been saved." All of these are in the past tense. However, as Schreiner argues, these "past-tense statements do not cancel out the eschatological dimension of salvation."[72] Rather,

> Paul most commonly assigns salvation to the future, but he can speak of salvation as past since the age to come has invaded this present evil age. The past dimension of salvation, therefore, should be understood within the eschatological framework of Paul's theology. And Romans 8:24 helps us understand that the reality of salvation in the past does not mean that salvation is now complete. Believers still hope for the future realization of their salvation for they have not yet received the full inheritance. Once we grasp the eschatological tension between the future and the present, it is understandable that Paul also describes

71. Ibid., 226.
72. Ibid., 228.

307

salvation as an ongoing process in the present. Through the gospel "you are being saved" (1 Cor. 15:2); and the eschatological tension of Paul's view is preserved in that such salvation will only be realized through perseverance. In 1 Corinthians 1:18 the gospel's power has seized "those who are being saved" (cf. 2 Cor. 2:15). Indeed, the gospel is the reason for their salvation.[73]

Schreiner's point is well taken. "Salvation" is fundamentally a future reality, but it has broken into the past and the present (already/not yet). As Sproul states, "We have been saved, are being saved, and shall be saved. There is a past, present, and future dimension to salvation."[74] Therefore, "salvation" is a soteriological category that is *broad*, covering not only the past and present but also the future, and therefore it is erroneous for Erickson, Lewis and Demarest, and avowed Arminians like Lemke and Keathley to define "salvation" so narrowly as to refer to the one instantaneous event of regeneration at initiation.[75] It is obvious that Arminians who equate "saved" with "regeneration" in their appeal to such passages have succumbed to a reductionistic interpretation."[76]

Placing Conversion before Regeneration Is Synergistic

In evaluating the work of Erickson, Lewis and Demarest, and Keathley, it is crucial to recognize that placing conversion before regeneration is synergistic because in this arrangement God's act of regeneration is logically and causally dependent upon and conditioned upon man's act of belief and repentance.[77] If conversion precedes regeneration, then it must be the case that the Spirit's regenerate act is in response to man's act

---

73. Ibid., 228.

74. R. C. Sproul, *What Is Reformed Theology?* (Grand Rapids: Baker, 1997), 198.

75. Snoeberger, "The Logical Priority of Regeneration," 60.

76. One could possibly object that even though "saved," reception of the "Holy Spirit," and "eternal life" are broadly defined, nevertheless, regeneration is included within such a broad definition and therefore would still come subsequent to belief. However, Snoeberger demonstrates that just because "saved," or reception of the "Spirit," or "life" follows faith "it does not follow that every single aspect" of "saved," "life," or reception of the "Spirit," must follow faith. In other words, while some aspects of "salvation" or "life" may follow faith it is also the case that other aspects precede faith. Snoeberger, "The Logical Priority of Regeneration," 61, 65.

77. Erickson, *Systematic Theology*, 945.

to repent and believe. This is the essence of Arminianism. Erickson and Lewis and Demarest in particular try to avoid full-fledged Arminianism by placing effectual calling prior to conversion, but this does not remove the dependence or conditionality of regeneration on man's willful choice, which is the fundamental principle of an Arminian soteriology.[78] Lewis and Demarest even concede this when they admit that their moderately Reformed scheme agrees with Arminians who place the sinner's free choice before regeneration.[79] Given the presence of this Arminian stream of synergism in the work of Erickson and Lewis and Demarest, we must conclude that, unlike any of the three views previously discussed (Murray, Berkhof, or Hoekema), which stand firmly within the Reformed tradition, it would be outside the limits of a Reformed understanding of monergism—and, more importantly, outside the view of Scripture itself (see chapter 4)—to argue that conversion is subsequent to effectual calling but prior to regeneration.

Monergism Wrongly Defined

Despite the fact that the modified view of Erickson and Lewis and Demarest diverges from the Reformed view by agreeing with Arminians that faith precedes regeneration, Lewis and Demarest do not hesitate to include their view as a legitimate option within the "Reformed Evangelical" position. In so doing, they give the impression that their view is monergistic like the Reformed view, but slightly modified. To make matters worse, Keathley, whom Roger Olson identifies as an Arminian, is insistent that he too can affirm the label "monergism," despite the fact that he completely rejects both the Calvinist position *and* the modified view in favor of a traditional Arminian view of resistible grace.[80]

---

78. I am not saying that Erickson and Lewis and Demarest are Arminians. Clearly they are not since they affirm a calling that is effectual and limited to the elect. Therefore, they are not *total* synergists. However, what I am arguing is that in placing conversion prior to regeneration they have borrowed the essence of Arminianism (or synergism). While they may begin as monergist (i.e., calling is effectual, preceding conversion) they end as synergists (i.e., in the end regeneration is still conditioned upon man's will in conversion). Perhaps to be accurate it would be best to categorize Erickson and Lewis and Demarest as *partial* or *soft* synergists.

79. Lewis and Demarest, *Integrative Theology*, 3:56–57.

80. "*God's grace is both monergistic and resistible.*" Keathley, *Salvation*, 11, emphasis original.

Monergism, according to Keathley, means that "God is the only worker and accomplisher of our redemption."[81] In Keathley's mind, then, monergism means nothing more than the fact that God alone is the author of redemption. Furthermore, says Keathley, though he affirms resistible grace, he claims that his view is still "monergistic because all that is necessary in this scenario is that a person *refrains* from acting."[82]

To summarize, for Keathley grace is monergistic if (1) God alone is the author of redemption and (2) if man refrains from acting or resisting. But is this how monergism has been defined, either theologically or historically? R. C. Sproul explains exactly why such a definition is misguided:

> The classic dispute over monergism and synergism is not over the question of who does the regenerating. Virtually everyone agrees that only God can do the work of regeneration proper. The issue focuses instead on what the unregenerate person can do to evoke the divine work of regeneration. Synergists hold that one can "choose Christ" or "believe in Christ" prior to regeneration. The choice or the act of faith is a condition for regeneration. It is at this point that they are synergistic. The grace of regeneration is offered, but the "efficacious" grace of regeneration is given only to those who first accept the offer or act in faith to receive it.[83]

In other words, the issue in debate is not merely whether God alone is the author of regeneration. Both Arminians and Calvinists agree on this. If, as Keathley thinks, this is the whole of how monergism is defined, then every Arminian is a monergist! To the contrary, the debate is over whether the Arminian is right in arguing that regeneration is contingent upon man's will to believe. It is clear that for Keathley regeneration *is* conditioned upon man's will to believe (faith); therefore, his view succumbs to synergism entirely.

81. Ibid. Also see 103.
82. Ibid., 105.
83. R. C. Sproul, *Willing to Believe* (Grand Rapids: Baker, 1997), 196.

Moreover, it is surprising that Keathley defines monergism as meaning that the "person merely refrains from resisting."[84] No Arminian would disagree with such a definition because this is the essence of synergism: divine grace is successful as long as man cooperates by refraining from resisting. Once again, if this is what monergism means, then every Arminian has the right to call himself a monergist. To the contrary, Keathley has not only defined monergism wrongly in theological terms, but also in historical terms, for as we saw in chapter 5, Arminians throughout history have defined grace as Keathley does but labeled it synergism. Therefore, for Keathley to say that he can affirm monergism is (1) a complete redefinition of monergism so that even Arminians can affirm such a label, and (2) misleading since his view, as already seen, is basic Arminian synergism wrapped in a new label he calls "overcoming grace." While this maneuver by Keathley may appear novel, history once again repeats itself. For example, seventeenth-century Dutch Reformed theologian Wilhelmus à Brakel (1635–1711) also noticed such a move by Arminians in his own day and saw through it.

> Moreover, the Arminians understand *effectual grace* to refer to the *result*. It is not effectual by the almighty power of God who would thus in actuality convert man, but only in reference to the result. If man repents and believes in Christ, his calling is effectual because of what man has done. . . . All of this, however, culminates in one thing: Free will remains lord and master, having ultimate power to either accept or reject. God is merely a servant or a friend who advises and urges him to act, whereas man himself determines whether or not he will allow himself to be persuaded. All of this we reject.[85]

Finally, "monergism" has been defined much differently than Erickson, Lewis and Demarest, and especially Keathley want to admit. As Sproul stated above, monergism does not merely mean that God alone is the author of redemption, but also—and significantly—that

---

84. Keathley, *Salvation*, 105.

85. Wilhelmus à Brakel, *The Christian's Reasonable Service*, ed. Joel R. Beeke, trans. Bartel Elshout (Grand Rapids: Reformation Heritage, 1993), 2:214–15.

regeneration precedes faith. Throughout its history, Reformed theology has consistently understood monergism in this way. An examination of Reformed theologians (as well as Reformed Baptist theologians) from not only the seventeenth century but also the eighteenth, nineteenth, and twentieth centuries[86] leaves us with the same conclusion: the consensus among Calvinists, both past and present, is that *regeneration precedes faith* in the *ordo salutis* and this is essential to monergism.[87] To deny this or to tinker with it is to deny Calvinism as it has traditionally been construed. Moreover, no contemporary Reformed theologian has even mentioned the modified view of Erickson and Lewis and Demarest as a possible option for Reformed theology, nor has any noted the possibility of redefining monergism as Keathley does.

86. E.g., James P. Boyce, *Abstract of Systematic Theology* (n.p., 1887; reprint, Cape Coral, FL: Founders, 2006), 374, 379, 513; John L. Dagg, *Manual of Theology* (1857; Harrisonburg, VA: Sprinkle, 2009; Gano Books, 1982), 332–33; Charles H. Spurgeon, "On *Regeneration*," *Founders Journal* 48 (2002): 29–32. More recently, consider: Wayne Grudem, *Systematic Theology* (Grand Rapids: Zondervan, 1994), 702–3; John Piper, *Finally Alive* (Fearn, Ross-shire, Great Britain: Christian Focus, 2009), 70, 102, 105, 107; Thomas R. Schreiner, "Does Regeneration Necessarily Precede Conversion?," accessed July 6, 2008, available from http://www.9marks.org/ejournal/does-regeneration-necessarily -precede-conversion; accessed 6 July 2008; Bruce A. Ware, "Divine Election to Salvation," in *Perspectives on Election: Five Views*, ed. Chad Owen Brand (Nashville: B&H Publishing Group, 2006), 19, 21.

87. E.g., Charles Hodge, *Systematic Theology*, 3 vols. (Grand Rapids: Eerdmans, 1982), 2:680, 688; A. A. Hodge, "The Ordo Salutis: or, Relation in the Order of Nature of Holy Character and Divine Favor," *The Princeton Review* 54 (1878): 313; A. A. Hodge, *Outlines of Theology* (Reprint: Grand Rapids: Eerdmans, 1959), 445–64; Benjamin B. Warfield, *Calvin and Calvinism*, vol. 5 of *The Works of Benjamin B. Warfield* (Grand Rapids: Baker, 2003), 359–60; Herman Bavinck, *Reformed Dogmatics*, ed. John Bolt, trans. John Vriend (Grand Rapids: Baker, 2006), 3:582; Shedd, *Dogmatic Theology*, 771–72. Also consider Archibald Alexander, Abraham Kuyper, and Robert L. Dabney. More recently, consider: Murray, *Redemption Accomplished and Applied*, 103; Berkhof, *Systematic Theology*, 473; Hoekema, *Saved by Grace*, 101, 144; Edwin H. Palmer, *The Person and Ministry of the Holy Spirit: The Traditional Calvinistic Perspective* (Grand Rapids: Baker, 1974), 83–84; R. C. Sproul, *Chosen by God* (Wheaton, IL: Tyndale, 1986), 118–19; James Montgomery Boice and Philip Graham Ryken, *The Doctrines of Grace: Rediscovering the Evangelical Gospel* (Wheaton, IL: Crossway, 2002), 135, 149; Robert L. Reymond, *A New Systematic Theology of the Christian Faith*, 2nd ed. (Nashville: Thomas Nelson, 1998), 708, 720; Michael S. Horton, "The *Sola*'s of the Reformation," in *Here We Stand! A Call from Confessing Evangelicals for a Modern Reformation*, ed. James Montgomery Boice and Benjamin E. Sasse (Phillipsburg, NJ: P&R Publishing, 1996), 120; Robert A. Peterson and Michael D. Williams, *Why I Am Not an Arminian* (Downers Grove, IL: InterVarsity, 2004), 188–89.

The reason for this is obvious: the modified position of Erickson and Lewis and Demarest deviates considerably in affirming certain aspects of Arminianism, and in Keathley's case, it affirms synergism entirely. Therefore, it is fitting to conclude that since Reformed theologians have never defined monergism as Erickson, Lewis and Demarest, or Keathley do, it is illegitimate to classify the modified view as falling within the parameters of Reformed theology or to accept Keathley's definition of monergism as accurate.

CONCLUSION

As we have seen from the evidence presented, attempts at a *tertium quid* or *via media* between Calvinism and Arminianism are unsuccessful, a point upon which both Arminians and Calvinists agree. As Reformed theologian W. Robert Godfrey explains,

> Some try to split the difference between Arminianism and Calvinism. They say something like "I want to be 75% Calvinist and 25% Arminian." If they mean that literally, then they are 100% Arminian since giving any determinative place to human will is Arminian. Usually they mean that they want to stress the grace of God and human responsibility. If that is what they mean, then they can be 100% Calvinists for Calvinism does teach both that God's grace is entirely the cause of salvation and that man is responsible before God to hear and heed the call to repentance and faith.[88]

Arminian Roger Olson says the same: "Consistent classical Arminians agree with Godfrey that their system of belief is incompatible with Calvinism and would argue that most people who declare themselves Calminians or 75 percent Calvinist and 25 percent Arminian are actually Arminian! Some are simply inconsistent and willing to embrace contradictory propositions."[89]

88. W. Robert Godfrey, "Who Was Arminius?," *Modern Reformation* 1 (1992): 24.
89. Roger E. Olson, *Arminian Theology* (Downers Grove, IL: InterVarsity, 2006), 67.

The modified attempts of Erickson, Lewis and Demarest, and especially Keathley are contemporary examples of the very point Godfrey and Olson make. Modifying monergism by borrowing from Arminian synergism results not merely in an unsuccessful attempt at Calminianism but, as Olson says, in a theology that is ultimately Arminian. Consequently, the "plain fact of the matter is that *on certain points* classical Calvinism and classical Arminianism simply disagree, and no bridge uniting them can be found; no hybrid of the two can be created."[90] The issue of monergism versus synergism is one of these points and, as we have seen, the hybrid models evaluated in this chapter simply cannot bridge this gulf.

90. Ibid., 68.

CONCLUSION

As we conclude this debate over the nature of divine grace, Herman Bavinck asks the most telling question of all, "One always has to face the question: at the end of all the interactions, who makes the final decision?" Bavinck's answer to this central question is exactly what we have found to be true in the course of this project.

> If it is the human person, then Pelagius is fundamentally correct and the decision concerning what is most important in human history—namely, eternal salvation—rests in human hands. If, however, the last word rests with God and his omnipotent grace, one sides with Augustine and accepts a preceding rebirth (internal grace) in which the human person is passive. In other words, by placing regeneration after faith and repentance, one does not escape the problem but wraps oneself in an insoluble contradiction.[1]

Though Pelagianism, Semi-Pelagianism, and Arminianism may differ, at the end of the day their answer to the question of who is the ultimate determiner in salvation is the same: man's will decides. Therefore, J. I. Packer's observation is invaluable:

> Arminianism is a slippery slope, and it is always arbitrary where one stops on the slide down. All Arminianisms start from a rationalistic hermeneutic which reads into the Bible at every point the philosophic axiom that to be responsible before God man's acts must be contingent in relation to him. All Arminianisms involve a

---

1. Herman Bavinck, *Reformed Dogmatics*, ed. John Bolt, trans. John Vriend (Grand Rapids: Baker, 2008), 4:66.

rationalistic restriction of the sovereignty of God and the efficacy of the cross, a restriction which Scripture seems directly to contradict. All Arminianisms involve a measure of synergism, if not strong (God helps me to save myself) then weak (I help God to save me). All Arminianisms imply the non-necessity of hearing the gospel, inasmuch as they affirm that every man can be saved by responding to what he knows of God here and now.[2]

Packer's words are strong but true and sobering. When it comes to who has the final say, Calvinism answers that it is God and God alone while the Arminian answers that it must be man. As already seen, the former exalts and preserves the sovereignty of grace and the glory of God while the latter restricts divine sovereignty and steals God's glory, giving it to man instead. The former only boasts in the Lord while the latter gives man room, even if it be slight, to boast in himself. Bruce Ware explains the difference precisely:

> But because "salvation is from the Lord" in every respect, from start to finish, and because to God alone belongs all glory and boasting for the gracious saving work he accomplishes and applies to sinners' lives (1 Cor. 1:26–31; Eph. 2:8–9), therefore the unconditional nature of God's election is highly valued by its advocates. Both the rightful glory of God and the proper humility of sinners are secured in salvation only when the work of salvation, from beginning to end, is grounded in God's unconditional elective purposes. With the psalmist, we proclaim, "Not to us, Lord, not to us, but to Your name give glory" (Ps. 115:1 HCSB). Only if God's election of those whom he determines to save is grounded on the good pleasure of God and not at all on any quality, decision, or action that will one day be true of those persons whom God creates can we proclaim, without qualification, that salvation is altogether from the Lord, and to him alone belongs exclusive glory.[3]

2. J. I. Packer, "Arminianisms," in *Puritan Papers*, vol.5, *1968–1969*, ed. J. I. Packer (Phillipsburg, NJ: P&R Publishing, 2005), 27–30.

3. Bruce A. Ware, "Divine Election to Salvation," in *Perspectives on Election: Five Views*, ed. Chad Owen Brand (Nashville: B&H Publishing Group, 2006), 5–6.

Ware's statement cannot be improved upon. Only when grace is unconditional, monergistic, and effectual, not only in election but also in special calling and regeneration, does God receive his rightful glory. Therefore, only the Calvinist can consistently say, "Not to us, Lord, not to us, but to Your name give glory" (Ps. 115:1), and, "it depends not on human will or exertion, but on God, who has mercy" (Rom. 9:16). While the synergist comes to God with his own autonomy in hand, the monergist, as Augustus Montague Toplady once wrote, comes to God saying,

> Nothing in my hand I bring,
> Simply to thy Cross I cling;
> Naked, come to thee for dress;
> Helpless, look to thee for grace;
> Foul, I to the fountain fly;
> Wash me, Saviour, or I die.

SELECT BIBLIOGRAPHY[1]

PRIMARY SOURCES

à Brakel, Wilhelmus. *The Christian's Reasonable Service*. 4 vols. Edited by Joel R. Beeke. Translated by Bartel Elshout. Grand Rapids: Reformation Heritage, 1992–95.

Arminius, James. "Apology Against Thirty-One Defamatory Articles." In vol. 2 of *The Writings of James Arminius*, trans. James Nichols and William Nichols, 276–380. London: 1825, 1828, 1875. Reprint, Grand Rapids: Baker, 1956.

_____. "Certain Articles to be Diligently Examined and Weighed." In vol. 2 of *The Writings of James Arminius*, trans. James Nichols and William Nichols, 479–511. London: 1825, 1828, 1875. Reprint, Grand Rapids: Baker, 1956.

_____. "A Declaration of the Sentiments of Arminius." In vol. 1 of *The Writings of James Arminius*, trans. James Nichols and William Nichols, 193–275. London: 1825, 1828, 1875. Reprint, Grand Rapids: Baker, 1956.

_____. "Epistolary Discussion, Concerning Predestination, between James Arminius, D. D., and Francis Junius, D. D." In vol. 3 of *The Writings of James Arminius*, trans. James Nichols and William Nichols, 7–278. London: 1825, 1828, 1875. Reprint, Grand Rapids: Baker, 1956.

_____. "Examination of a Treatise Concerning the Order and Mode of Predestination, and the Amplitude of Divine Grace, by William Perkins." In vol. 3 of *The Writings of James Arminius*, trans. James Nichols and William Nichols, 279–526. London: 1825, 1828, 1875. Reprint, Grand Rapids: Baker, 1956.

_____. "A Letter Addressed to Hippolytus A Collibus." In vol. 2 of *The Writings of James Arminius*, trans. James Nichols and William Nichols, 453–78. London: 1825, 1828, 1875. Reprint, Grand Rapids: Baker, 1956.

_____. "Seventy-Nine Private Disputations" In *The Writings of James Arminius*, trans. James Nichols and William Nichols, 9–193. London: 1825, 1828, 1875. Reprint, Grand Rapids: Baker, 1956.

1. For a more extensive bibliography, see *Reclaiming Monergism*, e-book, published by P&R Publishing.

_____. "Twenty-Five Public Disputations." In *The Writings of James Arminius*, trans. James Nichols and William Nichols, 390–669. London: 1825, 1828, 1875. Reprint, Grand Rapids: Baker, 1956.

_____. *The Writings of James Arminius.* 3 vols. Translated by James Nichols and William Nichols. London: 1825, 1828, 1875. Reprint, Grand Rapids: Baker, 1956.

Augustine. *Answer to Julian.* In *Answer to the Pelagians II*, part I, vol. 24 of *The Works of Augustine: A Translation for the Twenty-first Century*, ed. John E. Rotelle, trans. Roland J. Teske, 222–36. New York: New City, 1998.

_____. *Answer to the Two Letters of the Pelagians.* In *Answer to the Pelagians II.* Edited by John E. Rotelle. Translated by Roland J. Teske, 98–221. Part I, vol. 24 of *The Works of Saint Augustine: A Translation for the Twenty-first Century*, ed. Boniface Ramsey. New York: New City, 1998.

_____. *City of God.* Trans. Henry Bettenson. London: Penguin, 1984.

_____. *The Confessions.* Translated by Maria Boulding. Part 1, vol. 1 of *The Works of Saint Augustine: A Translation for the Twenty-first Century*, ed. Boniface Ramsey. New York: New City, 1997.

_____. *Confessions.* Translated by R. S. Pine-Coffin. New York: Penguin, 1961.

_____. *Confessions and Enchiridion.* Library of Christian Classics, vol. 7. Edited and translated by Albert C. Outler. Philadelphia: Westminster, 1955.

_____. *The Deeds of Pelagius.* In *Answer to the Pelagians I.* Edited by John E. Rotelle. Translated by Roland J. Teske, 309–72. Part I, vol. 23 of *The Works of Saint Augustine: A Translation for the Twenty-first Century*, ed. Boniface Ramsey. New York: New City, 1997.

_____. *Enchiridion.* In *Basic Writings of Saint Augustine*, vol. 1, ed. Whitney J. Oats, 656–730. New York: Random House, 1948.

_____. *Enchiridion on Faith, Hope, and Love.* Translated by Bruce Harbert. In *On Christian Belief*, part 1, vol. 8 of *The Works of Saint Augustine: A Translation for the Twenty-first Century*, ed. Boniface Ramsey, 273–344. New York: New City, 2005.

_____. *The Gift of Perseverance.* In *Answer to the Pelagians IV.* Edited by John E. Rotelle. Translated by Roland J. Teske, 191–240. Part I, vol. 26 of *The Works of Saint Augustine: A Translation for the Twenty-first Century*, ed. Boniface Ramsey. New York: New City, 1999.

_____. *Four Anti-Pelagian Writings.* Vol. 86 of *The Fathers of the Church*, trans. John A. Mourant and William J. Collinge. Washington, DC: The Catholic University of America Press, 1977.

_____. *Grace and Free Choice*. In *Answer to the Pelagians IV*. Edited by John E. Rotelle. Translated by Roland J. Teske, 70–107. Part I, vol. 26 of *The Works of Saint Augustine: A Translation for the Twenty-first Century*, ed. Boniface Ramsey. New York: New City, 1999.

_____. *The Grace of Christ and Original Sin*. In *Answer to the Pelagians I*. Edited by John E. Rotelle. Translated by Roland J. Teske, 373–450. Part I, vol. 23 of *The Works of Saint Augustine: A Translation for the Twenty-first Century*, ed. Boniface Ramsey. New York: New City, 1997.

_____. *The Happy Life*. Trans. Ludwig Schopp. London: B. Herder, 1939.

_____. *Letters*. Part 2, vols. 1–4 of *The Works of Saint Augustine: A Translation for the Twenty-first Century*, ed. John Rotelle (vol. 1) and Boniface Ramsey (vols. 2–4), trans. Roland J. Teske. New York: New City, 2001–2005.

_____. *Marriage and Desire*. In *Answer to the Pelagians II*. Edited by John E. Rotelle. Translated by Roland J. Teske, 12–97. Part 1, vol. 24 of *The Works of Saint Augustine: A Translation for the Twenty-first Century*, ed. Boniface Ramsey. New York: New City, 1998.

_____. *Nature and Grace*. In *Answer to the Pelagians I*. Edited by John E. Rotelle. Translated by Roland J. Teske, 197–268. Part I, vol. 23 of *The Works of Saint Augustine: A Translation for the Twenty-first Century*, ed. Boniface Ramsey. New York: New City, 1997.

_____. *The Nature and Origin of the Soul*. In *Answer to the Pelagians I*. Edited by John E. Rotelle. Translated by Roland J. Teske, 451–542. Part 1, vol. 23 of *The Works of Saint Augustine: A Translation for the Twenty-first Century*, ed. Boniface Ramsey. New York: New City, 1997.

_____. *On Free Choice of the Will*. Edited by Thomas Williams. Indianapolis, IN: Hackett, 1964.

_____. *On Rebuke and Grace*. In *Answer to the Pelagians IV*. Edited by John E. Rotelle. Translated by Roland J. Teske, 108–48. Part 1, vol. 26 of *The Works of Saint Augustine: A Translation for the Twenty-first Century*, ed. Boniface Ramsey. New York: New City, 1999.

_____. *The Perfection of Human Righteousness*. In *Answer to the Pelagians I*. Edited by John E. Rotelle. Translated by Roland J. Teske, 269–308. Part 1, vol. 23 of *The Works of Saint Augustine: A Translation for the Twenty-first Century*, ed. Boniface Ramsey. New York: New City, 1997.

_____. *The Predestination of the Saints*. In *Answer to the Pelagians IV*. Edited by John E. Rotelle. Translated by Roland J. Teske, 149–90. Part I, vol. 26 of *The Works of Saint Augustine: A Translation for the Twenty-first Century*, ed. Boniface Ramsey. New York: New City, 1999.

321

_____. *The Punishment and Forgiveness of Sins and the Baptism of Little Ones.* In *Answer to the Pelagians I.* Edited by John E. Rotelle. Translated by Roland J. Teske, 19–134. Part 1, vol. 23 of *The Works of Augustine: A Translation for the Twenty-first Century,* ed. Boniface Ramsey. New York: New City, 1997.

_____. *Revisions.* Translated by Boniface Ramsey. Part 1, vol. 2 of *The Works of Saint Augustine: A Translation for the Twenty-first Century,* ed. Boniface Ramsey. New York: New City Press, 2010.

_____. *Sermons 51–94: On the New Testament.* Edited by John E. Rotelle. Translated by Edmund Hill. Part 3, vol. 3 of *The Works of Saint Augustine: A Translation for the Twenty-first Century,* ed. Boniface Ramsey. New York: New City, 1991.

_____. *The Spirit and the Letter.* In *Answer to the Pelagians I.* Edited by John E. Rotelle. Translated by Roland J. Tesk, 135–96. Part I, vol. 23 of *The Works of Saint Augustine: A Translation for the Twenty-first Century,* ed. Boniface Ramsey. New York: New City, 1997.

_____. *Tractates on the Gospel of John 1–10.* Translated by John W. Rettig. The Fathers of the Church. Washington, DC: The Catholic University of America Press, 1988.

_____. *Tractates on the Gospel of John 11–27.* Translated by John W. Rettig. The Fathers of the Church. Washington, DC: The Catholic University of America Press, 1988

_____. *The Trinity: De Trinitate.* Edited by John E. Rotelle. Translated by Edmund Hill. Part 1, vol. 5 of *The Works of Saint Augustine: A Translation for the Twenty-first Century,* ed. Boniface Ramsey. New York: New City, 1991.

_____. *Unfinished Work in Answer to Julian.* In *Answer to the Pelagians III.* Edited by John E. Rotelle. Translated by Roland J. Teske, 13–726. Part 1, vol. 25 of *The Works of Saint Augustine: A Translation for the Twenty-first Century,* ed. Boniface Ramsey. New York: New City, 1999.

Bavinck, Herman. *The Doctrine of God.* Translated by William Hendriksen. Grand Rapids: Eerdmans, 1951.

_____. *Gereformeerde Dogmatiek.* 3rd ed. Kampen: Kok, 1918.

_____. *Reformed Dogmatics.* Edited by John Bolt. Translated by John Vriend. 4 vols. Grand Rapids: Baker, 2008.

_____. *Roeping en wedergeboorte.* Kampen: Zalsman, 1903.

_____. *Saved by Grace: The Holy Spirit's Work in Calling and Regeneration.* Edited by J. Mark Beach. Translated by Nelson D. Kloosterman. Grand Rapids: Reformation Heritage, 2008.

Beardslee, John W., III, ed. and trans. *Reformed Dogmatics*. A Library of Protestant Thought. New York: Oxford University Press, 1965.

Beeke, Joel R., and Sinclair B. Ferguson, eds. *Reformed Confessions Harmonized*. Grand Rapids: Baker, 1999.

Boyce, James P. *Abstract of Systematic Theology*. Philadelphia: American Baptist Publication Society, 1887. Reprint, Cape Coral, FL: Founders, 2006.

Bradwardine, Thomas. *De Causa Dei*. Edited by Henry Savile. Frankfurt: Gruyter, 1964.

Burns, J. Patout. *The Development of Augustine's Doctrine of Operative Grace*. Paris: Études augustiniennes, 1980.

————, ed. and trans. *Theological Anthropology*. Sources of Early Christian Thought. Philadelphia: Fortress, 1981.

Calvin, John. *The Bondage and Liberation of the Will: A Defense of the Orthodox Doctrine of Human Choice against Pighius*. Edited by A. N. S. Lane. Translated by G. Davies. Texts and Studies in Reformation and Post-Reformation Thought. Grand Rapids: Baker, 1996.

————. *Calvin's Calvinism: Treatises on 'The Eternal Predestination of God' and 'The Secret Providence of God.'* Edited and translated by Henry Cole. London: Sovereign Grace Union, 1927.

————. *Calvin's Commentaries*. 22 vols. Various editors. Edinburgh, Scotland: Calvin Translation Society, n.d. Reprint, Grand Rapids: Baker, 2005.

————. *Institutes of the Christian Religion*. 2 vols. Edited by John T. McNeill. Translated by Ford Lewis Battles. Library of Christian Classics, vols. 20–21. Philadelphia: Westminster John Knox, 1960.

————. *Commentary on the Book of Psalms*. 4 vols. Translated by James Anderson. Grand Rapids: Baker, 1996.

————. *Commentary on the Book of the Prophet Isaiah 33–66*. Edited and translated by William Pringle. Vol. 8 of *Calvin's Commentaries*. Edinburgh, Scotland: Calvin Translation Society: n.d. Reprint, Grand Rapids: Baker, 2005.

————. *Commentaries on the Epistles of Paul to the Galatians and Ephesians*. Translated by William Pringle. Grand Rapids: Eerdmans, 1948.

————. *Commentaries on the First Book of Moses Called Genesis*. 2 vols. Translated by John King. Grand Rapids: Baker, 1996.

————. *Commentary on the Gospel according to John 1–11*. Translated and edited by William Pringle. Vol. 17 of *Calvin's Commentaries*. Edinburgh, Scotland: Calvin Translation Society: n.d. Reprint, Grand Rapids: Baker, 2005.

_____. *The Epistles of Paul the Apostle to the Romans and to the Thessalonians*. Vol. 8 of *Calvin's New Testament Commentaries*. Edited by D. W. Torrance and T. F. Torrance. Translated by R. MacKenzie. Grand Rapids: Eerdmans, 1960.

_____. *The Gospel according to St. John*. Translated by T. H. L. Parker. 2 vols. Grand Rapids: Eerdmans, 1959.

_____. *Ioannis Calvini Opera quae supersunt omnia*. Edited by Wilhelm Baum, Eduard Cunitz, and Eduard Reuss. 59 vols. in 58. Corpus Reformatorum, vols. 29–87. Brunswick, NJ: E. C. Schwetschke and Son, 1863–1900. Reprint, New York: Johnston Reprint Corp., 1964.

_____. *Joannis Calvini Opera Selecta*. Edited by P. Barth, W. Niesel, and D. Scheuner. 5 vols. Munich: Chr. Kaiser, 1926–62.

_____. *The Secret Providence of God*. Edited by Paul Helm. Translated by Keith Goad. Wheaton, IL: Crossway, 2010.

_____. *Selected Works of John Calvin: Tracts and Letters*. 7 vols. Edited by Henry Beveridge and Jules Bonnet. N.p., 1858. Reprint, Grand Rapids: Baker, 1983.

_____. *Sermons on Election and Reprobation*. Translated by John Fielde. London: n.p., 1579. Reprint, Audobon, NJ: Old Paths, 1996.

_____. *Sermons on Ephesians*. Edinburgh: Banner of Truth, 1981.

_____. *Sermons on Galatians*. Edinburgh: Banner of Truth, 1997.

_____. *Theological Treatises*. Edited and translated by J. K. S. Reid. Library of Christian Classics, vol. 22. Louisville: Westminster John Knox, 1954.

_____. *Tracts and Letters*. 7 vols. Edited by Jules Bonnet. Translated by David Constable. Edinburgh: Banner of Truth, 2009.

Calvin, John, and Jerome Bolsec. *The Bolsec Controversy on Predestination, from 1551 to1555: The Statements of Jerome Bolsec, and the Responses of John Calvin, Theodore Beza, and Other Reformed Theologians*. Vol. 1, *Theological Currents, the Setting and Mood, and the Trial Itself*. Edited by Philip C. Holtrop. Lewiston: The Edwin Mellen Press, 1993.

Calvin, John, and Jacopo Sadoleto. *A Reformation Debate*. Edited by John C. Olin. Grand Rapids: Baker, 1966.

Cassian, John. *The Conferences*. Trans. Boniface Ramsey. Ancient Christian Writers, vol. 57. New York: Newman, 1997.

_____. *The Institutes*. Translated by Boniface Ramsey. Ancient Christian Writers, vol. 58. New York, NY: Newman, 2000.

Clarke, Adam. *Christian Theology*. New York: Eaton and Mains, 1835.

Cochrane, Arthur C., ed. *Reformed Confessions of the Sixteenth Century*. Louisville: Westminster John Knox, 2003.

Dabney, R. L. *The Five Points of Calvinism*. Harrisonburg, VA: Sprinkle, 1992.

_____. *Systematic Theology*. Edinburgh: Banner of Truth, 2002.

Dagg, John L. *Manual of Theology*. The Southern Baptist Publication Society, 1857. Reprint, Harrisonburg, VA: Gano Books, 1990.

Dennison, James, Jr., ed., *Reformed Confessions of the Sixteenth and Seventeenth Centuries in English Translation*, 3 vols. to date (Grand Rapids: Reformation Heritage, 2008–12).

Edwards, Jonathan. "A Divine and Supernatural Light Immediately Imparted to the Soul by the Spirit of God, Shown to be Both a Scriptural and Rational Doctrine." In vol. 2 of *The Works of Jonathan Edwards*, 12–17. Peabody, MA: Hendrickson, 2004.

_____. *Efficacious Grace*. In *Writings on the Trinity, Grace, and Faith*, ed. Sang Hyun Lee, 198–290. Vol. 21 of *The Works of Jonathan Edwards*. New Haven, CT: Yale University Press, 2003.

_____. *Freedom of the Will*. Edited by Paul Ramsey. Vol. 1 of *The Works of Jonathan Edwards*. New Haven, CT: Yale University Press, 1957.

_____. *The Great Christian Doctrine of Original Sin Defended*. In volume 1 of *The Works of Jonathan Edwards*, 143–233. Edinburgh, PA: Banner of Truth, 1979.

_____. *Original Sin*. Edited by Clyde A. Holbrook. Vol. 3 of *The Works of Jonathan Edwards*. New Haven, CT: Yale University Press, 1970.

_____. *The Works of Jonathan Edwards*. 2 vols. Edinburgh: Banner of Truth, 1979.

_____. *Writings on the Trinity, Grace, and Faith*. Edited by Sang Hyun Lee. Vol. 21 of *The Works of Jonathan Edwards*. New Haven: Yale University Press, 2003.

Episcopius, Simon. *The Confession of Faith of Those Called Arminians, or, a Declaration of the Opinions and Doctrines of the Ministers and Pastors, Which in the United Provinces are Known by the Name of Remonstrants Concerning the Chief Points of the Christian Religion*. London: n.p., 1684.

Erasmus. *Controversies: De Libero Arbitrio, Hyperaspistes 1*. Edited by Charles Trinkaus. Translated by Peter Macardle and Clarence H. Miller. Vol. 76 of the *Collected Works of Erasmus*. Toronto: University of Toronto Press, 1999.

_____. *Controversies: Hyperaspistes 2*. Edited by Charles Trinkaus. Translated by Peter Macardle and Clarence H. Miller. Vol. 77 of the *Collected Works of Erasmus*. Toronto: University of Toronto Press, 2000.

_____. *A Discussion of Free Will*. Translated by Peter MaCardle. Vol. 67 of the *Collected Works of Erasmus*. Toronto: University of Toronto Press, 1999.

The 1599 Geneva Bible. White Hall, WV: Tolle Lege, 2008.

Finney, Charles. *Finney's Systematic Theology*. Edited by J. H. Fairchild. Minneapolis: Bethany Fellowship, 1976.

Fletcher, John. *Checks to Antinomianism*. New York: J. Collard, 1837.

_____. *The New Birth*. Louisville: The Herald, n.d.

_____. *The Works of the Reverend John Fletcher*. 9 vols. New York: John Wilson and Daniel Hitt, 1809.

Fuller, Andrew. *The Complete Works of Reverend Andrew Fuller*. 3 vols. Edited by Joseph Belcher. Philadelphia: American Baptist Publication Society, 1845. Reprint, Harrisonburg, VA: Sprinkle, 1988.

The Geneva Bible: The Annotated New Testament. Edited by Gerald T. Sheppard. Cleveland: Pilgrim, 1989.

Girardeau, John L. *Calvinism and Evangelical Arminianism: Compared as to Election, Reprobation, Justification, and Related Doctrines*. New York: Baker and Taylor, 1890. Reprint, Harrisonburg, VA: Sprinkle, 1984.

Goodwin, Thomas. *A Discourse of Election*. In vol. 9 of *The Works of Thomas Goodwin*. Grand Rapids: Reformation Heritage, 2006.

Heppe, Heinrich. *Reformed Dogmatics: Set Out and Illustrated from the Sources*. Translated by G. T. Thomson. Revised and edited by Ernst Bizer. London: George Allen & Unwin, 1950. Reprint, Eugene, OR: Wipf and Stock, 2007.

Hodge, A. A. "The Ordo Salutis: or, Relation in the Order of Nature of Holy Character and Divine Favor." *The Princeton Review* 54 (1878): 304–21.

_____. *Outlines of Theology*. Grand Rapids: Eerdmans, 1959.

Hodge, Caspar Wistar. "Imputation." In *International Standard Bible Encyclopedia*. Edited by Geoffrey W. Bromiley. Grand Rapids: Eerdmans, 1982.

Hodge, Charles. *Ephesians*. Edited by Alister McGrath and J. I. Packer. Wheaton, IL: Crossway, 1994.

_____. "Regeneration." In *Princeton v. The New Divinity: The Meaning of Sin, Grace, Salvation, Revival: Articles from the* Princeton Review, 1–51. Edinburgh: Banner of Truth, 2001.

_____. *Romans*. The Crossway Classic Commentaries. Wheaton, IL: Crossway, 1993.

_____. *Systematic Theology*. 3 vols. New York: Scribner's, 1872–73. Reprint, Grand Rapids: Eerdmans, 1952.

Hopkins, Ezekiel. "The Nature and Necessity of Regeneration; or, the New-Birth." In vol. 2 of *The Works of Ezekiel Hopkins*, ed. Charles W. Quick, 221–98. Reprint, Morgan, PA: Soli Deo Gloria, 1997.

Leff, Gordon. *Bradwardine and the Pelagians: A Study of His "De Causa Dei" and Its Opponents*. Cambridge: Cambridge University Press, 1957.

Limborch, Philip. *A Complete System, or, Body of Divinity*. Translated by William Jones. London: John Darby, 1713.

Lumpkin, William L., ed. *Baptist Confessions of Faith*. Valley Forge, VA: Judson, 1969.

Luther, Martin. *The Bondage of the Will*. Edited and translated by J. I. Packer and O. R. Johnston. New York: Fleming H. Revell, 1957.

————. *The Bondage of the Will*. Vol. 33 of *Luther's Works*. Edited by Jaroslav Pelikan, Hilton C. Oswald, and Helmut T. Lehmann. Philadelphia: Fortress, 1957.

————. *What Luther Says*. Edited by Ewald M. Plass. St. Louis: Concordia, 1959.

Mastricht, Peter van. *A Treatise on Regeneration*. Edited by Brandon Withrow. Morgan, PA: Soli Deo Gloria, 2002.

Melanchthon, Philip. *Loci Communes 1543*. Translated by J. A. O. Preus. St. Louis: Concordia, 1992.

Miley, John. *Systematic Theology*. 3 vols. Peabody, MA: Hendrickson, 1989.

Owen, John. *The Death of Death in the Death of Christ*. Edinburgh: Banner of Truth, 2002.

————. *A Display of Arminianism; The Death of Death in the Death of Christ; Of the Death of Christ; A Diss. on Divine Justice*. Vol. 10 of *The Works of John Owen*, ed. William H. Goold. Edinburgh: Banner of Truth, 2000.

————. *The Doctrine of the Saints' Perseverance Explained and Confirmed*. Vol. 11 of *The Works of John Owen*, ed. William H. Goold. Edinburgh: Banner of Truth, 2000.

————. *Pneumatologia: or, A Discourse Concerning the Holy Spirit*. Vol. 3 of *The Works of John Owen*, ed. William H. Goold. Edinburgh: Banner of Truth, 2000.

————. *Vindiciae Evangelicae Mystery of the Gospel Vindicated; Of the Death of Christ, and of Justification; A Review of the Annotations of Grotius*. Vol. 12 of *The Works of John Owen*, ed. William H. Goold. Edinburgh: Banner of Truth, 2000.

Pelagius. *Pelagius's Commentary on St Paul's Epistle to the Romans*. Translated by Theodore De Bruyn. Oxford Early Christian Studies. Oxford: Clarendon, 1993.

Pelikan, Jaroslav, and Valerie R. Hotchkiss. *Creeds and Confessions of Faith in the Christian Tradition*. 3 vols. New Haven and London: Yale University Press, 2003.

Perkins, William. *A Christian and Plaine Treatise of the Manner and Order of Predestination and of the Largenes of Gods Grace*. London, 1606.

————. *A Golden Chaine; or, The Description of Theologie Containing the Order of the Causes of Salvation and Damnation, According to Gods Woord: A View of the Order Whereof, Is to Be Seene in the Table Annexed*. London, 1591.

————. *The Work of William Perkins*. Edited by Ian Breward. Courtenay Library of Christian Classics 3. Abingdon: Sutton Courtenay, 1970.

_____. *The Workes of That Famous and Worthie Minister of Christ, in the Universitie of Cambridge, Mr. W. Perkins*. Cambridge: Iohn Legate, 1608.

Polanus, Amandus. *Syntragma theologiae christianae*. 5th ed. Hanover: Aubry, 1624.

Pope, William Burton. *A Compendium of Christian Theology*. New York: Phillips & Hunt, n.d.

Prosper. *Grace and Free Will*. Vol. 7 of *The Fathers of the Church*, ed. Joseph Deferrari, trans. J. Reginald O'Donnell. New York: Fathers of the Church, 1947.

Ralston, Thomas. *Elements of Divinity*. Nashville: Cokesbury, 1924.

Raymond, Miner. *Systematic Theology*. 3 vols. New York, Phillips & Hunt, 1877–79.

Rees, B. R., ed. and trans. *The Letters of Pelagius and His Followers*. Rochester, NY: Boydell, 1991.

_____. *Pelagius: Life and Letters*. 2 vols. in one. Rochester, NY: Boydell, 1998.

Schaff, Philip, ed. *The Evangelical Protestant Creeds*. Vol. 3 of *The Creeds of Christendom*. Revised by David S. Schaff. Reprint, Grand Rapids: Baker, 1997.

Summers, Thomas O. *Systematic Theology: A Complete Body of Wesleyan Arminian Divinity*. 2 vols. Nashville: Methodist Episcopal Church, South, 1888.

Taylor, John. *The Scripture-Doctrine of Original Sin, Exposed to Free and Candid Examination*. London: n.p., 1740.

Tillett, Wilbur. *Personal Salvation*. Nashville: Barbee and Smith, 1902.

Turretin, Francis. *Institutes of Elenctic Theology*. Edited by James T. Dennison Jr. Translated by George Musgrave Giger. 3 vols. Phillipsburg, NJ: P&R Publishing, 1992–97.

Van Mastricht, Peter. *A Treatise on Regeneration*. Edited by Brandon Withrow. Morgan, PA: Soli Deo Gloria, 2002.

Warfield, Benjamin B. *Calvin and Calvinism*. Vol. 5 of *The Works of Benjamin B. Warfield*. Grand Rapids: Baker, 2003.

_____. *Calvin as a Theologian and Calvinism Today*. Grand Rapids: Evangelical Press, 1969.

_____. *The Plan of Salvation*. Eugene, OR: Wipf and Stock, 1989.

_____. "Regeneration," in vol. 2 of *Selected Shorter Writings of Benjamin B. Warfield*, ed. John E. Meeter, 321–23. Nutley, NJ: Presbyterian and Reformed, 1973.

_____. "Review of John Miley's *Systematic Theology*." In vol. 2 of *Selected Shorter Writings of Benjamin B. Warfield*, ed. John E. Meeter, 308–20. Nutley, NJ: Presbyterian and Reformed, 1973.

_____. *Studies in Tertullian and Augustine*. Vol. 4 of *The Works of Benjamin B. Warfield*. Grand Rapids: Baker, 1932.

_____. *Studies in Theology*. New York: Oxford University Press, 1932.

Watson, Richard. *Theological Institutes*. 3 vols. New York: Lane & Scott, 1851.

Wesley, John, ed. *The Arminian Magazine. Consisting of Extracts and Original Treatises on Universal Redemption*. 14 vols. London, 1778–91.

_____. "A Dialogue between a Predestinarian and His Friend." In vol. 10 of *The Works of John Wesley*, ed. T. Jackson, 259–65. Grand Rapids: Baker, 1978.

_____. "The Doctrine of Original Sin, according to Scripture, Reason, and Experience." In vol. 9 of *The Works of John Wesley*, ed. T. Jackson, 191–464. Grand Rapids: Baker, 1978.

_____. *Explanatory Notes Upon the New Testament*. 2 vols. Grand Rapids: Baker, 1981.

_____. "Free Grace." In vol. 7 of *The Works of John Wesley*, ed. T. Jackson, 373–86. Grand Rapids: Baker, 1978.

_____. "The General Spread of the Gospel." In vol. 2 of *The Works of John Wesley*, ed. T. Jackson, 488–89. Grand Rapids: Baker, 1978.

_____. "God's Love to Fallen Man." In vol. 6 of *The Works of John Wesley*, ed. T. Jackson, 231–40. Grand Rapids: Baker, 1978.

_____. "Heavenly Treasure in Earthen Vessels." In vol. 4 of *The Works of John Wesley*, ed. Albert C. Outler, 162–67. Nashville: Abingdon, 1986.

_____. "The New Birth." In vol. 6 of *The Works of John Wesley*, ed. T. Jackson, 65–77. Grand Rapids: Baker, 1978.

_____. "On Original Sin." In vol. 6 of *The Works of John Wesley*, ed. T. Jackson, 54–65. Grand Rapids: Baker, 1978.

_____. "On the Deceitfulness of the Human Heart." In vol. 7 of *The Works of John Wesley*, ed. T. Jackson, 335–43. Grand Rapids: Baker, 1978.

_____. "On the Fall of Man." In vol. 6 of *The Works of John Wesley*, ed. T. Jackson, 215–24. Grand Rapids: Baker, 1978.

_____. "On Working Out Our Own Salvation." In vol. 6 of *The Works of John Wesley*, ed. T. Jackson, 506–13. Grand Rapids: Baker, 1978.

_____. "Predestination Calmly Considered." In vol. 10 of *The Works of John Wesley*, ed. T. Jackson, 204–58. Grand Rapids: Baker, 1978.

_____. "The Question, 'What Is an Arminian?' Answered. By a Love of Free Grace." In vol. 10 of *The Works of John Wesley*, ed. T. Jackson, 358–60. Grand Rapids: Baker, 1978.

_____. "Some Remarks on 'A Defense of the Preface to the Edinburgh Edition of Aspasio Vindicated.'" In vol. 10 of *The Works of John Wesley*, ed. T. Jackson, 346–57. Grand Rapids: Baker, 1978.

————. "Some Remarks on Mr. Hill's 'Review of All the Doctrines Taught by John Wesley.'" In vol. 10 of *The Works of John Wesley*, ed. T. Jackson, 344–414. Grand Rapids: Baker, 1978.

————. "The Spirit of Bondage and of Adoption." In vol. 5 of *The Works of John Wesley*, ed. T. Jackson, 98–111. Grand Rapids: Baker, 1978.

————. "Thoughts upon Necessity." In vol. 10 of *The Works of John Wesley*, ed. T. Jackson, 457–73. Grand Rapids: Baker, 1978.

————. *Wesley's Standard Sermons*. Edited by Edward H. Sugden. London: Epworth, 1955–56.

————. *The Works of John Wesley*. Edited by T. Jackson. 14 vols. Grand Rapids: Baker, 1978.

————. *The Works of John Wesley*. Edited by Albert C. Outler. 24 vols. Nashville: Abingdon, 1986.

Wollebius, Johannes. *Compendium Theologiae Christianae*. Translated by Alexander Ross. London: n.p., 1650.

SECONDARY SOURCES

Abbott, T. K. *A Critical and Exegetical Commentary on the Epistles to the Ephesians and to the Colossians*. International Critical Commentary. Edinburgh: T&T Clark, 1979.

Achtemeier, P. J. *1 Peter*. Minneapolis: Fortress, 1996.

Adamson, James B. *The Epistle of James*. New International Commentary on the New Testament. Grand Rapids: Baker, 1976.

Akin, Daniel L. *1, 2, 3 John*. New American Commentary, vol. 38. Nashville: B&H, 2001.

————, ed. *A Theology for the Church*. Nashville: B&H Publishing Group, 2007.

Allen, David L., and Steve W. Lemke, eds. *Whosoever Will: A Biblical-Theological Critique of Five-Point Calvinism*. Nashville: B&H Publishing Group, 2010.

Allen, R. Michael. *Reformed Theology*. Edinburgh: T&T Clark, 2010.

Arnold, Clinton E. *Ephesians*. Zondervan Exegetical Commentary on the New Testament. Grand Rapids: Zondervan, 2010.

————. *Powers of Darkness: Principalities and Powers in Paul's Letters*. Leicester: InterVarsity, 1992.

Bangs, Carl. *Arminius: A Study in the Dutch Reformation*. Grand Rapids: Zondervan, 1985.

Barnett, Paul. *The Second Epistle to the Corinthians*. New International Commentary on the New Testament. Grand Rapids: Baker, 1997.

Barrett, C. K. *A Critical and Exegetical Commentary on The Acts of the Apostles 1–14*. The International Critical Commentary. Edinburgh: T&T Clark, 1994.

_____. *The Gospel according to St. John*. Philadelphia: Westminster, 1978.

Basinger, David, and Randall Basinger, ed. *Predestination and Free Will: Four Views of Divine Sovereignty and Human Freedom*. Downers Grove, IL: InterVarsity, 1986.

Beale, G. K. *The Book of Revelation*. New International Greek Testament Commentary. Grand Rapids: Eerdmans 1999.

Beeke, Joel R. *Living for God's Glory: An Introduction to Calvinism*. Orlando: Reformation Trust, 2008.

Beilby, James K., and Paul R. Eddy, eds. *Divine Foreknowledge: Four Views*. With contributions by Gregory A. Boyd, David Hunt, William Lane Craig, and Paul Helm. Downers Grove, IL: InterVarsity, 2001.

Benedict, Philip. *Christ's Churches Purely Reformed: A Social History of Calvinism*. New Haven: Yale University Press, 2002.

Berkhof, Louis. *The History of Christian Doctrines*. Grand Rapids: Eerdmans, 1949.

_____. *Systematic Theology*. Edinburgh: Banner of Truth, 2003.

Berkouwer, G. C. *Divine Election*. Translated by Hugo Bekker. Grand Rapids: Eerdmans, 1960.

_____. *Faith and Justification*. Grand Rapids: Eerdmans, 1954.

_____. *Faith and Sanctification*. Grand Rapids: Eerdmans, 1952.

_____. *Sin*. Grand Rapids: Eerdmans, 1971.

Bernard, J. H. *The Gospel according to St. John*. 2 vols. International Critical Commentary. Edinburgh: T&T Clark, 1928.

Best, E. *Ephesians*. International Critical Commentary. Edinburgh: T&T Clark, 1998.

Blass, F., and A. Debrunner. *A Greek Grammar of the New Testament*. Translated by R. W. Funk. Chicago: University of Chicago Press, 1961.

Block, Daniel I. *The Book of Ezekiel, Chapters 25–48*. The New International Commentary on the Old Testament. Grand Rapids: Eerdmans, 1998.

_____. *Judges, Ruth*. The New American Commentary, vol. 6. Nashville: B&H Publishing Group, 1999.

Blocher, Henri. *Original Sin: Illuminating the Riddle*. Grand Rapids: Eerdmans, 1997.

Bock, Darrell L. *Acts*. Baker Exegetical Commentary on the New Testament. Grand Rapids: Baker Academic, 2007.

_____. *Luke*. 2 vols. Baker Exegetical Commentary of the New Testament. Grand Rapids: Baker Academic, 1994–96.

Boettner, Loraine. *The Reformed Doctrine of Predestination*. Philadelphia: Presbyterian and Reformed, 1932.

Boice, James Montgomery, and Philip Graham Ryken. *The Doctrines of Grace: Rediscovering the Evangelical Gospel*. Wheaton, IL: Crossway, 2002.

Boice, James Montgomery, and Benjamin E. Sasse, eds. *Here We Stand! A Call from Confessing Evangelicals*. Grand Rapids: Baker, 1996.

Bonner, Gerald. *Freedom and Necessity: St. Augustine's Teaching on Divine Power and Human Freedom*. Washington, DC: The Catholic University of America Press, 2007.

————. *St. Augustine of Hippo: Life and Controversies*. Norwick: Canterbury Press, 1986.

Boyd, Gregory A. *God of the Possible*. Grand Rapids: Baker, 2000.

————. *Satan and the Problem of Evil*. Downers Grove, IL: InterVarsity, 2001.

Boyd Gregory A., and Paul R. Eddy. *Across the Spectrum: Understanding Issues in Evangelical Theology*. 2nd ed. Grand Rapids: Baker, 2009.

Brand, Chad, ed. *Perspectives on Election: Five Views*. With contributions by Jack W. Cottrell, Clark H. Pinnock, Robert L. Reymond, Thomas B. Talbot, and Bruce A. Ware. Nashville: B&H Publishing Group, 2006.

Brandt, C. *The Life of James Arminius, D.D.* Translated by John Cuthrie. London: n.p., 1854.

Brandt, Gerard. *The History of the Reformation and Other Ecclesiastical Transactions in and about the Low Countries, down to the Famous Synod of Dort*. 4 vols. London: n.p., 1720–23. Reprint, New York: AMS, 1979.

Bratt, John H., ed. *The Rise and Development of Calvinism*. Grand Rapids: Eerdmans, 1959.

Bray, Gerald. *The Doctrine of God*. Contours of Christian Theology. Downers Grove, IL: InterVarsity, 1993.

Brown, Peter. *Augustine of Hippo: A Biography*. Berkeley, CA: University of California Press, 2000.

Brown, Raymond E. *The Gospel according to John I–XII*. Anchor Bible, vol. 29. New York: Doubleday, 1966.

Bruce, F. F. *The Epistles to the Colossians, to Philemon, and to the Ephesians*. New International Commentary on the New Testament. Grand Rapids: Baker, 1989.

Bucke, Emory S., ed. *The History of American Methodism*. 3 vols. Nashville: Abingdon, 1964.

Burdick, Donald W. *Letters of John the Apostle*. Chicago: Moody, 1985.

Burge, Gary M. *The Letters of John*. The NIV Application Commentary. Grand Rapids: Zondervan, 1996.

Burson, Scott R., and Jerry L. Walls. *C. S. Lewis and Francis Schaeffer*. Downers Grove, IL: InterVarsity, 1998.

Cameron, Euan. *The European Reformation*. Oxford: Oxford University Press, 1991.

Cannon, William R. *The Theology of John Wesley: With Special Reference to the Doctrine of Justification*. New York: University Press of America, 1974.

Carson, D. A. *Divine Sovereignty and Human Responsibility: Biblical Perspectives in Tension*. Eugene, OR: Wipf and Stock, 1994.

————. *The Gospel according to John*. The Pillar New Testament Commentary. Grand Rapids: Eerdmans, 1991.

————. *How Long, O Lord?* Grand Rapids: Baker, 1990.

————. *Matthew*. The Expositor's Bible Commentary, vol. 8. Grand Rapids: Zondervan, 1984.

Carter, Charles W., ed. *A Contemporary Wesleyan Theology*. Grand Rapids: Asbury, 1983.

Cary, Phillip. *Inner Grace: Augustine in the Traditions of Plato and Paul*. Oxford: Oxford University Press, 2008.

Cell, George Croft. *The Rediscovery of John Wesley*. New York: H. Holt, 1935.

Chapell, Bryan. *Ephesians*. Reformed Expository Commentary. Phillipsburg, NJ: P&R Publishing, 2009.

Cheeseman, John. *Saving Grace*. Edinburgh: Banner of Truth, 1999.

Chiles, Robert E. *Theological Transition in American Methodism: 1790–1935*. Nashville: Abingdon, 1965.

Clark, Gordon H. *Predestination*. Phillipsburg, NJ: Presbyterian and Reformed, 1987.

Clarke, F. Stuart. *The Ground of Election: Jacobus Arminius' Doctrine of the Work and Person of Christ*. Waynesboro, GA: Paternoster, 2006.

Clendenen, E. Ray, and Brad J. Waggoner, ed. *Calvinism: A Southern Baptist Dialogue*. Nashville: B&H Publishing Group, 2008.

Cole, Graham A. *Engaging with the Holy Spirit: Real Questions, Practical Answers*. Wheaton, IL: Crossway, 2008.

————. *He Who Gives Life: The Doctrine of the Holy Spirit*. Foundations of Evangelical Theology, vol. 4. Wheaton, IL: Crossway, 2007.

Collins, Kenneth J. *A Faithful Witness: John Wesley's Homiletical Theology*. Wilmore, KY: Wesley Heritage, 1993.

_____. *The Scripture Way of Salvation: The Heart of John Wesley's Theology*. Nashville: Abingdon, 1997.

_____. *Wesley on Salvation: A Study in the Standard Sermons*. Grand Rapids: Zondervan, 1989.

Collins, Kenneth J., and John H. Tyson. *Conversion in the Wesleyan Tradition*. Nashville: Abingdon, 2001.

Cooper, Lamar E., Sr. *Ezekiel*. New American Commentary, vol. 17. Nashville: B&H Publishing Group, 1994.

Cottrell, Jack. *What the Bible Says about God the Redeemer*. Vol. 3 of *The Doctrine of God*. Eugene, OR: Wipf and Stock, 1987.

_____. *What the Bible Says about God the Ruler*. Vol. 2 of *The Doctrine of God*. Eugene, OR: Wipf and Stock, 1984.

Cowburn, John. *Free Will, Predestination and Determinism*. Milwaukee, WI: Marquette University Press, 2008.

Craig, William L. *Divine Foreknowledge and Human Freedom*. E. J. Brill's Studies in Intellectual History 19. Leiden: E. J. Brill, 1990.

Craigie, Peter C. *The Book of Deuteronomy*. The New International Commentary on the Old Testament. Grand Rapids: Eerdmans, 1976.

Cranfield, C. E. B. *A Critical and Exegetical Commentary on the Epistle to the Romans: Introduction and Commentary on Romans I–VIII*. International Critical Commentary. Edinburgh: T&T Clark, 1975.

Culver, Robert Duncan. *Systematic Theology: Biblical and Historical*. Fearn, Ross-shire, Great Britain: Christian Focus, 2005.

Custance, Arthur C. *The Sovereignty of Grace*. Brockville, ON: Doorway, 1979.

Davies, Philip R. *Faith and Obedience in Romans: A Study of Romans 1–4*. Journal for the Study of the New Testament Supplement. London: Sheffield Academic, 1990.

Davids, Peter H. *The Epistle of James*. New International Greek Testament Commentary. Grand Rapids: Eerdmans, 1982.

_____. *The First Epistle of Peter*. The New International Commentary on the New Testament. Grand Rapids: Eerdmans, 1990.

Dearman, J. Andrew. *Jeremiah and Lamentations*. The NIV Application Commentary. Grand Rapids: Zondervan, 2002.

De Jong, Peter Y., ed. *Crisis in the Reformed Churches: Essays in Commemoration of the Great Synod of Dort, 1618–1619*. Grand Rapids: Reformed Fellowship, 1968.

Demarest, Bruce. *The Cross and Salvation: The Doctrine of Salvation*. Foundations of Evangelical Theology, vol. 4. Wheaton, IL: Crossway, 1997.

den Boer, William. *God's Twofold Love: The Theology of Jacob Arminius (1559–1609)*. Translated by Albert Gootjes. Vol. 14 in Reformed Historical Theology, ed. Herman J. Selderhuis. Göttingen: Vandenhoeck & Ruprecht, 2010.

Doriani, Daniel M. *James*. Reformed Expository Commentary. Phillipsburg, NJ: P&R Publishing, 2007.

Duguid, Iain M. *Ezekiel*. The NIV Application Commentary. Grand Rapids: Zondervan, 1999.

Duncan, J. Ligon, III, ed. *The Westminster Confession into the Twenty-first Century: Essays in Remembrance of the 350th Anniversary of the Westminster Assembly*. 3 vols. to date. Fearn, Ross-shire, Great Britain: Christian Focus, 2003– .

Dunn, James D. G. *Romans 1–8*. Word Biblical Commentary, vol. 38A. Dallas: Word, 1988.

Dunning, H. Ray. *Grace, Faith, and Holiness: A Wesleyan Systematic Theology*. Kansas City, MO: Beacon Hill, 1988.

Edgar, William. *Truth in All Its Glory: Commending the Reformed Faith*. Phillipsburg, NJ: P&R Publishing, 2004.

Ellis, E. Earle. *The Sovereignty of God in Salvation*. New York: T&T Clark, 2009.

Erickson, Millard J. *Christian Theology*. 2nd ed. Grand Rapids: Baker, 1985.

Evans, G. R., ed. *The Medieval Theologians*. Oxford: Blackwell, 2001.

Evans, Robert F. *Four Letters of Pelagius*. New York: The Seabury Press, 1968.

————. *Pelagius: Inquiries and Reappraisals*. New York: The Seabury Press, 1968.

Evans, William B. *Imputation and Impartation: Union with Christ in American Reformed Theology*. Studies in Christian History and Thought. Carlisle, UK: Paternoster, 2008.

Fee, Gordon D. *Paul's Letter to the Philippians*. New International Commentary on the New Testament. Grand Rapids: Eerdmans, 1995.

Feinberg, John S. *No One Like Him: The Doctrine of God*. Foundations of Evangelical Theology, vol. 3. Wheaton, IL: Crossway, 2007.

Ferguson, John. *Pelagius: A Historical and Theological Study*. Cambridge: W. Heffer, 1956.

Ferguson, Sinclair. *The Christian Life: A Doctrinal Introduction*. Edinburgh: Banner of Truth, 1981.

————. *The Holy Spirit*. Contours of Christian Theology. Downers Grove, IL: InterVarsity, 1996.

Ferguson, Sinclair F., David F. Wright, and J. I. Packer, eds. *New Dictionary of Theology*. Downers Grove: InterVarsity, 1988.

Fesko, J. V. *Diversity Within the Reformed Tradition: Supra- and Infralapsarianism in Calvin, Dort, and Westminster*. Greenville, SC: Reformed Academic, 2003.

————. *Justification: Understanding the Classic Reformed Doctrine*. Phillipsburg, NJ: P&R Publishing, 2008.

Forde, Gerhard O. *The Captivation of the Will: Luther vs. Erasmus on Freedom and Bondage*. Edited by Steven Paulson. Grand Rapids: Eerdmans, 2005.

Frame, John M. *The Doctrine of God*. A Theology of Lordship. Phillipsburg, NJ: P&R Publishing, 2002.

————. *The Doctrine of the Knowledge of God*. A Theology of Lordship. Phillipsburg, NJ: P&R Publishing, 1987.

————. *No Other God: A Response to Open Theism*. Phillipsburg, NJ: P&R Publishing, 2001.

————. *Salvation Belongs to the Lord*. Phillipsburg, NJ: P&R Publishing, 2006.

France, R. T. *The Gospel of Matthew*. The New International Commentary on the New Testament. Grand Rapids: Eerdmans, 2007.

————. *The Gospel of Mark*. New International Greek Testament Commentary. Grand Rapids: Eerdmans, 2002.

Gaffin, Richard B., Jr. *By Faith, Not By Sight: Paul and the Order of Salvation*. Milton Keynes: Paternoster, 2006.

Gamble, Richard C. *God's Mighty Acts in the Old Testament*. Vol. 1 of *The Whole Counsel of God*. Phillipsburg, NJ: P&R Publishing, 2009.

Garland, David E. *1 Corinthians*. Baker Exegetical Commentary of the New Testament. Grand Rapids: Baker Academic, 2003.

————. *2 Corinthians*. New American Commentary, vol. 29. Nashville: B&H Publishing Group, 1999.

Geisler, Norman. *Chosen but Free: A Balanced View of Divine Election*. 2nd ed. Minneapolis: Bethany House, 2001.

Geldenhuys, Norval. *The Gospel according to Luke*. The New International Commentary on the New Testament. Grand Rapids: Eerdmans, 1979.

Genderen, J. Van, and W. H. Velema. *Reformed Dogmatics*. Translated by Gerrit Bilkes and Ed M. van der Maas. Phillipsburg, NJ: P&R Publishing, 2008.

George, Timothy. *Amazing Grace*. Wheaton, IL: Crossway, 2011.

————. *The Theology of the Reformers*. Nashville: B&H Publishing Group, 1988.

Gerstner, John. *A Predestination Primer*. Winona Lake, IN: Alpha, 1979.

————. *Wrongly Dividing the Word of Truth*. Brentwood, TN: Wolgemuth & Hyatt, 1991.

Goldingay, John. *Psalms*, vol. 1, *Psalms 1–41*. Baker Commentary on the Old Testament. Grand Rapids: Baker, 2006.

————. *Psalms*, vol. 2, *Psalms 42–89*. Baker Commentary on the Old Testament. Grand Rapids: Baker, 2007.

González, Justo L. *A History of Christian Thought*. 3 vols. Nashville: Abingdon, 1970.

————. *The Story of Christianity*. 2 vols. New York: HarperSanFrancisco, 1984.

Goppelt, L. A. *Commentary on 1 Peter*. Grand Rapids: Eerdmans, 1993.

Gordon, Bruce. *Calvin*. New Haven: Yale University Press, 2009.

Graham, Billy. *How to Be Born Again*. Waco, TX: Word, 1977.

————. *The World Aflame*. Minneapolis: Billy Graham Evangelistic Association, 1967.

Graham, W. Fred, ed. *Later Calvinism: International Perspectives*. Sixteenth-Century Essays and Studies, vol. 22. Kirksville, MO: Sixteenth-Century Journal, 1994.

Green, V. H. H. *John Wesley*. Nashville: Nelson, 1965.

Grider, J. Kenneth. *A Wesleyan-Holiness Theology*. Kansas City, MO: Beacon Hill, 1994.

Grosheide, F. W. *The First Epistle to the Corinthians*. The New International Commentary on the New Testament. Grand Rapids: Eerdmans, 1979.

Grudem, Wayne. *The First Epistle of Peter*. Tyndale New Testament Commentaries. Downers Grove, IL: InterVarsity, 1988.

————. *Systematic Theology*. Grand Rapids: Zondervan, 1994.

Guelzo, Allen C. *Edwards on the Will: A Century of American Theological Debate*. Middletown, CT: Wesleyan University Press, 1989.

Guthrie, Donald. *New Testament Theology*. Downers Grove, IL: InterVarsity, 1981.

————. *The Pastoral Epistles*. Leicester, England: Inter-Varsity, 1990.

Hafemann, Scott J. *2 Corinthians*. The New American Commentary. Nashville: B&H Publishing Group, 2000.

Hall, David W., and Peter A. Lillback, eds. *A Theological Guide to Calvin's Institutes: Essays and Analysis*. Phillipsburg, NJ: P&R Publishing, 2008.

Hamilton, James M., Jr. *God's Indwelling Presence: The Holy Spirit in the Old and New Testaments*. NAC Studies in Bible and Theology, vol. 1. Nashville: B&H Publishing Group, 2006.

Hamilton, Victor P. *The Book of Genesis, Chapters 1–17*. New International Commentary on the Old Testament. Grand Rapids: Eerdmans, 1990.

Hampton, Stephen. *Anti-Arminians*. Oxford Theological Monographs. New York: Oxford University Press, 2008.

Harnack, Adolph. *History of Dogma*, vol. 5. Translated by Neil Buchanan. Boston: Little, Brown, and Co., 1903.

Harris, Murray J. *The Second Epistle to the Corinthians*. New International Greek Testament Commentary. Grand Rapids: Eerdmans: 2005.

Harrison, A. W. *Arminianism*. London: Duckworth, 1937.

_____. *The Beginnings of Arminianism to the Synod of Dort*. London: University of London Press, 1926.

Hart, Darryl G., ed. *The Dictionary of Historical Theology*. Grand Rapids: Eerdmans, 2000.

Hartley, John E. *The Book of Job*. The New International Commentary on the Old Testament. Grand Rapids: Eerdmans, 1988.

Hartley, John E., and R. Larry Shelton, eds. *An Inquiry into Soteriology from a Biblical Theological Perspective*. Vol. 1 of *Wesleyan Theological Perspectives*. Anderson, IN: Warner, 1981.

Heitzenrater, Richard P. *Wesley and the People Called Methodists*. Nashville: Abingdon, 1995.

Helm, Paul. *Calvin and the Calvinists*. Edinburgh: Banner of Truth, 1982.

_____. *Calvin at the Centre*. New York: Oxford, 2010.

_____. *John Calvin: A Guide for the Perplexed*. London: T. & T. Clark, 2008.

_____. *John Calvin's Ideas*. New York: Oxford University Press, 2004.

Hendriksen, William. *Exposition of Paul's Epistle to the Romans*. Grand Rapids: Baker, 1980.

_____. *Exposition of the Gospel according to John*. New Testament Commentary. Grand Rapids: Baker Academic, 2002.

Hesselink, John I. *Calvin's First Catechism: A Commentary*. Louisville: Westminster John Knox, 1997.

Hoehner, Harold W. *Ephesians: An Exegetical Commentary*. Grand Rapids: Baker, 2002.

Hoekema, Anthony A. *Created in God's Image*. Grand Rapids: Eerdmans, 1986.

_____. *Saved by Grace*. Grand Rapids: William B. Eerdmans, 1989.

Hoeksema, Herman. *The Protestant Reformed Church in America*. 2nd ed. Grand Rapids: Baker, 1947.

_____. *Reformed Dogmatics*. Grand Rapids: Reformed Free Publishing Association, 1966.

_____. *Whosoever Will*. Grand Rapids: Eerdmans, 1945.

Hoeksema, Homer. *The Voice of Our Fathers: An Exposition of the Canons of Dordrecht*. Grandville, MI: Reformed Free Press, 1981.

Holifield, E. Brook. *Theology in America: Christian Thought From the Age of the Puritans to the Civil War*. New Haven: Yale University Press, 2003.

Holtzmann, H. J. *Lehrbuch der neutestamentlichen Theologie*. Tübingen: n.p., 1911.

Horton, Michael. *Covenant and Salvation: Union with Christ*. Louisville: Westminster John Knox, 2007.

————. *For Calvinism*. Grand Rapids: Zondervan, 2011.

————. *Putting Amazing Back into Grace*. Grand Rapids: Baker, 1994.

Hoskyns, E. C. *The Fourth Gospel*. 2nd ed. Edited by F. N. Davey. London: Faber and Faber, 1947.

Huey, Jr., F. B. *Jeremiah, Lamentations*. New American Commentary, vol. 16. Nashville: B&H Publishing Group, 1993.

Hughes, Philip E. *Paul's Second Epistle to the Corinthians*. The New International Commentary on the New Testament. Grand Rapids: Eerdmans, 1962.

Hunt, Dave, and James White. *Debating Calvinism: Five Points, Two Views*. Sisters, OR: Multnomah, 2004.

Jewett, Paul King. *Election and Predestination*. Grand Rapids: Eerdmans, 1985.

Jobes, Karen H. *1 Peter*. Baker Exegetical Commentary on the New Testament. Grand Rapids: Baker, 2005.

Johnson, Gary L. W., and R. Fowler White, eds. *Whatever Happened to the Reformation?* Phillipsburg, NJ: P&R Publishing, 2001.

Johnston, Robert K., L. Gregory Jones, and Jonathan R. Wilson, eds. *Grace Upon Grace: Essays in Honor of Thomas A. Langford*. Nashville: Abingdon, 1999.

Kane, Robert. *A Contemporary Introduction to Free Will*. New York: Oxford University Press, 2005.

————, ed. *The Oxford Handbook of Free Will*. New York: Oxford University Press, 2002.

————. *The Significance of Free Will*. New York: Oxford University Press, 1996.

Käsemann, E. *Commentary on Romans*. Edited and translated by G. W. Bromiley. Grand Rapids: Eerdmans, 1980.

Keathley, Kenneth. *Salvation and Sovereignty: A Molinist Approach*. Nashville: B&H Publishing Group, 2010.

Kelly, Douglas F. *Systematic Theology*, vol. 1, *Grounded in Holy Scripture and Understood in Light of the Church*. Fearn, Ross-shire, Great Britain: Christian Focus, 2008.

Kelly, J. N. D. *Early Christian Doctrines*. San Francisco: Harper & Row, 1978.

Knight, George W, III. *The Pastoral Epistles: A Commentary on the Greek Text*. New International Greek Testament Commentary. Grand Rapids: Eerdmans, 1992.

339

Köstenberger, Andreas J. *John*. Baker Exegetical Commentary on the New Testament. Grand Rapids: Baker Academic, 2004.

————. *A Theology of John's Gospel and Letters: The Word, the Christ, the Son of God*. Biblical Theology of the New Testament. Grand Rapids: Zondervan, 2009.

Kruse, Colin G. *The Letters of John*. Pillar New Testament Commentary. Grand Rapids: Eerdmans, 2000.

Kuiper, Herman. *By Grace Alone: A Study in Soteriology*. Grand Rapids: Eerdmans, 1955.

Kuyper, Abraham. *By Grace Alone*. Grand Rapids: Eerdmans, 1955.

————. *The Work of the Holy Spirit*. Translated by Henri De Vries. Grand Rapids: Eerdmans, 1941.

Laato, T. *Paul and Judaism: An Anthropological Approach*. Translated by T. McElwain. Atlanta: Scholars, 1995.

————. *Paulus und das Judentum: Anthropologische Erwägungen*. Åbo: Åbo Akademi Press, 1991.

Lane, William L. *The Gospel according to Mark*. New International Commentary on the New Testament. Grand Rapids: Eerdmans, 1974.

Langford, Thomas A. *Practical Divinity*. 2 vols. Nashville: Abingdon, 1998–99.

————. *Wesleyan Theology: A Sourcebook*. Durham, NC: The Labyrinth, 1984.

Lawson, Albert Brown. *John Wesley and the Anglican Evangelicals of the Eighteenth Century: A Study in Cooperation and Separation with Special Reference to the Calvinistic Controversies*. Durham: Pentland, 1994.

Lea, Thomas D., and Hayne P. Griffin. *1, 2 Timothy, Titus*. The New American Commentary, vol. 34. Nashville: B&H Publishing Group, 1992.

Lee, Umphrey. *John Wesley and Modern Religion*. Nashville: Cokesbury, 1936.

Letham, Robert. *The Westminster Assembly*. Phillipsburg, NJ: P&R Publishing, 2009.

Lewis, Gordon R., and Bruce A. Demarest. *Integrative Theology*. 3 vols. Grand Rapids: Zondervan, 1994.

Liefeld, Walter L. *1 and 2 Timothy, Titus*. The NIV Application Commentary. Grand Rapids: Zondervan, 1999.

Liefeld, Walter L., and David W. Pao. *Luke*. The Expositor's Bible Commentary, vol. 10. Rev. ed. Grand Rapids: Zondervan, 2007.

Lindberg, Carter. *The European Reformations*. Oxford: Blackwell, 1996.

————, ed. *The Reformation Theologians: An Introduction to Theology in the Early Modern Period*. Oxford: Blackwell, 2002.

Lindstrom, Harald. *Wesley and Sanctification: A Study in the Doctrine of Salvation.* London: Epworth, 1950.

Lloyd-Jones, D. Martyn, ed. *Puritan Papers,* vol. 1, *1956–1959.* Phillipsburg, NJ: P&R Publishing, 2001.

Longenecker, Richard N. *Acts.* The Expositor's Bible Commentary, vol. 9. Grand Rapids: Zondervan, 1981.

_____. *Galatians.* Word Biblical Commentary, vol. 41. Dallas: Word: 1990.

Longman, Tremper, III. *The Book of Ecclesiastes.* The New International Commentary on the Old Testament. Grand Rapids: Eerdmans, 1998.

_____. *Jeremiah, Lamentations.* New International Biblical Commentary. Peabody, MA: Hendrickson, 2008.

Machen, J. Gresham. *The Christian View of Man.* Edinburgh: Banner of Truth, 1984.

_____. *What Is Faith?* Edinburgh: Banner of Truth, 1991.

Maddox, Randy L. *Responsible Grace: John Wesley's Practical Theology.* Nashville: Kingswood, 1994.

Marshall, I. Howard. *A Critical and Exegetical Commentary on the Pastoral Epistles.* International Critical Commentary. Edinburgh: T&T Clark, 1999.

_____. *The Epistles of John.* New International Commentary on the New Testament. Grand Rapids: Eerdmans, 1978.

Mathews, Kenneth A. *Genesis 1–11:26.* The New American Commentary, vol. 1a. Nashville: B&H Publishing Group, 1996.

McCartney, Dan G. *James.* Baker Exegetical Commentary of the New Testament. Grand Rapids: Baker Academic, 2009.

McConville, J. G. *Deuteronomy.* Apollos Old Testament Commentary. Downers Grove, IL: InverVarsity, 2002.

McGonigle, Herbert Boyd. *Sufficient Saving Grace: John Wesley's Evangelical Arminianism.* Milton Keynes: Paternoster, 2001.

McGrath, Alister E. *Historical Theology: An Introduction to the History of Christian Thought.* Oxford: Blackwell, 1998.

_____. *The Intellectual Origins of the European Reformation.* Oxford: Blackwell, 1993.

_____. *Iustitia Dei: A History of the Christian Doctrine of Justification.* 3rd ed. New York: Cambridge, 2005.

_____. *A Life of John Calvin.* Oxford: Blackwell, 1990.

_____. *Reformation Thought: An Introduction.* 3rd ed. Oxford: Blackwell, 1999.

_____. *Studies in Doctrine.* Grand Rapids: Zondervan, 1997.

McNeil, John T. *The History and Character of Calvinism*. New York: Oxford University Press, 1954.

Melick, Richard R., Jr. *Philippians, Colossians, Philemon*. New American Commentary, vol. 32. Nashville: B&H Publishing Group, 1991.

Merrill, Eugene H. *Deuteronomy*. New American Commentary, vol. 4. Nashville: B&H Publishing Group, 1994.

Michaels, J. Ramsey. *The Gospel of John*. New International Commentary on the New Testament. Grand Rapids: Eerdmans, 2010.

Mickey, Paul A. *Essentials of Wesleyan Theology*. Grand Rapids: Zondervan, 1980.

Mitchell, Crichton T., ed. *The Wesley Century*. 2 vols. Kansas City, MO: Beacon Hill, 1984.

Monk, Robert C. *John Wesley: His Puritan Heritage*. Nashville: Abingdon, 1966.

Moo, Douglas. *The Epistle to the Romans*. New International Commentary on the New Testament. Grand Rapids: Eerdmans, 1996.

_____. *The Gospel according to John*. The New International Commentary on the New Testament. Grand Rapids: Eerdmans, 1971.

_____. *The Letters to the Colossians and to Philemon*. Pillar New Testament Commentary. Grand Rapids: Eerdmans, 2008.

_____. *The Letter of James*. The Pillar New Testament Commentary. Grand Rapids: Eerdmans, 2000.

Moreland, J. P., and William Lane Craig. *Philosophical Foundations for a Christian Worldview*. Downers Grove, IL: InterVarsity, 2003.

Morris, Leon. *Epistle to the Romans*. The Pillar New Testament Commentary. Grand Rapids: Eerdmans, 1988.

_____. *1 Corinthians*. Tyndale New Testament Commentaries. Downers Grove, IL: InterVarsity, 2008.

_____. *The First and Second Epistles to the Thessalonians*. The New International Commentary on the New Testament. Grand Rapids: Eerdmans, 1991.

_____. *The Gospel according to John*. The New International Commentary on the New Testament. Reprint, Grand Rapids: Eerdmans, 1971.

_____. *The Gospel according to Matthew*. The Pillar New Testament Commentary. Grand Rapids: William B. Eerdmans, 1992.

Moule, H. C. G. *The Epistle to the Romans*. The Expositor's Bible. New York: Armstrong & Son, 1894.

Moulton, J. H. *A Grammar of New Testament Greek*. 2 vols. Edinburgh: T&T Clark, 1908.

Mounce, Robert H. *The Book of Revelation*. New International Commentary on the New Testament. Grand Rapids: Baker, 1977.

_____. *John*. The Expositor's Bible Commentary, vol. 10. Grand Rapids: Zondervan, 2007.

_____. *Romans*. The New American Commentary, vol. 27. Nashville: B&H Publishing Group, 1995.

Mounce, William D. *Basics of Biblical Greek: Grammar*. Grand Rapids: Zondervan, 2003.

_____. *Pastoral Epistles*. Word Biblical Commentary, vol. 46. Nashville: Thomas Nelson, 2000.

Muller, Richard. *After Calvin: Studies in the Development of a Theological Tradition*. New York: Oxford University Press, 2003.

_____. *Christ and the Decree: Christology and Predestination in Reformed Theology from Calvin to Perkins*. Studies in Historical Theology 2. Durham, NC: Labyrinth, 1986. Reprint, Grand Rapids: Baker, 2008.

_____. *Dictionary of Latin and Greek Theological Terms: Drawn Principally from Protestant Scholastic Theology*. Grand Rapids: Baker, 2004.

_____. *God, Creation, and Providence in the Thought of Jacob Arminius: Sources and Directions of Scholastic Protestantism in the Era of Early Orthodoxy*. Grand Rapids: Baker, 1991.

_____. *Post-Reformation Reformed Dogmatics: The Rise and Development of Reformed Orthodoxy, ca. 1520–ca. 1725*. 4 vols. Grand Rapids: Baker, 2003.

_____. *The Unaccommodated Calvin: Studies in the Foundation of a Theological Tradition*. New York: Oxford University Press, 2000.

Mulsow, Marin, and Jan Rohls, eds. *Socinianism and Arminianism: Antitrinitarians, Calvinists and Cultural Exchange in Seventeenth-Century Europe*. Brill's Studies in Intellectual History 134. Leiden: E. J. Brill, 2005.

Murray, Iain H. *John Wesley and the Men Who Followed*. Edinburgh: Banner of Truth, 2003.

_____. *Spurgeon versus Hyper-Calvinism*. Edinburgh: Banner of Truth, 1995.

Murray, John. *Collected Writings of John Murray*. 4 vols. Edinburgh: Banner of Truth, 1976.

_____. *The Epistle to the Romans*. New International Commentary on the New Testament. Grand Rapids: Eerdmans, 1959.

_____. *The Imputation of Adam's Sin*. Grand Rapids: Eerdmans, 1959.

_____. *Redemption Accomplished and Applied*. Grand Rapids: Eerdmans, 1955.

Murray, John, and Ned Stonehouse. *The Free Offer of the Gospel*. Phillipsburg, NJ: Lewis J. Grotenhuis, 1948.

Niesel, Wilhelm. *The Theology of Calvin*. Translated by Harold Knight. Philadelphia: Westminster, 1956.

Nettles, Thomas J. *By His Grace and for His Glory: A Historical, Theological, and Practical Study of the Doctrines of Grace in Baptist Life*. Expanded and revised. Cape Coral, FL: Founders, 2006.

Nicole, Roger. *Our Sovereign Saviour: The Essence of the Reformed Faith*. Fearn, Ross-shire, UK: Christian Focus, 2002.

————. *Standing Forth: Collected Writings of Roger Nicole*. Fearn, Ross-shire, UK: Christian Focus, 2002.

Nygren, Anders. *Commentary on Romans*. Philadelphia: Fortress, 1972.

Oberman, Heiko A. *The Dawn of the Reformation: Essays in Late Medieval and Reformation Thought*. Edinburgh: T&T Clark, 1986.

————. *Forerunners of the Reformation: The Shape of Late Medieval Thought*. Translated by Paul L. Nyhus. Philadelphia: Fortress Press, 1981.

————. *The Harvest of Medieval Theology: Gabriel Biel and Late Medieval Nominalism*. Cambridge: Harvard University Press, 1963.

————. *Luther: Man between God and the Devil*. Translated by Eileen Walliser-Schwarzbart. New York: Image, 1992.

————. *Masters of the Reformation*. Translated by Dennis Martin. Cambridge: Cambridge University Press, 1981.

————. *The Reformation: Roots and Ramifications*. Translated by Andrew Colin Gow. Edinburgh: T&T Clark, 1994.

————. *The Two Reformations: The Journey from the Last Days to the New World*. Edited by Donald Weinstein. New Haven: Yale University Press, 2003.

O'Brien, Peter T. *Colossians, Philemon*. Word Biblical Commentary, vol. 44. Dallas: Word, 1982.

————. *The Epistle to the Philippians*. New International Greek Testament Commentary. Grand Rapids: Eerdmans, 1991.

————. *The Letter to the Ephesians*. The Pillar New Testament Commentary. Grand Rapids: Eerdmans, 1999.

————. *The Letter to the Hebrews*. Pillar New Testament Commentary. Grand Rapids: Eerdmans, 2010.

Oden, Thomas C. *John Wesley's Scriptural Christianity: A Plain Exposition of His Teaching on Christian Doctrine*. Grand Rapids: Zondervan, 1994.

_____. *Life in the Spirit*. Vol. 3 of *Systematic Theology*. New York: Harper-SanFrancisco, 1992.

_____. *Systematic Theology*. 3 vols. Peabody, MA: Hendrickson, 2006.

_____. *The Transforming Power of Grace*. Nashville: Abingdon, 1993.

Oliphint, K. Scott, ed. *Justified in Christ: God's Plan for Us in Justification*. Fearn, Ross-shire: Christian Focus, 2007.

Olson, Roger E. *Against Calvinism*. Grand Rapids: Zondervan, 2011.

_____. *Arminian Theology: Myths and Realities*. Downers Grove, IL: InterVarsity, 2006.

Osborne, Grant R. *Revelation*. Baker Exegetical Commentary on the New Testament. Grand Rapids: Baker, 2002.

Outler, Albert C. *Theology in the Wesleyan Spirit*. Nashville: Tidings, 1975.

Ozment, Steven E. *The Age of Reform, 1250–1550: An Intellectual and Religious History of Late Medieval and Reformation Europe*. New Haven: Yale University Press, 1980.

Packer, J. I., *Evangelism and the Sovereignty of God*. Downers Grove, IL: InterVarsity, 1961.

_____, ed. *Puritan Papers*, volumes 2–4. Phillipsburg, NJ: P&R Publishing, 2001–2005.

_____. *A Quest for Godliness: The Puritan Vision of the Christian Life*. Wheaton, IL: Crossway, 1990.

Palmer, Edwin H. *The Five Points of Calvinism: A Study Guide*. 2nd ed. Grand Rapids: Baker Academic, 2010.

_____. *The Person and Ministry of the Holy Spirit: The Traditional Calvinistic Perspective*. Grand Rapids: Baker, 1974.

Parker, T. H. L. *Calvin: An Introduction to His Thought*. Louisville: Westminster John Knox, 1995.

Parsons, Michael C. *Acts*. Grand Rapids: Baker, 2008.

Partee, Charles. *The Theology of John Calvin*. Louisville: Westminster John Knox, 2008.

Pelikan, Jaroslav. *The Christian Tradition: A History of the Development of Doctrine*. 5 vols. Chicago: University of Chicago Press, 1971–89.

Peterson, David G. *The Acts of the Apostles*. The Pillar New Testament Commentary. Grand Rapids: Eerdmans, 2009.

Peterson, Henry. *The Canons of Dort*. Grand Rapids: Baker, 1968.

Peterson, Robert A., and Michael D. Williams. *Why I Am Not an Arminian*. Downers Grove, IL: InterVarsity, 2004.

Picirilli, Robert E. *Grace, Faith, Free Will—Contrasting Views of Salvation: Calvinism and Arminianism*. Nashville: Randall House Publications, 2002.

Pink, A. W. *The Doctrine of Salvation*. Grand Rapids: Baker, 1975.

Pinnock, Clark H., ed. *The Grace of God and the Will of Man: A Case for Arminianism*. Minneapolis: Bethany House, 1989.

————. *Grace Unlimited*. Eugene, OR: Wipf and Stock, 1999.

————. *Most Moved Mover: A Theology of God's Openness*. Grand Rapids: Baker, 2001.

Pinnock, Clark H., Richard Rice, John Sanders, William Hasker, and David Basinger. *The Openness of God: A Biblical Challenge to the Traditional Understanding of God*. Downers Grove, IL: InterVarsity, 1994.

Piper, John. *Finally Alive*. Fearn, Ross-Shire, Scotland: Christian Focus, 2009.

————. *The Justification of God: An Exegetical and Theological Study of Romans 9:1–23*. 2nd ed. Grand Rapids: Baker, 1993.

————. *The Pleasures of God*. Sisters, OR: Multnomah, 2000.

Piper, John, and Justin Taylor, eds. *A God-Entranced Vision of All Things: The Legacy of Jonathan Edwards*. Wheaton, IL: Crossway, 1994.

Piper, John, Justin Taylor, and Paul Kjoss Helseth. *Beyond the Bounds: Open Theism and the Undermining of Biblical Christianity*. Wheaton, IL: Crossway, 2003.

Plantinga, Cornelius, Jr. *Not the Way It's Supposed to Be: A Breviary of Sin*. Grand Rapids: Eerdmans, 1995.

————. *A Place to Stand: A Reformed Study of Creeds and Confessions*. Grand Rapids: CRC Publications, 1979.

Ramm, Bernard. *Offense to Reason: A Theology of Sin*. Vancouver, BC: Regent College Publishing, 1985.

Rattenbury, J. E. *The Conversion of the Wesleys*. London: Epworth, 1938.

Reid, W. Standford, and Paul Woolley, eds. *John Calvin: His Influence in the Western World*. Grand Rapids: Zondervan, 1982.

Reymond, Robert L. *A New Systematic Theology of the Christian Faith*. 2nd ed. Nashville: Thomas Nelson, 1998.

Richardson, Kurt A. *James*. New American Commentary, vol. 36. Nashville: B&H, 1997.

Ridderbos, Herman. *The Epistle of Paul to the Churches of Galatia*. New International Commentary on the New Testament. Grand Rapids: Eerdmans, 1953.

————. *The Gospel according to John*. Translated by J. Vriend. Grand Rapids: Eerdmans, 1997.

————. *Paul: An Outline of His Theology.* Translated by J. R. de Witt. Grand Rapids: Eerdmans, 1975.

Robertson, A. T. *Grammar of the Greek New Testament in the Light of Historical Research.* Nashville: Broadman, 1934.

Robinson, Childs. *The Reformation: A Rediscovery of Grace.* Grand Rapids: Eerdmans, 1962.

Rohls, Jan. *Reformed Confessions.* Louisville: Westminster John Knox, 1998.

Ross, Alexander. *The Epistles of James and John.* The New International Commentary on the New Testament. Grand Rapids: Eerdmans, 1954.

Rost, Stephen, ed. *John Wesley.* Nashville: Thomas Nelson, 1989.

Runyon, Theodore. *The New Creation: John Wesley's Theology Today.* Nashville: Abingdon, 1998.

————, ed. *Wesleyan Theology Today.* Nashville: Kingswood Books, 1985.

Sailhamer, John H. *Genesis.* The Expositor's Bible Commentary, vol. 1. Grand Rapids: Zondervan, 2008.

Sanders, John. *The God Who Risks: A Theology of Providence.* Downers Grove, IL: InterVarsity, 1999.

Schaff, Philip. *The History of the Christian Church.* 8 vols. Peabody, MA: Hendrickson, 2006.

Schnackenburg, Rudolf. *The Gospel according to St. John.* 3 vols. Translated by K. Smith. New York: Crossroad, 1968.

Schreiner, Thomas R. *1, 2 Peter, Jude.* The New American Commentary, vol. 37. Nashville: B&H Publishing Group, 2003.

————. *Galatians.* Zondervan Exegetical Commentary on the New Testament. Grand Rapids: Zondervan, 2010.

————. *New Testament Theology: Magnifying God in Christ.* Grand Rapids: Baker, 2008.

————. *Paul: Apostle of God's Glory in Christ.* Downers Grove, IL: InterVarsity, 2001.

————. *Romans.* Baker Exegetical Commentary on the New Testament. Grand Rapids: Baker, 1998.

Schreiner, Thomas R., and Ardel B. Caneday. *The Race Set Before Us: A Biblical Theology of Perseverance and Assurance.* Downers Grove, IL: InterVarsity, 2001.

Schreiner, Thomas R., and Bruce A. Ware, eds. *Still Sovereign: Contemporary Perspectives on Election, Foreknowledge, and Grace.* Grand Rapids: Baker Academic, 2000.

347

————. *The Grace of God, the Bondage of the Will: Historical and Theological Perspectives on Calvinism*, vol. 2. Grand Rapids: Baker 1995.

Seeberg, Reinhold. *Text-Book of the History of Doctrines*. Translated by Charles E. Hay. 2 vols. Grand Rapids: Baker, 1977.

Selderhuis, Herman J., ed. *The Calvin Handbook*. Grand Rapids: Eerdmans, 2009.

Sell, Alan P. F. *The Great Debate: Calvinism, Arminianism, and Salvation*. Grand Rapids: Baker, 1982.

Shedd, William G. T. *Calvinism: Pure and Mixed*. Edinburgh: Banner of Truth, 1986.

————. *Dogmatic Theology*. 3rd ed. Edited by Alan W. Gomes. Phillipsburg, NJ: P&R Publishing, 2003.

————. *A History of Christian Doctrine*. 2 vols. Reprint, Vestavia Hills, AL: Solid Ground Christian, 2006.

Silva, Moisés. *Philippians*. 2nd ed. Baker Exegetical Commentary on the New Testament. Grand Rapids: Baker, 2005.

Simpson, E. K. *Commentary on the Epistle to the Ephesians*. New International Commentary on the New Testament. Grand Rapids: Baker, 1977.

Simpson, E. K., and F. F. Bruce. *The Epistles to the Ephesians and Colossians*. The New International Commentary on the New Testament. Grand Rapids: Eerdmans, 1977.

Slatte, Howard A. *The Arminian Arm of Theology: The Theologies of John Fletcher, First Methodist Theologian, and His Precursor, James Arminius*. Washington, DC: University Press of America, 1979.

Smalley, Stephen S. *1, 2, 3 John*. Word Biblical Commentary, vol. 51. Dallas: Word, 1984.

Smith, David L. *With Willful Intent: A Theology of Sin*. Eugene, OR: Wipf and Stock, 1994.

Smith, G. Abbott. *A Manual Greek Lexicon of the New Testament*. 3rd ed. Edinburgh: T&T Clark, 1968.

Smith, Timothy L. *Whitefield and Wesley on the New Birth*. Grand Rapids: Zondervan, 1986.

Souter, Alexander. *Pelagius's Expositions of Thirteen Epistles of St. Paul*. 3 vols. Cambridge: Cambridge University Press, 1922–31.

Southern Baptist Theological Seminary. *The Abstract of Principles*. Accessed October 16, 2012. http://www.sbts.edu/about/ truth/abstract/.

Spencer, Duane Edward. *Tulip: The Five Points of Calvinism in the Light of Scripture*. 2nd ed. Grand Rapids: Baker, 1979.

Sproul, R. C. *Chosen by God*. Wheaton, IL: Tyndale House, 1986.

————. *What Is Reformed Theology? Understanding the Basics*. Grand Rapids: Baker, 1997, 2005.

————. *Willing to Believe: The Controversy over Free Will*. Grand Rapids: Baker, 1997.

Sproul, R. C., and Sinclair Ferguson. "Questions and Answers #3." Session held at the annual meeting of the Ligonier Ministries National Conference, Orlando, Florida, March 21, 2009.

Sproul, R. C., Jr., ed. *After Darkness, Light*. Phillipsburg, NJ: P&R Publishing, 2003.

Stanglin, Keith D. *Arminius on the Assurance of Salvation: The Context, Roots, and Shape of the Leiden Debate, 1603–1609*. Brill's Series in Church History 27. Leiden: E. J. Brill, 2007.

————, and Thomas H. McCall. *Jacob Arminius: Theologian of Grace*. Oxford: Oxford University Press, 2012.

Steele, David N., Curtis C. Thomas, and S. Lance Quinn. *The Five Points of Calvinism: Defined, Defended, and Documented*. Phillipsburg, NJ: P&R Publishing, 2004.

Stein, Robert H. *Mark*. Baker Exegetical Commentary of the New Testament. Grand Rapids: Baker Academic, 2008.

Steinmetz, David C. *Luther in Context*. 2nd ed. Grand Rapids: Baker, 2002.

Stewart, Kenneth J. *Ten Myths about Calvinism: Recovering the Breadth of the Reformed Tradition*. Downers Grove, IL: InterVarsity, 2011.

Storms, Samuel C. *Chosen for Life: The Case for Divine Election*. Wheaton, IL: Crossway, 2007.

Stott, John R. W. *Baptism and Fullness: The Work of the Holy Spirit Today*. 3rd ed. Downers Grove, IL: InterVarsity, 2006.

————. *God's New Society*. Downers Grove, IL: InterVarsity, 1982.

————. *The Letters of John*. Grand Rapids: Eerdmans, 1988.

————. *Letters of John*. Tyndale New Testament Commentaries, vol. 19. Downers Grove, IL: InterVarsity, 1998.

————. *The Message of Acts*. Downers Grove, IL: InterVarsity, 1990, 263.

————. *Romans: God's Good News for the World*. Downers Grove, IL: InterVarsity, 1994.

Strong, Augustus Hopkins. *Systematic Theology: Three Volumes in One*. Philadelphia: Judson, 1907. Reprint, Old Tappan, NJ: Fleming H. Revell, 1976.

Thielman, Frank. *Ephesians*. Baker Exegetical Commentary on the New Testament. Grand Rapids: Baker, 2010.

————. *Paul and the Law: A Contextual Approach*. Downers Grove, IL: Inter-Varsity, 1994.

————. *Theology of the New Testament: A Canonical and Synthetic Approach*. Grand Rapids: Zondervan, 2005.

Thiessen, Henry C. *Lectures in Systematic Theology*. Grand Rapids: Eerdmans, 1979.

Thiselton, Anthony C. *The First Epistle to the Corinthians: A Commentary on the Greek Text*. The New International Greek Testament Commentary. Grand Rapids: Eerdmans, 2000.

Thompson, J. A. *The Book of Jeremiah*. The New International Commentary on the Old Testament. Grand Rapids: Eerdmans, 1980.

————. *Deuteronomy*. Tyndale Old Testament Commentaries, vol. 5. Downers Grove, IL: IVP Academic, 2008.

Thompson, M. M. *The God of the Gospel of John*. Grand Rapids: Eerdmans, 2001.

Thornwell, James H. *Election and Reprobation*. Jackson, MS: Presbyterian Reformation Society, 1961.

Thuesen, Peter J. *Predestination: The American Career of a Contentious Doctrine*. New York: Oxford University Press, 2009.

Toon, Peter. *Born Again: A Biblical and Theological Study of Regeneration*. Grand Rapids: Baker, 1987.

————. *The Emergence of Hyper-Calvinism in English Nonconformity, 1689–1765*. London: The Olive Tree, 1967.

Towner, Philip H. *The Letters to Timothy and Titus*. New International Commentary on the New Testament. Grand Rapids: Baker, 2006.

Tuell, Steven. *Ezekiel*. New International Biblical Commentary. Peabody, MA: Hendrickson, 2009.

Turner, David L. *Matthew*. Baker Exegetical Commentary of the New Testament. Grand Rapids: Baker Academic, 2008.

Tyacke, Nicholas. *Anti-Calvinists: The Rise of English Arminianism, c. 1590–1640*. Oxford: Oxford University Press, 1987.

Van Asselt, Willem J., J. Martin Bac, and Roelf T. te Velde, eds. *Reformed Thought on Freedom: The Concept of Free Choice in Early Modern Reformed Theology*. Texts and Studies in Reformation and Post-Reformation Thought. Grand Rapids: Baker, 2010.

VanGemeren, Willem A. *The Progress of Redemption: The Story of Redemption from Creation to the New Jerusalem*. Grand Rapids: Baker, 1988.

————. *Psalms*. The Expositor's Bible Commentary, vol. 5. Grand Rapids: Zondervan, 2008.

Van Groningen, Gerard. *Messianic Revelation in the Old Testament*. Grand Rapids: Baker, 1990.

Van Leeuwen, Marius, Keith D. Stanglin, and Marijke Tolsma, eds. *Arminius, Arminianism, and Europe: Jacob Arminius (1559/60–1609)*. Brill's Series in Church History 39. Leiden: E. J. Brill, 2010.

Wallace, Daniel B. *Greek Grammar: An Exegetical Syntax of the New Testament*. Grand Rapids: Zondervan, 1996.

Wallace, Dewey D., Jr. *Puritans and Predestination: Grace in English Protestant Theology, 1515–1695*. Chapel Hill: University of North Carolina Press, 1982.

Walls, Jerry L., and Joseph R. Dongell. *Why I Am Not a Calvinist*. Downers Grove, IL: InterVarsity, 2004.

Waltke, Bruce K. *The Book of Proverbs, Chapters 15–31*. The New International Commentary on the Old Testament. Grand Rapids: Eerdmans, 2005.

Wanamaker, Charles A. *The Epistles to the Thessalonians*. New International Greek Testament Commentary. Grand Rapids: Eerdmans, 1990.

Ware, Bruce A. *God's Greater Glory: The Exalted God of Scripture and the Christian Faith*. Wheaton, IL: Crossway, 2004.

————. *God's Lesser Glory: The Diminished God of Open Theism*. Wheaton, IL: Crossway, 2000.

————, ed. *Perspectives on the Doctrine of God: Four Views*. Nashville: B&H Publishing Group, 2008.

Watkin-Jones, Howard. *The Holy Spirit from Arminius to Wesley: A Study of Christian Teaching Concerning the Holy Spirit and His Place in the Trinity in the Seventeenth and Eighteenth Centuries*. London: Epworth, 1929.

Weaver, Rebecca Harden. *Divine Grace and Human Agency: A Study of the Semi-Pelagian Controversy*. Patristic Monograph Series 15. Macon, GA: Mercer University Press, 1996.

Wells, David F. *God the Evangelist: How the Holy Spirit Works to Bring Men and Women to Faith*. Grand Rapids: Eerdmans, 1987.

Wendel, François. *Calvin: Origins and Developments of His Religious Thought*. Translated by Philip Mairet. Grand Rapids: Baker, 1987.

Whedon, Daniel D. *Freedom of the Will: A Wesleyan Response to Jonathan Edwards*. Edited by John D. Wagner. Eugene, OR: Wipf & Stock, 2009.

White, James. *Drawn by the Father: A Study of John 6:35–45*. Southbridge, MA: Crowne, 1991.

————. *The Potter's Freedom: A Defense of the Reformation and a Rebuttal of Norman Geisler's* Chosen But Free. Amityville: Calvary, 2000.

White, Peter. *Predestination, Policy, and Polemic: Conflict and Consensus in the English Church from the Reformation to the Civil War.* Cambridge: Cambridge University Press, 1992.

Wiley, H. Orton. *Christian Theology.* 2 vols. Kansas City, MO: Beacon Hill, 1952.

Williams, Colin W. *John Wesley's Theology Today.* Nashville: Abingdon, 1960.

Witherington, Ben, III. *John's Wisdom.* Louisville: Westminster John Knox, 1995.

_____. *The Problem with Evangelical Theology: Testing the Exegetical Foundations of Calvinism, Dispensationalism, and Wesleyanism.* Waco, TX: Baylor University Press, 2005.

Wolff, Hans W. *Anthropology of the Old Testament.* Mifflintown, PA: Sigler, 1996.

Wright, N. T. *The Epistles of Paul to the Colossians and to Philemon.* Tyndale New Testament Commentaries. Downers Grove, IL: InterVarsity, 1986.

Wright, R. K. McGregor. *No Place for Sovereignty: What's Wrong with Freewill Theism.* Downers Grove, IL: Inter Varsity, 1996.

Yarbrough, Robert W. *1–3 John.* Baker Exegetical Commentary on the New Testament. Grand Rapids: Baker, 2008.

Zerwick, M. *Biblical Greek Illustrated by Examples.* Rome: Pontificii Instituti Biblici, 1963.

ARTICLES

Baker, Lynne Rudder. "Why Christians Should Not Be Libertarians: An Augustinian Challenge." *Faith and Philosophy* 20 (2003): 460–78.

Bangs, Carl. "Arminius and the Scholastic Tradition." *Calvin Theological Journal* 24 (1989): 263–77.

_____. "Arminius as a Reformed Theologian." In *The Heritage of John Calvin*, ed. John H. Bratt, 209–22. Grand Rapids: Eerdmans, 1973.

_____. "Jacobus Arminius." In *The Oxford Encyclopedia of the Reformation*, ed. Hans J. Hillerbrand. Oxford: Oxford University Press, 1996.

Basinger, David. "Middle Knowledge and Classical Christian Thought." In *Religious Studies* 22 (1986): 407–22.

Basinger, Randall G. "Exhaustive Divine Sovereignty: A Practical Critique." In *The Grace of God and the Will of Man: A Case for Arminianism*, ed. Clark H. Pinnock, 191–206. Minneapolis: Bethany House, 1989.

Bennett, David. "How Arminian was John Wesley?" *Evangelical Quarterly* 72, 3 (2000): 237–48.

Bevins, Winfield H. "Pneumatology in John Wesley's Theological Method." *The Asbury Theological Journal* 58 (2003): 101–14.

Bryant, Barry E. "Original Sin." In *The Oxford Handbook of Methodist Studies*, ed. William J. Abraham and James E. Kirby, 522–39. Oxford: Oxford University Press, 2009.

Callen, Barry L. "A Mutuality Model of Conversion." In *Conversion in the Wesleyan Tradition*, ed. Kenneth J. Collins and John H. Tyson, 145–59. Nashville: Abingdon, 2001.

Carson, D. A. "How Can We Reconcile the Love and the Transcendent Sovereignty of God?" In *God Under Fire: Modern Scholarship Reinvents God*, ed. Douglas S. Huffman and Eric L. Johnson, 279–312. Grand Rapids: Zondervan, 2002.

Clark, R. Scott. "Janus, the Well-Meant Offer of the Gospel, and Westminster Theology." In *The Pattern of Sound Doctrine: Systematic Theology at the Westminster Seminaries: Essays in Honor of Robert B. Strimple*, ed. David VanDrunen, 149–80. Phillipsburg, NJ: P&R Publishing, 2004.

Clarke, F. Stuart. "Arminius's Understanding of Calvin." *Evangelical Quarterly* 54 (1982): 25–35.

————. "Theology of Arminius." *London Quarterly and Holborn Review* 185 (1960): 248–53.

Collinge, William J. "Introduction." In *Saint Augustine: Four Anti-Pelagian Writings*, trans. John A. Mourant and William J. Collinge, 3–99. Washington, DC: The Catholic University of America Press, 1992.

Collins, G. N. M. "Order of Salvation." *Evangelical Dictionary of Theology*. Edited by Walter A. Elwell. Grand Rapids: Baker Academic, 2001.

Combs, William W. "Does the Bible Teach Prevenient Grace?" *Detroit Baptist Seminary Journal* 10 (2005): 3–18.

Cossee, Eric H. "Arminius and Rome." In *Arminius, Arminianism, and Europe: Jacob Arminius (1559/60–1609)*, ed. Marius van Leeuwen, Keith D. Stanglin, and Marijke Tolsma, 73–88. Brill's Series in Church History 39. Leiden: E. J. Brill, 2010.

————. "Our Liberal Protestant Heritage, A European Perspective." *The Non-Subscribing Presbyterian* 15 (1997): 96–101.

Cottrell, Jack W. "The Classical Arminian View of Election." In *Perspectives on Election: Five Views*, ed. Chad O. Brand, 70–134. Nashville: B&H Publishing Group, 2006.

————. "Conditional Election." In *Grace Unlimited*, ed. Clark H. Pinnock, 51–73. Eugene, OR: Wipf and Stock, 1999.

————. "The Nature of the Divine Sovereignty." In *The Grace of God and the Will of Man: A Case for Arminianism*, ed. Clark H. Pinnock, 97–120. Minneapolis: Bethany House, 1989.

Cowan, Steven B. "Common Misconceptions of Evangelicals Regarding Calvinism." *Journal of the Evangelical Theological Society*, 33 (1990): 189–95.

Cox, Leo G. "John Wesley's Concept of Sin." *Journal of the Evangelical Theological Society* 7, 3 (1966): 8–24.

————. "Prevenient Grace—A Wesleyan View." *Journal of the Evangelical Theological Society* 12 (1969): 143–49.

Cracknell, Kenneth. "The Spread of Wesleyan Methodism." In *The Cambridge Companion to John Wesley*, ed. Randy L. Maddox and Jason E. Vickers, 245–61. Cambridge: Cambridge University Press, 2010.

Cross, Richard. "Anti-Pelagianism and the Resistibility of Grace." *Faith and Philosophy* 22 (2005): 199–210.

Cushman, Robert E. "Salvation for All." In *Methodism*, ed. William Anderson, 105–11. Nashville/New York: Abingdon/Cokesbury, 1947.

Davies, Rupert E. "The People Called Methodist: 'Our Doctrines.'" In *History of Methodist Church in Great Britain*, ed. Rupert Davies, George A. Raymond, and Rupp Gordon, 1:145–80. London: Epworth, 1965.

De Jong, Peter Y. "The Rise of the Reformed Churches in the Netherlands." In *Crisis in the Reformed Churches: Essays in Commemoration of the Great Synod of Dort, 1618–1619*, ed. Peter Y. De Jong, 1–21. Grand Rapids: Reformed Fellowship, 1968.

Dekker, Eef. "Was Arminius a Molinist?" *Sixteenth-Century Journal* 27 (1996): 337–52.

de Witt, John R. "The Arminian Conflict and the Synod of Dort." In *Puritan Papers*, vol. 5: *1968–1969*, ed. J. I. Packer. Phillipsburg, NJ: P&R Publishing, 2005.

Dieter, Melvin E. "The Wesleyan Perspective." In *Five Views on Sanctification*, ed. Melvin E. Dieter, 9–58. Grand Rapids: Zondervan, 1987.

Duncan, J. Ligon, III. "The Resurgence of Calvinism in America." In *Calvin for Today*, ed. Joel R. Beeke, 227–40. Grand Rapids: Reformation Heritage, 2009.

Elliott-Binns, L. "James 1.18: Creation or Redemption?" *New Testament Studies* 3 (1955): 148–61.

Ellis, Mark A. "Introduction." In *The Arminian Confession of 1621*, ed. Mark A. Ellis, viii-ix. Princeton Theological Monograph Series. Eugene, OR: Wipf and Stock, 2005.

English, John C. "References to St. Augustine in the Works of John Wesley," *Ashland Theological Journal* 60, 2 (2005): 5–24

Evans, C. Stephen. "Salvation, Sin, and Human Freedom in Kierkegaard." In *The Grace of God and the Will of Man: A Case for Arminianism*, ed. Clark H. Pinnock, 181–90. Minneapolis: Bethany House, 1989.

Feinberg, John. "God, Freedom, and Evil in Calvinist Thinking." In *The Grace of God, the Bondage of the Will: Historical and Theological Perspectives on Calvinism*, ed. Thomas R. Schreiner and Bruce A. Ware, 2:459–84. Grand Rapids: Baker, 1995.

————. "God Ordains All Things." In *Predestination and Free Will: Four Views of Divine Sovereignty and Human Freedom*, ed. David Basinger and Randall Basinger, 17–60. Downers Grove, IL: InterVarsity, 1986.

Ferguson, Sinclair B. "Ordo Salutis." In *New Dictionary of Theology*. Edited by S. B. Ferguson and D. F. Wright. Downers Grove, IL: InterVarsity, 1988.

————. "Repentance, Recovery, and Confession." In *Here We Stand: A Call from Confessing Evangelicals for a Modern Reformation*, ed. James Montgomery Boice and Benjamin E. Sasse, 131–56. Phillipsburg, NJ: P&R Publishing, 1996.

Foster, Herbert Darling. "Liberal Calvinism: the Remonstrants at the Synod of Dort in 1618." *Harvard Theological Review* 16 (1973): 1–37.

Fuhrman, Eldon R. "The Wesleyan Doctrine of Grace." In *The Word and Doctrine*, ed. Kenneth E. Geiger, 139–54. Kansas City: Beacon Hill, 1965.

Gaffin, Richard B. "Justification and Union with Christ (3.11–19)." In *A Theological Guide to Calvin's Institutes*, ed. David W. Hall and Peter A. Lillback, 248–69. Phillipsburg, NJ: P&R Publishing, 2008.

————. "Some Epistological Reflection on 1 Cor 2:6–16." *Westminster Theological Journal* 57 (1995): 103–24.

Geisler, Norman. "A Moderate Calvinist View." In *Four Views on Eternal Security*, ed. J. Matthew Pinson, 61–134. Grand Rapids: Zondervan, 2002.

George, Timothy. "John Gill." In *Theologians of the Baptist Tradition*, ed. Timothy George and David S. Dockery, 11–33. Nashville: B&H Publishing Group, 2001.

Gerstner, John H. "Augustine, Luther, Calvin, and Edwards on the Bondage of the Will." In *The Grace of God, the Bondage of the Will: Historical and Theological Perspectives on Calvinism*, ed. Thomas R. Schreiner and Bruce A. Ware, 2:279–94. Grand Rapids: Baker, 1995.

Godfrey, W. Robert. "Who Was Arminius?" *Modern Reformation* 1 (1992): 24.

Goudriaan, Aza. " 'Augustine Asleep' or 'Augustine Awake'? James Arminius's Reception of Augustine." In *Arminius, Arminianism, and Europe: Jacob Arminius (1559/60–1609)*, ed. Marius van Leeuwen, Keith D. Stanglin, and Marijke Tolsma, 51–72. Brill's Series in Church History 39. Leiden: E. J. Brill, 2010.

Gregory, Thomas M. "The Presbyterian Doctrine of Total Depravity." In *Soli Deo Gloria: Essays in Reformed Theology: Festschrift for John H. Gerstner*, ed. R. C. Sproul, 36–54. Nutley, NJ: Presbyterian and Reformed, 1976.

Grider, J. K. "Arminianism." In *Evangelical Dictionary of Theology*. Edited by Walter A. Elwell. Grand Rapids: Baker, 1984.

Gunter, W. Stephen. "John Wesley, A Faithful Representative of Jacobus Arminius." *Wesleyan Theological Journal* 42, 2 (2007): 65–82.

Hansen, Gary N. "Regeneration." In *Theologians of the Reformation*, ed. R. Ward Holder, 76–77. Louisville: Westminster John Knox, 2010.

Harper, Steve. "Cross Purposes: Wesley's View of the Atonement." In *Basic United Methodist Beliefs: An Evangelical View*, ed. James V. Heidinger II, 39–45. Wilmore, KY: Good News, 1986.

Hasker, William. "A Philosophical Perspective." In *The Openness of God: A Biblical Challenge to the Traditional Understanding of God*, by Clark H. Pinnock, Richard Rice, John Sanders, William Hasker, and David Basinger, 126–54. Downers Grove, IL: InterVarsity, 1994.

Heitzenrater, Richard P. "God with Us: Grace and the Spiritual Senses in John Wesley's Theology." In *Grace Upon Grace: Essays in Honor of Thomas A. Langford*, ed. Robert K. Johnston, L. Gregory Jones, and Jonathan R. Wilson, 87–110. Nashville: Abingdon, 1999.

Helm, Paul. "Augustine's Griefs." *Faith and Philosophy* 20 (2003): 448–59.

_____. "Calvin, English Calvinism and the Logic of Doctrinal Development." *Scottish Journal of Theology* 34 (1981): 179–85.

_____. "Calvin (and Zwingli) on Divine Providence." *Calvin Theological Journal* 29 (1994): 388–405.

_____. "Classical Calvinist Doctrine of God." In *Perspectives on the Doctrine of God: Four Views*, ed. Bruce A. Ware, 5–52. Nashville: B&H, 2008.

_____. "The Great Christian Doctrine (*Original Sin*)." In *A God Entranced Vision of All Things*, ed. John Piper and Justin Taylor, 175–200. Wheaton, IL: Crossway, 2004.

Hempton, David. "John Wesley (1703–1791)." In *The Pietist Theologians*, ed. Carter Lindberg, 256–72. Oxford: Blackwell, 2005.

Hendricks, M. Elton. "John Wesley and Natural Theology." *Wesley Theological Journal* 18 (1983): 7–17.

Hesselink, I. John. "Calvin's Theology." In *The Cambridge Companion to John Calvin*, ed. Donald K. McKim, 74–92. New York: Cambridge University Press, 2004.

Hoenderdaal, Gerrit Jan. "The Debate about Arminius outside the Netherlands." In *Leiden University in the Seventeenth Century*, ed. Th. H. Lunsingh Scheurleer and G. H. M. Posthumus Meyjes, 1–20. Leiden: E. J. Brill, 1975.

_____. "The Life and Struggle of Arminius in the Dutch Republic." In *Man's Faith and Freedom: The Theological Influence of Jacobus Arminius*, ed. Gerald O. McCulloh, 11–26. Eugene, OR: Wipf & Stock, 2007.

Horton, Michael. "Evangelical Arminianism." *Modern Reformation* 1, 3 (1992): 15–19.

_____. "A Shattered Vase: The Tragedy of Sin in Calvin's Thought." In *A Theological Guide to Calvin's Institutes*, ed. David W. Hall and Peter A. Lillback, 151–67. Phillipsburg, NJ: P&R Publishing, 2008.

_____. "Sola Gratia." In *After Darkness, Light: Distinctives of Reformed Theology, Essays in Honor of R. C. Sproul*, ed. R. C. Sproul Jr., 111–33. Phillipsburg, NJ: P&R Publishing, 2003.

_____. "The *Sola's* of the Reformation." In *Here We Stand! A Call from Confessing Evangelicals for a Modern Reformation*, ed. James Montgomery Boice and Benjamin E. Sasse, 99–130. Phillipsburg, NJ: P&R Publishing, 1996.

_____. "Who Saves Whom?" *Modern Reformation* 1, 3 (1992): 1–3.

Hughes, Philip E.. "Another Dogma Falls." *Christianity Today* 23 (May 1969): 13.

_____. "But for the Grace of God: Divine Initiative and Human Need." In *Christian Foundations*, 1:1–94. Philadelphia: Westminster, 1964.

Johnston, R. K. "Imputation." In *Evangelical Dictionary of Theology*, ed. Walter A. Elwell, 554–55. Grand Rapids: Baker, 1984.

Keathley, Kenneth. "A Molinist View of Election, or How to Be a Consistent Infralapsarian." In *Calvinism: A Southern Baptist Dialogue*, ed. E. Ray Clendenen and Brad J. Waggoner, 195–215. Nashville: B&H Academic, 2008.

_____. "The Work of God: Salvation." In *A Theology for the Church*, ed. Daniel L. Akin, David P. Nelson, and Peter R. Schemm, 686–785. Nashville: B&H Publishing Group, 2007.

Keefer, Luke L. "Characteristics of Wesley's Arminianism." *Wesleyan Theological Journal* 22, 1 (1987): 88–100.

_____. "John Wesley and English Arminianism." *Evangelical Journal* 4, 1 (1986): 15–28.

Kistemaker, Simon. "Leading Figures at the Synod of Dort." In *Crisis in the Reformed Churches: Essays in Commemoration of the Great Synod of Dort, 1618–1619*, ed. Peter Y. De Jong, 39–51. Grand Rapids: Reformed Fellowship, 1968.

Klooster, Fred H. "Doctrinal Deliverances of Dort." In *Crisis in the Reformed Churches: Essays in Commemoration of the Great Synod of Dort, 1618–1619*, ed. Peter Y. De Jong, 52–94. Grand Rapids: Reformed Fellowship, 1968.

Knickerbocker, Waldo E. "Arminian Anglicanism and John and Charles Wesley." *Memphis Theological Seminary Journal* 29, 3 (1991): 79–97.

Knight, Henry H., III. "The Transformation of the Human Heart: The Place of Conversion in Wesley's Theology." In *Conversion in the Wesleyan Tradition*, ed. Kenneth J. Collins and John H. Tyson, 43–55. Nashville: Abingdon, 2001.

Lake, Donald M. "Jacob Arminius' Contribution to a Theology of Grace." In *Grace Unlimited*, ed. Clark H. Pinnock, 223–42. Eugene, OR: Wipf and Stock, 1999.

Lane, Anthony N. S. "Anthropology." In *The Calvin Handbook*, ed. Herman J. Selderhuis, 275–88. Grand Rapids: Eerdmans, 2009.

Lemke, Steve W. "A Biblical and Theological Critique of Irresistible Grace." In *Whosoever Will: A Biblical-Theological Critique of Five-Point Calvinism*, ed. David L. Allen and Steve W. Lemke, 109–62. Nashville: B&H Publishing Group, 2010.

Lindars, Barnabas. "The Fourth Gospel an Act of Contemplation." In *Studies in the Fourth Gospel*, ed. F. L. Cross, 23–35. London: A. R. Mowbray, 1957.

Logan, James C. "After Wesley: The Middle Period (1791–1849)." In *Grace Upon Grace: Essays in Honor of Thomas A. Langford*, ed. Robert K. Johnston, L. Gregory Jones, and Jonathan R. Wilson, 111–23. Nashville: Abingdon, 1999.

MacDonald, William G. "The Spirit of Grace." In *Grace Unlimited*, ed. Clark H. Pinnock, 74–94. Eugene, OR: Wipf and Stock, 1999.

Maddox, Randy L. "Wesley and the Question of Truth or Salvation Through Other Religions." *Wesleyan Theological Journal* 27 (1992): 14–18.

McGowan, A. T. B. "Justification and the *Ordo Salutis*." In *Justification in Perspective*, ed. Bruce L. McCormack, 147–63. Grand Rapids: Baker, 2006.

Marshall, I. Howard. "Predestination in the New Testament." In *Grace Unlimited*, ed. Clark H. Pinnock, 127–43. Eugene, OR: Wipf and Stock, 1999.

Miller, Samuel. "Introductory Essay." In *The Articles of the Synod of Dort*, ed. Thomas Scott and Samuel Miller, 5–78. Philadelphia: Presbyterian Board of Publication, 1856.

Motyer, Stephen. "Call, Calling." In *The Evangelical Dictionary of Biblical Theology*. Edited by Walter A. Elwell. Grand Rapids: Baker, 1996.

Mulder, John M. "Conversion." In *The Westminster Handbook to Reformed Theology*. Edited by Donald K. McKim. Louisville: Westminster John Knox, 2001.

Muller, Richard A. "Arminius and Arminianism." In *The Dictionary of Historical Theology*. Edited by Trevor A. Hart. Grand Rapids: Eerdmans, 2000.

_____. "Arminius and the Reformed Tradition." *Westminster Theological Journal* 70 (2008): 19–48.

————. "Arminius and the Scholastic Tradition." *Calvin Theological Journal* 24 (1989): 263–77.

————. "*Fides* and *Cognitio* in Relation to the Problem of Intellect and Will in the Theology of John Calvin." *Calvin Theological Journal* 25 (1990): 207–24.

————. "Freedom." In *The Westminster Handbook to Reformed Theology*. Edited by Donald K. McKim. Louisville: Westminster John Knox, 2001.

————. "God, Predestination, and the Integrity of the Created Order: A Note on Patterns in Arminius' Theology." In *Later Calvinism: International Perspectives*, ed. W. Fred Graham, 431–46. Kirksville, MO: Sixteenth-Century Journal Publishers, 1994.

————. "Grace, Election, and Contingent Choice: Arminius's Gambit and the Reformed Response." In *The Grace of God, the Bondage of the Will: Historical and Theological Perspectives on Calvinism*, ed. Thomas R. Schreiner and Bruce A. Ware, 2:251–78. Grand Rapids: Baker, 1995.

————. "Jonathan Edwards and the Absence of Free Choice: A Parting of Ways in the Reformed Tradition." *Jonathan Edwards Studies* 1, 1 (2011): 3–22.

————. "Liberum Arbitrium." In *Dictionary of Latin and Greek Theological Terms: Drawn Principally from Protestant Scholastic Theology*, by Richard A. Muller. Grand Rapids: Baker, 1985.

————. "The Myth of 'Decretal Theology.'" *Calvin Theological Journal* 30 (1995): 159–67.

————. "Perkins' *A Golden Chaine*: Predestination System or Schematized *Ordo Salutis*?" *Sixteenth-Century Journal* 9 (1978): 69–81.

————. "Predestination." In *The Oxford Encyclopedia of the Reformation*. Edited by Hans J. Hillerbrand. Oxford: Oxford University Press, 1996.

————. "The Priority of the Intellect in the Soteriology of James Arminius," *Westminster Theological Journal* 55 (1993): 55–72.

————. "Reformation, Augustinianism in the." In *Augustine through the Ages: An Encyclopedia*. Edited by Allan D. Fitzgerald. Grand Rapids: Eerdmans, 1999.

————. "Synergismus." In *Dictionary of Latin and Greek Theological Terms: Drawn Principally from Protestant Scholastic Theology*, by Richard A. Muller, 294. Grand Rapids: Baker, 2004.

————. "The Use and Abuse of a Document: Beza's Tabula Preaedestinationis, the Bolsec Controversy, and the Origins of Reformed Orthodoxy." In *Protestant Scholasticism: Essays in Reassessment*, ed. Carl R. Trueman and R. Scott Clark, 33–61. Carlisle, England: Paternoster, 1999.

_____. "Vocatio." In *Dictionary of Latin and Greek Theological Terms: Drawn Principally from Protestant Scholastic Theology*, by Richard A. Muller. Grand Rapids: Baker, 1985.

Murray, John. "The Call." In vol. 2 of *Collected Writings of John Murray*, 161–66. Edinburgh: Banner of Truth, 1976.

_____. "Calvin, Dort and Westminster–A Comparative Study." In *Crisis in the Reformed Churches: Essays in Commemoration of the Great Synod of Dort, 1618–1619*, ed. Peter Y. De Jong, 150–60. Grand Rapids: Reformed Fellowship, 1968.

_____. "Common Grace." In vol. 2 of *Collected Writings of John Murray*, 93–96. Edinburgh: Banner of Truth, 1976.

_____. "Irresistible Grace." In *Soli Deo Gloria: Essays in Reformed Theology: Festschrift for John H. Gerstner*, ed. R. C. Sproul, 55–62. Nutley, NJ: Presbyterian and Reformed, 1976.

_____. "Regeneration." In vol. 2 of *Collected Writings of John Murray*, 167–201. Edinburgh: Banner of Truth, 1976.

Nettles, Thomas J. "John Wesley's Contention with Calvinism." In *The Grace of God, the Bondage of the Will: Historical and Theological Perspectives on Calvinism*, ed. Thomas R. Schreiner and Bruce A. Ware, 2:297–322. Grand Rapids: Baker, 1995.

_____. "Preaching Irresistible Grace." In *Reclaiming the Gospel and Reforming Churches: The Southern Baptist Founders Conference, 1982–2002*, ed. Thomas K. Ascol, 383–404. Cape Coral, FL: Founders, 2003.

Norris, Robert M. "The Thirty-Nine Articles at the Westminster Assembly." In *The Westminster Confession into the Twenty-first Century: Essays in Remembrance of the 350th Anniversary of the Westminster Assembly*, vol. 3, ed. J. Ligon Duncan III, 139–74. Fearn, Ross-shire, Great Britain: Christian Focus, 2009.

Oepke, Albrecht. "*Elkō*." In *Theological Dictionary of the New Testament*, ed. and trans. Gerhard Kittel and Geoffrey W. Bromiley. Grand Rapids: Eerdmans, 1964.

Olson, Roger E. "The Classical Free Will Theist Model of God." In *Perspectives on the Doctrine of God: Four Views*, ed. Chad O. Brand, 148–72. Nashville: B&H Publishing Group, 2008.

_____. "Conversion," "Election/Predestination," "Faith," "Freedom/Free Will," "Grace," "Repentance," "Salvation," "Sin/Original Sin," "The Story of Evangelical Theology." In *The Westminster Handbook to Evangelical Theology*, ed. Roger Olson. Louisville: Westminster John Knox, 2004.

Osborne, Grant R. "Exegetical Notes on Calvinist Texts." In *Grace Unlimited*, ed. Clark H. Pinnock, 167–89. Eugene, OR: Wipf and Stock, 1999.

_____. "Soteriology in the Gospel of John." In *The Grace of God and the Will of Man: A Case for Arminianism*, ed. Clark H. Pinnock, 243–60. Minneapolis: Bethany House, 1989.

Outler, Albert C. "The Wesleyan Quadrilateral in John Wesley." In *The Wesleyan Theological Heritage: Essays of Albert C. Outler*, ed. Thomas C. Oden and Leicester R. Longden, 21–38. Grand Rapids: Zondervan, 1991.

Packer, J. I. "Arminianisms." In *Puritan Papers*, vol. 5: *1968–1969*, ed. J. I. Packer, 25–41. Phillipsburg, NJ: P&R Publishing, 2000.

_____. "Call, Called, Calling." In *Baker's Dictionary of Theology*, ed. Everett F. Harrison, 184. Grand Rapids: Baker, 1973.

_____. "Calvin the Theologian." In *John Calvin: A Collection of Essays*, ed. Gervase E. Duffield, 149–75. Abingdon: Sutton Courtenay, 1966.

_____. "Introductory Essay." In *The Death of Death in the Death of Christ*, by John Owen. London: Banner of Truth, 1959.

_____. "The Love of God: Universal and Particular." In *Still Sovereign: Contemporary Perspectives on Election, Foreknowledge, and Grace*, ed. Thomas R. Schreiner and Bruce A. Ware, 277–94. Grand Rapids: Baker, 2000.

_____. "Regeneration." In *Evangelical Dictionary of Theology*, ed. Walter A. Elwell, 925. Grand Rapids: Baker, 2001.

Pinnock, Clark H. "Divine Election as Corporate, Open, and Vocational." In *Perspectives on Election: Five Views*, ed. Chad O. Brand, 276–314. Nashville: B&H Publishing Group, 2006.

_____. "From Augustine to Arminius: A Pilgrimage in Theology." In *The Grace of God and the Will of Man: A Case for Arminianism*, ed. Clark H. Pinnock, 15–30. Minneapolis: Bethany House, 1989.

_____. "Responsible Freedom and the Flow of Biblical History." In *Grace Unlimited*, ed. Clark H. Pinnock, 95–109. Eugene, OR: Wipf and Stock, 1999.

Pinson, J. Matthew. "The Righteousness of Saving Faith: Arminian versus Remonstrant Grace." *Evangelical Journal* 9 (1991):27–39.

_____. "Will the Real Arminius Please Stand Up? A Study of the Theology of Jacobus Arminius in Light of His Interpreters." *Integrity* 2 (2003): 121–39.

Pipa, Joseph A., Jr. "Calvin on the Holy Spirit." In *Calvin for Today*, ed. Joel R. Beeke, 51–90. Grand Rapids: Reformation Heritage, 2009.

Pitkin, Barbara. "Faith and Justification" In *The Calvin Handbook*, ed. Herman J. Selderhuis, 288–98. Grand Rapids: Eerdmans, 2009.

Praamsma, Louis. "Background of Arminian Controversy." In *Crisis in the Reformed Churches: Essays in Commemoration of the Great Synod of Dort, 1618–1619*, ed. Peter Y. De Jong, 22–38. Grand Rapids: Reformed Fellowship, 1968.

Rakeshaw, Robert V. "John Wesley as a Theologian of Grace." *Journal of the Evangelical Theological Society* 27 (1984): 193–203.

Reichenbach, Bruce R. "Freedom, Justice, and Moral Responsibility." In *The Grace of God and the Will of Man: A Case for Arminianism*, ed. Clark H. Pinnock, 286. Minneapolis: Bethany House, 1989.

_____. "God Limits His Power." In *Predestination and Free Will: Four Views of Divine Sovereignty and Human Freedom*, ed. David Basinger and Randall Basinger, 99–140. Downers Grove, IL: InterVarsity, 1986.

Ritchie, Rick. "A Lutheran Response to Arminianism." *Modern Reformation* 1, 3 (1992): 11–13.

Robertson, O. Palmer. "The Holy Spirit in the Westminster Confession." In *The Westminster Confession into the Twenty-first Century: Essays in Remembrance of the 350th Anniversary of the Westminster Assembly*, vol. 1, ed. J. Ligon Duncan III, 57–100. Fearn, Ross-shire, Great Britain: Christian Focus, 2003.

Rohls, Jan. "Calvinism, Arminianism and Socinianism in the Netherlands until the Synod of Dort." In *Socinianism and Arminianism: Antitrinitarians, Calvinists and Cultural Exchange in Seventeenth-Century Europe*, ed. Martin Mulsow and Jan Rohls, 3–48. Brill's Studies in Intellectual History 134. Leiden: Brill, 2005.

Schreiner, Thomas R. "Does Romans 9 Teach Individual Election to Salvation?" In *Still Sovereign: Contemporary Perspectives on Election, Foreknowledge, and Grace*, ed. Thomas R. Schreiner and Bruce A. Ware, 89–106. Grand Rapids: Baker Academic, 2000.

_____. "Does Scripture Teach Prevenient Grace in the Wesleyan Sense?" In *Still Sovereign: Contemporary Perspectives on Election, Foreknowledge, and Grace*, ed. Thomas R. Schreiner and Bruce A. Ware, 229–46. Grand Rapids: Baker Academic, 2000.

Shipley, David C. "Development of Theology in American Methodism in the Nineteenth Century." *The London Quarterly and Holborn Review* (1959): 249–64.

_____. "Wesley and Some Calvinistic Controversies." *Drew Gateway* 25, 4 (1955): 195–210.

Smalley, S. S. "'The Paraclete': Pneumatology in the Johannine Gospel and Apocalypse." In *Exploring the Gospel of John*, ed. R. A. Culpepper and C. C. Black, 289–300. Louisville: Westminster John Knox, 1996.

Smith, J. Weldon, III. "Some Notes on Wesley's Doctrine of Prevenient Grace." *Religion in Life* 34 (1964–65): 70–74.

Snoeberger, Mark A. "The Logical Priority of Regeneration to Saving Faith in a Theological *Ordo Salutis*." *Detroit Baptist Seminary Journal* 7 (2002): 49–94.

Spurgeon, Charles H. "On *Regeneration*." *Founders Journal* 48 (2002): 29–32.

Stafford, Gilbert W. "Salvation in the General Epistles." In *Wesleyan Theological Perspectives*, ed. John E. Hartley and R. Larry Shelton, 1:195–224. Anderson, IN: Warner, 1981.

Stanglin, Keith D. "Arminius Avant la Lettre: Peter Baro, Jacob Arminius, and the Bond of Predestinarian Polemic." *Westminster Theological Journal* 67 (2005): 51–74.

Steers, David. "Arminianism amongst Protestant Dissenters in England and Ireland in the Eighteenth Century." In *Arminius, Arminianism, and Europe: Jacob Arminius (1559/60–1609)*, ed. Marius van Leeuwen, Keith D. Stanglin, and Marijke Tolsma, 159–202. Brill's Series in Church History 39. Leiden: E. J. Brill, 2010.

Stewart, Kenneth. "The Doctrine of Regeneration in Evangelical Theology: The Reformation to 1800," *JBTM* 8, 1 (2011): 42–57.

Storms, Sam. "Jonathan Edwards on the Freedom of the Will." *Trinity Journal* 3, 2 (1982): 131–69.

————. "The Will: Fettered Yet Free (*Freedom of the Will*)." In *A God Entranced Vision of All Things*, ed. John Piper and Justin Taylor, 201–20. Wheaton, IL: Crossway, 2004.

Strehle, Stephen. "Universal Grace and Amyraldianism." *Westminster Theological Journal* 51 (1989): 345–57.

Suchocki, Marjorie. "Wesleyan Grace." In *The Oxford Handbook of Methodist Studies*. Edited by William J. Abraham and James E. Kirby, 540–53. Oxford: Oxford University Press, 2009.

Talbot, Mark R. "True Freedom: The Liberty That Scripture Portrays as Worth Having." In *Beyond the Bounds: Open Theism and the Undermining of Biblical Christianity*, ed. John Piper, Justin Taylor, and Paul Kjoss Helseth, 77–110. Wheaton, IL: Crossway, 2003.

Toon, Peter. "Regeneration." In *The Westminster Handbook to Reformed Theology*. Edited by Donald K. McKim. Louisville: Westminster John Knox, 2001.

Trueman, Carl R. "Calvin and Reformed Orthodoxy." In *The Calvin Handbook*, ed. Herman J. Selderhuis, 472–78. Grand Rapids: Eerdmans, 2009.

Vanderschaaf, Mark E. "Predestination and Certainty of Salvation in Augustine and Calvin," *Review of Religion* 30 (1976–77):1–8.

Van Dixhoorn, Chad B. "The Rise of Arminianism Reconsidered." *Past and Present*, 33 (1987): 201–29.

Vanhoozer, Kevin J. "Effectual Call or Causal Effect? Summon, Sovereignty and Supervenient Grace." *Tyndale Bulletin* 49 (1998): 213–51.

Van Leeuwen, Th. Marius. "Introduction: Arminius, Arminianism, and Europe." In *Arminius, Arminianism, and Europe: Jacob Arminius (1559/60–1609)*, ed. Marius van Leeuwen, Keith D. Stanglin, and Marijke Tolsma, ix-2. Brill's Series in Church History 39. Leiden: E. J. Brill, 2010.

Van Til, Cornelius. "The Significance of Dort for Today." In *Crisis in the Reformed Churches: Essays in Commemoration of the Great Synod of Dort, 1618–1619*, ed. Peter Y. De Jong, 181–96. Grand Rapids: Reformed Fellowship, 1968.

Vickers, Jason E. "Wesley's Theological Emphasis." In *The Cambridge Companion to John Wesley*, ed. Randy L. Maddox and Jason E. Vickers, 190–206. Cambridge: Cambridge University Press, 2010.

Wainwright, Geoffrey. "Charles Wesley and Calvinism." In *Charles Wesley: Life, Literature and Legacy*, ed. Kenneth G. C. Newport and Ted A. Campbell, 184–203. Peterborough: Epworth, 2007.

Walls, Jerry L. "Divine Commands, Predestination, and Moral Intuition." In *The Grace of God and the Will of Man: A Case for Arminianism*, ed. Clark H. Pinnock, 261–76. Minneapolis: Bethany House, 1989.

Ware, Bruce A. "Divine Election to Salvation." In *Perspectives on Election: Five Views*, ed. Chad O. Brand, 1–58. Nashville: B&H Publishing Group, 2006.

_____. "Effectual Calling and Grace." In *Still Sovereign: Contemporary Perspectives on Election, Foreknowledge, and Grace*, ed. Thomas R. Schreiner and Bruce A. Ware, 203–28. Grand Rapids: Baker, 2000.

_____. "A Modified Calvinist Doctrine of God." In *Perspectives on the Doctrine of God: Four Views*, ed. Bruce A. Ware, 76–120. Nashville: B&H Publishing Group, 2008.

Warren, Scott C. "Ability and Desire: Reframing Debates Surrounding Freedom and Responsibility." *Journal of the Evangelical Theological Society* 52 (2009): 551–67.

Wellum, Stephen J. "The Importance of Nature of Divine Sovereignty for Our View of Scripture." *Southern Baptist Journal of Theology* 4, 2 (2000): 76–90.

Welty, Greg. "Election and Calling: A Biblical Theological Study." In *Calvinism: A Southern Baptist Dialogue*, ed. E. Ray Clendenen and Brad J. Waggoner, 216–46. Nashville: B&H Publishing Group, 2008.

Witherington, Ben, III. "New Creation or New Birth? Conversion in the Johannine and Pauline Literature." In *Conversion in the Wesleyan Tradition*, ed. Kenneth J. Collins and John H. Tyson, 119–42. Nashville: Abingdon, 2001.

Wolfson, Harry A. "Philosophical Implications of the Pelagian Controversy." In *Doctrines of Human Nature, Sin, and Salvation in the Early Church*, ed. Everett Ferguson, 170–78. New York: Garland, 1993.

Wood, A. Skevington. "The Contribution of John Wesley's Theology of Grace." In *Grace Unlimited*, ed. Clark H. Pinnock, 209–22. Eugene, OR: Wipf and Stock, 1999.

DISSERTATIONS AND THESES

Bryant, B. E. "John Wesley's Doctrine of Sin." PhD diss., University of London, 1992.

Chamberlain, Mary Ava. "Jonathan Edwards Against the Antinomians and Arminians." PhD diss., Columbia University, 1990.

Crow, E. P. "John Wesley's Conflict with Antinomianism in Relation to the Moravians and Calvinists." PhD diss., University of Manchester, 1963.

Eaton, D. E. "Arminianism in the Theology of John Wesley." PhD diss., Duke University, 1988.

Ellis, Mark A. "Simon Episcopius and the Doctrine of Original Sin." PhD diss., Dallas Theological Seminary, 2002.

Heitzenrater, R. P. "Wesley and the Oxford Methodists, 1725–1735." PhD diss., Duke University, 1972.

Hicks, John M. "The Theology of Grace in the Thought of Jacobus Arminius and Philip van Limborch: A Study in the Development of Seventeenth-Century Dutch Arminianism." PhD diss., Westminster Theological Seminary, 1985.

Hoon, P. W. "The Soteriology of John Wesley." PhD diss., University of Edinburgh, 1936.

Ireson, R. W. "The Doctrine of Faith in John Wesley and the Protestant Tradition." PhD diss., University of Manchester, 1973.

Knight, John A. "John William Fletcher and the Early Methodist Tradition." PhD diss., Vanderbilt University, 1966.

Pask, A. H. S. "The Influence of Arminius Upon the Theology of John Wesley." PhD diss., University of Edinburgh, 1940.

Rogers, C. A. "The Concept of Prevenient Grace in the Theology of John Wesley." PhD diss., Duke University, 1967.

Royster, Mark. "John Wesley's Doctrine of Prevenient Grace in Missiological Perspective." PhD diss., Asbury Theological Seminary, 1989.

Shermer, R. C. "John Wesley's Speaking and Writing on Predestination and Free Will." PhD diss., Southern Illinois University, 1969.

Shipley, D. C. "Methodist Arminianism in the Theology of John Fletcher." PhD diss., Yale University, 1942.

Witt, William Gene. "Creation, Redemption and Grace in the Theology of Jacob Arminius." 2 vols. PhD diss., University of Notre Dame, 1993.

BOOK REVIEWS

Bangs, Carl. Review of *God, Creation, and Providence in the Thought of Jacob Arminius*, by Richard Muller. *Church History* 66 (1997): 118–20.

Nicole, Roger. Review of *Grace, Faith, Free Will: Contrasting Views of Salvation: Calvinism and Arminianism*, by Robert E. Picirilli. *Founders Journal* 52 (2003): 26–29.

Olson, Roger. Review of *Whosoever Will: A Biblical-Theological Critique of Five-Point Calvinism*, ed. by David L. Allen and Steve W. Lemke (Nashville: B&H Publishing Group, 2010). Available online from Baptist Theology. Accessed November 1, 2010. http://www.baptisttheology.org/WhosoeverWill.cffm.

INTERNET ARTICLES

Schreiner, Thomas. "Does Regeneration Necessarily Precede Conversion?" From 9Marks: Building Healthy Churches. Accessed July 6, 2008. http://www.9marks.org /journal/does-regeneration-necessarily-precede-conversion.

INDEX OF SCRIPTURE

377

INDEX OF SUBJECTS AND NAMES